DATSUN
240-280Z
1970-1978
SHOP MANUAL

By
ALAN AHLSTRAND

ERIC JORGENSEN
Editor

JEFF ROBINSON
Publisher

CLYMER PUBLICATIONS

*World's largest publisher of books
devoted exclusively to automobiles and motorcycles*

12860 MUSCATINE STREET · P.O. BOX 20 · ARLETA, CALIFORNIA 91331

FIRST EDITION
Published November, 1972

SECOND EDITION
Revised by Alan Ahlstrand to include 1973-1974 models
Published March, 1975

THIRD EDITION
Revised by Alan Ahlstrand to include 1975-1976 models
Published February, 1977

FOURTH EDITION
Revised by Alan Ahlstrand to include 1977-1978 models
Published October, 1978

FIFTH EDITION
Revised by Alan Ahlstrand
First Printing October, 1979
Second Printing September, 1980

SIXTH EDITION
Revised by Alan Ahlstrand
First Printing October, 1981
Second Printing December, 1982
Third Printing September, 1983

Printed in U.S.A.

ISBN: 0-89287-290-X

Production Coordinator, Christopher McIntire

Photos and illustrations courtesy of Nissan Motor Corporation in U.S.A.

CONTENTS

DATSUN
240-280Z
1970-1978
SHOP MANUAL

QUICK REFERENCE DATA

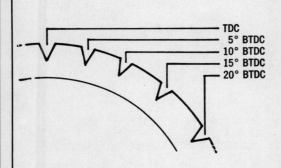

TIMING MARKS (EARLY MODELS)

TDC
5° BTDC
10° BTDC
15° BTDC
20° BTDC

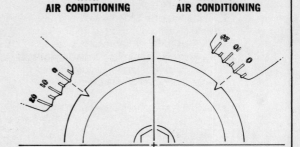

TIMING MARKS (LATE MODELS)

WITH AIR CONDITIONING

WITHOUT AIR CONDITIONING

CYLINDER HEAD TIGHTENING SEQUENCE

```
12   8   4   2   6   10   14

11   7   3   1   5   9    13
```

TUNE-UP SPECIFICATIONS

Cylinder Head Torque

240Z through engine No. L24-027600*	43-51 ft.-lb. (6-7 mkg)
240Z from engine No. L24-027601*	51-61 ft.-lb. (7.0-8.5 mkg)
260Z	47-61 ft.-lb. (6.5-8.5 mkg)
1975-1976 280Z	54-61 ft.-lb. (7.5-8.5 mkg)
1977 and later 280Z	51-61 ft.-lb. (7.0-8.5 mkg)

Valve Clearance (Cold)

Intake	0.008 in. (0.20mm)
Exhaust	0.010 in. (0.25mm)

(continued)

Valve Clearance (Hot)

Intake	0.010 in. (0.25mm)
Exhaust	0.012 in. (0.30mm)

Ignition Timing

1970-1972 manual	5° BTDC at 750 rpm
1971-1972 automatic (advanced)	10° BTDC at 600 rpm in Drive
1971-1972 automatic (retarded)	0° (TDC) at 600 rpm in Drive
1973-1974 manual	7° BTDC at 750 rpm
1973-1974 automatic (advanced)	15° BTDC at 600 rpm in Drive
1973 automatic (retarded)	5° BTDC at 600 rpm in Drive
1974 automatic (retarded)	8° BTDC at 600 rpm in Drive
1975-1976 California cars (manual)	10° BTDC at 800 rpm
1975-1976 California cars (automatic)	10° BTDC at 700 rpm in Drive
1975-1976 non-California manual (advanced)	13° BTDC at 800 rpm
1975-1976 non-California manual (retarded)	7° BTDC at 800 rpm
1975-1976 non-California automatic (advanced)	13° BTDC at 700 rpm in Drive
1975-1976 non-California automatic (retarded)	7° BTDC at 700 rpm in Drive
1977 and later manual	10° BTDC at 800 rpm
1977 and later automatic	10° BTDC at 700 rpm in Drive

Spark Plug Gap

1970-1975	0.031-0.035 in. (0.8-0.9mm)
1976	0.028-0.031 in. (0.7-0.8mm)
1977 and later	0.039-0.043 in. (1.0-1.1mm)

Distributor Point Gap (240Z only)   0.018-0.021 in. (0.45-0.55mm)

Reluctor Air Gap

260Z	0.012-0.016 in. (0.3-0.4mm)
280Z	0.008-0.016 in. (0.2-0.4mm)

Dwell Angle (240Z only)

Manual transmission	35-41°
Automatic transmission	33-39°

Idle Speed

1970-1974 manual	750 rpm
1971-1974 automatic	600 rpm in Drive
1975 and later manual	800 rpm
1975 and later automatic	700 rpm in Drive
Firing order	1-5-3-6-2-4 (No. 1 front)

*Late type cylinder head bolts have a circular groove stamped in the top surface of the bolt head. Early type cylinder head bolts do not.

RECOMMENDED LUBRICANTS

Engine	API Service SD or SE
Manual transmission	API GL-4
Automatic transmission	Dexron
Differential	API GL-5
Brake and clutch fluid	DOT 3

LUBRICANT VISCOSITY

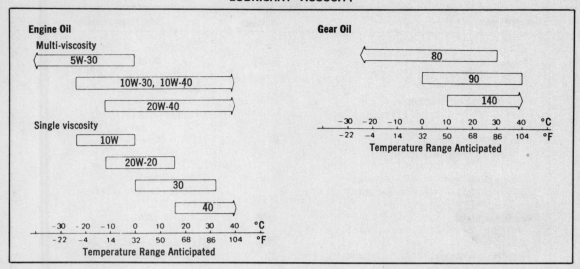

Engine Oil

Multi-viscosity

5W-30

10W-30, 10W-40

20W-40

Single viscosity

10W

20W-20

30

40

$-30 \quad -20 \quad -10 \quad 0 \quad 10 \quad 20 \quad 30 \quad 40 \quad °C$
$-22 \quad -4 \quad 14 \quad 32 \quad 50 \quad 68 \quad 86 \quad 104 \quad °F$

Temperature Range Anticipated

Gear Oil

80

90

140

$-30 \quad -20 \quad -10 \quad 0 \quad 10 \quad 20 \quad 30 \quad 40 \quad °C$
$-22 \quad -4 \quad 14 \quad 32 \quad 50 \quad 68 \quad 86 \quad 104 \quad °F$

Temperature Range Anticipated

APPROXIMATE REFILL CAPACITIES

Engine oil

1970-1973
    With filter change   5⅛ qt. (4.9 liters)
    Without filter change   4¼ qt. (4 liters)
1974-1977
    With filter change   5 qt. (4.7 liters)
    Without filter change   4¼ qt. (4 liters)
1978
    With filter change   4¾ qt. (4.5 liters)
    Without filter change   4¼ qt. (4 liters)

Manual transmission oil

    Four-speed   3⅝ pt. (1.7 liters)
    Five-speed   4¼ pt. (2 liters)

Differential oil

    240-260Z   2⅛ pt. (1 liter)
    1975-1976 280Z   2¾ pt. (1.3 liter)
    1977-1978 280Z
        With manual transmission   2¾ pt. (1.3 liter)
        With automatic transmission   2⅛ pt. (1 liter)

Cooling system

    1970-1973   10½ qt. (9.9 liters)
    1974-1975   10 qt. (9.4 liters)
    1976   11 qt. (10.4 liters)
    1977-1978
        Manual transmission   10⅞ qt. (10.3 liters)
        Automatic transmission   10⅝ qt. (10.1 liters)

BULB CHART

Application	Wattage	SAE trade number
Headlights	50/40	6012
Front parking/turn signals	23/8	1034
Side markers	8	67
License plate light	7.5	89
Tail/brake lights	23/8	1034
Rear turn signals	23	1073
Back-up lights	23	1073
Gauge lights	3.4	57X

TIRE PRESSURES

	Above 100 mph	Below 100 mph
Regular tires (175 SR-14, 175 HR-14, 195/70 HR-14, 195/70 VR-14)	32 psi	28 psi
1977 and later spare tire* (C78-14)	—	28 psi

*Do not use the spare tire at speeds above 50 mph.

INTRODUCTION

This detailed, comprehensive manual covers all 1970-1978 Datsun 240Z's, 260Z's and 280Z's. The expert text gives complete information on maintenance, repair, and overhaul. Hundreds of photos and drawings guide you through every step. The book includes all you need to know to keep your car running right.

Where repairs are practical for the owner/mechanic, complete procedures are given. Equally important, difficult jobs are pointed out. Such operations are usually more economically performed by a dealer or independent garage.

A shop manual is a reference. You want to be able to find information fast. As in all Clymer books, this one is designed with this in mind. All chapters are thumb tabbed. Important items are indexed at the rear of the book. Finally, all the most frequently used specifications and capacities are summarized on the *Quick Reference* pages at the front of the book.

Keep the book handy. Carry it in your glove box. It will help you to better understand your car, lower repair and maintenance costs, and generally improve your satisfaction with your vehicle.

CHAPTER ONE

GENERAL INFORMATION

The troubleshooting, tune-up, maintenance, and step-by-step repair procedures in this book are written for the owner and home mechanic. The text is accompanied by useful photos and diagrams to make the job as clear and correct as possible.

Troubleshooting, tune-up, maintenance, and repair are not difficult if you know what tools and equipment to use and what to do. Anyone not afraid to get their hands dirty, of average intelligence, and with some mechanical ability can perform most of the procedures in this book.

In some cases, a repair job may require tools or skills not reasonably expected of the home mechanic. These procedures are noted in each chapter and it is recommended that you take the job to your dealer, a competent mechanic, or machine shop.

MANUAL ORGANIZATION

This chapter provides general information and safety and service hints. Also included are lists of recommended shop and emergency tools as well as a brief description of troubleshooting and tune-up equipment.

Chapter Two provides methods and suggestions for quick and accurate diagnosis and repair of problems. Troubleshooting procedures discuss typical symptoms and logical methods to pinpoint the trouble.

Chapter Three explains all periodic lubrication and routine maintenance necessary to keep your vehicle running well. Chapter Three also includes recommended tune-up procedures, eliminating the need to constantly consult chapters on the various subassemblies.

Subsequent chapters cover specific systems such as the engine, transmission, and electrical systems. Each of these chapters provides disassembly, repair, and assembly procedures in a simple step-by-step format. If a repair requires special skills or tools, or is otherwise impractical for the home mechanic, it is so indicated. In these cases it is usually faster and less expensive to have the repairs made by a dealer or competent repair shop. Necessary specifications concerning a particular system are included at the end of the appropriate chapter.

When special tools are required to perform a procedure included in this manual, the tool is illustrated either in actual use or alone. It may be possible to rent or borrow these tools. The inventive mechanic may also be able to find a suitable substitute in his tool box, or to fabricate one.

The terms NOTE, CAUTION, and WARNING have specific meanings in this manual. A NOTE provides additional or explanatory information. A CAUTION is used to emphasize areas where equipment damage could result if proper precautions are not taken. A WARNING is used to stress those areas where personal injury or death could result from negligence, in addition to possible mechanical damage.

SERVICE HINTS

Observing the following practices will save time, effort, and frustration, as well as prevent possible injury.

Throughout this manual keep in mind two conventions. "Front" refers to the front of the vehicle. The front of any component, such as the transmission, is that end which faces toward the front of the vehicle. The "left" and "right" sides of the vehicle refer to the orientation of a person sitting in the vehicle facing forward. For example, the steering wheel is on the left side. These rules are simple, but even experienced mechanics occasionally become disoriented.

Most of the service procedures covered are straightforward and can be performed by anyone reasonably handy with tools. It is suggested, however, that you consider your own capabilities carefully before attempting any operation involving major disassembly of the engine.

Some operations, for example, require the use of a press. It would be wiser to have these performed by a shop equipped for such work, rather than to try to do the job yourself with makeshift equipment. Other procedures require precision measurements. Unless you have the skills and equipment required, it would be better to have a qualified repair shop make the measurements for you.

Repairs go much faster and easier if the parts that will be worked on are clean before you begin. There are special cleaners for washing the engine and related parts. Brush or spray on the cleaning solution, let it stand, then rinse it away with a garden hose. Clean all oily or greasy parts with cleaning solvent as you remove them.

WARNING
Never use gasoline as a cleaning agent. It presents an extreme fire hazard. Be sure to work in a well-ventilated area when using cleaning solvent. Keep a fire extinguisher, rated for gasoline fires, handy in any case.

Much of the labor charge for repairs made by dealers is for the removal and disassembly of other parts to reach the defective unit. It is frequently possible to perform the preliminary operations yourself and then take the defective unit in to the dealer for repair, at considerable savings.

Once you have decided to tackle the job yourself, make sure you locate the appropriate section in this manual, and read it entirely. Study the illustrations and text until you have a good idea of what is involved in completing the job satisfactorily. If special tools are required, make arrangements to get them before you start. Also, purchase any known defective parts prior to starting on the procedure. It is frustrating and time-consuming to get partially into a job and then be unable to complete it.

Simple wiring checks can be easily made at home, but knowledge of electronics is almost a necessity for performing tests with complicated electronic testing gear.

During disassembly of parts keep a few general cautions in mind. Force is rarely needed to get things apart. If parts are a tight fit, like a bearing in a case, there is usually a tool designed to separate them. Never use a screwdriver to pry apart parts with machined surfaces such as cylinder head and valve cover. You will mar the surfaces and end up with leaks.

Make diagrams wherever similar-appearing parts are found. You may think you can remember where everything came from — but mistakes are costly. There is also the possibility you may get sidetracked and not return to work for days or even weeks — in which interval, carefully laid out parts may have become disturbed.

Tag all similar internal parts for location, and mark all mating parts for position. Record number and thickness of any shims as they are removed. Small parts such as bolts can be identified by placing them in plastic sandwich bags that are sealed and labeled with masking tape.

Wiring should be tagged with masking tape and marked as each wire is removed. Again, do not rely on memory alone.

When working under the vehicle, do not trust a hydraulic or mechanical jack to hold the vehicle up by itself. Always use jackstands. See **Figure 1**.

Disconnect battery ground cable before working near electrical connections and before disconnecting wires. Never run the engine with the battery disconnected; the alternator could be seriously damaged.

Protect finished surfaces from physical damage or corrosion. Keep gasoline and brake fluid off painted surfaces.

Frozen or very tight bolts and screws can often be loosened by soaking with penetrating oil like Liquid Wrench or WD-40, then sharply striking the bolt head a few times with a hammer and punch (or screwdriver for screws). Avoid heat unless absolutely necessary, since it may melt, warp, or remove the temper from many parts.

Avoid flames or sparks when working near a charging battery or flammable liquids, such as brake fluid or gasoline.

No parts, except those assembled with a press fit, require unusual force during assembly. If a part is hard to remove or install, find out why before proceeding.

Cover all openings after removing parts to keep dirt, small tools, etc., from falling in.

When assembling two parts, start all fasteners, then tighten evenly.

The clutch plate, wiring connections, brake shoes, drums, pads, and discs should be kept clean and free of grease and oil.

When assembling parts, be sure all shims and washers are replaced exactly as they came out.

Whenever a rotating part butts against a stationary part, look for a shim or washer. Use new gaskets if there is any doubt about the condition of old ones. Generally, you should apply gasket cement to one mating surface only, so the parts may be easily disassembled in the future. A thin coat of oil on gaskets helps them seal effectively.

Heavy grease can be used to hold small parts in place if they tend to fall out during assembly. However, keep grease and oil away from electrical, clutch, and brake components.

High spots may be sanded off a piston with sandpaper, but emery cloth and oil do a much more professional job.

Carburetors are best cleaned by disassembling them and soaking the parts in a commercial carburetor cleaner. Never soak gaskets and rubber parts in these cleaners. Never use wire to clean out jets and air passages; they are easily damaged. Use compressed air to blow out the carburetor, but only if the float has been removed first.

Take your time and do the job right. Do not forget that a newly rebuilt engine must be broken in the same as a new one. Refer to your owner's manual for the proper break-in procedures.

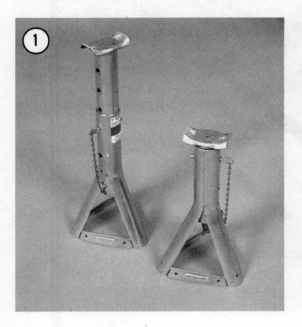

SAFETY FIRST

Professional mechanics can work for years and never sustain a serious injury. If you observe a few rules of common sense and safety, you can enjoy many safe hours servicing your vehicle. You could hurt yourself or damage the vehicle if you ignore these rules.

1. Never use gasoline as a cleaning solvent.

2. Never smoke or use a torch in the vicinity of flammable liquids such as cleaning solvent in open containers.

3. Never smoke or use a torch in an area where batteries are being charged. Highly explosive hydrogen gas is formed during the charging process.

4. Use the proper sized wrenches to avoid damage to nuts and injury to yourself.

5. When loosening a tight or stuck nut, be guided by what would happen if the wrench should slip. Protect yourself accordingly.

6. Keep your work area clean and uncluttered.

7. Wear safety goggles during all operations involving drilling, grinding, or use of a cold chisel.

8. Never use worn tools.

9. Keep a fire extinguisher handy and be sure it is rated for gasoline (Class B) and electrical (Class C) fires.

EXPENDABLE SUPPLIES

Certain expendable supplies are necessary. These include grease, oil, gasket cement, wiping rags, cleaning solvent, and distilled water.

Also, special locking compounds, silicone lubricants, and engine cleaners may be useful. Cleaning solvent is available at most service stations and distilled water for the battery is available at most supermarkets.

SHOP TOOLS

For proper servicing, you will need an assortment of ordinary hand tools (**Figure 2**).

As a minimum, these include:

a. Combination wrenches
b. Sockets
c. Plastic mallet
d. Small hammer
e. Snap ring pliers
f. Gas pliers
g. Phillips screwdrivers
h. Slot (common) screwdrivers
i. Feeler gauges
j. Spark plug gauge
k. Spark plug wrench

Special tools necessary are shown in the chapters covering the particular repair in which they are used.

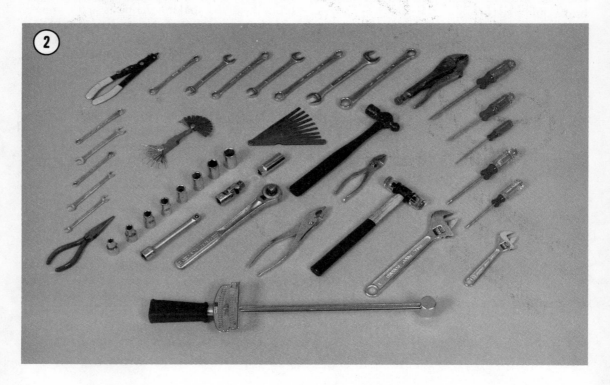

Engine tune-up and troubleshooting procedures require other special tools and equipment. These are described in detail in the following sections.

EMERGENCY TOOL KIT

A small emergency tool kit kept in the trunk is handy for road emergencies which otherwise could leave you stranded. The tools listed below and shown in **Figure 3** will let you handle most roadside repairs.

   a. Combination wrenches

   b. Crescent (adjustable) wrench

   c. Screwdrivers — common and Phillips

   d. Pliers — conventional (gas) and needle nose

   e. Vise Grips

   f. Hammer — plastic and metal

   g. Small container of waterless hand cleaner

   h. Rags for clean up

   i. Silver waterproof sealing tape (duct tape)

   j. Flashlight

   k. Emergency road flares — at least four

   l. Spare drive belts (water pump, alternator, etc.)

TROUBLESHOOTING AND TUNE-UP EQUIPMENT

Voltmeter, Ohmmeter, and Ammeter

For testing the ignition or electrical system, a good voltmeter is required. For automotive use, an instrument covering 0-20 volts is satisfac-

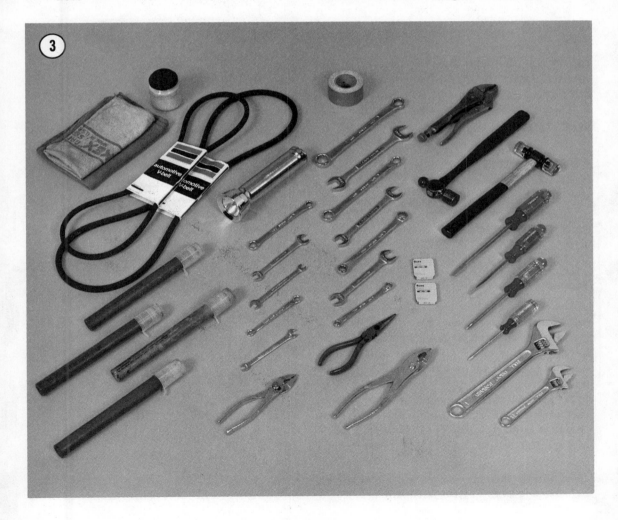

tory. One which also has a 0-2 volt scale is necessary for testing relays, points, or individual contacts where voltage drops are much smaller. Accuracy should be ± ½ volt.

An ohmmeter measures electrical resistance. This instrument is useful for checking continuity (open and short circuits), and testing fuses and lights.

The ammeter measures electrical current. Ammeters for automotive use should cover 0-50 amperes and 0-250 amperes. These are useful for checking battery charging and starting current.

Several inexpensive VOM's (volt-ohm-milliammeter) combine all three instruments into one which fits easily in any tool box. See **Figure 4**. However, the ammeter ranges are usually too small for automotive work.

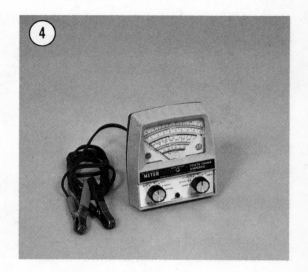

Hydrometer

The hydrometer gives a useful indication of battery condition and charge by measuring the specific gravity of the electrolyte in each cell. See **Figure 5**. Complete details on use and interpretation of readings are provided in the electrical chapter.

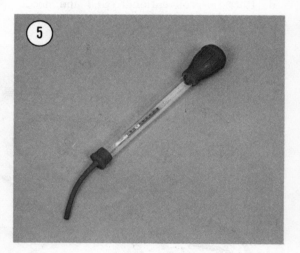

Compression Tester

The compression tester measures the compression pressure built up in each cylinder. The results, when properly interpreted, can indicate general cylinder and valve condition. See **Figure 6**.

Vacuum Gauge

The vacuum gauge (**Figure 7**) is one of the easiest instruments to use, but one of the most difficult for the inexperienced mechanic to interpret. The results, when interpreted with other findings, can provide valuable clues to possible trouble.

To use the vacuum gauge, connect it to a vacuum hose that goes to the intake manifold. Attach it either directly to the hose or to a T-fitting installed into the hose.

NOTE: *Subtract one inch from the reading for every 1,000 ft. elevation.*

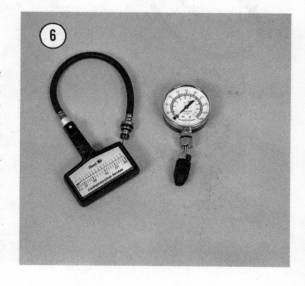

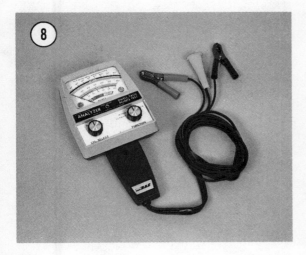

Fuel Pressure Gauge

This instrument is invaluable for evaluating fuel pump performance. Fuel system trouble-shooting procedures in this manual use a fuel pressure gauge. Usually a vacuum gauge and fuel pressure gauge are combined.

Dwell Meter (Contact Breaker Point Ignition Only)

A dwell meter measures the distance in degrees of cam rotation that the breaker points remain closed while the engine is running. Since this angle is determined by breaker point gap, dwell angle is an accurate indication of breaker point gap.

Many tachometers intended for tuning and testing incorporate a dwell meter as well. See **Figure 8**. Follow the manufacturer's instructions to measure dwell.

Tachometer

A tachometer is necessary for tuning. See **Figure 8**. Ignition timing and carburetor adjustments must be performed at the specified idle speed. The best instrument for this purpose is one with a low range of 0-1,000 or 0-2,000 rpm for setting idle, and a high range of 0-4,000 or more for setting ignition timing at 3,000 rpm. Extended range (0-6,000 or 0-8,000 rpm) instruments lack accuracy at lower speeds. The instrument should be capable of detecting changes of 25 rpm on the low range.

Strobe Timing Light

This instrument is necessary for tuning, as it permits very accurate ignition timing. The light flashes at precisely the same instant that No. 1 cylinder fires, at which time the timing marks on the engine should align. Refer to Chapter Three for exact location of the timing marks for your engine.

Suitable lights range from inexpensive neon bulb types ($2-3) to powerful xenon strobe lights ($20-40). See **Figure 9**. Neon timing lights are difficult to see and must be used in dimly lit areas. Xenon strobe timing lights can be used outside in bright sunlight. Both types work on this vehicle; use according to the manufacturer's instructions.

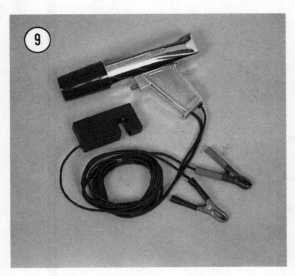

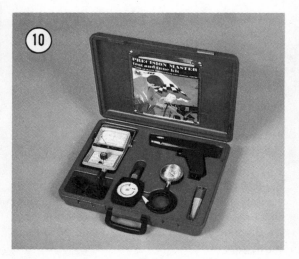

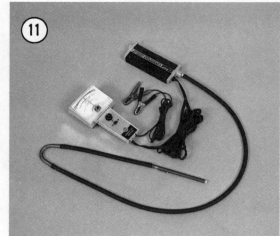

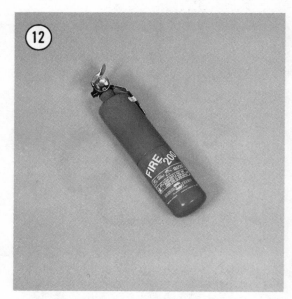

Tune-up Kits

Many manufacturers offer kits that combine several useful instruments. Some come in a convenient carry case and are usually less expensive than purchasing one instrument at a time. **Figure 10** shows one of the kits that is available. The prices vary with the number of instruments included in the kit.

Exhaust Gas Analyzer

Of all instruments described here, this is the least likely to be owned by a home mechanic. This instrument samples the exhaust gases from the tailpipe and measures the thermal conductivity of the exhaust gas. Since different gases conduct heat at varying rates, thermal conductivity of the exhaust is a good indication of gases present.

An exhaust gas analyzer is vital for accurately checking the effectiveness of exhaust emission control adjustments. They are relatively expensive to buy ($70 and up), but must be considered essential for the owner/mechanic to comply with today's emission laws. See **Figure 11**.

Fire Extinguisher

A fire extinguisher is a necessity when working on a vehicle. It should be rated for both *Class B* (flammable liquids — gasoline, oil, paint, etc.) and *Class C* (electrical — wiring, etc.) type fires. It should always be kept within reach. See **Figure 12**.

CHAPTER TWO

TROUBLESHOOTING

Troubleshooting can be a relatively simple matter if it is done logically. The first step in any troubleshooting procedure must be defining the symptoms as closely as possible. Subsequent steps involve testing and analyzing areas which could cause the symptoms. A haphazard approach may eventually find the trouble, but in terms of wasted time and unnecessary parts replacement, it can be very costly.

The troubleshooting procedures in this chapter analyze typical symptoms and show logical methods of isolation. These are not the only methods. There may be several approaches to a problem, but all methods must have one thing in common — a logical, systematic approach.

STARTING SYSTEM

The starting system consists of the starter motor and the starter solenoid. The ignition key controls the starter solenoid, which mechanically engages the starter with the engine flywheel, and supplies electrical current to turn the starter motor.

Starting system troubles are relatively easy to find. In most cases, the trouble is a loose or dirty electrical connection. **Figures 1 and 2** provide routines for finding the trouble.

CHARGING SYSTEM

The charging system consists of the alternator (or generator on older vehicles), voltage regulator, and battery. A drive belt driven by the engine crankshaft turns the alternator which produces electrical energy to charge the battery. As engine speed varies, the voltage from the alternator varies. A voltage regulator controls the charging current to the battery and maintains the voltage to the vehicle's electrical system at safe levels. A warning light or gauge on the instrument panel signals the driver when charging is not taking place. Refer to **Figure 3** for a typical charging system.

Complete troubleshooting of the charging system requires test equipment and skills which the average home mechanic does not possess. However, there are a few tests which can be done to pinpoint most troubles.

Charging system trouble may stem from a defective alternator (or generator), voltage regulator, battery, or drive belt. It may also be caused by something as simple as incorrect drive belt tension. The following are symptoms of typical problems you may encounter.

1. *Battery dies frequently, even though the warning lamp indicates no discharge* — This can be caused by a drive belt that is slightly too

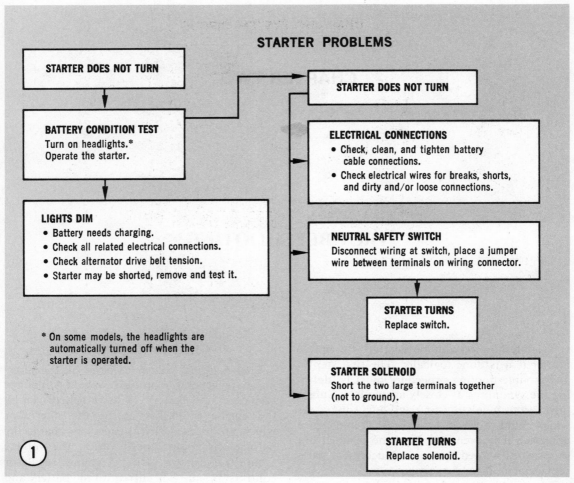

STARTER PROBLEMS

STARTER DOES NOT TURN

BATTERY CONDITION TEST
Turn on headlights.*
Operate the starter.

LIGHTS DIM
- Battery needs charging.
- Check all related electrical connections.
- Check alternator drive belt tension.
- Starter may be shorted, remove and test it.

* On some models, the headlights are automatically turned off when the starter is operated.

STARTER DOES NOT TURN

ELECTRICAL CONNECTIONS
- Check, clean, and tighten battery cable connections.
- Check electrical wires for breaks, shorts, and dirty and/or loose connections.

NEUTRAL SAFETY SWITCH
Disconnect wiring at switch, place a jumper wire between terminals on wiring connector.

STARTER TURNS
Replace switch.

STARTER SOLENOID
Short the two large terminals together (not to ground).

STARTER TURNS
Replace solenoid.

①

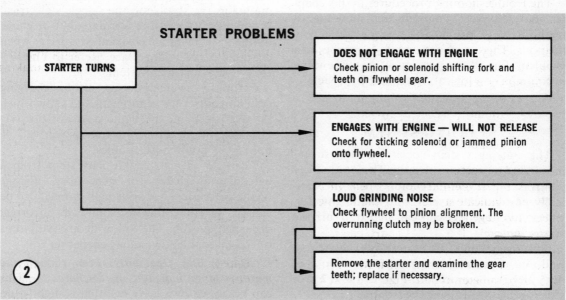

STARTER PROBLEMS

STARTER TURNS

DOES NOT ENGAGE WITH ENGINE
Check pinion or solenoid shifting fork and teeth on flywheel gear.

ENGAGES WITH ENGINE — WILL NOT RELEASE
Check for sticking solenoid or jammed pinion onto flywheel.

LOUD GRINDING NOISE
Check flywheel to pinion alignment. The overrunning clutch may be broken.

Remove the starter and examine the gear teeth; replace if necessary.

②

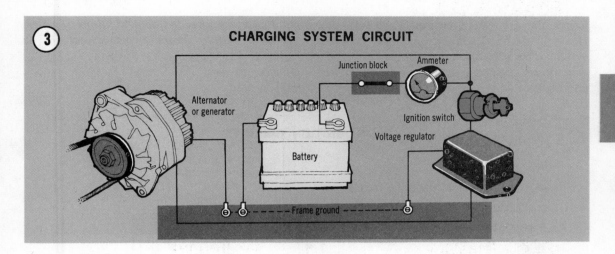

③ **CHARGING SYSTEM CIRCUIT**

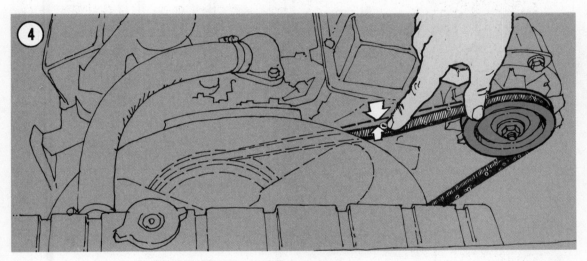

④

loose. Grasp the alternator (or generator) pulley and try to turn it. If the pulley can be turned without moving the belt, the drive belt is too loose. As a rule, keep the belt tight enough that it can be deflected about ½ in. under moderate thumb pressure between the pulleys (**Figure 4**). The battery may also be at fault; test the battery condition.

2. *Charging system warning lamp does not come on when ignition switch is turned on* — This may indicate a defective ignition switch, battery, voltage regulator, or lamp. First try to start the vehicle. If it doesn't start, check the ignition switch and battery. If the car starts, remove the warning lamp; test it for continuity with an ohmmeter or substitute a new lamp. If the lamp is good, locate the voltage regulator

and make sure it is properly grounded (try tightening the mounting screws). Also the alternator (or generator) brushes may not be making contact. Test the alternator (or generator) and voltage regulator.

3. *Alternator (or generator) warning lamp comes on and stays on* — This usually indicates that no charging is taking place. First check drive belt tension (**Figure 4**). Then check battery condition, and check all wiring connections in the charging system. If this does not locate the trouble, check the alternator (or generator) and voltage regulator.

4. *Charging system warning lamp flashes on and off intermittently* — This usually indicates the charging system is working intermittently.

Check the drive belt tension (**Figure 4**), and check all electrical connections in the charging system. Check the alternator (or generator). *On generators only*, check the condition of the commutator.

5. *Battery requires frequent additions of water, or lamps require frequent replacement* — The alternator (or generator) is probably overcharging the battery. The voltage regulator is probably at fault.

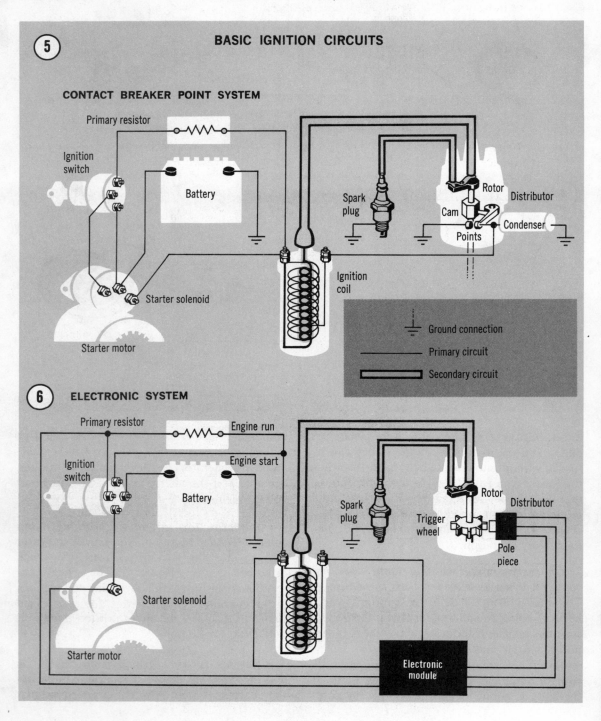

⑤ **BASIC IGNITION CIRCUITS**

CONTACT BREAKER POINT SYSTEM

Primary resistor

Ignition switch

Battery

Spark plug

Rotor

Distributor

Cam

Condenser

Points

Ignition coil

Starter solenoid

Starter motor

Ground connection

Primary circuit

Secondary circuit

⑥ **ELECTRONIC SYSTEM**

Primary resistor

Engine run

Ignition switch

Engine start

Battery

Spark plug

Rotor

Distributor

Trigger wheel

Pole piece

Starter solenoid

Starter motor

Electronic module

6. *Excessive noise from the alternator (or generator)* — Check for loose mounting brackets and bolts. The problem may also be worn bearings or the need of lubrication in some cases. If an alternator whines, a shorted diode may be indicated.

IGNITION SYSTEM

The ignition system may be either a conventional contact breaker type or an electronic ignition. See electrical chapter to determine which type you have. **Figures 5 and 6** show simplified diagrams of each type.

Most problems involving failure to start, poor performance, or rough running stem from trouble in the ignition system, particularly in contact breaker systems. Many novice troubleshooters get into trouble when they assume that these symptoms point to the fuel system instead of the ignition system.

Ignition system troubles may be roughly divided between those affecting only one cylinder and those affecting all cylinders. If the trouble affects only one cylinder, it can only be in the spark plug, spark plug wire, or portion of the distributor associated with that cylinder. If the trouble affects all cylinders (weak spark or no spark), then the trouble is in the ignition coil, rotor, distributor, or associated wiring.

The troubleshooting procedures outlined in **Figure 7** (breaker point ignition) or **Figure 8**

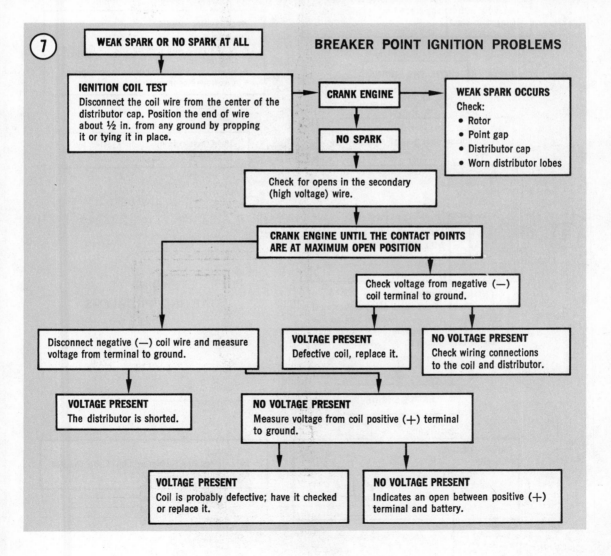

(electronic ignition) will help you isolate ignition problems fast. Of course, they assume that the battery is in good enough condition to crank the engine over at its normal rate.

ENGINE PERFORMANCE

A number of factors can make the engine difficult or impossible to start, or cause rough running, poor performance and so on. The majority of novice troubleshooters immediately suspect the carburetor or fuel injection system. In the majority of cases, though, the trouble exists in the ignition system.

The troubleshooting procedures outlined in **Figures 9 through 14** will help you solve the majority of engine starting troubles in a systematic manner.

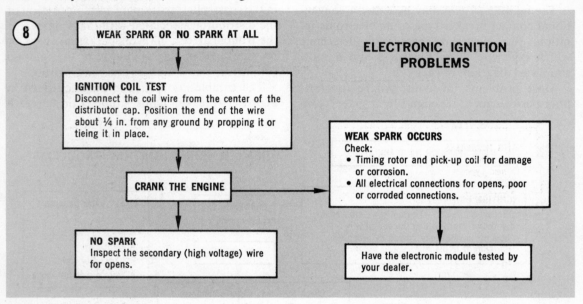

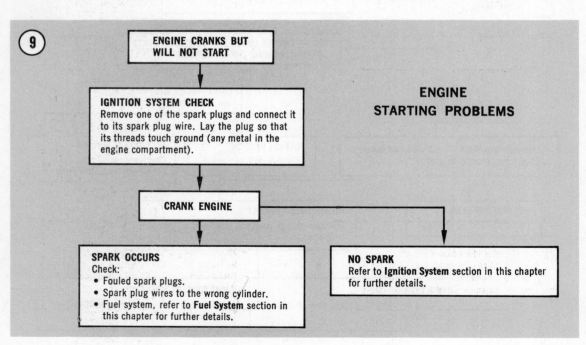

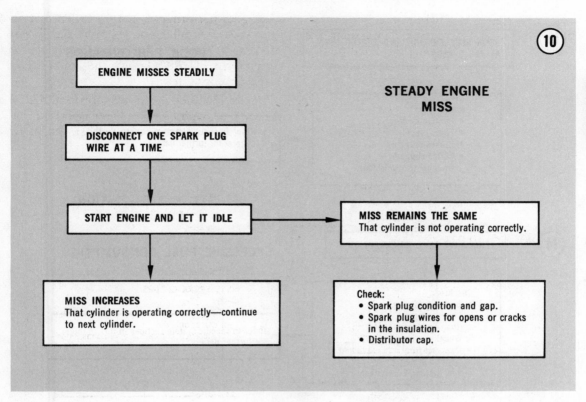

(10)

ENGINE MISSES STEADILY

STEADY ENGINE MISS

DISCONNECT ONE SPARK PLUG WIRE AT A TIME

START ENGINE AND LET IT IDLE

MISS REMAINS THE SAME
That cylinder is not operating correctly.

MISS INCREASES
That cylinder is operating correctly—continue to next cylinder.

Check:
• Spark plug condition and gap.
• Spark plug wires for opens or cracks in the insulation.
• Distributor cap.

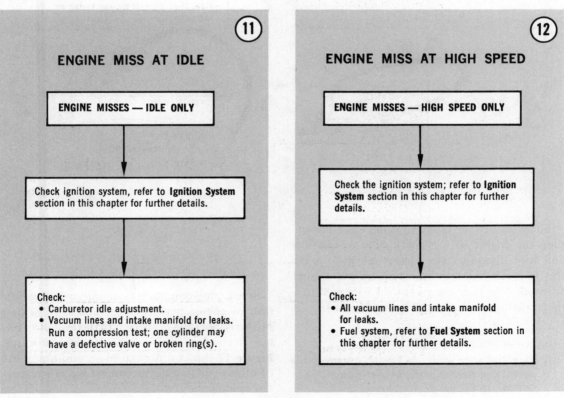

(11)

ENGINE MISS AT IDLE

ENGINE MISSES — IDLE ONLY

Check ignition system, refer to **Ignition System** section in this chapter for further details.

Check:
• Carburetor idle adjustment.
• Vacuum lines and intake manifold for leaks. Run a compression test; one cylinder may have a defective valve or broken ring(s).

(12)

ENGINE MISS AT HIGH SPEED

ENGINE MISSES — HIGH SPEED ONLY

Check the ignition system; refer to **Ignition System** section in this chapter for further details.

Check:
• All vacuum lines and intake manifold for leaks.
• Fuel system, refer to **Fuel System** section in this chapter for further details.

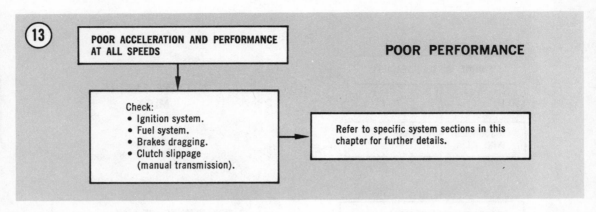

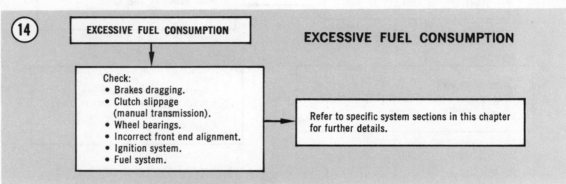

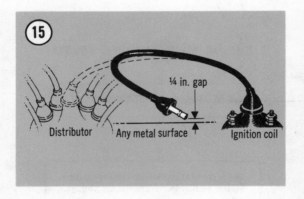

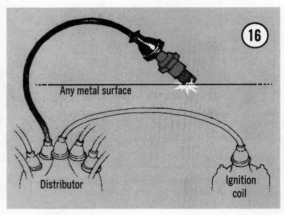

Some tests of the ignition system require running the engine with a spark plug or ignition coil wire disconnected. The safest way to do this is to disconnect the wire with the engine stopped, then prop the end of the wire next to a metal surface as shown in **Figures 15 and 16**.

WARNING
Never disconnect a spark plug or ignition coil wire while the engine is running. The high voltage in an ignition system, particularly the newer high-energy electronic ignition systems could cause serious injury or even death.

Spark plug condition is an important indication of engine performance. Spark plugs in a properly operating engine will have slightly pitted electrodes, and a light tan insulator tip. **Figure 17** shows a normal plug, and a number of others which indicate trouble in their respective cylinders.

NORMAL
• Appearance—Firing tip has deposits of light gray to light tan.
• Can be cleaned, regapped and reused.

CARBON FOULED
• Appearance—Dull, dry black with fluffy carbon deposits on the insulator tip, electrode and exposed shell.
• Caused by—Fuel/air mixture too rich, plug heat range too cold, weak ignition system, dirty air cleaner, faulty automatic choke or excessive idling.
• Can be cleaned, regapped and reused.

OIL FOULED
• Appearance—Wet black deposits on insulator and exposed shell.
• Caused by—Excessive oil entering the combustion chamber through worn rings, pistons, valve guides or bearings.
• Replace with new plugs (use a hotter plug if engine is not repaired).

LEAD FOULED
• Appearance — Yellow insulator deposits (may sometimes be dark gray, black or tan in color) on the insulator tip.
• Caused by—Highly leaded gasoline.
• Replace with new plugs.

LEAD FOULED
• Appearance—Yellow glazed deposits indicating melted lead deposits due to hard acceleration.
• Caused by—Highly leaded gasoline.
• Replace with new plugs.

OIL AND LEAD FOULED
• Appearance—Glazed yellow deposits with a slight brownish tint on the insulator tip and ground electrode.
• Replace with new plugs.

FUEL ADDITIVE RESIDUE
• Appearance — Brown colored hardened ash deposits on the insulator tip and ground electrode.
• Caused by—Fuel and/or oil additives.
• Replace with new plugs.

WORN
• Appearance — Severely worn or eroded electrodes.
• Caused by—Normal wear or unusual oil and/or fuel additives.
• Replace with new plugs.

PREIGNITION
• Appearance — Melted ground electrode.
• Caused by—Overadvanced ignition timing, inoperative ignition advance mechanism, too low of a fuel octane rating, lean fuel/air mixture or carbon deposits in combustion chamber.

PREIGNITION
• Appearance—Melted center electrode.
• Caused by—Abnormal combustion due to overadvanced ignition timing or incorrect advance, too low of a fuel octane rating, lean fuel/air mixture, or carbon deposits in combustion chamber.
• Correct engine problem and replace with new plugs.

INCORRECT HEAT RANGE
• Appearance—Melted center electrode and white blistered insulator tip.
• Caused by—Incorrect plug heat range selection.
• Replace with new plugs.

2

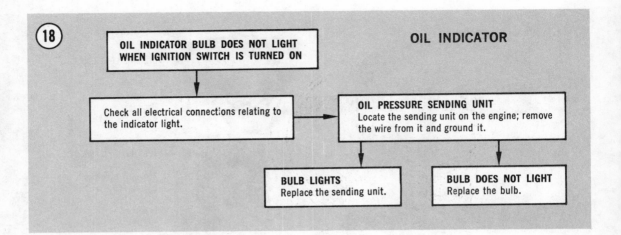

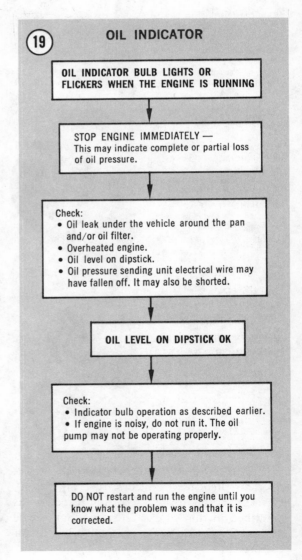

ENGINE OIL
PRESSURE LIGHT

Proper oil pressure to the engine is vital. If oil pressure is insufficient, the engine can destroy itself in a comparatively short time.

The oil pressure warning circuit monitors oil pressure constantly. If pressure drops below a predetermined level, the light comes on.

Obviously, it is vital for the warning circuit to be working to signal low oil pressure. Each time you turn on the ignition, but before you start the car, the warning light should come on. If it doesn't, there is trouble in the warning circuit, not the oil pressure system. See **Figure 18** to troubleshoot the warning circuit.

Once the engine is running, the warning light should stay off. If the warning light comes on or acts erratically while the engine is running there is trouble with the engine oil pressure system. *Stop the engine immediately*. Refer to **Figure 19** for possible causes of the problem.

FUEL SYSTEM
(CARBURETTED)

Fuel system problems must be isolated to the fuel pump (mechanical or electric), fuel lines, fuel filter, or carburetor. These procedures assume the ignition system is working properly and is correctly adjusted.

1. *Engine will not start* — First make sure that fuel is being delivered to the carburetor. Remove the air cleaner, look into the carburetor throat, and operate the accelerator

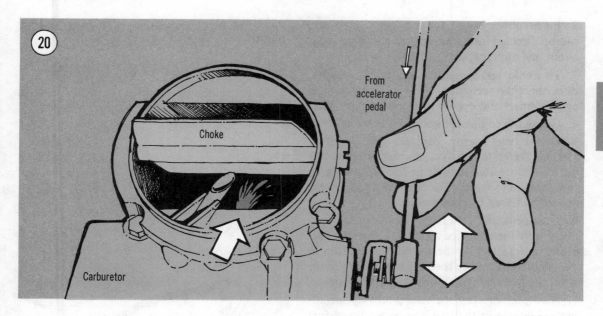

linkage several times. There should be a stream of fuel from the accelerator pump discharge tube each time the accelerator linkage is depressed (**Figure 20**). If not, check fuel pump delivery (described later), float valve, and float adjustment. If the engine will not start, check the automatic choke parts for sticking or damage. If necessary, rebuild or replace the carburetor.

2. *Engine runs at fast idle* — Check the choke setting. Check the idle speed, idle mixture, and decel valve (if equipped) adjustment.

3. *Rough idle or engine miss with frequent stalling* — Check idle mixture and idle speed adjustments.

4. *Engine "diesels" (continues to run) when ignition is switched off* — Check idle mixture (probably too rich), ignition timing, and idle speed (probably too fast). Check the throttle solenoid (if equipped) for proper operation. Check for overheated engine.

5. *Stumbling when accelerating from idle* — Check the idle speed and mixture adjustments. Check the accelerator pump.

6. *Engine misses at high speed or lacks power* — This indicates possible fuel starvation. Check fuel pump pressure and capacity as described in this chapter. Check float needle valves. Check for a clogged fuel filter or air cleaner.

7. *Black exhaust smoke* — This indicates a badly overrich mixture. Check idle mixture and idle speed adjustment. Check choke setting. Check for excessive fuel pump pressure, leaky floats, or worn needle valves.

8. *Excessive fuel consumption* — Check for overrich mixture. Make sure choke mechanism works properly. Check idle mixture and idle speed. Check for excessive fuel pump pressure, leaky floats, or worn float needle valves.

FUEL SYSTEM (FUEL INJECTED)

Troubleshooting a fuel injection system requires more thought, experience, and know-how than any other part of the vehicle. A logical approach and proper test equipment are essential in order to successfully find and fix these troubles.

It is best to leave fuel injection troubles to your dealer. In order to isolate a problem to the injection system make sure that the fuel pump is operating properly. Check its performance as described later in this section. Also make sure that fuel filter and air cleaner are not clogged.

FUEL PUMP TEST (MECHANICAL AND ELECTRIC)

1. Disconnect the fuel inlet line where it enters the carburetor or fuel injection system.

2. Fit a rubber hose over the fuel line so fuel can be directed into a graduated container with about one quart capacity. See **Figure 21**.

3. To avoid accidental starting of the engine, disconnect the secondary coil wire from the coil or disconnect and insulate the coil primary wire.

4. Crank the engine for about 30 seconds.

5. If the fuel pump supplies the specified amount (refer to the fuel chapter later in this book), the trouble may be in the carburetor or fuel injection system. The fuel injection system should be tested by your dealer.

6. If there is no fuel present or the pump cannot supply the specified amount, either the fuel pump is defective or there is an obstruction in the fuel line. Replace the fuel pump and/or inspect the fuel lines for air leaks or obstructions.

7. Also pressure test the fuel pump by installing a T-fitting in the fuel line between the fuel pump and the carburetor. Connect a fuel pressure gauge to the fitting with a short tube **(Figure 22)**.

8. Reconnect the coil wire, start the engine, and record the pressure. Refer to the fuel chapter later in this book for the correct pressure. If the pressure varies from that specified, the pump should be replaced.

9. Stop the engine. The pressure should drop off very slowly. If it drops off rapidly, the outlet valve in the pump is leaking and the pump should be replaced.

EMISSION CONTROL SYSTEMS

Major emission control systems used on nearly all U.S. models include the following:

a. Positive crankcase ventilation (PCV)

b. Thermostatic air cleaner

c. Air injection reaction (AIR)

d. Fuel evaporation control

e. Exhaust gas recirculation (EGR)

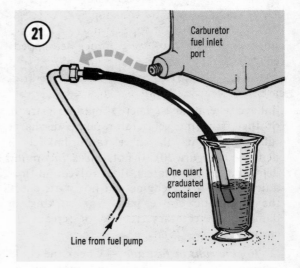

Carburetor fuel inlet port

One quart graduated container

Line from fuel pump

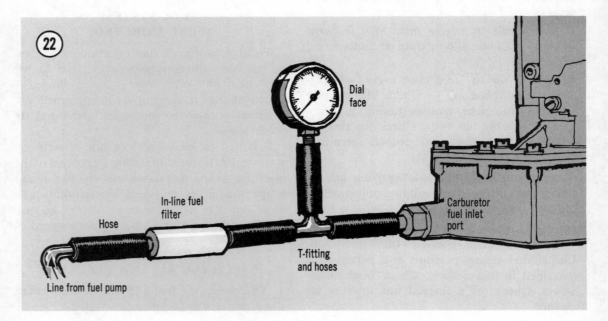

Dial face

In-line fuel filter

Hose

Carburetor fuel inlet port

T-fitting and hoses

Line from fuel pump

Emission control systems vary considerably from model to model. Individual models contain variations of the four systems described here. In addition, they may include other special systems. Use the index to find specific emission control components in other chapters.

Many of the systems and components are factory set and sealed. Without special expensive test equipment, it is impossible to adjust the systems to meet state and federal requirements.

Troubleshooting can also be difficult without special equipment. The procedures described below will help you find emission control parts which have failed, but repairs may have to be entrusted to a dealer or other properly equipped repair shop.

With the proper equipment, you can test the carbon monoxide and hydrocarbon levels.

Figure 23 provides some sources of trouble if the readings are not correct.

Positive Crankcase Ventilation

Fresh air drawn from the air cleaner housing scavenges emissions (e.g., piston blow-by) from the crankcase, then the intake manifold vacuum draws emissions into the intake manifold. They can then be reburned in the normal combustion process. **Figure 24** shows a typical system. **Figure 25** provides a testing procedure.

Thermostatic Air Cleaner

The thermostatically controlled air cleaner maintains incoming air to the engine at a predetermined level, usually about 100°F or higher. It mixes cold air with heated air from the exhaust manifold region. The air cleaner in-

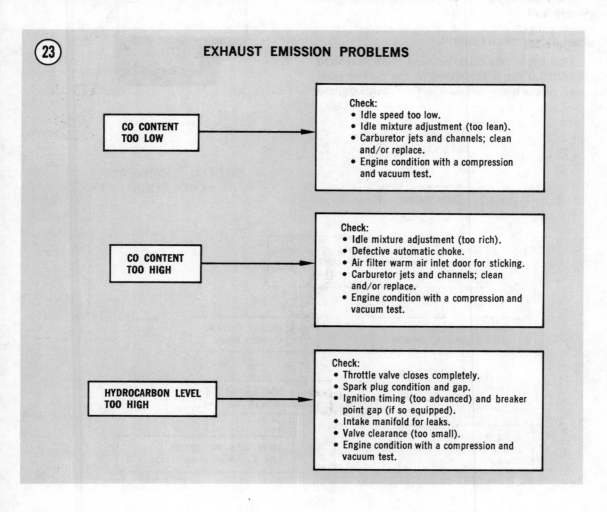

(23) **EXHAUST EMISSION PROBLEMS**

CO CONTENT TOO LOW

Check:
- Idle speed too low.
- Idle mixture adjustment (too lean).
- Carburetor jets and channels; clean and/or replace.
- Engine condition with a compression and vacuum test.

CO CONTENT TOO HIGH

Check:
- Idle mixture adjustment (too rich).
- Defective automatic choke.
- Air filter warm air inlet door for sticking.
- Carburetor jets and channels; clean and/or replace.
- Engine condition with a compression and vacuum test.

HYDROCARBON LEVEL TOO HIGH

Check:
- Throttle valve closes completely.
- Spark plug condition and gap.
- Ignition timing (too advanced) and breaker point gap (if so equipped).
- Intake manifold for leaks.
- Valve clearance (too small).
- Engine condition with a compression and vacuum test.

cludes a temperature sensor, vacuum motor, and a hinged door. See **Figure 26**.

The system is comparatively easy to test. See **Figure 27** for the procedure.

Air Injection Reaction System

The air injection reaction system reduces air pollution by oxidizing hydrocarbons and carbon monoxide as they leave the combustion chamber. See **Figure 28**.

The air injection pump, driven by the engine, compresses filtered air and injects it at the exhaust port of each cylinder. The fresh air mixes with the unburned gases in the exhaust and promotes further burning. A check valve prevents exhaust gases from entering and damaging the air pump if the pump becomes inoperative, e.g., from a fan belt failure.

Figure 29 explains the testing procedure for this system.

Fuel Evaporation Control

Fuel vapor from the fuel tank passes through the liquid/vapor separator to the carbon canister. See **Figure 30**. The carbon absorbs and

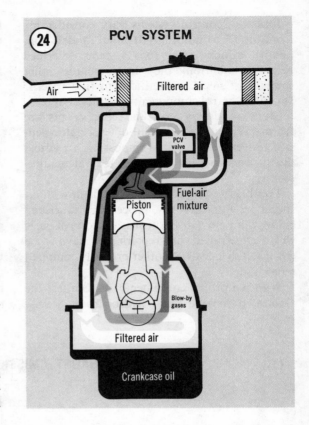

(24) PCV SYSTEM

Air → Filtered air

PCV valve

Fuel-air mixture

Piston

Blow-by gases

Filtered air

Crankcase oil

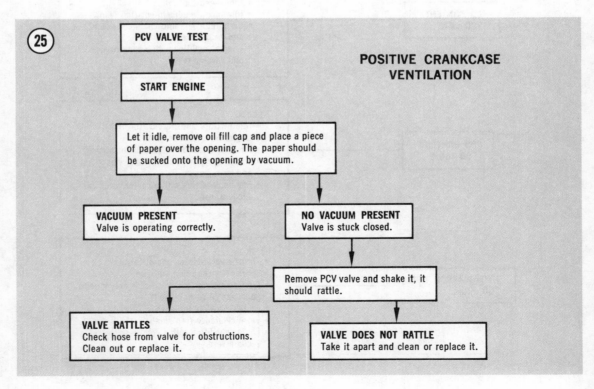

(25) POSITIVE CRANKCASE VENTILATION

PCV VALVE TEST
↓
START ENGINE
↓
Let it idle, remove oil fill cap and place a piece of paper over the opening. The paper should be sucked onto the opening by vacuum.

VACUUM PRESENT
Valve is operating correctly.

NO VACUUM PRESENT
Valve is stuck closed.

Remove PCV valve and shake it, it should rattle.

VALVE RATTLES
Check hose from valve for obstructions. Clean out or replace it.

VALVE DOES NOT RATTLE
Take it apart and clean or replace it.

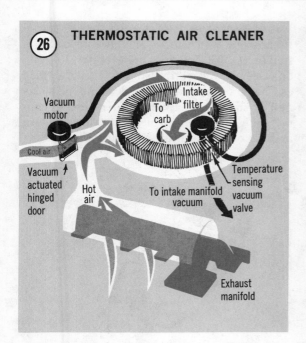

THERMOSTATIC AIR CLEANER (26)

- Vacuum motor
- Cool air
- Intake filter
- To carb
- Vacuum actuated hinged door
- Hot air
- To intake manifold vacuum
- Temperature sensing vacuum valve
- Exhaust manifold

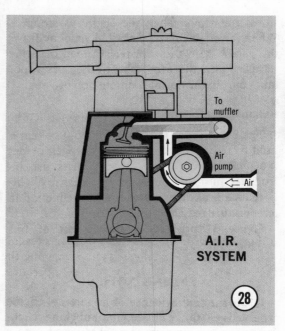

(28)

- To muffler
- Air pump
- Air

A.I.R. SYSTEM

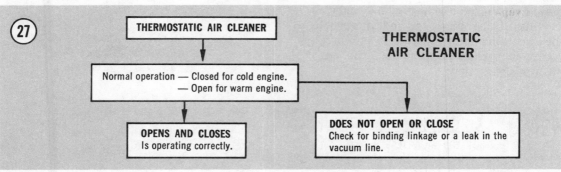

(27)

THERMOSTATIC AIR CLEANER

Normal operation — Closed for cold engine.
— Open for warm engine.

OPENS AND CLOSES
Is operating correctly.

DOES NOT OPEN OR CLOSE
Check for binding linkage or a leak in the vacuum line.

THERMOSTATIC AIR CLEANER

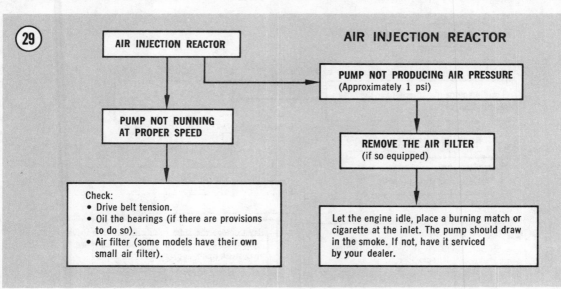

(29)

AIR INJECTION REACTOR

AIR INJECTION REACTOR

PUMP NOT PRODUCING AIR PRESSURE
(Approximately 1 psi)

PUMP NOT RUNNING AT PROPER SPEED

REMOVE THE AIR FILTER
(if so equipped)

Check:
- Drive belt tension.
- Oil the bearings (if there are provisions to do so).
- Air filter (some models have their own small air filter).

Let the engine idle, place a burning match or cigarette at the inlet. The pump should draw in the smoke. If not, have it serviced by your dealer.

stores the vapor when the engine is stopped. When the engine runs, manifold vacuum draws the vapor from the canister. Instead of being released into the atmosphere, the fuel vapor takes part in the normal combustion process.

Exhaust Gas Recirculation

The exhaust gas recirculation (EGR) system is used to reduce the emission of nitrogen oxides (NOx). Relatively inert exhaust gases are introduced into the combustion process to slightly reduce peak temperatures. This reduction in temperature reduces the formation of NOx.

Figure 31 provides a simple test of this system.

ENGINE NOISES

Often the first evidence of an internal engine trouble is a strange noise. That knocking, clicking, or tapping which you never heard before may be warning you of impending trouble.

While engine noises can indicate problems, they are sometimes difficult to interpret correctly; inexperienced mechanics can be seriously misled by them.

Professional mechanics often use a special stethoscope which looks similar to a doctor's stethoscope for isolating engine noises. You can do nearly as well with a "sounding stick" which can be an ordinary piece of doweling or a section of small hose. By placing one end in contact with the area to which you want to listen and the other end near your ear, you can hear

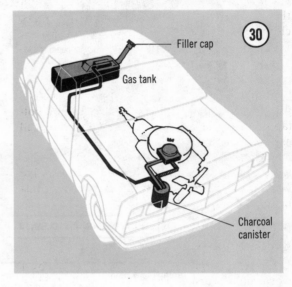

30

Filler cap

Gas tank

Charcoal canister

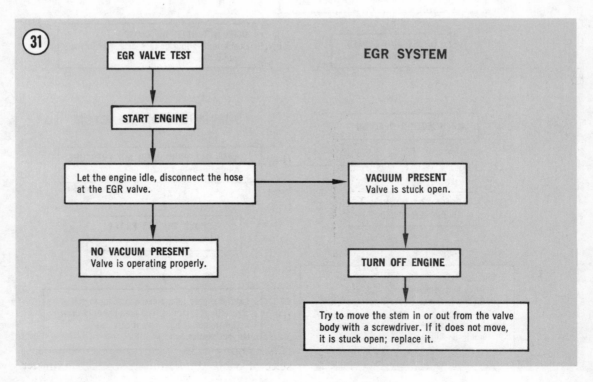

31

| EGR VALVE TEST | | EGR SYSTEM |

START ENGINE

Let the engine idle, disconnect the hose at the EGR valve.

VACUUM PRESENT
Valve is stuck open.

NO VACUUM PRESENT
Valve is operating properly.

TURN OFF ENGINE

Try to move the stem in or out from the valve body with a screwdriver. If it does not move, it is stuck open; replace it.

sounds emanating from that area. The first time you do this, you may be horrified at the strange noises coming from even a normal engine. If you can, have an experienced friend or mechanic help you sort the noises out.

Clicking or Tapping Noises

Clicking or tapping noises usually come from the valve train, and indicate excessive valve clearance.

If your vehicle has adjustable valves, the procedure for adjusting the valve clearance is explained in Chapter Three. If your vehicle has hydraulic lifters, the clearance may not be adjustable. The noise may be coming from a collapsed lifter. These may be cleaned or replaced as described in the engine chapter.

A sticking valve may also sound like a valve with excessive clearance. In addition, excessive wear in valve train components can cause similar engine noises.

Knocking Noises

A heavy, dull knocking is usually caused by a worn main bearing. The noise is loudest when the engine is working hard, i.e., accelerating hard at low speed. You may be able to isolate the trouble to a single bearing by disconnecting

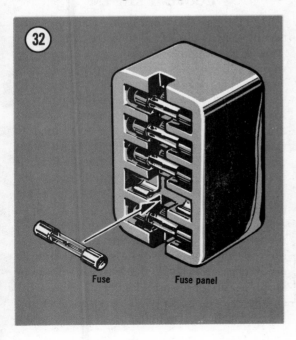

Fuse   Fuse panel

the spark plugs one at a time. When you reach the spark plug nearest the bearing, the knock will be reduced or disappear.

Worn connecting rod bearings may also produce a knock, but the sound is usually more "metallic." As with a main bearing, the noise is worse when accelerating. It may even increase further just as you go from accelerating to coasting. Disconnecting spark plugs will help isolate this knock as well.

A double knock or clicking usually indicates a worn piston pin. Disconnecting spark plugs will isolate this to a particular piston, however, the noise will *increase* when you reach the affected piston.

A loose flywheel and excessive crankshaft end play also produce knocking noises. While similar to main bearing noises, these are usually intermittent, not constant, and they do not change when spark plugs are disconnected.

Some mechanics confuse piston pin noise with piston slap. The double knock will distinguish the piston pin noise. Piston slap is identified by the fact that it is always louder when the engine is cold.

ELECTRICAL ACCESSORIES

Lights and Switches (Interior and Exterior)

1. *Bulb does not light* — Remove the bulb and check for a broken element. Also check the inside of the socket; make sure the contacts are clean and free of corrosion. If the bulb and socket are OK, check to see if a fuse has blown or a circuit breaker has tripped. The fuse panel **(Figure 32)** is usually located under the instrument panel. Replace the blown fuse or reset the circuit breaker. If the fuse blows or the breaker trips again, there is a short in that circuit. Check that circuit all the way to the battery. Look for worn wire insulation or burned wires.

If all the above are all right, check the switch controlling the bulb for continuity with an ohmmeter at the switch terminals. Check the switch contact terminals for loose or dirty electrical connections.

2. *Headlights work but will not switch from either high or low beam* — Check the beam selector switch for continuity with an ohmmeter

at the switch terminals. Check the switch contact terminals for loose or dirty electrical connections.

3. *Brake light switch inoperative* — On mechanically operated switches, usually mounted near the brake pedal arm, adjust the switch to achieve correct mechanical operation. Check the switch for continuity with an ohmmeter at the switch terminals. Check the switch contact terminals for loose or dirty electrical connections.

4. *Back-up lights do not operate* — Check light bulb as described earlier. Locate the switch, normally located near the shift lever. Adjust switch to achieve correct mechanical operation. Check the switch for continuity with an ohmmeter at the switch terminals. Bypass the switch with a jumper wire; if the lights work, replace the switch.

Directional Signals

1. *Directional signals do not operate* — If the indicator light on the instrument panel burns steadily instead of flashing, this usually indicates that one of the exterior lights is burned out. Check all lamps that normally flash. If all are all right, the flasher unit may be defective. Replace it with a good one.

2. *Directional signal indicator light on instrument panel does not light up* — Check the light bulbs as described earlier. Check all electrical connections and check the flasher unit.

3. *Directional signals will not self-cancel* — Check the self-cancelling mechanism located inside the steering column.

4. *Directional signals flash slowly* — Check the condition of the battery and the alternator (or generator) drive belt tension (**Figure 4**). Check the flasher unit and all related electrical connections.

Windshield Wipers

1. *Wipers do not operate* — Check for a blown fuse or circuit breaker that has tripped; replace or reset. Check all related terminals for loose or dirty electrical connections. Check continuity of the control switch with an ohmmeter at the switch terminals. Check the linkage and arms

for loose, broken, or binding parts. Straighten out or replace where necessary.

2. *Wiper motor hums but will not operate* — The motor may be shorted out internally; check and/or replace the motor. Also check for broken or binding linkage and arms.

3. *Wiper arms will not return to the stowed position when turned off* — The motor has a special internal switch for this purpose. Have it inspected by your dealer. Do not attempt this yourself.

Interior Heater

1. *Heater fan does not operate* — Check for a blown fuse or circuit breaker that has tripped. Check the switch for continuity with an ohmmeter at the switch terminals. Check the switch contact terminals for loose or dirty electrical connections.

2. *Heat output is insufficient* — Check the heater hose/engine coolant control valve usually located in the engine compartment; make sure it is in the open position. Ensure that the heater door(s) and cable(s) are operating correctly and are in the open position. Inspect the heat ducts; make sure that they are not crimped or blocked.

COOLING SYSTEM

The temperature gauge or warning light usually signals cooling system troubles before there is any damage. As long as you stop the vehicle at the first indication of trouble, serious damage is unlikely.

In most cases, the trouble will be obvious as soon as you open the hood. If there is coolant or steam leaking, look for a defective radiator, radiator hose, or heater hose. If there is no evidence of leakage, make sure that the fan belt is in good condition. If the trouble is not obvious, refer to **Figures 33 and 34** to help isolate the trouble.

Automotive cooling systems operate under pressure to permit higher operating temperatures without boil-over. The system should be checked periodically to make sure it can withstand normal pressure. **Figure 35** shows the equipment which nearly any service station has for testing the system pressure.

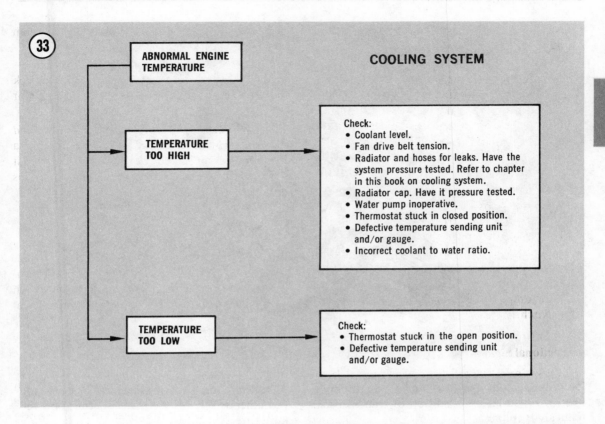

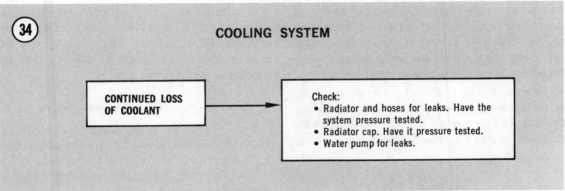

CLUTCH

All clutch troubles except adjustments require transmission removal to identify and cure the problem.

1. *Slippage* — This is most noticeable when accelerating in a high gear at relatively low speed. To check slippage, park the vehicle on a level surface with the handbrake set. Shift to 2nd gear and release the clutch as if driving off. If the clutch is good, the engine will slow and stall. If the clutch slips, continued engine speed will give it away.

Slippage results from insufficient clutch pedal free play, oil or grease on the clutch disc, worn pressure plate, or weak springs.

2. *Drag or failure to release* — This trouble usually causes difficult shifting and gear clash, especially when downshifting. The cause may be excessive clutch pedal free play, warped or bent pressure plate or clutch disc, broken or

loose linings, or lack of lubrication in pilot bearing. Also check condition of transmission main shaft splines.

3. *Chatter or grabbing* — A number of things can cause this trouble. Check tightness of engine mounts and engine-to-transmission mounting bolts. Check for worn or misaligned pressure plate and misaligned release plate.

4. *Other noises* — Noise usually indicates a dry or defective release or pilot bearing. Check the bearings and replace if necessary. Also check all parts for misalignment and uneven wear.

MANUAL TRANSMISSION/TRANSAXLE

Transmission and transaxle troubles are evident when one or more of the following symptoms appear:

 a. Difficulty changing gears
 b. Gears clash when downshifting
 c. Slipping out of gear
 d. Excessive noise in NEUTRAL
 e. Excessive noise in gear
 f. Oil leaks

Transmission and transaxle repairs are not recommended unless the many special tools required are available.

Transmission and transaxle troubles are sometimes difficult to distinguish from clutch troubles. Eliminate the clutch as a source of trouble before installing a new or rebuilt transmission or transaxle.

AUTOMATIC TRANSMISSION

Most automatic transmission repairs require considerable specialized knowledge and tools. It is impractical for the home mechanic to invest in the tools, since they cost more than a properly rebuilt transmission.

Check fluid level and condition frequently to help prevent future problems. If the fluid is orange or black in color or smells like varnish, it is an indication of some type of damage or failure within the transmission. Have the transmission serviced by your dealer or competent automatic transmission service facility.

BRAKES

Good brakes are vital to the safe operation of the vehicle. Performing the maintenance speci-

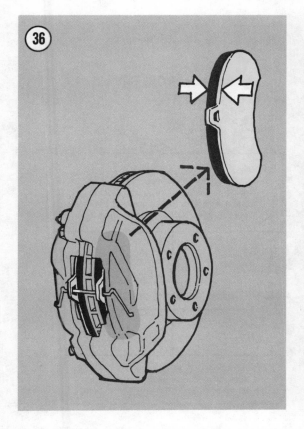

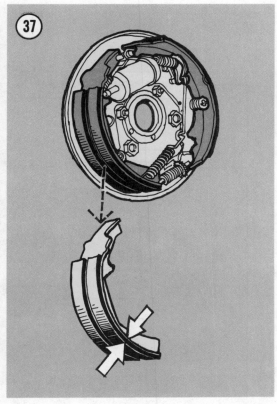

fied in Chapter Three will minimize problems with the brakes. Most importantly, check and maintain the level of fluid in the master cylinder, and check the thickness of the linings on the disc brake pads (**Figure 36**) or drum brake shoes (**Figure 37**).

If trouble develops, **Figures 38 through 40** will help you locate the problem. Refer to the brake chapter for actual repair procedures.

STEERING AND SUSPENSION

Trouble in the suspension or steering is evident when the following occur:

a. Steering is hard
b. Car pulls to one side
c. Car wanders or front wheels wobble
d. Steering has excessive play
e. Tire wear is abnormal

Unusual steering, pulling, or wandering is usually caused by bent or otherwise misaligned suspension parts. This is difficult to check without proper alignment equipment. Refer to the suspension chapter in this book for repairs that you can perform and those that must be left to a dealer or suspension specialist.

If your trouble seems to be excessive play, check wheel bearing adjustment first. This is the most frequent cause. Then check ball-joints (refer to Suspension chapter). Finally, check tie rod end ball-joints by shaking each tie rod. Also check steering gear, or rack-and-pinion assembly to see that it is securely bolted down.

TIRE WEAR ANALYSIS

Abnormal tire wear should be analyzed to determine its causes. The most common causes are the following:

a. Incorrect tire pressure
b. Improper driving
c. Overloading
d. Bad road surfaces
e. Incorrect wheel alignment

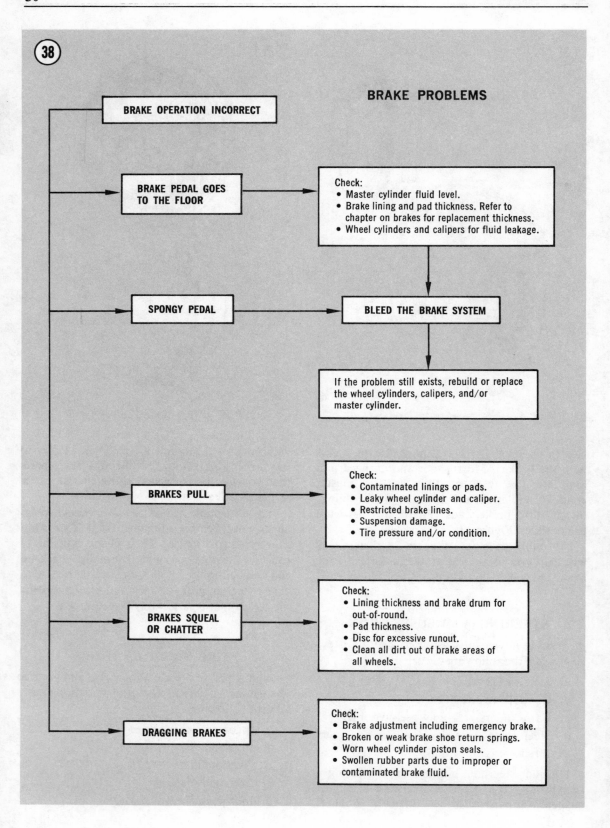

(38)

BRAKE PROBLEMS

BRAKE OPERATION INCORRECT

BRAKE PEDAL GOES TO THE FLOOR → Check:
- Master cylinder fluid level.
- Brake lining and pad thickness. Refer to chapter on brakes for replacement thickness.
- Wheel cylinders and calipers for fluid leakage.

SPONGY PEDAL → **BLEED THE BRAKE SYSTEM**

If the problem still exists, rebuild or replace the wheel cylinders, calipers, and/or master cylinder.

BRAKES PULL → Check:
- Contaminated linings or pads.
- Leaky wheel cylinder and caliper.
- Restricted brake lines.
- Suspension damage.
- Tire pressure and/or condition.

BRAKES SQUEAL OR CHATTER → Check:
- Lining thickness and brake drum for out-of-round.
- Pad thickness.
- Disc for excessive runout.
- Clean all dirt out of brake areas of all wheels.

DRAGGING BRAKES → Check:
- Brake adjustment including emergency brake.
- Broken or weak brake shoe return springs.
- Worn wheel cylinder piston seals.
- Swollen rubber parts due to improper or contaminated brake fluid.

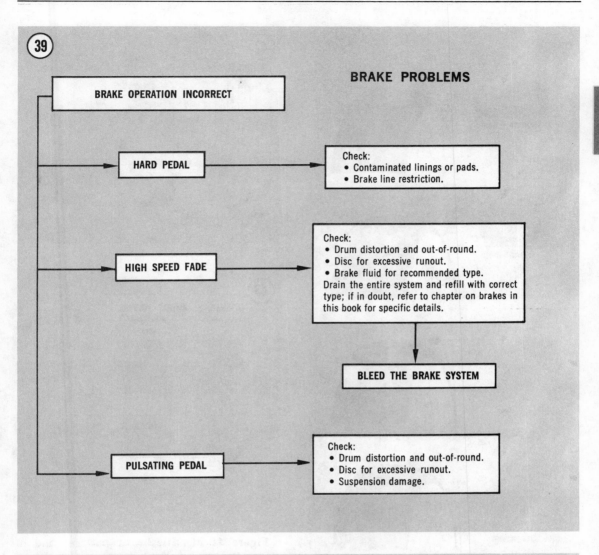

BRAKE PROBLEMS

BRAKE OPERATION INCORRECT

HARD PEDAL

Check:
• Contaminated linings or pads.
• Brake line restriction.

HIGH SPEED FADE

Check:
• Drum distortion and out-of-round.
• Disc for excessive runout.
• Brake fluid for recommended type.
Drain the entire system and refill with correct type; if in doubt, refer to chapter on brakes in this book for specific details.

BLEED THE BRAKE SYSTEM

PULSATING PEDAL

Check:
• Drum distortion and out-of-round.
• Disc for excessive runout.
• Suspension damage.

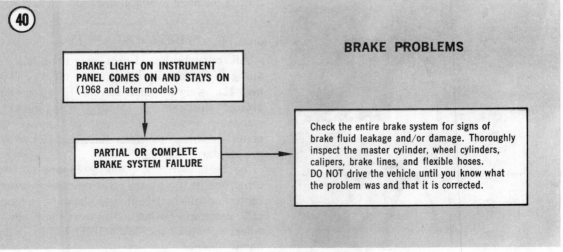

BRAKE PROBLEMS

BRAKE LIGHT ON INSTRUMENT PANEL COMES ON AND STAYS ON
(1968 and later models)

PARTIAL OR COMPLETE BRAKE SYSTEM FAILURE

Check the entire brake system for signs of brake fluid leakage and/or damage. Thoroughly inspect the master cylinder, wheel cylinders, calipers, brake lines, and flexible hoses.
DO NOT drive the vehicle until you know what the problem was and that it is corrected.

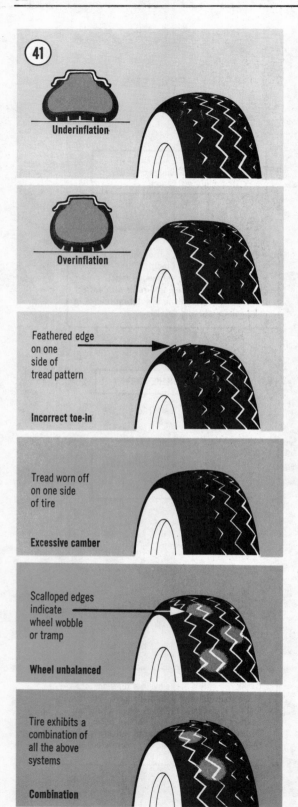

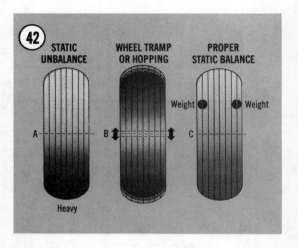

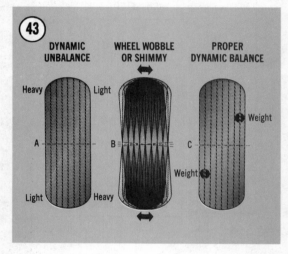

Figure 41 identifies wear patterns and indicates the most probable causes.

WHEEL BALANCING

All four wheels and tires must be in balance along two axes. To be in static balance (**Figure 42**), weight must be evenly distributed around the axis of rotation. (A) shows a statically unbalanced wheel; (B) shows the result — wheel tramp or hopping; (C) shows proper static balance.

To be in dynamic balance (**Figure 43**), the centerline of the weight must coincide with the centerline of the wheel. (A) shows a dynamically unbalanced wheel; (B) shows the result — wheel wobble or shimmy; (C) shows proper dynamic balance.

CHAPTER THREE

LUBRICATION, MAINTENANCE, AND TUNE-UP

This chapter deals with all the normal maintenance necessary to keep your car running properly. It includes summaries of service intervals in table form (**Tables 1, 2, 3, 4, and 5**).

ROUTINE CHECKS

The following checks should be performed at each stop for gas.

1. Check engine oil level (**Figure 1**). Top up to the "H" mark on the dipstick if necessary, using a grade recommended in **Tables 6 and 7**.
2. Check coolant level. On cars without coolant recovery systems, it should be one inch below the radiator filler neck. On cars with recovery systems, it should be above the LOW mark on the reservoir tank.

WARNING
Do not remove the radiator cap quickly while the engine is warm. Cover the cap with a rag and turn it ¼ turn counter-clockwise. After cooling system pressure has been released, press the cap down, turn counterclockwise, and re-move. If the engine is very hot, let it cool down before removing the cap.

3. Check the battery electrolyte level. It should be up to the mark indicated on the battery case. If topping up is necessary, lift the right front apron and remove the cover from

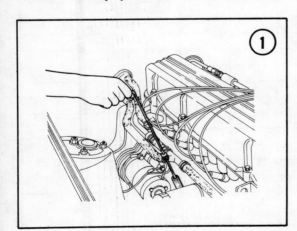

Table 1	FUEL STOP CHECKS
Item	**Procedure**
Engine oil	Check level
Coolant	Check level
Battery electrolyte	Check level
Windshield washers	Check container level
Brake fluid	Check level
Tire pressures	Check

Table 2   SCHEDULED MAINTENANCE, 240Z

Service	Months or Thousands of Miles				
	3	6	12	24	30
Engine oil	X				
Man. trans. oil, auto. trans. fluid	X				
Differential oil	X				
Hydraulic systems	X				
Fuel lines				X	
Spark plugs, distributor points	X				
Ignition timing	X				
Carburetor	X				
Valve clearances		X			
Engine leak inspection		X			
Drive belts			X		
Throttle linkage		X			
Steering rack, suspension		X			
Hinges, latches, locks		X			
PCV system			X		
Steering grease reservoir			X		
EGR system			X		
Evaporative emission control system			X		
Cooling system			X		
Vacuum lines			X		
ATC air cleaner			X		
Fuel filter				X	
Spark timing control system				X	
Throttle opener			X		
Brake fluid, brake booster			X		
Battery			X		
Brake inspection	X		X		
Shock absorbers			X		
Drive shaft			X		
Wheel alignment			X		
Pedals			X		
Engine compression			X		
Coolant				X	
Air cleaner element				X	
Air injection system				X	
Proportioning valve				X	
Steering rack, suspension ball-joints					X
Wheel bearings					X
Manual transmission					X
Differential, rear axle shafts					X
Headlights					X
Drive shaft					X
Tune-up			X		

Table 3   SCHEDULED MAINTENANCE, 260Z

Service	4	8	12	24	36
		Months or Thousands of Miles			
Engine oil	X				
Manual transmission oil	X				
Automatic transmission fluid	X				
Differential oil	X				
Hydraulic systems	X				
Fuel lines				X	
Engine leak inspection	X				
Drive belts			X		
Throttle linkage		X			
Steering rack, suspension	X				
Hinges, latches, locks		X			
PCV system			X		
EGR system			X		
Evaporative emission control system			X		
Cooling system			X		
Vacuum lines			X		
ATC air cleaner			X		
Fuel filter				X	
Spark timing control system				X	
Throttle opener			X		
Brake fluid			X		
Brake booster			X		
Battery		X			
Brake inspection	X		X		
Drive shaft					X
Wheel alignment		X			
Engine compression			X		
Coolant				X	
Air cleaner element				X	
Air injection system				X	
Proportioning valve				X	
Steering linkage, suspension ball-joints				X	
Wheel bearings				X	
Manual transmission					X
Differential					X
Rear axle shafts					X
Drive shaft					X
Headlights					X
Tune-up			X		

Table 4   SCHEDULED MAINTENANCE — 1975-1977 280Z

Service	Thousands of Miles (Months)		
	6.25 (6)	12.5 (12)	25 (24)
Engine oil	X		
Manual transmission oil	X		
Automatic transmission fluid	X		
Differential oil	X		
Hydraulic systems	X		
Fuel lines		X	
Drive belts		X	
Hinges, latches, locks	X		
PCV system			X
Evaporative emission control system			X
Cooling system		X	
Vacuum lines		X	
Fuel filter			X
Spark timing control system			X
Boost controlled deceleration device		X	
Brake fluid		X	
Brake booster		X	
Brake inspection	X	X	
Wheel alignment		X	
Coolant		X	
Air cleaner element			X
Proportioning valve	X		
Steering linkage, suspension ball-joints			X
Wheel bearings			X
Manual transmission			X
Differential			X
Tune-up		X	

Table 5   SCHEDULED MAINTENANCE — 1978 280Z

Interval	Service
Every 7,500 miles (6 months)	Engine oil and filter Manual transmission oil Automatic transmission fluid Differential oil Hydraulic systems Front brake pads, booster, proportioning valve Hinges, latches, locks Engine leak inspection
Every 15,000 miles (12 months)	Drive belts Coolant hoses and connections Vacuum lines Brake fluid Steering linkage and suspension tightness Drive shaft tightness Wheel alignment Rear brakes Tune-up
Every 30,000 miles (24 months)	Coolant Brake booster hoses and check valve Air cleaner element Fuel filter Evaporative emission control system PCV valve Ball-joints Rear axle shaft U-joints Front wheel bearings Manual transmission oil change Differential oil change

the battery cell caps as shown in **Figure 2**. Top up with distilled water only.

4. Check the level of the windshield washer container. It should be kept full.

5. Check the brake and clutch fluid level. Since the master cylinder reservoirs are translucent, this can be done at a glance. The clutch master cylinder is located to the left of the brake master cylinder and behind the windshield washer container (**Figure 3**). Make sure the fluid level is up to the upper line on each reser-voir. If low, top up with brake fluid marked DOT 3 or DOT 4. The same fluid is used for clutch and brakes.

CAUTION
Do not remove reservoir caps unless topping up fluid. Clean the area around the reservoir caps before removing.

6. Check tire pressures. This should be done when the tires are cold. Recommended pressures are listed in **Table 8**.

Table 6 LUBRICANT VISCOSITY

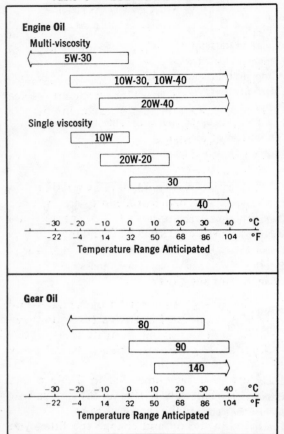

Engine Oil

Multi-viscosity
- 5W-30
- 10W-30, 10W-40
- 20W-40

Single viscosity
- 10W
- 20W-20
- 30
- 40

| −30 | −20 | −10 | 0 | 10 | 20 | 30 | 40 | °C |
| −22 | −4 | 14 | 32 | 50 | 68 | 86 | 104 | °F |

Temperature Range Anticipated

Gear Oil
- 80
- 90
- 140

| −30 | −20 | −10 | 0 | 10 | 20 | 30 | 40 | °C |
| −22 | −4 | 14 | 32 | 50 | 68 | 86 | 104 | °F |

Temperature Range Anticipated

Table 7 RECOMMENDED LUBRICANTS

Engine	SD or SE
Manual transmission	API GL-4
Automatic transmission	Dexron
Differential	API GL-5
Brake and clutch fluid	DOT 3

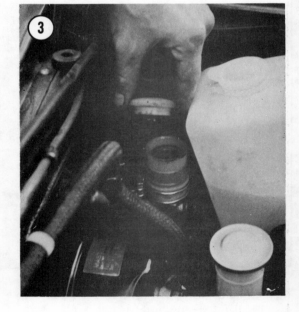

Table 8 TIRE PRESSURES

	Above 100 mph	Below 100 mph
Regular tires (175 SR-14, 175 HR-14, 195/70 HR-14, 195/70 VR-14)	32 psi	28 psi
1977 and later spare tire* (C78-14)	—	28 psi
*Do not use the spare tire at speeds above 50 mph.		

PERIODIC CHECKS
AND MAINTENANCE

The following procedures are done at specified intervals of miles or time. Refer to **Tables 1** through **5**.

These service schedules are intended for cars given normal use. More frequent service is required under the following conditions:

- a. Stop-and-go driving
- b. Constant high-speed driving
- c. Severe dust
- d. Rough or salted roads
- e. Very hot, very cold, or rainy weather

Some maintenance procedures are included in the *Tune-up* section of this chapter, and detailed instructions will be found there.

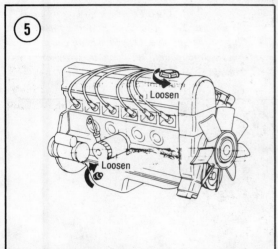

Engine Oil and Filter

If the car is given normal use, change the oil when recommended in **Tables 2-5**. If it is used for stop-and-go driving, in dusty areas, or left idling for long periods, change the oil every 3,000 miles or 3 months.

Use an oil recommended in **Table 6** and **Table 7**. The rating (SE or SF is usually printed on top of the can (**Figure 4**).

To drain the oil and change the filter, you will need:

- a. Drain pan
- b. Oil can spout or can opener and funnel
- c. Filter wrench
- d. 5 quarts of oil
- e. Oil filter

There are several ways to discard the old oil safely. The easiest is to pour it from the drain pan into a gallon bleach or milk bottle. The oil can be taken to a service station for dumping or, where permitted, thrown in your household trash.

1. Warm the engine to operating temperature, then shut if off.

2. Put the drain pan under the drain plug (**Figure 5**). Remove the plug and let the oil drain for at least 10 minutes.

3. Unscrew the oil filter (**Figure 6**) counterclockwise. Use a filter wrench if the filter is too tight to remove by hand.

4. Wipe the gasket surface on the engine block clean with a lint-free cloth.

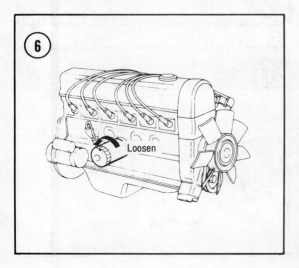

5. Coat the neoprene gasket on the new filter with clean engine oil. See **Figure 7**.

6. Screw the filter onto the engine *by hand* until the gasket just touches the engine block. At this point, there will be a very slight resistance when turning the filter.

7. Tighten the filter 2/3 turn more *by hand.* If the filter wrench is used, the filter will probably be overtightened. This will cause an oil leak.

8. Install the oil pan drain plug. Tighten it securely.

9. Remove the oil filler cap (**Figure 5**).

10. Pour oil into the engine. Capacity is listed in **Table 9**.

11. Start the engine and let it idle. The instrument panel oil pressure light will remain on for 15-30 seconds, then go out.

> *CAUTION*
> *Do not rev the engine to make the oil pressure light go out. It takes time for the oil to reach all areas of the engine and revving it could damage dry parts.*

12. While the engine is running, check the drain plug and oil filter for leaks.

13. Turn the engine off. Let the oil settle for several minutes, then check level on the dipstick. See **Figure 8**. Add oil if necessary to bring the level up to the "H" mark, but *do not* overfill.

Manual Transmission Oil Level

To check, remove the filler plug. On F4W71A transmissions (manufactured through September, 1972) the plug is on the right side of the transmission, just in front of the backup light switch. On F4W71B and FS5W71B transmissions (manufactured after September, 1972), the plug is on the left side. Oil level should be within 1/4 in. of the bottom of the filler plug hole. Top up with an oil recommended in **Table 6** and **Table 7** if it is low.

Automatic Transmission Fluid Level

With the car on a level surface, start the engine and let it run for about 10 minutes. Apply the brakes and move the shift lever through all gear positions; stop at P. Check the transmission fluid level on the dipstick (**Figure 9**) with the engine idling. If necessary, top up to "F" line using Dexron type automatic transmission fluid.

> *CAUTION*
> *Do not use Type A or Type F, and do not fill past the "F" line. Overfilling can cause the fluid to foam, resulting in wear or damage.*

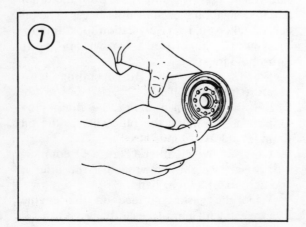

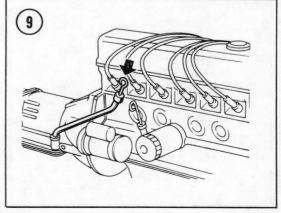

Differential Oil

To check, remove the filler plug from the inspection plate at the back of the differential. Check to make sure the level is 1/4 in. below the filler plug threads. Top up with an oil recommended in **Table 6** and **Table 7**.

Hydraulic Systems

Check for leaks. Inspect the brake master cylinders, calipers, and wheel cylinders for wetness. Do the same for the clutch master and operating cylinders, and all hydraulic line connections.

Engine Leak Inspection

The engine should be checked visually for leaks. Check the oil drain plug, oil pan gasket, oil filter, and front cover and oil pump assembly. Greasy-looking dirt at these points may indicate an oil leak. Inspect the radiator and hose connections for coolant residue or rust. Check the fuel connections (fuel filter, fuel pump, carburetors, or injectors) for wetness that indicates gasoline leakage.

Drive Belts

Check the fan belt tension by pressing down on the belt halfway between alternator and

3

Table 9 APPROXIMATE REFILL CAPACITIES

Engine oil	
1970-1973	
With filter change	5⅛ qt. (4.9 liters)
Without filter change	4¼ qt. (4 liters)
1974-1977	
With filter change	5 qt. (4.7 liters)
Without filter change	4¼ qt. (4 liters)
1978	
With filter change	4¾ qt. (4.5 liters)
Without filter change	4¼ qt. (4 liters)
Manual transmission oil	
Four-speed	3⅝ pt. (1.7 liters)
Five-speed	4¼ pt. (2 liters)
Differential oil	
240-260Z	2⅛ pt. (1 liter)
1975-1976 280Z	2¾ pt. (1.3 liter)
1977-1978 280Z	
With manual transmission	2¾ pt. (1.3 liter)
With automatic transmission	2⅛ pt. (1 liter)
Cooling system	
1970-1973	10½ qt. (9.9 liters)
1974-1975	10 qt. (9.4 liters)
1976	11 qt. (10.4 liters)
1977-1978	
Manual transmission	10⅞ qt. (10.3 liters)
Automatic transmission	10⅝ qt. (10.1 liters)

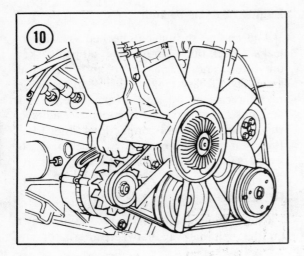

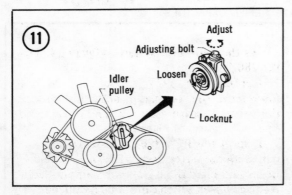

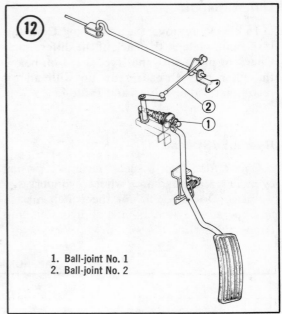

1. Ball-joint No. 1
2. Ball-joint No. 2

fan. See **Figure 10**. The belt should move approximately 1/2-3/4 in. (15-20 mm). If necessary, loosen the alternator mounting and adjusting bolts. Pull the alternator away from the engine to tighten the belt; push it toward the engine to loosen.

On 1970-1974 models, adjust the air pump belt in the same manner as the alternator belt.

On air-conditioned cars, press down on the belt between the idler pulley and air conditioning compressor. See **Figure 11**. The belt should move approximately 1/3-1/2 in. (8-12 mm). To adjust, loosen the idler pulley locknut. Turn the idler pulley adjusting bolt in or out to raise or lower the pulley. Then tighten the locknut.

Throttle Linkage (240-260Z)

Check throttle linkage ball-joints (**Figure 12**) for binding. Lubricate as needed with multipurpose grease.

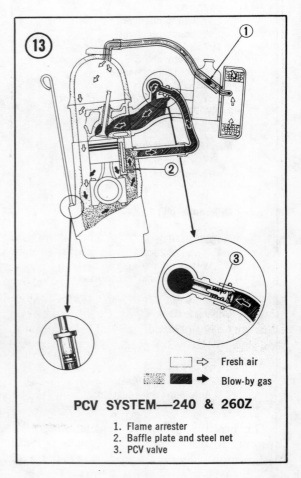

⬜ ⇨ Fresh air
▨ ■ ➡ Blow-by gas

PCV SYSTEM—240 & 260Z

1. Flame arrester
2. Baffle plate and steel net
3. PCV valve

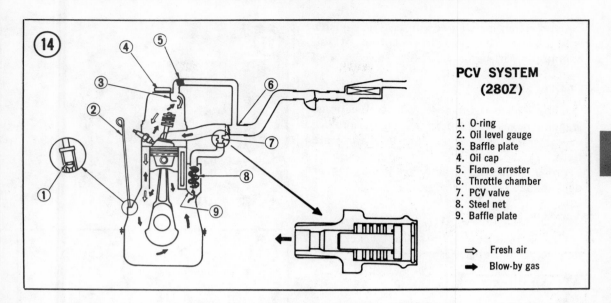

PCV SYSTEM (280Z)

1. O-ring
2. Oil level gauge
3. Baffle plate
4. Oil cap
5. Flame arrester
6. Throttle chamber
7. PCV valve
8. Steel net
9. Baffle plate

⇨ Fresh air
➡ Blow-by gas

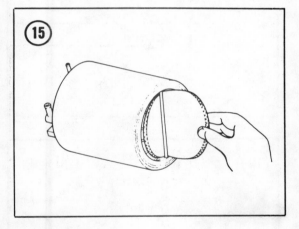

Hinges, Latches and Locks

Lightly grease the hood latch and tailgate lock with molybdenum disulfide based grease. Apply 1-2 drops of oil to hinges on doors, hood, and tailgate. Lubricate striker plates with a nonstaining stick lube such as Door Ease. Lubricate lock tumblers by applying a thin coat of Lubriplate, lock oil, or graphite to the key. Insert and work the lock several times. Wipe the key clean.

PCV System

The positive crankcase ventilation (PCV) system routes crankcase emissions into combustion chambers for burning. **Figure 13**

shows the 240-260Z system. **Figure 14** shows the 280Z design.

1. Replace the PCV valve. To do this, disconnect the ventilator hose and unscrew the valve. Discard the valve and install a new one.

2. Inspect the PCV hoses for leaks and loose connections. After inspection, disconnect the hoses and blow them out with compressed air. Replace hoses which cannot be unplugged.

Steering Grease Reservoir (240Z)

Check the plastic grease reservoir located on the steering rack-and-pinion housing. Detach the reservoir and fill with grease if it is low. Replace the reservoir if cracked or otherwise damaged.

EGR System

Inspect the exhaust gas recirculation system as described in Chapter Five.

Evaporative Emission Control System

Inspect fuel vapor lines, starting at the fuel tank and working forward. Tighten loose connections and replace damaged lines. Make sure the lines are secure in their clips and do not rub against any part of the car. On 1974 and later models, remove the carbon canister filter (**Figure 15**) from the bottom of the canister. Then install a new filter. The canister is located at the right front corner of the engine compartment. See **Figure 16**.

Cooling System

Inspect all coolant hoses and connections. Replace hoses that are cracked, deteriorated, or extremely soft. Make sure all clamps are tight.

Flush, drain, and refill the cooling system as described in Chapter Six.

Vacuum Lines

Check vacuum lines for cracks or deterioration. Replace as needed.

ATC Air Cleaner

The automatic temperature control air cleaner is used on 1972-1974 models. To check, look down the air cleaner throat. Make sure the flap valve closes when the engine is cold, and opens when the engine is warm.

Fuel Filter

Figure 17 shows the 240Z fuel filter. **Figure 18** shows the 260Z filter. To remove, disconnect the inlet line and plug it. Then disconnect the outlet line and pull the filter out of its clip. Install in the reverse order.

Figure 19 shows the 280Z fuel filter. Since the fuel in the lines is under high pressure, the pressure must be relieved before the lines can be disconnected. Proceed as follows.

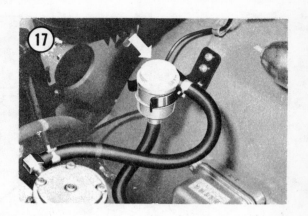

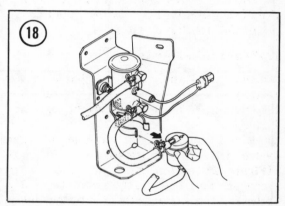

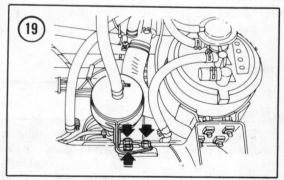

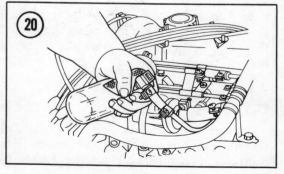

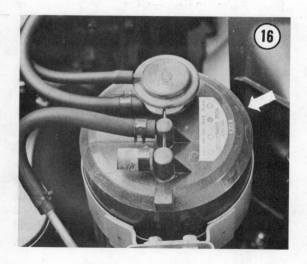

1975-1976 Models

1. Disconnect the negative cable from the battery.
2. Disconnect black wire from the fuel pump.
3. Disconnect the wire running from starter solenoid to starter motor. Leave the other starter wires connected.
4. Remove 2 screws securing the cold start valve to the manifold. Place the valve in a container (**Figure 20**).
5. Reconnect the battery cable. Turn the key to start and let the fuel run into the container.
6. Disconnect the lines from the fuel filter. Remove 3 securing bolts and take it out.
7. Install in the reverse order.

1977 and Later Models

1. Disconnect the negative cable from the battery.
2. Disconnect the wires from the cold start valve.
3. Run 2 jumper wires from the cold start valve terminals to the battery terminals (**Figure 21**). Connect the wires for a few seconds. This operates the cold start valve, releasing pressurized fuel into the intake manifold.
4. Disconnect the lines from the fuel filter. Remove its mounting screws and take it out.
5. Install in the reverse order.

Spark Timing Control System

Test as described in Chapter Seven.

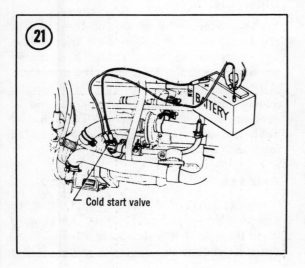

Cold start valve

Throttle Opener or BCDD

The throttle opener (240-260Z) or boost controlled deceleration device (280Z) reduces emissions during deceleration. To check, raise engine to 3,000-3,500 rpm, then release the throttle suddenly. Engine speed should drop to idle in a few seconds. If speed drops instantly or the throttle hangs open, the device probably requires adjustment. Take the job to a Datsun dealer.

Brake Fluid

Pump out all the old brake fluid and replace it with new fluid. See *Brake Bleeding*, Chapter Ten.

Brake Booster

Test brake booster, hose, and check valve as described under *Vacuum Booster*, Chapter Ten.

Battery

Check battery specific gravity as described under *Battery Testing*, Chapter Seven.

Brake Inspection

Inspect front brakes at 3,000 miles (1970-1972), 4,000 miles (1974), 6,250 miles (1975-1977), or 7,500 miles (1978).

Inspect rear brakes at 12,000 miles (1970-1974), 12,500 miles (1975-1977), or 15,000 miles (1978). Inspection procedures are described in Chapter Ten.

Shock Absorbers

As a quick check, lean on each corner of the car, then release it. If it bounces more than once, the shock absorbers probably need to be replaced. Also check for fluid leaks from the shocks.

Drive Shaft

Check the drive shaft for wear. The easiest way to do this is to shake the drive shaft while watching the universal joints. If play can be detected in the U-joints, disassemble and repair them as described in Chapter Twelve.

After checking for U-joint wear, tighten the bolts attaching the drive shaft to the differential flange.

Wheel Alignment

Have wheel alignment checked and adjusted if necessary by a dealer or front-end specialist.

Pedals

Using multipurpose grease, lubricate brake and clutch pedals at their pivot points. Also lubricate the pivot points (in the pedals) of the brake and clutch master cylinder pushrods.

Engine Compression

Test as described in this chapter.

Air Cleaner Element

On all models, the air cleaner element is a viscous paper type. Do not attempt to clean it between replacements.

To replace, remove the cover wing nuts, lift off the cover, and take out the element. Install in the reverse order.

Air Injection System

Inspect as described in Chapter Five.

Proportioning Valve

Test as described under *Brake Lines, Warning Switch, and Proportioning Valve*, Chapter Ten.

Steering Rack, Suspension Ball-Joints

Check the rack-and-pinion mechanism and tie rods for looseness. Check the bolts holding the rack-and-pinion mechanism to the frame, and the nuts attaching the tie rod ends to the knuckle arms. Check the bolts attaching the lower joint assembly to the upper steering column and to the pinion.

Check all fasteners in the front and rear suspensions for looseness. See Chapters Eleven and Twelve for specified tightening torques.

On 240Z's, remove the plug from each end of the steering rack and install a grease nipple. Inject multipurpose grease until a small amount is forced from the boot outlet hole. Also remove the grease reservoir and repack it with multipurpose grease.

On all Z's, lubricate the suspension and tie rod ball-joints with multipurpose grease. To do this, remove the filler plug from the bottom of each suspension ball-joint, and from the side of each tie rod ball-joint. Install grease nipples in place of the filler plugs. Inject grease with a grease gun until all the old grease is forced out. Be careful not to rupture the rubber dust covers on the ball-joints.

Wheel Bearings

Inspect, clean, repack, and adjust the wheel bearings. See Chapter Eleven.

Manual Transmission

To change the oil, first warm it up by driving a short distance. Then remove the filler and drain plugs and drain the oil. Reinstall the drain plug and fill it with an oil recommended in **Table 6** and **Table 7**. Capacity is listed in **Table 9**. When the transmission is full, reinstall filler plug.

> *NOTE*
> *Check the old transmission oil for such signs of damage as gear teeth and pieces of brass from synchronizers.*

Differential

This procedure is much like that used to change the transmission oil. First drive the car a short distance to warm the oil. Then remove the filler and drain plugs from the inspection plate on the back of the differential. When the oil has drained, reinstall the drain plug and fill with an oil recommended in **Table 6** and **Table 7**. Capacity is listed in **Table 9**. Reinstall the filler plug after filling.

Rear Axle Shafts

Check the rear axle shaft universal joints and dust boots for grease leakage. Thoroughly clean the axle shafts, then slide the dust boots down far enough to inspect the splines. If they are dry or the grease appears dirty, disassemble, clean, and lubricate the axle shafts as described in Chapter Twelve.

On 280Z's, remove the plugs from the universal joints, and install grease nipples. Inject multipurpose grease, then remove the nipples and reinstall the plugs.

Headlights

Have the aim of the headlights checked by a Datsun dealer or certified light adjusting station.

Drive Shaft

1. Securely block both front wheels so the car will not roll in either direction. Jack up the rear end and place jackstands beneath the frame.
2. Place the transmission in NEUTRAL and release the handbrake.
3. Rotate the drive shaft by turning a rear tire. Check for noise or rough movement. Check U-joints for looseness and for grease leaks. On 240-260Z's, replace the U-joints if any of these defects is found. On 280Z's, replace the drive shaft.

ENGINE TUNE-UP

Under normal conditions, a complete tune-up should be done every 12,000 miles (1970-1974), every 12,500 miles (1975-1977) or every 15,000 miles (1978). More frequent tune-ups may be needed if the car is used under the severe conditions described earlier in this chapter.

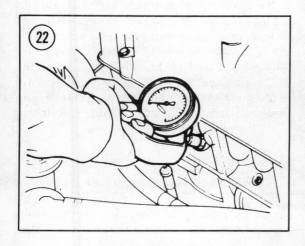

Since different engine systems interact, procedures should be done in the following order:

   a. Test compression
   b. Tighten cylinder head bolts
   c. Adjust valve clearances
   d. Work on ignition system
   e. Adjust carburetor

COMPRESSION TEST

There are 2 types of compression test: "wet" and "dry." These tests are intepreted together to isolate problems in cylinders and valves. The dry compression test is done first. Test as follows.

1. Warm the engine to normal operating temperature.
2. Remove the air cleaner as described in Chapter Five. On 240-260Z's, make sure the choke valves are completely open.
3. Remove the spark plugs.
4. Connect the compression tester to one cylinder following manufacturer's instructions. **Figure 22** shows a hand-held compression tester in use. You can also use the screw-in type described in Chapter One.

NOTE
Hand-held compression testers require 2 people—one to hold the compression tester and one to crank the engine. Screw-in compression testers only require one person.

5. Crank the engine over until there is no further increase in compression reading.
6. Remove the tester and write down the reading.
7. Repeat Steps 4-6 for each cylinder. Compare results with **Table 10** in this chapter.

When interpreting the results, actual readings are not as important as the differences in readings. Low readings, although they may be even, are a sign of wear. Low readings in 2 adjacent cylinders may indicate a defective head gasket. No cylinder should test at less than 80 percent of the highest cylinder. A greater difference indicates worn or broken rings, leaky or sticking valves, a defective head gasket, or a combination of all.

Table 10   TUNE-UP SPECIFICATIONS

Cylinder Head Torque

240Z through engine No. L24-027600*	43-51 ft.-lb. (6-7 mkg)
240Z from engine No. L24-027601*	51-61 ft.-lb. (7.0-8.5 mkg)
260Z	47-61 ft.-lb. (6.5-8.5 mkg)
1975-1976 280Z	54-61 ft.-lb. (7.5-8.5 mkg)
1977 and later 280Z,	51-61 ft.-lb. (7.0-8.5 mkg)

Compression Specifications

240, 260Z	171-185 psi (12-13 kg/cm^2)
280Z	164-178 psi (11 1/2-12 1/2 kg/cm^2)

Valve Clearance (Cold)

Intake	0.008 in. (0.20mm)
Exhaust	0.010 in. (0.25mm)

Valve Clearance (Hot)

Intake	0.010 in. (0.25mm)
Exhaust	0.012 in. (0.30mm)

Ignition Timing

1970-1972 manual	5° BTDC at 750 rpm
1971-1972 automatic (advanced)	10° BTDC at 600 rpm in Drive
1971-1972 automatic (retarded)	0° (TDC) at 600 rpm in Drive
1973-1974 manual	7° BTDC at 750 rpm
1973-1974 automatic (advanced)	15° BTDC at 600 rpm in Drive
1973 automatic (retarded)	5° BTDC at 600 rpm in Drive
1974 automatic (retarded)	8° BTDC at 600 rpm in Drive
1975-1976 California cars (manual)	10° BTDC at 800 rpm
1975-1976 California cars (automatic)	10° BTDC at 700 rpm in Drive
1975-1976 non-California manual (advanced)	13° BTDC at 800 rpm
1975-1976 non-California manual (retarded)	7° BTDC at 800 rpm
1975-1976 non-California automatic (advanced)	13° BTDC at 700 rpm in Drive
1975-1976 non-California automatic (retarded)	7° BTDC at 700 rpm in Drive
1977 and later manual	10° BTDC at 800 rpm
1977 and later automatic	10° BTDC at 700 rpm in Drive

Spark Plug Gap

1970-1975	0.031-0.035 in. (0.8-0.9mm)
1976	0.028-0.031 in. (0.7-0.8mm)
1977 and later	0.039-0.043 in. (1.0-1.1mm)

Distributor Point Gap (240Z only)   0.018-0.021 in. (0.45-0.55mm)

Reluctor Air Gap

260Z	0.012-0.016 in. (0.3-0.4mm)
280Z	0.008-0.016 in. (0.2-0.4mm)

Dwell Angle (240Z only)

Manual transmission	35-41°
Automatic transmission	33-39°

Idle Speed

1970-1974 manual	750 rpm
1971-1974 automatic	600 rpm in Drive
1975 and later manual	800 rpm
1975 and later automatic	700 rpm in Drive
Firing order	1-5-3-6-2-4 (No. 1 front)

*Late type cylinder head bolts have a circular groove stamped in the top surface of the bolt head. Early type cylinder head bolts do not.

If the dry compression test indicates a problem, isolate the cause with a wet compression test. This is done in the same way as the dry compression test, except that about one tablespoon of oil is poured down the spark plug holes before performing Steps 4-6. If the wet compression readings are much greater than the dry readings, the trouble is probably due to worn or broken rings. If there is little difference between wet and dry readings, the trouble is probably due to leaky or sticking valves. If 2 adjacent cylinders are low and the wet and dry readings are close, the head gasket may be damaged.

Cylinder Head Bolts

The engine must be cool enough to touch before tightening head bolts. Back each bolt off 1/4 turn to make sure it hasn't seized. Then tighten to specifications (**Table 10**). Follow the sequence shown in **Figure 23**.

Valve Clearance Adjustment

Valves are adjusted with the engine off. On 1970-1977 models, adjust the valves first with the engine cold, then at operating temperature. On 1978 models, the cold adjustment can be skipped.

Valve clearances are measured between the camshaft lobes and a friction surface on the center of each rocker. Adjust as follows.

1. Remove the valve cover and all 6 spark plugs. Removing the plugs makes it easier to turn the engine by hand.
2. Turn the engine in the normal direction (clockwise, viewed from the front) until the front camshaft lobe points straight up. Slip the feeler gauge between the rocker arm and the base of the cam lobe. Compare clearance with **Table 10**.

NOTE
Counting from the front of the engine, the valves are: 1—exhaust; 2—intake; 3—intake; 4—exhaust; 5—intake; 6—exhaust; 7—exhaust; 8—intake; 9—exhaust; 10—intake; 11—intake; 12—exhaust.

3. If the clearance is incorrect, loosen the rocker arm locknut with a 17 mm open-end wrench. See **Figure 24**. Turn the adjusting nut with a 14mm open-end wrench to change clearance, then tighten the locknut. If the 17mm crow's foot socket shown in **Figure 24** is available, tighten the locknut to 36-43 ft.-lb. (4.9-5.9 mkg). If it is not available, tighten the locknut securely with an open-end wrench.
4. Turn the engine so each cam lobe in turn points straight up, and adjust clearance for its valve. Continue this until all valves have been adjusted.
5. On 1970-1977 models, warm up the engine and recheck clearances. Adjust if necessary.

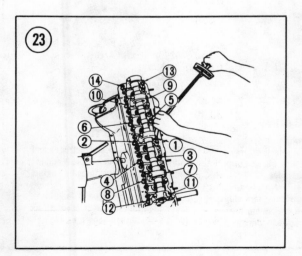

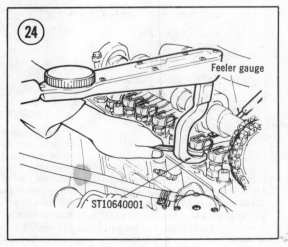

Feeler gauge

ST10640001

SPARK PLUG CONDITION

25

NORMAL
• Identified by light tan or gray deposits on the firing tip.
• Can be cleaned.

GAP BRIDGED
• Identified by deposit buildup closing gap between electrodes.
• Caused by oil or carbon fouling. If deposits are not excessive, the plug can be cleaned.

OIL FOULED
• Identified by wet black deposits on the insulator shell bore electrodes.
• Caused by excessive oil entering combustion chamber through worn rings and pistons, excessive clearance between valve guides and stems, or worn or loose bearings. Can be cleaned. If engine is not repaired, use a hotter plug.

CARBON FOULED
• Identified by black, dry fluffy carbon deposits on insulator tips, exposed shell surfaces and electrodes.
• Caused by too cold a plug, weak ignition, dirty air cleaner, defective fuel pump, too rich a fuel mixture, improperly operating heat riser, or excessive idling. Can be cleaned.

LEAD FOULED
• Identified by dark gray, black, yellow, or tan deposits or a fused glazed coating on the insulator tip.
• Caused by highly leaded gasoline. Can be cleaned.

WORN
• Identified by severely eroded or worn electrodes.
• Caused by normal wear. Should be replaced.

FUSED SPOT DEPOSIT
• Identified by melted or spotty deposits resembling bubbles or blisters.
• Caused by sudden acceleration. Can be cleaned.

OVERHEATING
• Identified by a white or light gray insulator with small black or gray brown spots and with bluish-burnt appearance of electrodes.
• Caused by engine overheating, wrong type of fuel, loose spark plugs, too hot a plug, low fuel pump pressure, or incorrect ignition timing. Replace the plug.

PREIGNITION
• Identified by melted electrodes and possibly blistered insulator. Metallic deposits on insulator indicate engine damage.
• Caused by wrong type of fuel, incorrect ignition timing or advance, too hot a plug, burned valves, or engine overheating. Replace the plug.

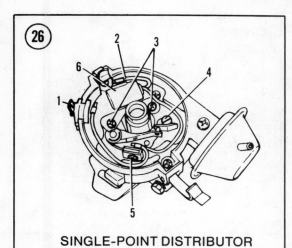

26

SINGLE-POINT DISTRIBUTOR

1. Primary lead terminal
2. Ground lead wire
3. Setscrew
4. Adjuster
5. Screw
6. Condenser

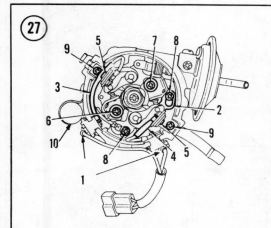

27

DUAL-POINT DISTRIBUTOR

1. Lead wire terminal setscrews
2. Adjuster plate
3. Primary lead wire
   (advanced points)
4. Primary lead wire
   (retarded points)
5. Primary lead terminals
6. Setscrew (advanced points)
7. Setscrew (retarded points)
8. Adjuster plate setscrews
9. Breaker plate setscrews
10. Condenser

Spark Plugs

Examine the plugs and compare their condition to **Figure 25**. Then discard the plugs. Their condition is an indicator of engine condition and can warn of developing trouble. Check the gap on the new plugs and compare to **Table 10**. Adjust the gap if needed, then install the plugs. Tighten plugs to 11-14 ft.-lb. (1.5-2.0 mkg).

Distributor Cap and Rotor

Pry back the distributor cap clips and remove the cap. Label the spark plug and coil wires so that they can be reconnected properly, then pull them out of the cap. Remove dirt and corrosion from the wire terminals and the terminals inside the cap. If the cap and the rotor are damaged or excessively worn, replace them. Replace the wires if insulation is cracked, melted, or brittle.

Breaker Points, Condenser

Breaker point ignition is used on 240Z's only. Manual transmission cars use a single set of points; automatics use 2 sets.

1. Loosen the screw on the primary lead terminal(s). See **Figure 26** (single-point distributors) or **Figure 27** (dual-point distributors). Slide the points lead wire(s) off the terminal(s).

2. Remove 2 screws securing the points (2 screws from each set of points on dual-point distributors). Carefully note how the points were positioned, then lift them out of the distributor. Install new points exactly as the old ones were.

3. Apply a *small* amount of distributor cam lubricant to the cam lobes.

4. Remove the condenser and install a new one.

5. Using a crayon or felt pen, make alignment marks on the distributor body and engine. Then loosen the distributor clamp bolt and carefully turn the distributor by hand until a cam lobe opens the points to the maximum

gap. Insert a feeler gauge in the gap (**Figure 28**) and adjust by turning the eccentric adjusting screw. On dual-point distributors, adjust both point sets in this manner.

6. After setting the point gap, rotate the distributor back to its original position and tighten the clamp bolt.

7. Install the distributor rotor and cap. Be sure the spark plug and coil wires are connected properly.

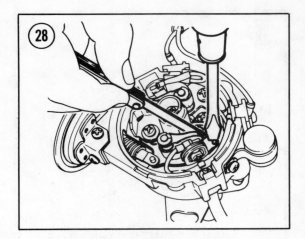

Reluctor, Pickup Coil

The reluctor and pickup coil are part of the breakerless ignition system used on 260-280Z's.

The gap between reluctor and pickup coil should be checked at each tune-up. To measure, insert a feeler gauge as shown in **Figure 29**. Adjustment is usually unnecessary, since there is no friction between reluctor and pickup coil. To adjust, loosen the pickup coil screw and pivot the coil in or out as needed. On dual-pickup distributors, adjust both gaps in the same manner.

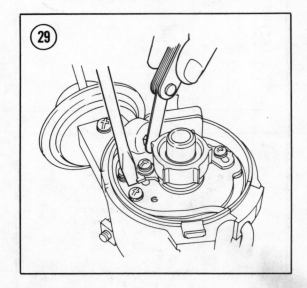

Ignition Timing
(Single Points or Single Pickup)

Single points are used on manual transmission 240Z's. Single pickups are used on manual transmission 260Z's, 1975-1976 California 280Z's, and all 1977-1978 280Z's.

Ignition timing requires a stroboscopic timing light of the type described in Chapter Two. Connect the light according to the manufacturer's instructions.

1. Clean the crankshaft pulley and timing marks. Early L-series engines have timing marks on the crankshaft pulley and a pointer on the engine front cover (**Figure 30**). Late models have a notch in the pulley and marks on the pointer (**Figure 31**).

2. Find the correct timing setting in **Table 10** at the end of the chapter. Apply chalk or white paint to the mark and to the pointer or crankshaft pulley notch.

3. Disconnect the vacuum line from the distributor. Plug the line with tape.

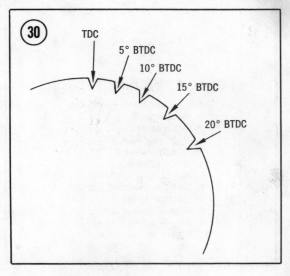

TDC
5° BTDC
10° BTDC
15° BTDC
20° BTDC

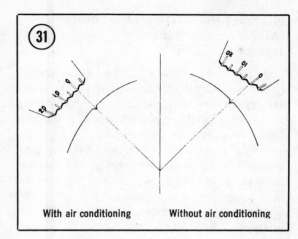

With air conditioning   Without air conditioning

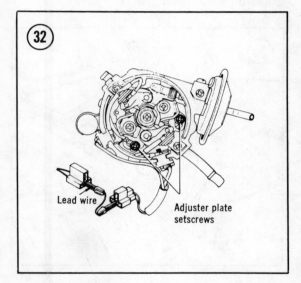

Lead wire

Adjuster plate
setscrews

4. Start the engine. If necessary, adjust idle speed to specifications (**Table 10**). Loosen the distributor clamp bolt and turn the distributor until the correct timing mark aligns with the timing pointer. Tighten the clamp bolt, shut the engine off, and reconnect the vacuum line.

Ignition Timing
(Dual Points or Dual Pickups)

Dual points are used on automatic transmission 240Z's. Dual pickups are used on automatic transmission 260Z's, and 1975-1976 non-California 280Z's.

1. Clean the crankshaft pulley and timing marks. Early L-series engines have timing marks on the crankshaft pulley and a timing pointer on the front cover (**Figure 30**). Late models have a notch in the pulley and marks on the front cover (**Figure 31**).

2. Find the correct advanced and retarded timing setting in **Table 10** at the end of the chapter. Apply paint or chalk to the timing marks and pointer so they will be easy to see. Use different colors so the marks can be told apart under the timing light.

3. Disconnect the vacuum line from the distributor. Plug the line with tape.

4. Start the engine. Compare idle speed with **Table 10** and adjust if necessary.

5. The retarded points normally function with the engine warm and idling. To set timing, however, the advanced points must be made to function. On 240Z's, disconnect the primary leads from the distributor and connect a jumper wire as shown in **Figure 32**. On 260Z's, disconnect the green wire from the water temperature switch in the thermostat housing. On 280Z's, disconnect the red wire from the temperature switch. Ground the harness end of the wire (not the switch end) to the engine with a jumper wire. See **Figure 33**.

6. Point the timing light at the crankshaft pulley and check timing. It should be at the advanced setting. If not, loosen the distributor fixing bolt and turn the distributor to change timing. Then tighten the fixing bolt.

7. On 240Z's, disconnect the jumper wire from the distributor side of the primary lead connector. Connect the jumper wire to the

other terminal in the distributor side of the connector.

8. On 260Z's, connect a jumper wire between the terminals of the water temperature switch's harness connector. See **Figure 34**.

9. On 280Z's, disconnect the temperature switch wire from the engine, but leave it disconnected from the switch.

10. Point the timing light at the crankshaft pulley. Ignition timing should now be at the retarded setting listed in **Table 10**. If so, no further steps are necessary.

11. If retarded timing is incorrect, adjust the phase difference (difference between advanced and retarded setting). This requires moving the retarded breaker points or pickup coil.

12. To adjust, loosen the adjuster plate setscrews. See **Figure 35** (240Z), **Figure 36** (260Z), or **Figure 37** (280Z). Insert a screwdriver in the slot and turn as needed to change the setting. See **Figure 38** (240Z), **Figure 39** (260Z), or **Figure 40** (280Z). Moving the adjuster plate counterclockwise increases phase difference (retards retarded timing). Moving the plate clockwise decreases phase difference (advances retarded timing).

To gauge the adjustment, refer to the graduations on the breaker plate. See **Figure 41** (240Z), or **Figure 42** (260-280Z).

Idle Speed and Mixture Adjustments (All 240Z's and Manual Transmission 260Z's)

Before performing these adjustments, check and adjust valve clearances, and make all ignition adjustments. A tune-up tachometer of the type described in Chapter One is required, as well as a timing light and Uni-Syn gauge. An exhaust gas analyzer should also be used, since correct idle mixture is based on the percentage of carbon monoxide in the exhaust gas. Mixture adjustments can be made without the gas analyzer, but it is necessary to ensure emission control compliance.

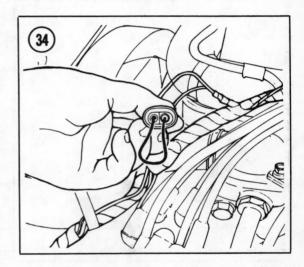

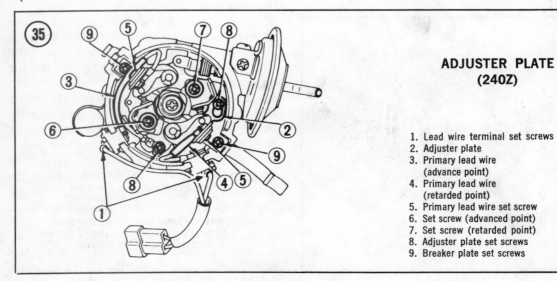

ADJUSTER PLATE (240Z)

1. Lead wire terminal set screws
2. Adjuster plate
3. Primary lead wire (advance point)
4. Primary lead wire (retarded point)
5. Primary lead wire set screw
6. Set screw (advanced point)
7. Set screw (retarded point)
8. Adjuster plate set screws
9. Breaker plate set screws

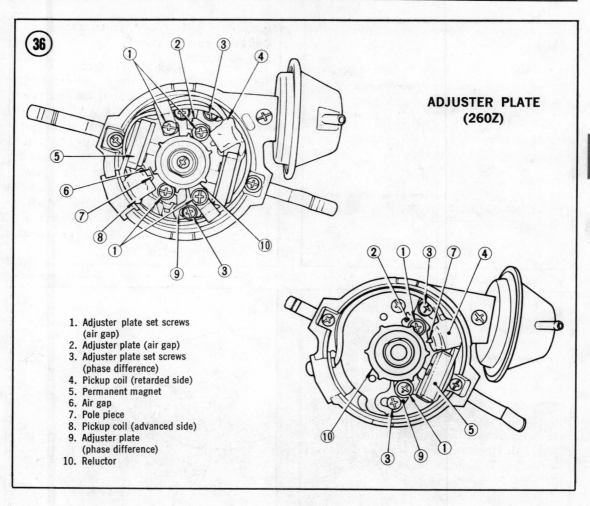

**ADJUSTER PLATE
(260Z)**

3

1. Adjuster plate set screws
   (air gap)
2. Adjuster plate (air gap)
3. Adjuster plate set screws
   (phase difference)
4. Pickup coil (retarded side)
5. Permanent magnet
6. Air gap
7. Pole piece
8. Pickup coil (advanced side)
9. Adjuster plate
   (phase difference)
10. Reluctor

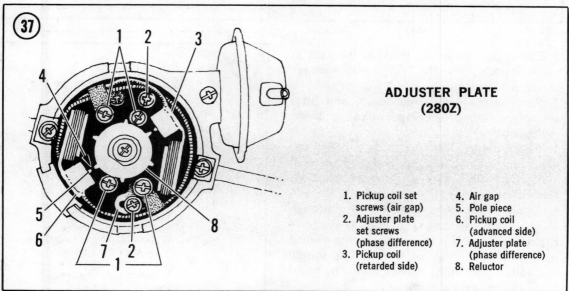

**ADJUSTER PLATE
(280Z)**

1. Pickup coil set
   screws (air gap)
2. Adjuster plate
   set screws
   (phase difference)
3. Pickup coil
   (retarded side)
4. Air gap
5. Pole piece
6. Pickup coil
   (advanced side)
7. Adjuster plate
   (phase difference)
8. Reluctor

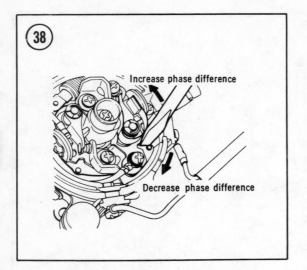

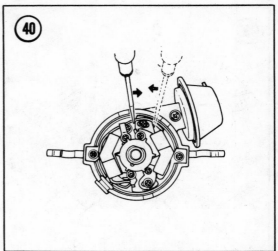

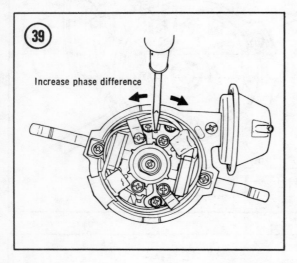

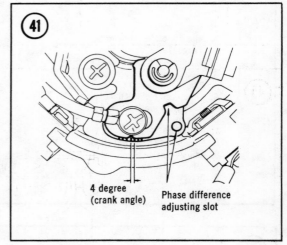

1. Drive the car for at least 20 minutes at approximately 30 mph. This is necessary for correct adjustments.

2. Remove the air cleaner cover and filter element. Remove the damper oil cap as shown in **Figure 43**.

3. Check damper oil level. If it is below the lower line on the plunger rod, top up with SAE 20 or 10W-30 oil. Do not use a heavier grade of oil.

4. Check piston movement. On cars through 1972, push up on the piston lifters as shown in **Figure 44**. On 1973-1974 cars, pry the pistons up with a soft metal bar. The pistons should rise and fall smoothly. A click should be heard when the pistons hit bottom.

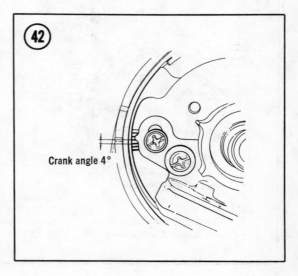

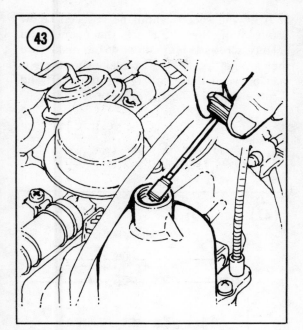

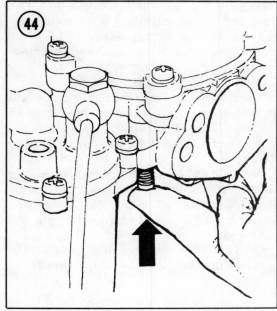

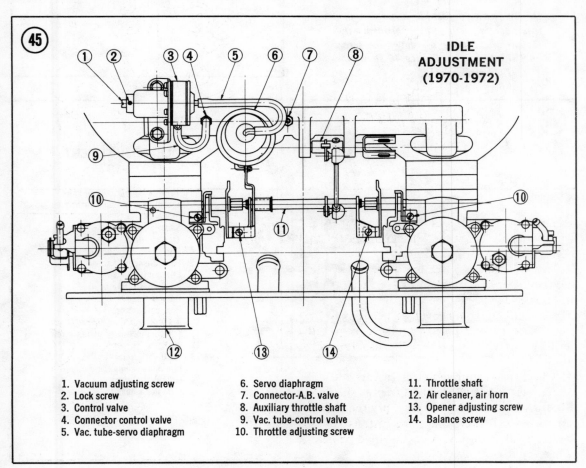

IDLE ADJUSTMENT (1970-1972)

1. Vacuum adjusting screw
2. Lock screw
3. Control valve
4. Connector control valve
5. Vac. tube-servo diaphragm
6. Servo diaphragm
7. Connector-A.B. valve
8. Auxiliary throttle shaft
9. Vac. tube-control valve
10. Throttle adjusting screw
11. Throttle shaft
12. Air cleaner, air horn
13. Opener adjusting screw
14. Balance screw

On 1970-1972 carburetors, disassemble and clean the suction chambers if the pistons do not move smoothly. On 1973-1974 carburetors, this is not recommended; if inspection indicates a mechanical problem, the entire carburetor must be replaced.

5. Completely loosen the balance screw and throttle opener adjusting screw. See **Figure 45** (1970-1972) or **Figure 46** (1973-1974).

6. Connect a tachometer and timing light to the engine.

7. On 1970-1972 cars, set engine idle speed at 600-700 rpm with the front and rear throttle adjusting screws (10, **Figure 45**). The engine should be at the lowest speed at which it will run smoothly.

On 1973-1974 cars, set idle speed at 750 rpm with the idle speed screw (4, **Figure 46**).

NOTE
Do not touch the fast idle screw. Turning this screw will unsynchronize the carburetors. Figure 47 shows the screw on 1970-1972 cars; Figure 46 shows the 1973-1974 arrangement.

8. If engine speed cannot be reduced below 750 rpm in Step 7, check the opener and balance screws (**Figure 45 or 46**) to make sure they are not too tight. Also make sure there is play between the auxiliary throttle shaft and throttle shafts as shown in **Figure 48**.

NOTE
The next two steps are applicable to 1970-1972 cars only.

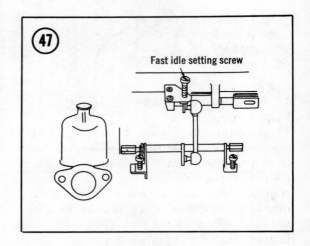

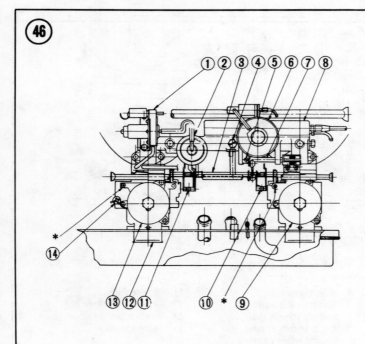

IDLE ADJUSTMENT
(1973-1974)

1. Throttle opener control valve assembly (Manual transmission models only)
2. Servo diaphragm
3. Throttle shaft
4. Idle speed adjusting screw
5. Fast idle setting screw
6. EGR control valve
7. Auxiliary throttle shaft
8. Balance tube
9. Rear carburetor
10. Balance adjusting screw
11. Throttle opener adjusting screw
12. Air horn
13. Front carburetor
14. Idle mixture adjusting screw (Idle limiter cap)
 * Do not adjust

9. Apply the Uni-Syn gauge to one of the air horns as shown in **Figure 49**. Turn the adjuster in the center of the gauge so that gauge float is centered in the calibrated tube.

10. Apply the Uni-Syn to the front and rear air horns and compare the height of the gauge float. If float height is not the same for both carburetors, adjust by turning the rear throttle adjusting screw.

NOTE
Since the Uni-Syn restricts air flow, apply it for only 1 or 2 seconds at a time. Longer applications will result in inaccurate readings.

11. Check ignition timing as described in this chapter. Adjust if necessary.

12. Referring to **Figure 45** or **Figure 46**, disconnect the control valve vacuum tube from the intake manifold connection. Then disconnect the servo diaphragm tube from the control valve and attach it to the intake manifold connection. This will cause manifold vacuum to operate the servo diaphragm and increase engine speed.

13. Engine speed should be approximately 1,400 rpm. Adjust if necessary by turning the throttle opener adjusting screw. See **Figure 45** (1970-1972) or **Figure 46** (1973-1974).

14. Measure air flow at front and rear air horns with the Uni-Syn (**Figure 49**). If uneven, adjust with the balance screw (**Figure 45** or **46**).

NOTE
Apply the Uni-Syn for only 1 or 2 seconds at a time to prevent inaccurate readings.

15. On 1973-1974 cars, install air cleaner cover.

16. Race the engine briefly at 3,000 rpm, then let engine speed drop. Turn the opener adjusting screw to increase engine speed to 1,700 rpm. Then gradually lower engine speed to 1,400 rpm with the opener adjusting screw.

17. Disconnect short hose from the air injection check valve. Plug the hole in check valve.

18. Check CO level with the exhaust gas analyzer. It must be 1.0-1.6 percent for manual transmission models, and 0.6-1.2 percent for automatics.

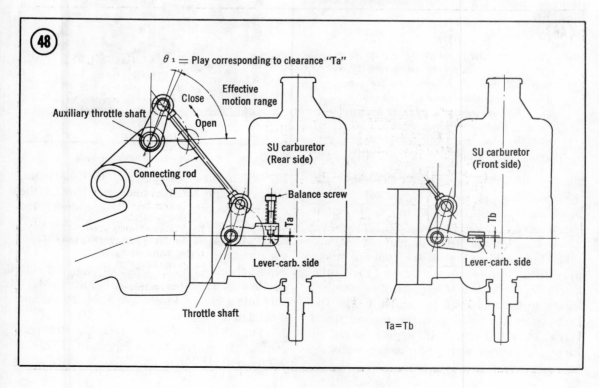

48

$\theta_1 =$ Play corresponding to clearance "Ta"

Effective motion range
Close
Open
Auxiliary throttle shaft
Connecting rod
SU carburetor (Rear side)
Balance screw
Lever-carb. side
Throttle shaft
Ta

SU carburetor (Front side)
Tb
Lever-carb. side
Ta=Tb

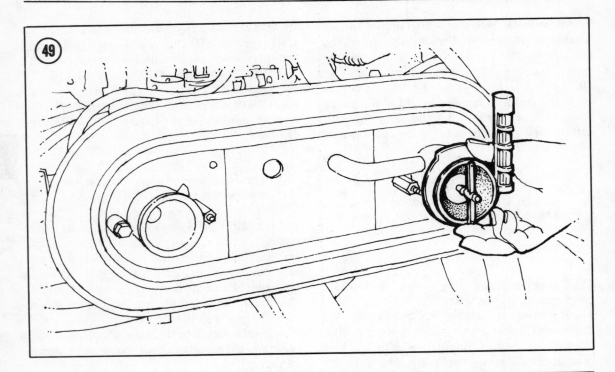

19. On 1970-1972 cars, if CO level is too high, turn the idle mixture adjusting nuts (**Figure 50**) to reduce it. Turn the nuts simultaneously, 1/8 turn at a time, clockwise (upward).

> *NOTE*
> *If a gas analyzer is not available, turn the idle adjusting nuts all the way to the top, then back them off 3 turns. Turn the nuts back up, simultaneously, 1/8 turn at a time, until the engine reaches its highest, most stable speed (approximately 2 1/2 turns). Do not use this procedure unless absolutely necessary.*

20. On 1973-1974 cars, adjust CO level with the idle mixture screw (14, **Figure 46**).

21. Reconnect the tube to the air injection check valve.

22. Disconnect the servo diaphragm vacuum tube (**Figure 45** or **Figure 46**) from the intake manifold connection. Leave the tube disconnected for a few seconds, then attach it to the manifold connection again. Check the tachometer to make sure the engine speed stays at 1,400 rpm. If engine speed is incorrect, adjust with the opener adjusting screw.

23. When the engine speed is 1,400 rpm, reconnect the throttle opener tubing in the normal position. To do this, connect the control valve tube to intake manifold connection, and connect the servo diaphragm vacuum tube to the control valve.

24. Recheck with the Uni-Syn to make sure air flow is even for both carburetors. Make sure idle speed is correct. See **Table 10**. Adjust if needed.

25. On 1973-1974 cars, recheck CO percentage. It must be below 3 percent (1973) or 2.7 percent (1974).

Idle Speed and Mixture Adjustments (Automatic Transmission 260Z's)

1. Perform Steps 1 through 11 of the previous adjustment procedure.

2. Raise engine speed to approximately 1,400 rpm with the fast idle screw (**Figure 51**).

NOTE
Count the number of turns required to raise idle speed to 1,400 rpm. Write this figure down for later use.

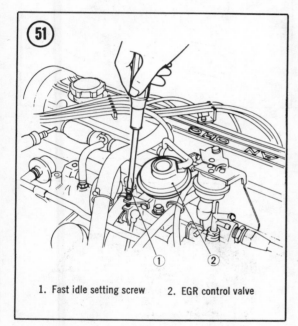

1. Fast idle setting screw   2. EGR control valve

1. Carburetor
2. Idle mixture adjusting screw

3. Measure airflow at both carburetors with a Uni-Syn gauge (**Figure 49**). If uneven, adjust with the balance screw (10, **Figure 46**).

4. Install the air cleaner cover.

5. Race the engine briefly at 3,000 rpm. Using the fast idle screw, raise engine speed to 1,700 rpm, then lower to 1,400 rpm.

6. Disconnect the inlet hose from the air injection check valve. Plug the hole in check valve.

7. Check CO percentage with the exhaust gas analyzer. It should be between 0.6-1.2 percent.

8. If the gas analyzer is not available, turn the idle mixture screw (**Figure 52**) counterclockwise until the engine just begins to idle roughly. Turn it back just enough to obtain a smooth idle. This procedure does not ensure compliance with emission standards, and should not be used unless absolutely necessary.

9. Turn the fast idle screw back to its original position, referring to the figure written down in Step 2.

10. Idle speed should be 600 rpm with the transmission in DRIVE. Adjust if necessary with the idle speed screw (**Figure 53**).

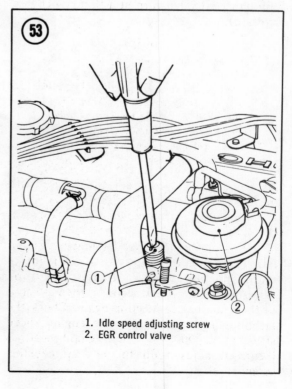

1. Idle speed adjusting screw
2. EGR control valve

Idle Speed Adjustment (280Z)

1. Warm the engine to normal operating temperature. Connect a tune-up tachometer.
2. On automatic transmissions, have an assistant hold the brake pedal down (or block the wheels) and shift to DRIVE. Leave manual transmissions in NEUTRAL.
3. Set idle speed (**Table 10**) to specifications with the idle speed screw. See **Figure 54**.

Idle Mixture Adjustment (280Z)

Idle mixture is not adjustable on 1975-1976 models. In 1977 and later models, it is adjustable, but the procedure is complicated and requires a CO meter. If the car doesn't idle smoothly after a tune-up, take it to a Datsun dealer or mechanic familiar with Bosch fuel injection.

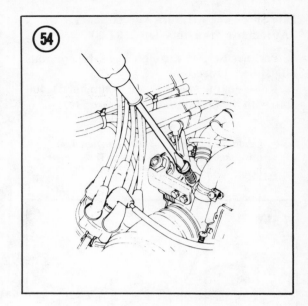

CHAPTER FOUR

ENGINE

All models use 6-cylinder versions of Datsun's L-series engine. The L24, used in the 240Z, displaces 146.0 cu. in. (2393cc). The L26, used in the 260Z, displaces 156.52 cu. in. (2565cc). The L28, used in the 280Z displaces 168.0 cu. in. (2753cc). **Table 1** and **Table 2** are at the end of the chapter.

The cylinder head is aluminum alloy. A forged steel crankshaft is supported by 7 main bearings. The camshaft, supported by 5 aluminum brackets, operates the valves through pivot-type rocker arms. The camshaft is driven by a double-row chain and 2 sprockets. Chain tension is controlled by a tensioner operated by a spring and oil pressure.

The lubrication system consists of an externally mounted rotor-type oil pump and cartridge filter. The oil pump is driven by the distributor driving spindle, which in turn is driven by a worm gear on the crankshaft. The oil pump pickup is inside the oil pan near the bottom.

A few special tools are used in this chapter. All are available through your dealer. A few are manufactured by Kent-Moore Tool Division, 29784 Little Mack, Roseville, Michigan, 48066 and may be ordered direct from them.

ENGINE REMOVAL

Although it is possible to remove the engine separately from the transmission, it is much easier to remove engine and transmission as a single unit and separate them. To remove the engine/transmission, proceed as follows.

1. Scribe alignment marks around the hood hinges onto the hood, then remove the hood. The marks will make hood installation easier.

2. Completely drain the cooling system.

3. Drain engine and transmission oil.

4. On 240-260Z's, disconnect both battery cables.

5. Remove the radiator (Chapter Six).

6. If equipped with a mechanical fuel pump, disconnect the inlet line (Chapter Five).

NOTE: *Step 7 applies to 1975-1976 models only.*

7. Eliminate pressure in the fuel lines. To do this, disconnect the black wire from the fuel pump, and the thin wire from the starter solenoid. Remove the cold start valve (Chapter Five) and place it in a container (**Figure 1**). Turn the ignition key to START and let the fuel run out.

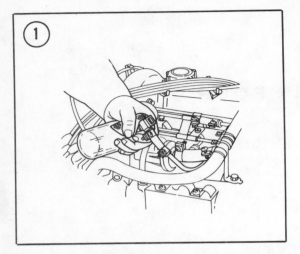

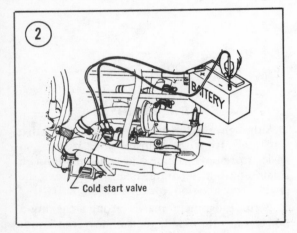

Cold start valve

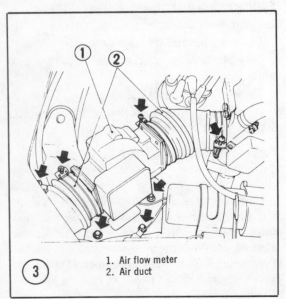

1. Air flow meter
2. Air duct

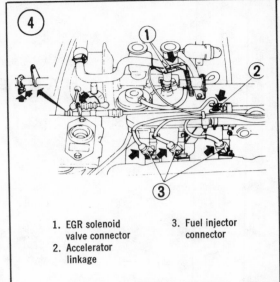

1. EGR solenoid valve connector
2. Accelerator linkage
3. Fuel injector connector

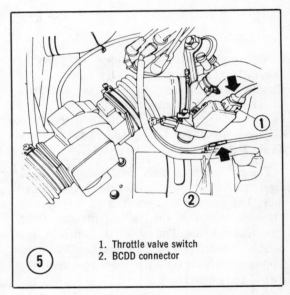

1. Throttle valve switch
2. BCDD connector

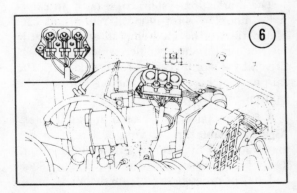

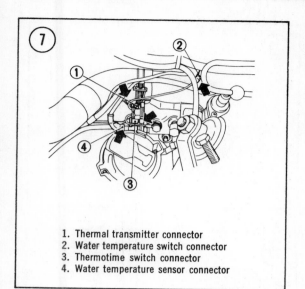

1. Thermal transmitter connector
2. Water temperature switch connector
3. Thermotime switch connector
4. Water temperature sensor connector

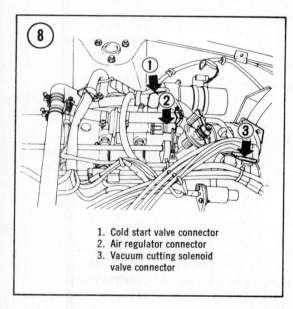

1. Cold start valve connector
2. Air regulator connector
3. Vacuum cutting solenoid
   valve connector

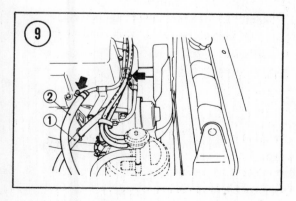

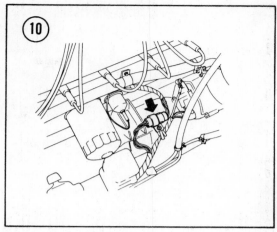

4

NOTE: *Steps 8-10 apply to 1977 and later models only.*

8. Disconnect the negative cable from the battery.

9. Disconnect the wires from the cold start valve.

10. Run 2 jumper wires from the cold start valve terminals to the battery terminals (**Figure 2**). Connect the wires for a few seconds. This operates the cold start valve, releasing pressurized fuel into the intake manifold.

NOTE: *Steps 11-15 apply to 1975 and later models only.*

11. Disconnect the battery cables.

12. Remove the air flow meter (**Figure 3**).

13. Disconnect the fuel injection component wires. See **Figures 4 through 8**.

14. Disconnect the fuel inlet (2) and return (1) lines (**Figure 9**).

15. Disconnect the connector for oil pressure sender and manual transmission switches (**Figure 10**).

16. On 240-260Z's with manual transmission, disconnect the wires from the electrical switches on the right-hand side of the transmission.

17. If equipped with automatic transmission, disconnect the wires from the inhibitor switch and downshift solenoid.

18. Disconnect the wires from the starter, alternator, ignition coil, oil pressure switch (240-260Z only), and coolant temperature sender.

19. On 1973-1974 cars, disconnect the wire from the exhaust gas recirculation solenoid (**Figure 11**).

20. On all 1973 cars and 260Z's with manual transmission, disconnect the throttle opener solenoid wire (**Figure 12**).

21. Remove the clutch operating cylinder (Chapter Eight).

22. Unscrew the speedometer cable union nut from the transmission.

23. On manual transmissions, remove the shift lever. See *Transmission Removal/Installation,* Chapter Nine.

24. On automatic transmissions, disconnect the linkage lever from the side of the transmission.

25. Disconnect the exhaust pipe from the exhaust manifold (Chapter Five). Hang the front end of the pipe from the car's frame with wire.

26. On 240Z's, disconnect the center exhaust pipe from the main muffler. Remove the front exhaust pipe, premuffler, and center exhaust pipe. See Chapter Five.

27. On 280Z's, disconnect the front exhaust tube bracket from the rear end of the transmission. Then unbolt the top half of the front tube's heat shield and let it hang on the tube.

28. Disconnect the drive shaft from the differential, then slide it backwards out of the transmission (Chapter Twelve).

29. Place a jack under the transmission. Jack the transmission up slightly. Working through the access hole in the center of the rear mounting member (**Figure 13**), remove the nut attaching the mounting member to the transmission. Then unbolt the mounting member from the car and remove it.

30. Unbolt the engine mounting brackets from the rubber insulators.

NOTE: *At this point, there should be no wires, hoses, or linkages attaching the engine or transmission to the body. Recheck this to be sure nothing will hamper engine removal.*

31. Attach a hoist to the engine slinger brackets at the front and rear of the cylinder head. Gradually lower the jack under the transmis-

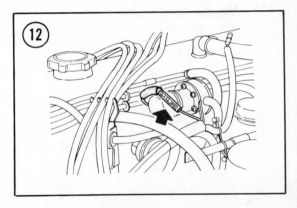

sion while raising the engine. Remove the jack from beneath transmission. Continue raising engine, tilting as necessary, until it is clear of the car.

CAUTION
Do not let the engine strike equipment installed on the engine compartment walls while removing.

32. Once the engine and transmission are clear of the car, lower them to a suitable support or stand and disconnect the hoist.

33. Remove the bolts attaching the transmission to the engine.

34. Inspect the rubber mounting insulators for wear or damage. Replace if these conditions are detected.

ENGINE INSTALLATION

Engine installation is simply the reverse of removal. Fasten the engine securely to its mounts before connecting anything else. Bleed the clutch and adjust as described in Chapter

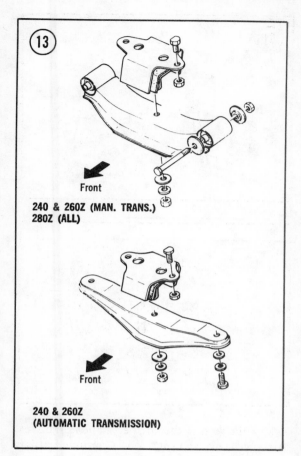

240 & 260Z (MAN. TRANS.)
280Z (ALL)

240 & 260Z
(AUTOMATIC TRANSMISSION)

Eight. Fill the engine and transmission with lubricants recommended in Chapter Three. Fill the cooling sysem with a 50/50 mixture of anti-freeze and water.

DISASSEMBLY SEQUENCES

The following three sequences are basic outlines that tell how much of the engine to remove and disassemble to perform a specific type of service. They are designed to keep engine disassembly to a minimum, thus avoiding unnecessary work. The major assemblies mentioned in these sequences are covered in detail under their own headings in this chapter, unless otherwise noted.

To use these sequences, first determine what type of service you plan to do (valve job, for example). Then turn to the sequence for that type of service. To perform a step within the sequence, turn to the section covering the major assembly mentioned in that step, and perform

the removal and inspection procedures. Do the same for each step until all necessary dis-assembly has been completed. To reassemble, reverse the sequences, performing the installation procedure for each major assembly mentioned.

Decarbonizing or Valve Service

1. Remove the exhaust and intake manifolds (Chapter Five).
2. Remove the rocker arms and camshaft.
3. Remove the cylinder head.
4. Remove and inspect valves. Inspect valve guides and valve seat inserts. Replace when necessary.
5. Assemble by reversing Steps 1-4.

Valve and Ring Service

1. Perform Steps 1-4 for valve service.
2. Remove the oil pan.
3. Remove the pistons together with the connecting rods.
4. Remove the piston rings. It is not necessary to separate the pistons from the connecting rods unless a piston, connecting rod, or piston pin needs repair or replacement.
5. Assemble by reversing Steps 1-4.

General Overhaul

1. Remove the engine and transmission and separate them. Remove the clutch (Chapter Eight) from manual transmission cars.
2. Remove the oil filter, oil pressure sender, and dipstick from the right-hand side of the cylinder block. Remove both motor mounts.
3. On 240-260Z's, remove the fuel pump (Chapter Five).
4. Remove the fan, water pump, and thermostat (Chapter Six).
5. Remove the alternator and the distributor (Chapter Seven).
6. Remove the air pump (Chapter Five).
7. Remove the air cleaner, intake manifold, and exhaust manifold (Chapter Five).
8. Remove rocker arms and camshaft.
9. Remove the cylinder head.
10. Remove the flywheel and rear end plate.

4

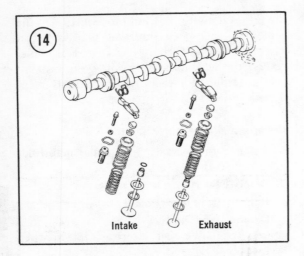

Intake   Exhaust

11. Remove the oil pan and strainer.

12. Remove oil pump and its driving spindle.

13. Remove the engine front cover.

14. Remove the timing chain, tensioner, chain guides, and crankshaft sprocket.

15. Remove piston/connecting rod assemblies.

16. Remove the main bearing caps, crankshaft and side rear oil seals, and crankshaft.

17. Inspect the cylinder block.

18. Assembly is the reverse of these steps.

CAMSHAFT AND ROCKER ARMS

Figure 14 shows the camshaft and rocker arm components, as well as valve components.

Rocker Arm Removal

1. Remove the springs looped over the tops of the rocker arms.

2. Loosen the locknut on the rocker arm pivot. Compress the valve springs by using a heavy-bladed screwdriver as a lever and the camshaft as a fulcrum. See **Figure 15**.

3. Withdraw the rocker arm while holding the valve springs down with the screwdriver. Be careful not to lose the rocker arm guide located between the rocker arm and the top of the valve stem.

4. If the rocker pivot is visibly worn, unscrew it from the cylinder head, together with its locknut.

5. Install by reversing Steps 1-4.

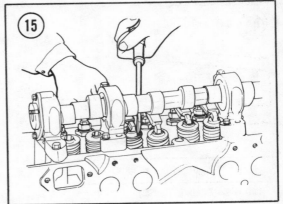

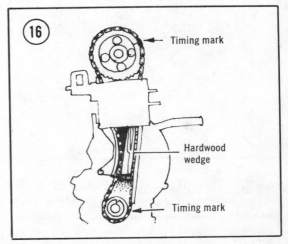

Timing mark

Hardwood wedge

Timing mark

Rocker Arm Inspection

Examine the rocker arm for visible wear on its cam contact surface, pivot contact surface, and valve contact surface. If wear or any defects can be seen, replace the rocker arm. If the rocker arm pivot is visibly worn, both the pivot and its corresponding rocker arm must be replaced.

Camshaft Removal

1. Remove the valve rocker cover.

2. On 240-260Z's, remove the fuel pump (Chapter Five).

3. Turn the engine over by hand until the timing marks on the camshaft and timing chain are aligned. See **Figure 16**.

4. Remove all rocker arms as described earlier.

5. Insert a hardwood wedge, such as Datsun tool ST17420001 (Kent-Moore J25660-01), be-

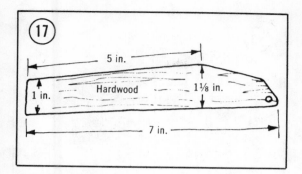

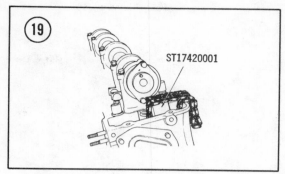

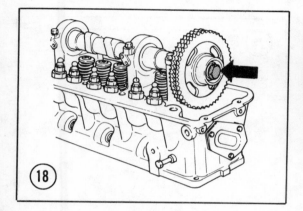

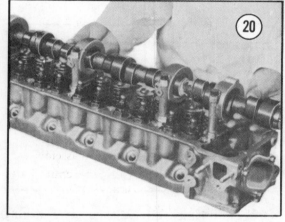

tween the sides of the chain. **Figure 16** shows the tool in place; **Figure 17** shows it alone. The tool keeps timing marks on crankshaft sprocket and chain aligned. It also prevents the chain tensioner piston from falling out. If the chain slips off the sprocket, or if the piston falls out, the front cover and oil pan must be removed to reinstall them.

NOTE: *If you make your own tool, use hardwood, not plywood. Plywood may leave fragments in the engine. Also, drill a hole in the top of the tool so it can be pulled out with a wire hook.*

6. Remove the bolt from the front end of the camshaft (**Figure 18**). Remove the fuel pump cam (240-260Z only) and camshaft sprocket. Take the sprocket out of the chain and drape the chain over the tool as shown in **Figure 19**.

7. Remove 2 bolts and take the camshaft locate plate off the front camshaft bracket.

8. Carefully withdraw the camshaft toward the front of the engine (**Figure 20**). Rotate the camshaft slowly while removing, and do not scratch the bearing surfaces.

CAUTION
Never remove camshaft brackets from the cylinder head, even though removal looks easy. If the brackets are removed, it will be extremely difficult, if not impossible, to realign the bearing centers.

Camshaft Inspection

1. Measure the inner diameter of the camshaft bearings (**Figure 21**). This figure must be between 1.8898-1.8904 in. (48.00-48.016mm). If any bearings are worn beyond the maximum, the entire cylinder head must be replaced.

2. Measure outer diameter of the camshaft journals. Subtract these figures from the bearing inner diameter to determine oil clearance. Normal oil clearance is 0.0015-0.0026 in. (0.038-0.067mm). If the bearings were within specifications in Step 1, and oil clearance exceeds 0.004 in (0.1mm), the camshaft must be replaced.

3. Measure camshaft bend. Rotate the camshaft between accurate centers (such as V-

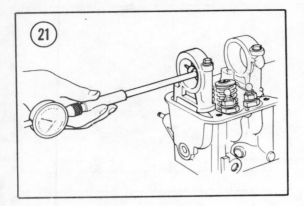

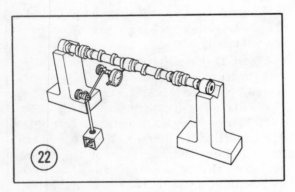

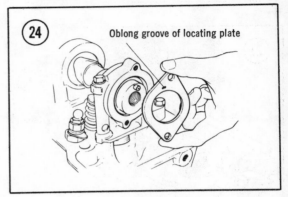

Oblong groove of locating plate

blocks or a lathe) with a dial gauge contacting the center journal. See **Figure 22**. Actual bend is half the reading shown on the dial gauge when the camshaft is rotated one full turn. Replace camshaft if bend exceeds 0.002 in. (0.05mm).

4. Check the camshaft sprocket for runout. Measure with the sprocket installed on the camshaft, as shown in **Figure 23**. Replace the sprocket if runout exceeds 0.004 in. (0.1mm).

Camshaft Installation

1. Coat the camshaft journals and bearing surfaces with clean engine oil.

2. Carefully install the camshaft in the brackets. Rotate the camshaft slowly while inserting to ease installation.

3. Install the camshaft locate plate **(Figure 24)** and secure it with 2 bolts. The groove in the locating plate goes on top, as shown in **Figure 24**.

4. Install the rocker arms as described earlier.

5. Lift up the timing chain and remove the support tool. Place the camshaft sprocket in the chain, making sure the timing marks on chain and sprocket are aligned.

6. Slide the sprocket onto the camshaft. Make sure the 3 locating holes in the sprocket are at top, left, and bottom as viewed from the front of the engine. See **Figure 25**.

7. Install the fuel pump cam. Install the bolt in the front of the camshaft. Tighten the bolt to 86-116 ft.-lb. (12-16 mkg) on 240Z's; 94-108 ft.-lb. (13-15 mkg) on 260-280Z's.

8. Install the fuel pump (240-260Z) and valve rocker cover.

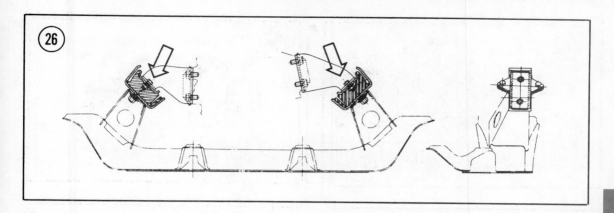

5. Remove bolts attaching the oil pan to the engine. Lower the pan and take it out from under the car.

6. **Figure 27** shows the oil strainer installed on the cylinder block. Remove if necessary by taking out 2 bolts and lockwashers.

7. Installation is the reverse of these steps. Use a new oil pan gasket coated on both sides with gasket sealer. Be sure there is enough sealer at front and rear ends of the gasket. Tighten the motor mount bolts to specifications given in **Table 2** at the end of the chapter.

OIL PAN AND STRAINER

Removal/Installation

Oil pan removal requires raising the engine slightly with a hoist. The hoist must be capable of supporting the engine for the entire time the oil pan is off. Hydraulic hoists, available from tool rental dealers, work well for this.

1. Attach the hoist to the engine slinger brackets at the front and rear of the cylinder head.

2. Loosen the bolts attaching the engine mounting brackets to the rubber insulators (**Figure 26**).

3. Raise the engine enough to take the load off the motor mounts, then remove the bolts shown in **Figure 26**.

4. Raise the engine far enough so the pan can be removed.

CAUTION
Do not raise the engine far enough to damage any wires, hoses, or linkages.

FRONT COVER, TIMING CHAIN, AND SPROCKETS

Front Cover Removal

1. Remove the radiator and fan (Chapter Six). Remove the air pump belt.

2. Remove the distributor (Chapter Seven).

3. Remove the oil pump and its driving spindle as described later in this chapter.

4. Remove the oil pan as described earlier.

5. Remove crankshaft pulley bolt. Then remove pulley with a puller such as Datsun ST 16540000 (**Figure 28**).

6. Remove the bolts attaching the front cover to cylinder block and head.

7. Withdraw the front cover forward and down (**Figure 29**). Water pump removal is not necessary to remove the front cover.

Front Cover Installation

Front cover installation is the reverse of removal, plus the following.

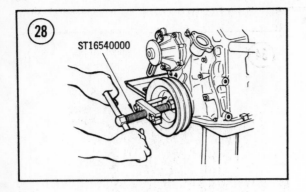

ST16540000

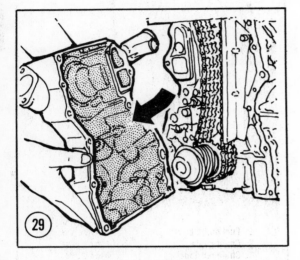

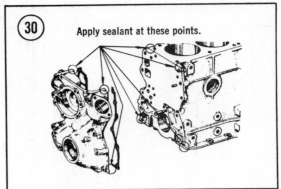

Apply sealant at these points.

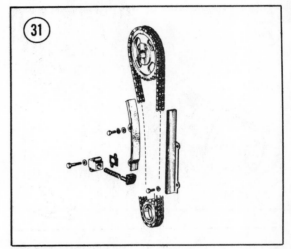

1. Use new left and right cover gaskets, coated on both sides with gasket sealer. Apply small amounts of sealer to the corners of the front cover. See **Figure 30**.

2. Install a new front cover oil seal as described in the next procedure. This should be done whenever the front cover is removed.

3. Take care not to bend the front portion of the head gasket when installing the cover. Be sure to install the cylinder head-to-cover bolts.

4. Fill the engine with oil and the radiator with coolant.

Front Oil Seal Replacement

1. Remove the front cover as described earlier.

2. Carefully pry out the old oil seal. Do not gouge the aluminum front cover.

3. Press in a new oil seal. Coat the seal lip with multipurpose grease.

4. Install the front cover as described earlier.

Sprocket and Chain Removal

1. Remove the valve rocker cover.

2. Remove the fuel pump (Chapter Five).

3. Remove the oil pump and driving spindle as described later in this chapter.

4. Remove the oil pan and front cover as described earlier.

5. Turn the engine over by hand until the timing marks in chain and sprockets are aligned. See **Figure 16**.

6. Referring to **Figure 31**, remove 2 bolts and lockwashers that attach the chain tensioner to the block.

7. Remove 4 bolts and lockwashers holding the left and right chain guides to the block. Remove the guides.

8. Remove the bolt that holds the fuel pump cam and camshaft sprocket to the front of the camshaft.

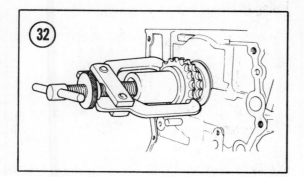

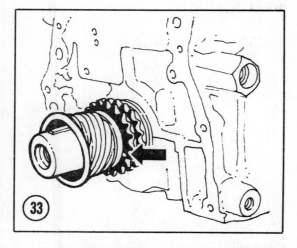

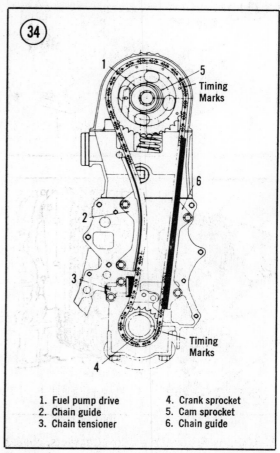

1. Fuel pump drive
2. Chain guide
3. Chain tensioner
4. Crank sprocket
5. Cam sprocket
6. Chain guide

9. Lift the timing chain aside and remove the camshaft sprocket and fuel pump cam from the camshaft.

10. Remove the timing chain from the crankshaft sprocket.

11. Remove the crankshaft sprocket, distributor drive gear, and oil thrower with a puller as shown in **Figure 32**.

CAUTION
Do not rotate the camshaft and crankshaft separately, or the valves may strike the piston tops.

Inspection

1. Thoroughly clean all parts in solvent before inspection.

2. Inspect the chain tensioner assembly and chain guides for wear or damage. Replace if these are evident.

3. Inspect the sprockets, distributor, drive gear, and oil thrower for wear or damage. Replace as needed.

4. Check the chain for wear, damage, or stretching of the roller links. Replace the chain if visibly defective. Check again for stretching as described in the next procedure.

Installation and Chain Inspection

1. Install the Woodruff keys in the crankshaft keyways if they have been removed.

2. Install the crankshaft sprocket, distributor drive gear, and oil thrower. See **Figure 33**.

NOTE: *Be sure the timing mark on the crankshaft sprocket faces the front.*

3. Install the timing chain over the crankshaft and camshaft sprockets. Make sure the timing marks on the chain are aligned with the timing marks on the sprockets (**Figure 34**).

4. Slide the camshaft sprocket onto the camshaft. Make sure the crankshaft and camshaft keys point straight up.

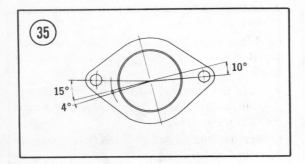

5. Bolt the chain guides to the cylinder block.

6. Install the chain tensioner.

7. Set No. 1 piston at top dead center on its compression stroke.

8. Refer to **Figures 35 and 36** for this step. **Figure 35** is a diagram of the camshaft locate plate and **Figure 36** shows the front side of the camshaft sprocket. Looking at the engine from the front, note whether the camshaft locating notch in the sprocket (**Figure 36**) is on the counterclockwise side of the left end of the oblong groove in the camshaft locate plate (**Figure 36**). If it is, the chain is stretched excessively. Perform Steps 9-11 to adjust it. If the camshaft locating notch is not past the left end of the oblong groove, the timing chain is satisfactory and Steps 9-11 may be skipped.

9. Remove the camshaft sprocket and reinstall it, using No. 2 locating hole. No. 2 hole should now be at the right end of the oblong groove.

10. If the locating hole position still is not correct, remove the camshaft sprocket again and reinstall it, this time using No. 3 locating hole. No. 3 hole should now be at the right end of the oblong groove.

11. If the hole still is not in the correct position, the timing chain is stretched beyond use and must be replaced. Install the new chain as described in Steps 3 and 4, using No. 1 locating hole in the camshaft sprocket.

12. Install the front cover as described earlier.

13. Install the oil pump driving spindle in the front cover, then install the oil pump. The pump driving spindle, which also drives the distributor, must be positioned as shown under *Distributor Installation*, Chapter Seven.

14. Install the oil pan as described earlier.

15. Install the distributor (Chapter Seven).

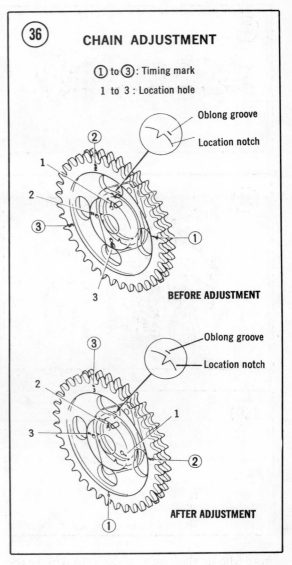

16. Install the fuel pump (240-260Z).

17. Install the valve rocker cover.

18. Install the fan and radiator (Chapter Six).

19. Fill the engine with oil and the radiator with coolant.

CYLINDER HEAD

Some of the following procedures must be performed by a dealer or machine shop, since they require special knowledge and expensive machine tools. Other procedures, while possible for the home mechanic, are difficult or time-consuming. A general practice among

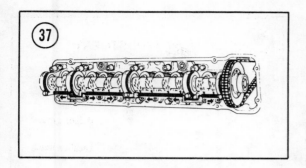

37

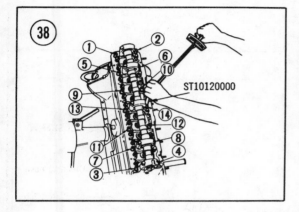

38

ST10120000

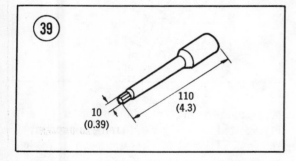

39

110
(4.3)

10
(0.39)

5. Detach the heater hoses from the right rear of the cylinder head.

6. Remove the thermostat housing and water outlet elbow from the left front of cylinder head.

7. Turn the camshaft so its key is straight up. This aligns crankshaft and camshaft sprockets for later installation.

8. Remove the camshaft and rocker arms as described earlier.

9. Unbolt the oil spray tube (if so equipped) from the camshaft brackets. See **Figure 37**.

10. Remove 2 bolts attaching the front of the cylinder head to the engine front cover.

11. Remove the 14 cylinder head bolts (**Figure 38**) working inward from the end in 2 or 3 stages. Head bolt removal requires a 10mm Allen socket, shown in **Figure 39**.

> NOTE: *There are 3 head bolt lengths on early engines, and 2 lengths on late engines. Tag them as they are removed, so they can be reinstalled in the same holes later.*

12. Once the head bolts are removed, lift the cylinder head off the engine. If the head is difficult to remove, tap it gently with a rubber mallet.

CAUTION
Never remove the camshaft brackets from the cylinder head, even though removal appears easy. If the brackets are removed, it will be extremely difficult if not impossible to realign the bearing centers.

Cylinder Head Inspection

1. Check the head for water leaks before cleaning.

2. Clean cylinder head thoroughly in solvent. While cleaning, check for cracks or other visible damage. Look for corrosion or foreign material in oil and water passages. Clean the passages with a stiff spiral wire brush, then blow them out with compressed air.

3. Check the cylinder head bottom (block mating) surface for flatness. Place an accurate straightedge along the surface. If there is any gap between the straightedge and cylinder head

those who do their own service is to remove the cylinder head, perform all disassembly except valve removal, and take the head to a machine shop for inspection and service. Since the cost is low in relation to the required effort and equipment, this may be the best approach, even for more experienced owners.

Cylinder Head Removal

1. Completely drain the cooling system.

2. Remove all spark plugs.

3. Remove the valve rocker cover.

4. Remove the fuel pump, air cleaner, and intake and exhaust manifolds (Chapter Five).

4

surface, measure it with a feeler gauge. Normal gap is 0.002 in. (0.05mm) or less. Maximum permissible is 0.004 in. (0.1mm). If the gap is beyond the limit, have the head resurfaced by a dealer or machine shop.

> NOTE: *If the block is not being resurfaced, up to 0.008 in. (0.2mm) may be removed from the cylinder head. If the block is also being resurfaced, metal removed from block and head may not total more than 0.008 in. (0.2mm).*

4. Check studs in the cylinder head for general condition. Replace damaged studs.

Decarbonizing

1. Without removing valves, remove all deposits from the combustion chambers, intake ports, and exhaust ports. Use a wire brush dipped in solvent. Be careful not to gouge or scratch the aluminum cylinder head.

2. After all carbon is removed from the combustion chambers and ports, clean the entire head in solvent.

3. Clean away all carbon on the piston tops. Do not remove the carbon ridge at the top of the cylinder bore.

Installation

1. Be sure the cylinder head, block, and cylinder bores are clean. Check all visible oil passages for cleanliness.

2. Install the camshaft and rocker arms in the cylinder head. Turn the camshaft so the key is straight up. This must be done before the cylinder head is installed to position the valves so they will not strike the piston tops.

3. Install a new cylinder head gasket. Never reuse an old head gasket. *Do not* use gasket sealer on the head gasket.

4. Install the cylinder head. On early engines, place the bolts in their holes according to the labels made during removal. On late engines, place the 5 long bolts in the "A" holes (**Figure 40**); place the 9 short bolts in the "B" holes.

> NOTE: *When positioning the cylinder head, look at the valves and make sure none are open far enough to strike the piston tops.*

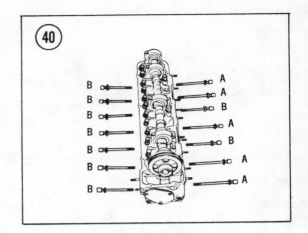

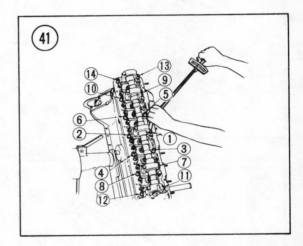

5. Tighten the head bolts in the order given in **Figure 41**. Perform the tightening sequence in 3 stages. Tightening torques are listed in **Table 2** at the end of the chapter.

6. Install the timing chain, camshaft sprocket, and fuel pump cam (240-260Z) as described earlier.

7. Install the oil spray tube, bolting it to the camshaft brackets.

8. Install the thermostat housing and water outlet elbow on the left front of the cylinder head.

9. Install the intake and exhaust manifolds and air cleaner.

10. Install the fuel pump (Chapter Five).

11. Attach the heater hoses at the right rear of the cylinder head.

12. Install spark plugs and valve rocker cover.

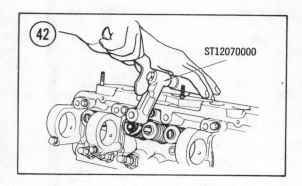

ST12070000

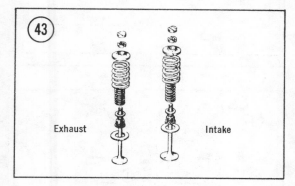

Exhaust   Intake

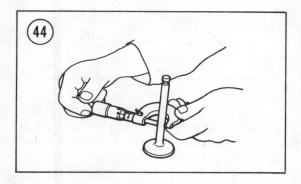

(Kent-Moore J-25631). See **Figure 42**. Remove the valve keepers and release the spring tension. Remove the spring washer, oil seals, inner and outer valve springs, and spring seat. Remove the valve through the combustion chamber. Be sure to keep all parts in order of removal. **Figure 43** shows the valve components.

CAUTION
Remove any burrs from valve stem grooves before removing valves. Otherwise the valve guides will be damaged.

Valve and Valve Guide Inspection

1. Clean the valves with a wire brush and solvent. Discard all the cracked, warped, or burned valves.

2. Measure the valve stems at the bottom, center, and top for wear. Use a micrometer as shown in **Figure 44**, or have measurements done by a dealer or machine shop. Also measure the length of each valve, and measure the diameter of each valve face.

3. If necessary, have the valve faces and valve stem ends refaced by a dealer or machine shop. Do not grind valve face thinner than 0.020 in. (0.05mm). No more than 0.020 in. (0.05mm) may be removed from valve stem ends.

4. Remove all carbon and varnish from valve guides with a stiff spiral wire brush.

NOTE: *The next step assumes that all valve stems have been measured and are within specifications. Replace any valves with worn stems before performing this step.*

13. Fill the cooling system with a 50/50 mixture of ethylene glycol-based anti-freeze and water. Check the oil level and top up if needed with a grade recommended in Chapter Three.

VALVES
AND VALVE SEAT INSERTS

Valve Removal

1. Remove the cylinder head, rocker arms, and camshaft as described earlier.

2. Compress each valve spring with a valve spring compressor such as Datsun ST 12070000

5. Insert each valve into the valve guide from which it was removed. Hold the valve just slightly off its seat and rock it back and forth in a direction parallel with the rocker arms. This is the direction where the greatest wear normally occurs. If the valve stem rocks more than 0.008 in. (0.2mm), its valve guide is worn and should be replaced.

6. If there is any doubt about valve guide condition after performing Step 5, measure the valve guide at top, center, and bottom with a bore gauge. Compare these figures with valve stem diameter to determine stem-to-guide clearance. Normal clearance for exhaust valves

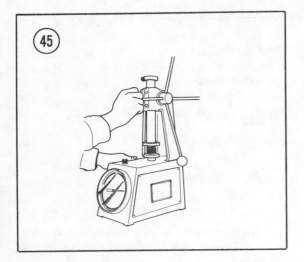

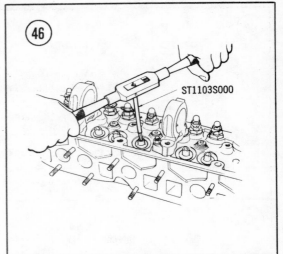

ST1103S000

is 0.0016-0.0029 in. (0.040-0.073mm). Normal clearance for intake valves is 0.0008-0.0021 in. (0.020-0.053mm). Maximum tolerance for exhausts and intakes is 0.004 in. (0.1mm). If any valve guides are worn past this tolerance, have them replaced as described later in this section.

7. Measure the height of the valve springs. Replace outer springs that are shorter than 1.968 in. (49.98mm). Replace any inner springs shorter than 1.766 in. (44.85mm).

8. Check the springs for deformation with a square. On L24 engines, replace any springs that are bent more than 0.063 in. (1.6mm). On L26 and L28 engines, replace inner springs bent more than 0.047 in. (1.2mm), and outer springs bent more than 0.087 in. (2.2mm).

9. Test the valve springs under load with a spring tester (**Figure 45**). Compare spring loaded lengths with specifications in the table at the end of the chapter. Replace any spring that does not meet specifications.

10. Inspect valve seat inserts. If worn or burned, they must be reconditioned. This should be done by a dealer or machine shop, although the procedure is described later in this section.

Valve Guide Replacement

This procedure requires a press capable of 4,400 lb. (2 metric tons) pressure and a valve guide reaming set such as Datsun ST 11030000 (Kent-Moore J-25618-02). If you do not have such equipment, take the job to a dealer or machine shop.

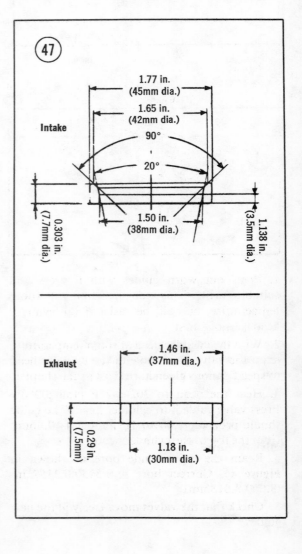

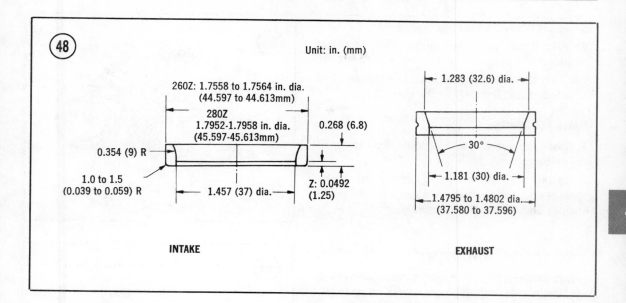

(48)   Unit: in. (mm)

260Z: 1.7558 to 1.7564 in. dia.
(44.597 to 44.613mm)
280Z
1.7952-1.7958 in. dia.
(45.597-45.613mm)   0.268 (6.8)

0.354 (9) R

1.0 to 1.5
(0.039 to 0.059) R   1.457 (37) dia.   Z: 0.0492
(1.25)

1.283 (32.6) dia.

30°

1.181 (30) dia.

1.4795 to 1.4802 dia.
(37.580 to 37.596)

INTAKE   **EXHAUST**

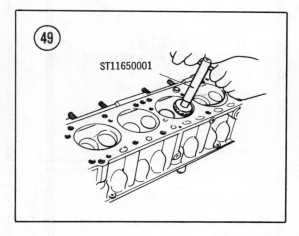

(49)

ST11650001

1. Press out worn guides with a press and suitable drift. This can be done at room temperature, but will be easier if the cylinder head is heated first.

2. With the cylinder head at room temperature, ream the valve guide hole in the cylinder head to specifications given at the end of the chapter.

3. Heat the head to 302-392°F (150-200°C). Press valve guide into cylinder head. The guide should protrude 0.409-0.417 in. (10.4-10.6mm) from the top of the cylinder head.

4. Ream the valve guide bore as shown in **Figure 46**. Correct bore is 0.3150-0.3157 in. (8.000-8.018mm).

5. Check that the valves move freely in the new guides.

Valve Seat Reconditioning

This job is best left to a Datsun dealer or automotive machine shop. They have the special knowledge and equipment required for this precise job. The following procedure is provided in the event that you are not near a dealer and your local machine shop is not familiar with the 240-280Z. Valve seat inserts that are too badly worn to be refaced can be replaced as follows:

1. Remove the old valve seat insert by boring it out until it collapses. Be sure not to cut the cylinder head during boring.

2. Select a valve seat insert and check its outside diameter. Compare with dimensions given in **Figure 47** (240Z) or **Figure 48** (all others). Inserts with a 0.020 in. (0.05mm) oversize diameter are available as replacement parts.

3. Machine the cylinder head recess diameter to fit the valve seat insert, using the valve guide as an axis.

4. Heat cylinder head to 302-392°F (150-200°C).

5. Install the valve seat insert, making sure it beds securely on the cylinder head.

6. Cut the valve seats to the dimensions given at the end of the chapter. Use a valve seat cutter such as ST 11650001 (**Figure 49**) or use a special stone.

7. Coat the corresponding valve face with Prussian blue.

8. Insert the valve into the valve guide.

9. Rotate the valve under light pressure about ¼ turn.

10. Lift the valve out. If it seats properly, the blue will transfer evenly to the valve face.

Valve Installation

1. Coat the valves with oil and insert them in the cylinder head.

2. Install the valve spring seats, oil seals, springs and spring washers. Compress the valve springs and install the keepers.

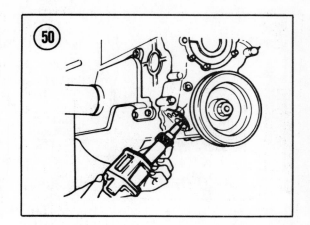

OIL PUMP

The rotor-type oil pump is attached to the bottom of the engine front cover by 4 bolts. The pump is driven by the distributor driving spindle. **Figure 50** shows the pump.

Removal/Installation

1. Turn the engine over by hand until No. 1 piston is at TDC on its compression stroke.

2. Remove the distributor (Chapter Seven).

3. Drain the engine oil.

4. Remove the splash shield panel located under the front of the car.

5. Remove 4 pump mounting bolts. Take out the pump and its driving spindle.

6. Installation is the reverse of these steps. Make sure the punched mark on the distributor driving spindle faces the front of the engine. Tighten the pump mounting bolts to 11-15 ft.-lb. (240Z) or 8-11 ft.-lb. (260-280Z). Install the distributor as described in Chapter Seven. Fill the engine with an oil recommended in Chapter Three.

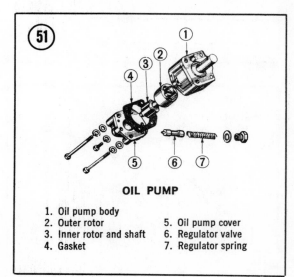

OIL PUMP

1. Oil pump body
2. Outer rotor
3. Inner rotor and shaft
4. Gasket
5. Oil pump cover
6. Regulator valve
7. Regulator spring

Disassembly/Inspection/Assembly

1. Remove one securing bolt to separate the pump cover from the body.

2. Lift out the inner and outer pump rotors. **Figure 51** shows the disassembled pump components.

3. Clean all parts in solvent. Check the distributor driving spindle and pump rotors for wear, scoring, or visible damage. Check oil

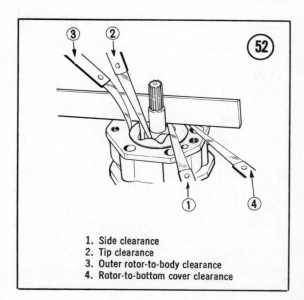

1. Side clearance
2. Tip clearance
3. Outer rotor-to-body clearance
4. Rotor-to-bottom cover clearance

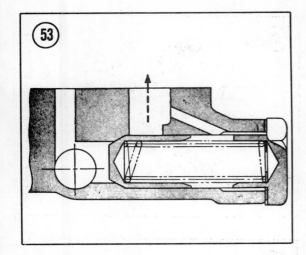

pump clearances (**Figure 52**) and compare with specifications.

4. Insert the inner rotor in the pump. Place the outer rotor over it. Install a new gasket coated on both sides with gasket sealer.

5. Place the cover on the pump body and secure it with the bolt. Be careful not to fold the gasket.

OIL PRESSURE RELIEF VALVE

The non-adjustable oil pressure relief valve is located on the bottom of the oil pump. When the valve opens, it allows oil to flow through a passage on the pump cover to the inlet side of the pump (**Figure 53**). To remove the valve, undo the cap bolt and take out the spring. The valve can then be taken out. Check spring tension by measuring the length of the spring. It should be 2.24 in. (57mm) on 240Z's; 2.06 in. (52.5mm) on 260-280Z's. If it is too long or short, replace it. When installing the relief valve, tighten the cap bolt to 22-25 ft.-lb. (240Z) or 29-36 ft.-lb. (260-280Z).

FLYWHEEL

Removal/Installation

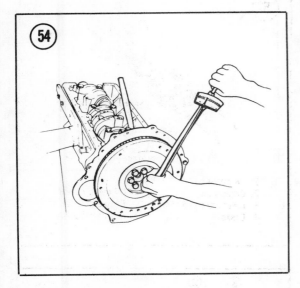

1. Remove the engine or transmission.

2. Remove the clutch from the flywheel. See Chapter Eight.

3. Unbolt the flywheel from the crankshaft (**Figure 54**).

4. Install by reversing Steps 1-3. Tighten the flywheel bolts to specifications. Tighten the bolts gradually in a diagonal pattern.

Inspection

1. Check the flywheel for scoring and wear. If the surface is glazed or slightly scratched, have it resurfaced by a machine shop. Replace the flywheel if damage is severe.

2. Measure the flywheel runout with a dial indicator (**Figure 55**). Replace the flywheel if runout exceeds 0.004 in. (0.1mm) on 240Z's, or 0.006 in. (0.15mm) on 260-280Z's.

3. Inspect the flywheel ring gear teeth. If the teeth are chipped, broken, or excessively worn, have a new starter ring shrunk onto the

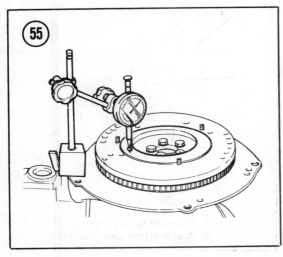

flywheel by a dealer or machine shop. The ring should be shrunk on at about 356-392°F (180-200°C).

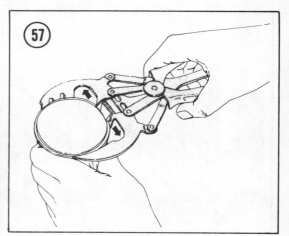

TORQUE CONVERTER DRIVE PLATE

The torque converter drive plate is fastened to the crankshaft with 6 bolts in the same manner as the flywheel. The drive plate bolts are torqued to 101-116 ft.-lb. (14-16 mkg).

Drive plate runout is measured in the same manner as flywheel runout. Replace the drive plate if runout exceeds 0.020 in. (0.05mm). The drive plate must also be replaced if the ring gear is damaged or worn excessively.

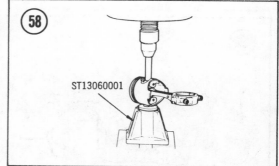

ST13060001

PISTON/CONNECTING ROD ASSEMBLIES

Piston Removal

1. Remove the cylinder head and oil pan as described earlier.

2. Remove the carbon ridge at the tops of the cylinder bores with a ridge reamer.

3. Rotate the crankshaft so the connecting rod is centered in the bore.

4. Unbolt the connecting rod cap **(Figure 56)** and push the piston and connecting rod out the

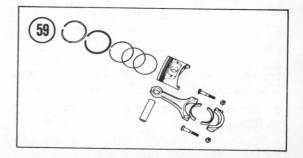

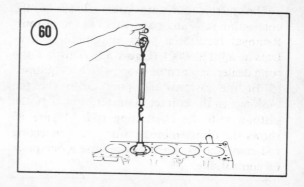

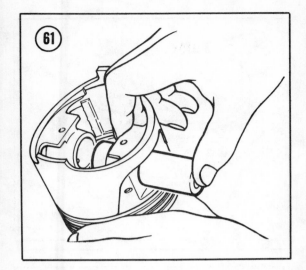

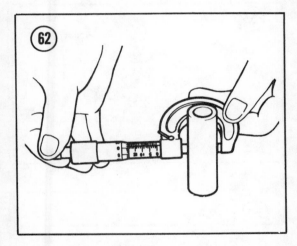

top of the bore. Tap the connecting rod with a wooden hammer handle if necessary.

5. Remove the rings with a ring remover as shown in **Figure 57**.

Piston Pin Removal/Installation

The piston pins are press fitted to the connecting rods and hand-fitted to the pistons. Removal requires a press and stand such as Datsun ST 13060001 (**Figure 58**). This is a job for a dealer or machine shop, which is equipped to fit the pistons and pins, ream the pin bushings to the correct diameter, and align the pistons with the connecting rods. **Figure 59** shows the disassembled piston and connecting rod components. Early engines use a one-piece oil control ring.

Piston Clearance Check

This procedure should be performed at room temperature. Pistons and cylinder walls must be clean and dry. Normal piston clearance is 0.0010-0.0018 in. (0.025-0.045mm).

1. Referring to **Figure 60**, insert the piston without rings upside down in the cylinder bore. Insert a 0.0016 in. feeler gauge between piston and cylinder wall and attach a spring scale as shown.

2. Pull on the spring scale. Note the amount of force required to pull the feeler gauge out of the cylinder. The pull should range from 0.44-3.30 lb. (0.2-1.5 kg). If the force is greater than this range, piston clearance is less than specified. If the force is less, piston clearance is greater.

3. Repeat the procedure for all 6 cylinders and pistons.

Piston Pin Clearance Check

1. Push the piston pin into the piston by hand (**Figure 61**). The pin should be tight enough not to wobble, but not too tight to press in with a thumb.

2. If there is any doubt about piston pin fit, measure the piston pin diameter with a micrometer (**Figure 62**). Then measure diameter of the piston pin hole in the piston and determine difference between the 2 measurements. Compare with specifications in **Table 1** at the end of the chapter. Replace both piston and pin if clearance exceeds this range.

Piston Ring Fit/Installation

1. Check the ring gap of each piston ring. To do this, first press the ring about one inch down the bore and square it by tapping gently with an inverted piston.

> NOTE: *If the cylinders have not been rebored, check the gap at the bottom of the ring travel, where the cylinder is least worn.*

2. Measure ring gap with a feeler gauge as shown in **Figure 63**. Compare with specifications at the end of the chapter.

3. Check side clearance of the rings as shown in **Figure 64**. Place the feeler gauge alongside the

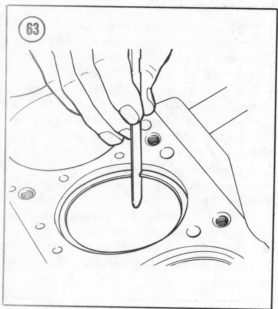

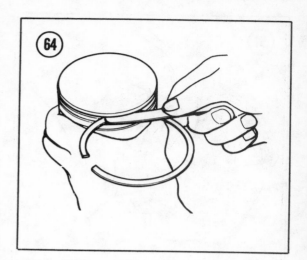

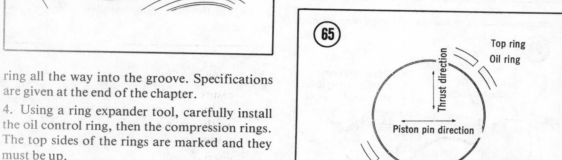

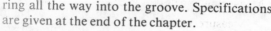

ring all the way into the groove. Specifications are given at the end of the chapter.

4. Using a ring expander tool, carefully install the oil control ring, then the compression rings. The top sides of the rings are marked and they must be up.

5. Turn the ring gaps 180° from each other. Turn the gaps so they are not in the front-rear direction of an installed piston. See **Figure 65**.

Connecting Rod Inspection

1. Check all connecting rods for bends or twisting with a connecting rod aligner (**Figure 66**). Realign or replace as necessary. This can be done by an automotive machine shop. The maximum allowable bend or twist in connecting rod is 0.002 in. (0.05mm) per 3.94 in. (10 cm) of connecting rod length.

2. Install the connecting rods and bearings on the crankshaft. Insert a feeler gauge between the connecting rod big end and crankshaft and measure the clearance (**Figure 67**). If clearance exceeds the maximum specified in **Table 1**, replace the connecting rod.

3. Weigh the connecting rods, especially if any have been replaced. Weight difference between the connecting rods must be 0.212 oz. (6 grams) or less on 240Z's; 0.247 oz. (7 grams) or less on all others.

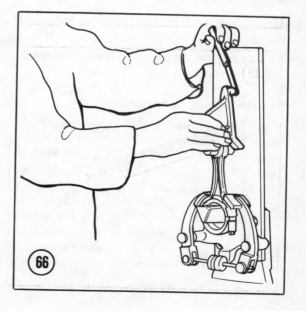

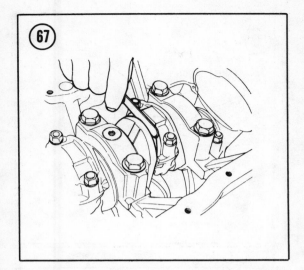

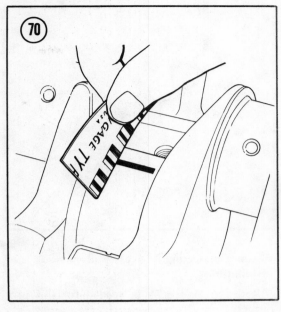

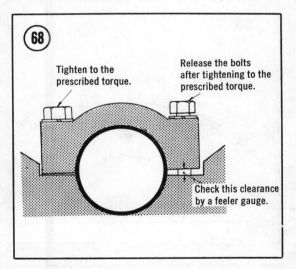

Tighten to the prescribed torque.

Release the bolts after tightening to the prescribed torque.

Check this clearance by a feeler gauge.

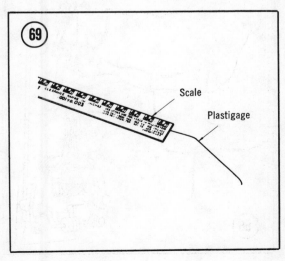

Scale

Plastigage

Measuring Bearing Clearance

1. Measure connecting rod bearing crush. To do this, install connecting rods, bearings, and caps on the proper crankpins. Tighten the cap nuts to specifications.

2. Loosen one nut on each connecting rod cap. Measure the gap between cap and connecting rod (**Figure 68**). Normal measurement is 0.0006-0.0018 in. (0.015-0.045mm). Replace the bearings if the gap is not within double this figure.

3. Assemble connecting rods with bearings on the proper crankpins. Do not tighten.

4. Cut a piece of Plastigage wire (**Figure 69**) the width of the bearing. Insert the Plastigage between the crankpin and bearing.

> NOTE: *Do not place the Plastigage over the crankpin oil hole.*

5. Install the connecting rod cap and tighten to specifications (see tightening torques at end of chapter). Do not rotate the crankshaft while the Plastigage is in place.

6. Remove the connecting rod cap. Bearing clearance is determined by comparing the width of the flattened Plastigage to markings on the envelope (**Figure 70**). If clearance exceeds specifications (end of chapter), the crankshaft must be reground.

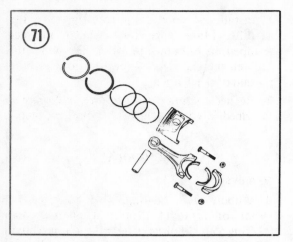

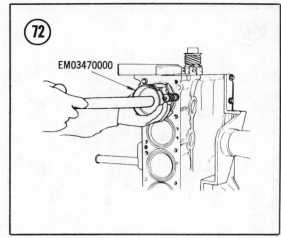

Piston/Connecting Rod Assembly
Installation

Refer to **Figure 71** as needed for this procedure.

1. Ensure that the ring gaps are 180° from each other, and not in a line from front to rear of the cylinder block **(Figure 65)**.

> NOTE: *On 1974 and later models, the top ring has a chrome-plated friction surface. The second ring is tapered. The upper and lower oil ring rails are interchangeable.*

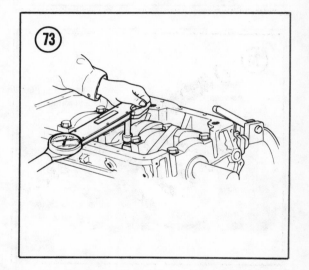

2. Immerse the entire piston in clean engine oil. Coat the cylinder wall with oil.

3. Slide a ring compressor over the rings. Compress the rings into the grooves.

4. Install the piston/connecting rod assembly in its cylinder as shown in **Figure 72**. Tap lightly with a wooden hammer handle to insert the piston. Be sure the number on the connecting rod corresponds with the cylinder number (counting from the front of the engine). Be sure the "F" mark on the piston faces the front, and the oil hole in the connecting rod big end faces the right-hand side of the engine.

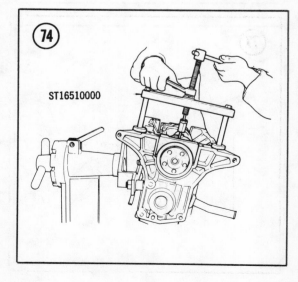

> CAUTION
> *Use extreme care not to let the connecting rod nick the crankshaft journal.*

5. Clean the connecting rod bearings carefully, including the back sides. Coat the crankpins and bearings with clean engine oil. Place the bearings in the connecting rod and cap.

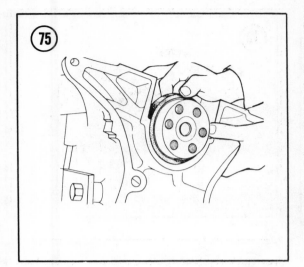

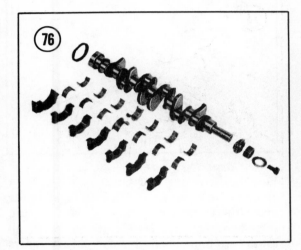

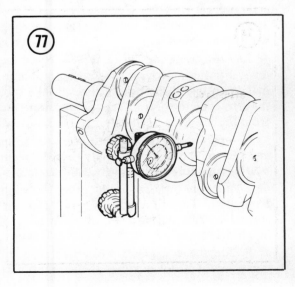

6. Install the connecting rod cap. See **Figure 73**. Make sure the cylinder numbers stamped on rod and cap are on the same side. Tighten the cap nuts to specifications given at the end of the chapter.

7. Recheck connecting rod big end play as described in *Connecting Rod Inspection*, Step 2.

CRANKSHAFT

Removal

1. Unbolt main bearing caps. Place caps in order of removal. Removal of rear main bearing cap requires a puller such as Datsun ST 16510000 (Kent-Moore J-25647). See **Figure 74**. If you do not have such a tool, take the engine to a Datsun dealer and have him remove the cap.

2. Remove crankshaft rear oil seal (**Figure 75**).

3. Lift out the crankshaft. Position the main bearings, caps, bolts, crankshaft, rear oil seal, crankshaft sprocket, distributor drive gear, and oil thrower on a workbench. **Figure 76** shows the arrangement.

Inspection

1. Clean the crankshaft thoroughly in solvent. Blow out the oil passages with compressed air.

2. Examine crankpins and main bearing journals for wear, scoring, or cracks. Check all journals against the specifications at the end of the chapter for out-of-roundness, taper, and wear. If necessary, have crankshaft reground.

3. Check the crankshaft for bending. Mount the crankshaft between accurate centers (such as V-blocks or a lathe) and rotate it one full turn with a dial gauge contacting the center journal. See **Figure 77**. Actual bend is half the reading shown on the gauge. Maximum permissible bend is 0.002 in. (0.05mm) on 240Z's, and 0.004 in. (0.1mm) on other models. The crankshaft must be reground if beyond the maximum.

4. Measure crankshaft end play. Install the crankshaft in the block and insert a feeler gauge between the center journal and the flange on the center bearing (**Figure 78**). Replace the center bearing if end play exceeds specifications given at the end of the chapter.

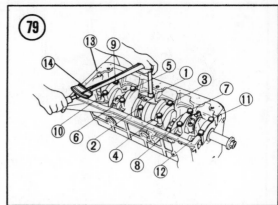

Measuring Main Bearing Clearance

1. Install the crankshaft, bearings, and bearing caps in the block. Tighten the caps to specifications found at end of chapter.

2. Loosen one bolt on each cap and measure the gap between cap and cylinder block. See **Figure 68**. Normal gap is zero-0.0012 in. (zero-0.03mm). Replace the bearings if the gap is not within double this figure.

3. Remove the main bearing caps and lower bearing halves.

4. Cut a piece of Plastigage the width of each main bearing. Lay a piece on each main bearing journal, then install the caps and tighten to specifications.

> NOTE: *Do not place Plastigage across crankshaft oil holes. Do not rotate the crankshaft while Plastigage is in place.*

5. Remove bearing caps. Compare the width of the flattened Plastigage to the markings on the envelope to determine bearing clearance. See **Figure 70**. Compare with specifications. The crankshaft must be reground if clearance is beyond the maximum.

Installation

1. Thoroughly clean main bearings, including the back sides.

2. Place the bearings in appropriate holders in the block. The center bearing is flanged to control crankshaft end play. Bearings 2, 3, 5, and 6 are identical. On 240Z's, No. 1 bearing appears identical to No. 7, but No. 1 has an oil

hole and No. 7 does not. On 260-280Z's, No. 1 and No. 7 are the same. On 240Z's, all upper and lower bearings except No. 1 are interchangeable. On 260Z's, all uppers and all lowers are interchangeable. On 280Z's uppers and lowers are not interchangeable.

3. Coat the bearings and crankshaft journals with clean engine oil.

4. Lay the crankshaft in the block. Place the lower bearing halves on the appropriate journals, then install the bearing caps. Make sure the arrows on the bearing caps point toward the front of the engine. Install the cap bolts loosely.

5. Gently push the crankshaft toward the front and rear of the engine to verify that the main bearing caps are properly aligned and seated.

6. Tighten the cap bolts in the order shown in **Figure 79**. Tighten gradually in 3 separate stages, working outward from the center bearing. Final torque is 33-40 ft.-lb. (4.5-5.5 mkg).

7. Rotate the crankshaft while tightening to make sure it is not binding. If the crankshaft

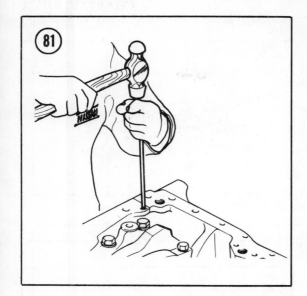

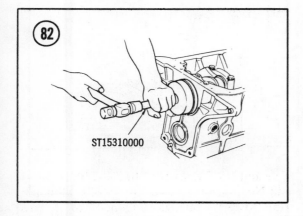

ST15310000

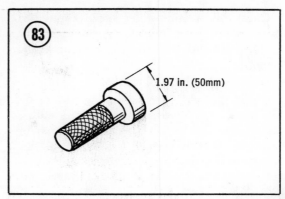

1.97 in. (50mm)

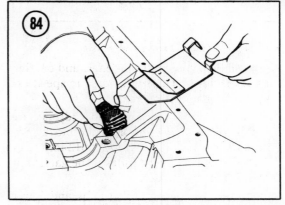

becomes difficult to turn, stop and find out why before continuing. Make absolutely certain that bearings are the correct size for the crankshaft, especially if it has been reground. Never use undersize bearings if the crankshaft has not been reground.

8. Recheck crankshaft end play (**Figure 80**).

9. Tap the side oil seals into the rear main cap and cylinder block (**Figure 81**).

10. Install the rear oil seal with a drift such as Datsun ST 15310000 (Kent-Moore J-25640-01). See **Figure 82**. **Figure 83** shows the drift. Coat the lip of the seal with lithium grease.

Pilot Bushing

The pilot bushing, located inside the rear end of the crankshaft, supports the transmission in-

put shaft on manual transmission models. Inspect the bushing for visible wear or damage. Have it replaced by a Datsun dealer or machine shop if defects are apparent.

CYLINDER BLOCK INSPECTION

1. Prior to inspection, remove the crankcase oil separator from the block (**Figure 84**). Wash it in solvent.

2. Clean the block thoroughly with solvent and check all freeze plugs for leaks. Replace any freeze plugs that are suspect. It is a good idea to replace all of them. While cleaning, check oil and water passages for dirt, sludge, and corrosion. If the passages are very dirty, the block should be boiled out by a dealer or by a machine shop.

NOTE: *Block boiling necessitates replacement of all freeze plugs. However, a block dirty enough to need boiling almost certainly needs new freeze plugs anyway.*

3. Check oil pressure relief valve (**Figure 85**) for cracks or other damage. If damaged, pry the valve out with a screwdriver and tap a new one in.

4. Examine the block for cracks.

5. Check the cylinder head mating surface on the block for flatness. Use an accurate straightedge and a feeler gauge as shown in **Figure 86**. Normal warp is less than 0.002 in. (0.05mm). The maximum permissible warp is 0.004 in. (0.1mm). Have the block resurfaced if beyond the maximum.

> NOTE: *If the block alone is being resurfaced, up to 0.008 in. (0.2mm) may be removed from it. If the block and head are being resurfaced, metal removed from both may not total more than 0.008 in. (0.2mm).*

6. Measure the cylinder bores for out-of-roundness or excessive wear with a bore gauge. See **Figure 87**. Measure the bores at top, center, and bottom, in front-rear and side-to-side directions. See **Figure 88**. Compare the measurement to specifications at the end of the chapter. If the cylinders exceed maximum tolerances, they must be rebored. Reboring is also necessary if the cylinder walls are badly scuffed or scored.

> NOTE: *If one cylinder is bored out, all cylinders must be bored to the same diameter. Cylinders must be bored in the following order: 1-5-3-6-2-4. When the cylinders are too badly worn to be bored further, undersize cylinder liners can be fitted.*

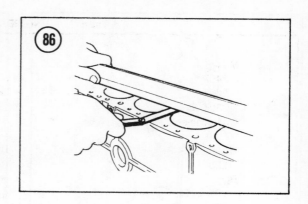

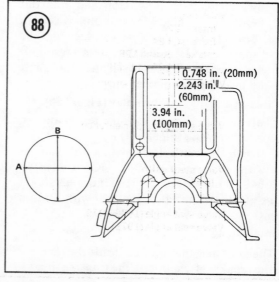

Table 1   ENGINE SPECIFICATIONS

Model	
240Z	L24 engine
260Z	L26 engine
280Z	L28 engine
Displacement	
L24	146.0 cu. in. (2,393cc)
L26	156.52 cu. in. (2,565cc)
L28	168.0 cu. in. (2,753cc)
Bore	
L24, L26	3.267 in. (83mm)
L28	3.39 in. (86mm)
Stroke	
L24	2.902 in. (73.7mm)
L26, L28	3.11 in. (79mm)
Firing order	1-5-3-6-2-4
Compression ratio	
Through 1971	9.0:1
1972-1974	8.8:1
1975-1976	8.3:1
Oil pressure (hot at 2,000 rpm)	50-57 psi (3.5-4.0 kg/cm²)

Valves	
Head diameter	
Intake, L24 and L26	1.65 in. (42mm)
Intake, L28	1.73 in. (44mm)
Exhaust, L24	1.30 in. (33mm)
Exhaust, L26 and L28	1.38 in. (35mm)
Valve stem diameter	
Intake, L24	0.3137-0.3142 in. (7.97-7.98mm)
Exhaust, L24	0.3126-0.3134 in. (7.94-7.96mm)
Intake, L26 and L28	0.3134-0.3142 in. (7.96-7.98mm)
Exhaust, L26 and L28	0.3126-0.3134 in. (7.94-7.96mm)
Valve length	
Intake, L24	4.59 in. (116.5mm)
Exhaust, L24	4.63 in. (117.5mm)
Intake, L26 and L28	4.524-4.535 in. (114.9-115.2mm)
Exhaust, L26 and L28	4.555-4.567 in. (115.7-116.0mm)
Valve spring loaded length	
Outer	1.16 in. at 108.03 lb. (29.5mm at 49 kg)
Inner	0.96 in. at 56.22 lb. (24.5mm at 25.5 kg)
Valve stem to guide clearance	
Intake	0.0008-0.0021 in. (0.020-0.053mm)
Exhaust	0.0016-0.0029 in. (0.040-0.073mm)
Valve stem width	
Intake	0.055-0.063 in. (1.4-1.6mm)
Exhaust	0.071-0.087 in. (1.8-2.2mm)
Valve seat angle (1970-1978)	45°
Valve seat angle (1979)	45° 30´

(continued)

Table 1   ENGINE SPECIFICATIONS (continued)

Camshaft
End play   0.003-0.015 in. (0.08-0.38mm)
Lobe lift   0.275 in. (7mm)

Connecting Rods
Big end play   0.008-0.012 in. (0.2-0.3mm)
Permissible weight variation
L24   0.18 oz. (6 gm)
L26 and L28   0.25 oz. (7 gm)

Crankshaft
Journal diameter   2.1631-2.1636 in. (54.942-54.955mm)
Journal taper and out-of-round
L24   Less than 0.0012 in. (0.03mm)
L26 and L28   Less than 0.0004 in. (0.01mm)
Crankshaft free end play   0.002-0.007 in. (0.05-0.18mm)
Maximum permissible end play   0.012 in. (0.3mm)
Crankpin diameter   1.9670-1.9675 in. (49.961-49.974mm)
Crankpin taper and out-of-round
L24   Less than 0.0012 in. (0.03mm)
L26 and L28   Less than 0.0004 in. (0.01mm)
Main bearing clearance
Standard   0.0008-0.0028 in. (0.020-0.072mm)
Maximum   0.005 in. (0.12mm)
Connecting rod bearing clearance
Standard   0.0010-0.0022 in. (0.025-0.055mm)
Maximum   0.005 in. (0.12mm)

Cylinders
Bore, L24 and L26   3.2677-3.2679 in. (83.00-83.05mm)
Bore, L28   3.3858-3.3878 in. (86.00-86.05mm)
Wear limit   0.0079 in. (0.2mm)
Taper or out-of-round   0.0006 in. (0.015mm)
Maximum difference between bores   0.0079 in. (0.2mm)

Pistons
Standard diameter, L24 and L26   3.267-3.269 in. (82.99-83.04mm)
Standard diameter, L28   3.3852-3.3872 in. (85.985-86.035mm)
Ring groove width
Compression   0.079 in. (2mm)
Oil control   0.157 in. (4mm)
Ring side clearance
Top compression   0.0018-0.0031 in. (0.045-0.078mm)
Second compression   0.0012-0.0025 in. (0.030-0.063mm)
Oil control (one-piece ring, early models)   0.0010-0.0025 in. (0.025-0.063mm)
Ring gap
Top compression   0.0091-0.0150 in. (0.23-0.38mm)
Second compression   0.0059-0.0118 in. (0.15-0.30mm)
Oil control   0.0059-0.0118 in. (0.15-0.30mm)
Maximum (all models)   0.039 in. (1mm)

Table 2 TIGHTENING TORQUES

	Ft.-lb.	Mkg
Camshaft locate plate bolts	4-6	0.5-0.8
Camshaft sprocket bolts		
L24	101-116	14-16
L26 and L28	94-108	13-15
Connecting rod big end nuts		
Early L24 (bolt head marked T13)	20-24	2.7-3.3
Late L24 (bolt head marked T12)	33-40	4.5-5.5
L26	27-31	3.7-4.3
L28	33-40	4.5-5.5
Crankshaft pulley bolt		
L24	86-116	12-16
L26 and L28	94-108	13-15
Cylinder head bolts		
L24 through engine No. L24-027600*		
First stage	33	4.5
Second stage	47	6.5
Third stage	47-51	6.5-7.0
L24 from engine No. L24-027601*		
First stage	33	4.5
Second stage	47	6.5
Third stage	51-61	7.0-8.5
L26 and L28 (through 1976)		
First stage	29	4.0
Second stage	47	6.5
Third stage	54-61	7.5-8.5
L28 (1977 and later)		
First stage	29	4.0
Second stage	43	6.0
Third stage	51-61	7.0-8.5
Flywheel bolts		
L24	101-116	14-16
L26 and L28	94-108	13-15
Front cover bolts		
Small bolts	3-6	0.4-0.6
Large bolts	7-12	1.0-1.6
Main bearing cap bolts	33-40	4.5-5.5
Oil pan bolts	4½-7	0.6-1.0
Oil pan drain plug	14-22	2.0-3.0
Oil pump bolts	8-11	1.1-1.5
Oil strainer bolts		
L24	6-9	0.8-1.2
L26 and L28 (through 1976)	3-4	0.4-0.6
L28 (1977-1978)	6-8	0.8-1.1
Rocker pivot locknuts	36-43	5-6

*Late L24 head bolts have a circular groove stamped in the top
surface of the bolt head. Early L24 head bolts do not.

4

CHAPTER FIVE

FUEL AND EXHAUST SYSTEMS

The 240Z fuel system consists of a fuel tank mounted beneath the rear floor section, which is connected through a line to a fuel strainer, then to a pump which delivers fuel to two SU-type Hitachi carburetors. The air cleaner used through 1972 is a manually-controlled hot air type. The 1973 cars use an automatic temperature control air cleaner.

The 260Z fuel system is similar to the 240Z's, but includes an auxiliary electric fuel pump.

The 280Z uses a Bosch L-Jetronic fuel injection system; the letter "L" stands for the German word "Luft" (air). Air flow into the engine is the primary factor in injection system operation.

Fuel system-related emission control devices include an evaporative emission control system, throttle opener or boost controlled deceleration device, and air injection system (240-260Z only). An exhaust gas recirculation system is used on 1973 and later cars, except 1975-1976 non-California models.

The 240-260Z exhaust system consists of manifold, front tube, combined pre-muffler and center tube, and combined main muffler and tailpipe. The 280Z system is similar to this, but uses either a separate premuffler (non-California cars) or catalytic converter (California models).

This chapter includes service procedures for the air cleaner, carburetors, fuel pumps, fuel system-related emission controls, and exhaust system. The 280Z fuel injection system is described and explained.

CARBURETOR AIR CLEANER

The 1970-1972 air cleaner setting is controlled by moving the control lever as shown in **Figure 1**. When turned to the winter setting, the control valve blocks the normal air intake. Hot air from near the exhaust manifold is then drawn into the air cleaner.

The 1973-1974 air cleaner is similar, but regulates incoming air temperature automatically.

Air Cleaner Removal/Installation

1. Remove the air cleaner cover and filter element.

2. On 1970-1972 air cleaners, disconnect the following from the air cleaner backplate: air

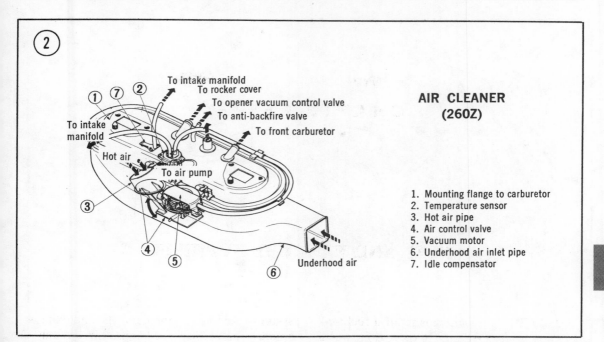

**AIR CLEANER
(260Z)**

To intake manifold
To rocker cover
To opener vacuum control valve
To anti-backfire valve
To front carburetor
To intake manifold
Hot air
To air pump
Underhood air

1. Mounting flange to carburetor
2. Temperature sensor
3. Hot air pipe
4. Air control valve
5. Vacuum motor
6. Underhood air inlet pipe
7. Idle compensator

5

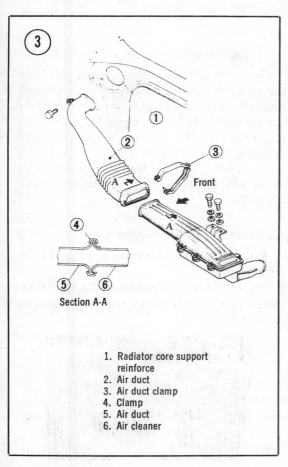

Front
A
A
Section A-A

1. Radiator core support reinforce
2. Air duct
3. Air duct clamp
4. Clamp
5. Air duct
6. Air cleaner

pump hose, PCV hose, float chamber overflow tubes, and tube to the flow guide valve.

3. On 1973-1974 air cleaners, disconnect the following from the backplate: 2 air pump hoses, carbon canister hose, hose to front carburetor, 2 hoses to intake manifold, one hose to rocker cover, duct to exhaust manifold, and hose to throttle opener control valve (not used on automatic transmission 260Z's). See **Figure 2**.

4. Remove the nut attaching the backplate to the carburetors, then lift off the backplate.

5. To install the air cleaner, reverse the preceding steps.

FUEL INJECTION AIR CLEANER

The fuel injection air cleaner is mounted at the front of the engine compartment.

Removal/Installation

1. On 1977 and later models, disconnect the intake duct (**Figure 3**).

2. Detach the air cleaner body and lift it out. See **Figure 4** and **Figure 5**.

3. Installation is the reverse of removal.

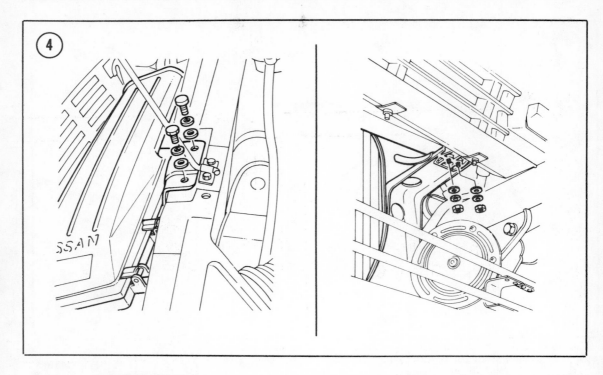

CARBURETORS

The 1970-1974 models use SU-type side-draft carburetors. The design used through 1972 uses a separate float chamber, mounted to one side of the carburetor. The choke mechanism works by lowering the jet in each carburetor, allowing more fuel to enter.

The 1973-1974 carburetors use integral float chambers located beneath the carburetor. This is intended to stabilize fuel level during hard cornering and acceleration. Choke action is provided by a butterfly valve in each carburetor. These restrict air flow when closed. A power valve in each carburetor supplements the piston-damper enrichment system during acceleration from medium speeds.

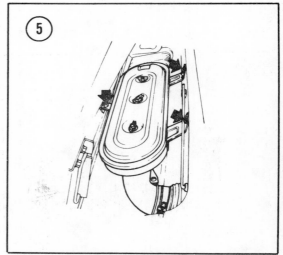

Basic Principles

The carburetors automatically vary the air venturi area and fuel jet size according to engine demands. **Figure 6** shows a simplified carburetor diagram. Note the movable piston which changes the effective area of the venturi. (A) shows the carburetor at idle. The throttle valve is open slightly, and the suction piston and jet needle are all the way down. This produces a small venturi and jet area, and as a result, only small amounts of air and fuel are admitted to the carburetor.

As the throttle valve is opened further (B), vacuum behind the suction piston increases. This increases vacuum above the piston and the piston rises, increasing venturi area. The tapered jet needle in the base of the piston is lifted together with the piston, thus increasing effective jet size. As a result, more fuel and air are admitted.

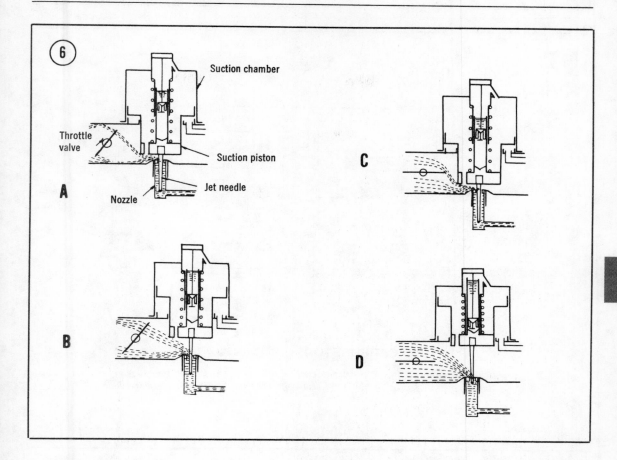

5

(C) shows the carburetor when the accelerator has been depressed rapidly. The piston attempts to rise rapidly, but the hydraulic damping mechanism in the suction chamber slows it down. This enriches the mixture temporarily.

(D) shows the carburetor under high speed driving conditions. The throttle valve is fully open, and the suction piston together with its jet needle have been lifted all the way up. This gives maximum venturi area and jet size, resulting in maximum air and fuel flow.

CARBURETOR OVERHAUL
(1970-1972)

Removal/Installation

1. Remove the air cleaner.

2. Detach the fuel lines from the float chambers.

3. Disconnect the servo diaphragm from the throttle linkage.

4. Disconnect the rod between the auxiliary throttle shaft and throttle shaft. See **Figure 7**.

5. Remove 4 nuts attaching each carburetor to the intake manifold. See **Figure 8**.

> NOTE: *On 1972 models, drain approximately ½ gallon of coolant to prevent coolant from seeping into the cylinders. If this happens, immediately remove all spark plugs and turn the engine over with the starter until all coolant is blown out of the cylinders.*

6. Lift the carburetors and throttle shaft away from the engine simultaneously. Separate the carburetors from the throttle shaft.

7. Installation is the reverse of these steps.

Description

Each carburetor consists of three main sections: float chamber, suction chamber, and jet nozzle. Disassembly, inspection, and repair

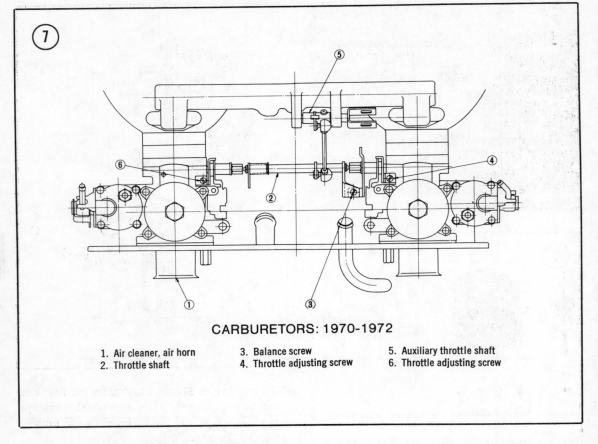

CARBURETORS: 1970-1972

1. Air cleaner, air horn
2. Throttle shaft
3. Balance screw
4. Throttle adjusting screw
5. Auxiliary throttle shaft
6. Throttle adjusting screw

procedures for the three sections, as well as for the throttle and choke levers follow.

The construction of SU-type carburetors is considerably more simple than that of other types. However, the carburetors are precision instruments. Clean working conditions are extremely important for carburetor overhaul. In addition, parts must never be switched from one carburetor to the other. Disassemble and reassemble one carburetor at a time to prevent mixing parts.

Disassembly

1. Referring to **Figure 9**, unscrew the oil cap nut and lift out the plunger.

2. Remove 4 setscrews and lift off the suction chamber.

3. Take the suction spring and nylon washer off the piston.

4. Lift the piston out of the carburetor, together with the jet needle.

CAUTION
Do not bend the jet needle when removing. A bent needle will seriously affect carburetor performance.

5. Do not remove the jet needle from the piston unless it is worn or incorrectly installed. To remove, loosen the setscrew in the side of the piston. Then hold the needle with pliers at a point 0.08 in. (2mm) or less from the piston. Turn and pull gently until the needle is out. Be careful not to bend the needle.

6. Detach the fuel line from the base of the float chamber. Detach the overflow tube from the top of the float chamber.

7. Referring to **Figure 10**, remove the fuel line fitting from the top of the float chamber. This fitting includes a fuel return tube, designed to prevent vapor lock.

8. Referring to **Figure 11**, remove 4 setscrews attaching the float chamber cover to the bowl. Lift off the cover together with the float.

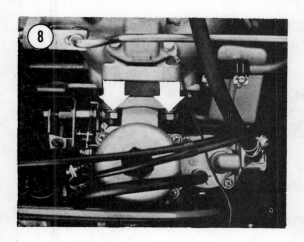

1. Oil cap nut
2. Suction chamber
3. Suction spring
4. Suction piston
5. Jet needle

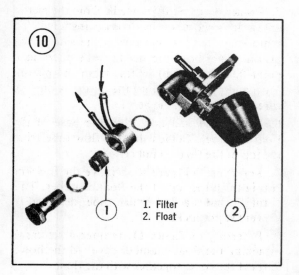

1. Filter
2. Float

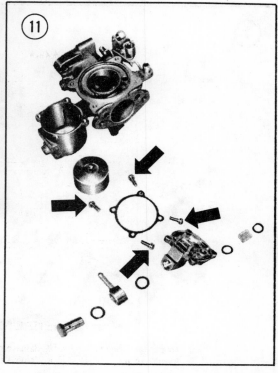

9. Referring to **Figure 12**, detach the fuel line from the jet nozzle. Then remove the Phillips screw attaching the choke lever to the nozzle, and take the nozzle out.

10. Unscrew the idle adjusting nut. Take the nut and spring off the idle sleeve.

> NOTE: *Installation of nozzle sleeve is difficult. Do not remove it unless absolutely necessary.*

11. If necessary, disassemble the throttle and choke levers. Disassembly should not be required unless a component is bent or otherwise damaged. **Figure 13** shows the throttle lever components, and **Figure 14** shows the choke lever components.

Inspection and Assembly

1. Thoroughly clean all parts in solvent and blow dry with compressed air. Do not use any abrasives for cleaning.

2. Inspect the inside of the suction chamber and the piston friction surface for scratches, dents, and wear. Replace the carburetor if any of these conditions is found.

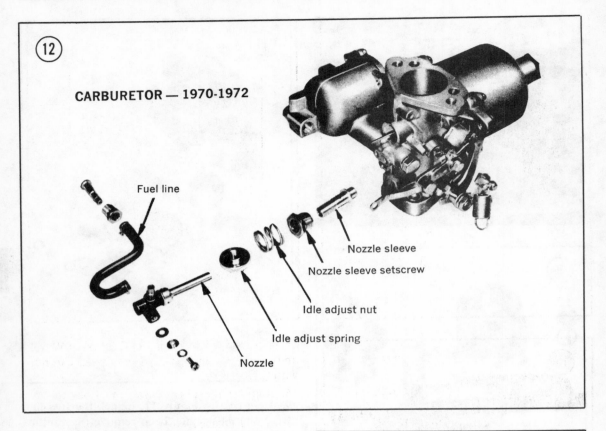

⑫

CARBURETOR — 1970-1972

Fuel line

Nozzle sleeve

Nozzle sleeve setscrew

Idle adjust nut

Idle adjust spring

Nozzle

3. Check the jet needle for wear. Also check for scuffs or worn streaks which indicate incorrect installation. If the needle is not worn, install it in the piston as shown in **Figure 15**. Use a straightedge to ensure that the shoulder of the needle is flush with the piston surface. Tighten the setscrew to lock the needle in place.

4. Install the jet nozzle sleeve (if removed), washer, and securing nut. Do not tighten the nut.

5. Inspect the jet nozzle on the outside for signs of wear. Carefully check the inside of the nozzle bore for wear and out-of-roundness. If they are even slightly suspect, replace the nozzle and jet needle.

6. Temporarily install the jet nozzle in the sleeve without the spring or idle adusting nut.

7. Temporarily install the suction chamber and piston without the spring.

8. Raise the piston with a finger and let it drop slowly. It should hit the bridge with an audible click. If it does not drop freely, recenter the nozzle and drop the piston again. Keep tighten-

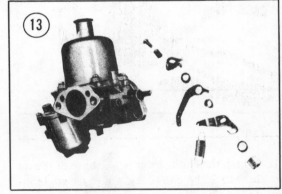

⑬

ing the securing nut, and testing centering by lifting and dropping the piston until the nut is tight and the piston drops freely.

9. Remove the jet nozzle. Install the spring and idle adjusting nut. Install the jet nozzle. Turn the idle adjusting nut so the distance between the nozzle head and jet bridge, dimension (A) in **Figure 16**, is approximately 0.087 in. (2.2mm).

10. Connect the fuel line to the base of the jet nozzle.

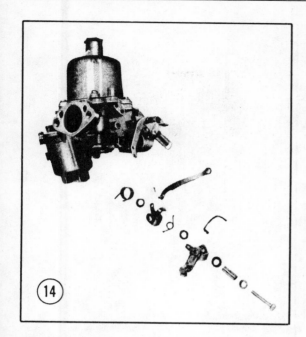

(14)

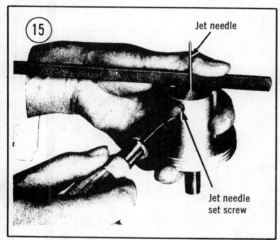

(15)

Jet needle

Jet needle
set screw

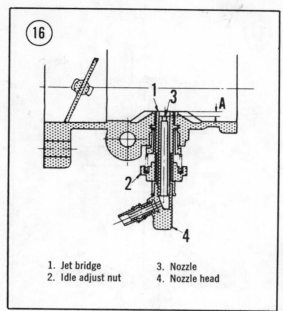

(16)

1. Jet bridge
2. Idle adjust nut
3. Nozzle
4. Nozzle head

11. Attach the choke lever to the base of the jet nozzle. Move the choke lever slightly while inserting the screw to ensure that the small spacer is centered in the hole in the lower end of the choke lever.

12. Place the nylon washer and the spring on the piston.

13. Apply a few drops of light oil to the outside of the piston damper. Do not put any oil at all on the inside of the suction chamber, or on the friction surface of the piston.

14. Install the suction chamber and secure it with 4 screws.

15. Fill damper with oil (SAE 20 or 10W-30) and install the plunger. Tighten the oil cap nut with fingers only.

16. Remove the pin holding the float to the float chamber cover. Inspect the needle valve for wear. Replace if worn or in doubt.

17. Check the float for dents or leaks. If the float is satisfactory, reassemble needle and float.

18. Place the float chamber cover and float on a workbench so the float is on top. Lift the float with a finger and lower it so the float just touches the needle valve. The distance from the float lever to the float chamber inside surface, dimension (H) in **Figure 17**, should be 0.55-0.59 in. (14-15mm). This will set the float level at 0.906 in. (23mm) as shown in **Figure 18**. If necessary, adjust the float level by bending the float lever.

19. Install the float chamber cover and fuel line fitting.

CARBURETOR OVERHAUL
(1973-1974)

Removal/Installation

1. Remove the air cleaner as described earlier.

2. Disconnect the fuel inlet and idle speed hoses from both carburetors. Disconnect the air

5

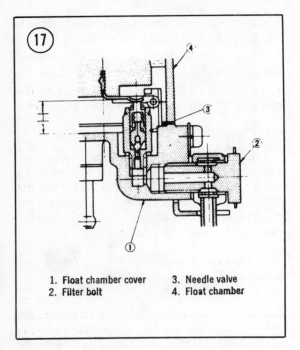

1. Float chamber cover   3. Needle valve
2. Filter bolt   4. Float chamber

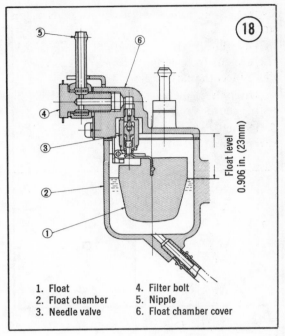

Float level
0.906 in. (23mm)

1. Float   4. Filter bolt
2. Float chamber   5. Nipple
3. Needle valve   6. Float chamber cover

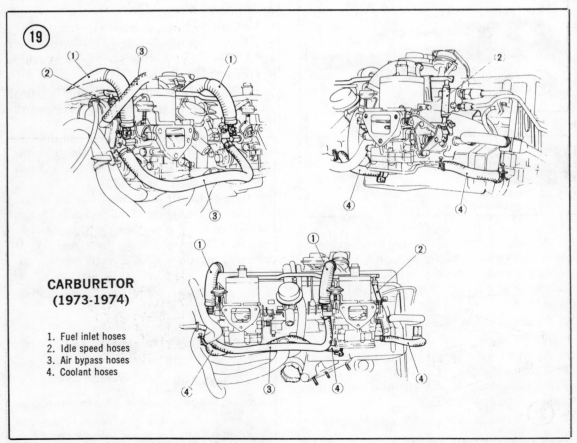

CARBURETOR
(1973-1974)

1. Fuel inlet hoses
2. Idle speed hoses
3. Air bypass hoses
4. Coolant hoses

bypass hose from front carburetor. See **Figure 19**.

3. Disconnect the distributor vacuum tube (**Figure 20**) from front carburetor. On 260Z's, disconnect the carbon canister as well.

4. Disconnect the EGR vacuum tube from the rear carburetor. See **Figure 20**.

5. Detach the coolant hoses from front and rear carburetors. **Figure 19** shows the hoses.

6. Remove 4 nuts attaching each carburetor to the manifold. Lift both carburetors off.

7. To separate carburetors, remove the coolant and air bypass hoses running between them.

8. Installation is the reverse of these steps. Use new gaskets between carburetors and manifold.

Description

The 1973-1974 carburetors require specialized equipment to assemble the fuel metering system. Because of this, the factory does not recommend major disassembly. The only removable components are the float chamber cover, power valve, and linkage parts.

Float Chamber Cover
Removal/Installation

The float chamber cover is removed to adjust the float level and to clean the chamber. On 1973 carburetors, the float and needle valve can be removed. On the 1974 carburetors, only the cover is removable.

1. Remove the carburetor as described earlier.

2. Remove the float chamber screws, then lift off the cover and gasket. See **Figure 21** (1973) or **Figure 22** (1974).

3. On 1973 carburetors, push out the float pivot pin, then remove the float. Remove the

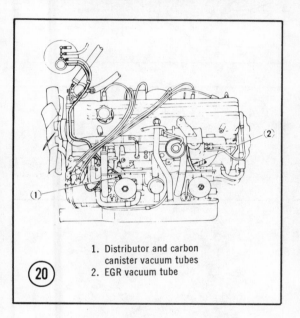

1. Distributor and carbon canister vacuum tubes
2. EGR vacuum tube

20

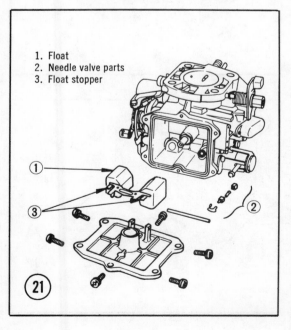

1. Float
2. Needle valve parts
3. Float stopper

21

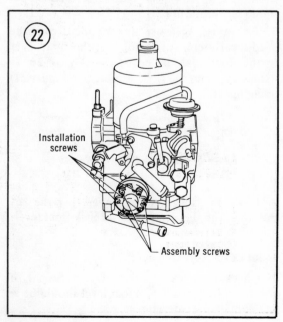

22

Installation screws

Assembly screws

needle valve securing clip and take out the needle valve. Inspect all parts and replace as needed.

> CAUTION
> *Do not move the jet needle adjusting nut or bend the float stoppers.*

4. If necessary, adjust float level as described later in this chapter.

5. Installation is the reverse of these steps. Use a new chamber cover gasket.

Power Valve Removal/Installation

1. Remove the carburetor as described earlier.

2. Remove 3 screws attaching the power valve to the carburetor. See **Figure 23** (1973) or **Figure 24** (1974).

3. Remove 3 screws holding the power valve together. Remove and examine the diaphragm. Replace the power valve if the diaphragm is worn or damaged.

4. Install in the reverse order.

Float Level Adjustment (1973)

1. To check float level, hold a mirror up to the sight glass on the side of the carburetor while the engine is running. See **Figure 25**. Fuel level should be ¼ in. (6mm) below the level of the sight glass centerline.

2. To adjust, measure the distance from the needle valve contact surface on the float lever to the float chamber cover. See **Figure 26**. If necessary, bend the float stoppers (3, **Figure 21**) to change it.

> NOTE: *Lowering the float stopper 0.009 in. (0.23mm) will raise the float level 0.039 in. (1mm). Raising the float stopper 0.009 in. will lower float level 0.039 in.*

3. Install the float chamber cover, then the carburetor. Run the engine and recheck float level.

Float Level Adjustment (1974)

1. Check float level as described in Step 1 of the previous procedure. Float level should be at the sight glass centerline.

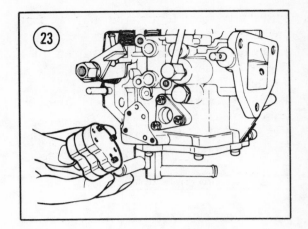

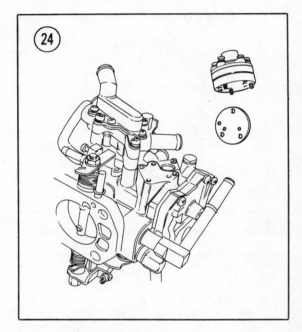

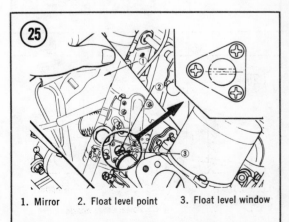

1. Mirror   2. Float level point   3. Float level window

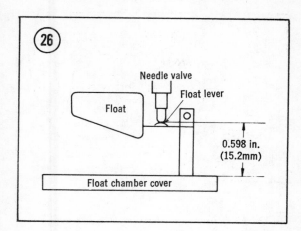

26

Needle valve

Float lever

Float

0.598 in.
(15.2mm)

Float chamber cover

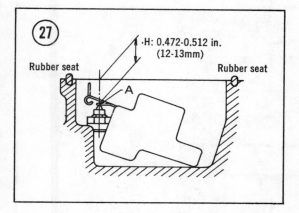

27

·H: 0.472-0.512 in.
(12-13mm)

Rubber seat

Rubber seat

A

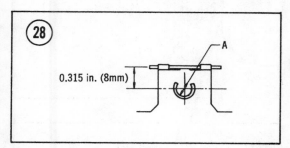

28

A

0.315 in. (8mm)

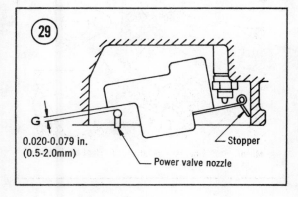

29

G

0.020-0.079 in.
(0.5-2.0mm)

Stopper

Power valve nozzle

2. Remove the float chamber cover and turn the carburetor upside down. Measure dimension (H), **Figure 27**. This is the distance from point (A) of float lever tongue to float chamber end surface. **Figure 28** shows point (A).

3. If dimension (H) is incorrect, bend the float lever tongue as necessary to change it.

4. Turn the carburetor right side up. Measure dimension (G), **Figure 29**. If incorrect, bend the float stopper as needed to change it. Recheck dimension (H) to make sure it has not changed.

5. Install the float chamber cover, then the carburetor. Run the engine and recheck float level.

CARBURETOR HEATING SYSTEM

On 1972-1974 models, the carburetors are heated by engine coolant routed through passages in the carburetor bases and intake manifold. **Figure 30** is a cross-sectional view of the coolant passages. **Figure 31** is a diagram of the 1972 system. The 1973-1974 version is similar.

Temperature is controlled by a thermostat which cuts off coolant flow when the coolant temperature reaches 150° F. The thermostat should only be removed for testing when it appears defective.

Thermostat Removal/Installation

Figure 31 shows the thermostat in position. To remove, loosen the small hose at the rear end of thermostat, then unscrew the thermostat. Install in the reverse order.

> NOTE: *To avoid spilling, drain approximately ½ gallon of coolant before removing the thermostat.*

Thermostat Testing

1. Referring to **Figure 32**, attach a tube to the rear of the thermostat.

2. Immerse the thermostat for several minutes in water heated to 175 °F (80 °C) or more.

3. Try to blow into the tube. Little or no air should pass through the thermostat. Replace the thermostat if air can be easily blown through it.

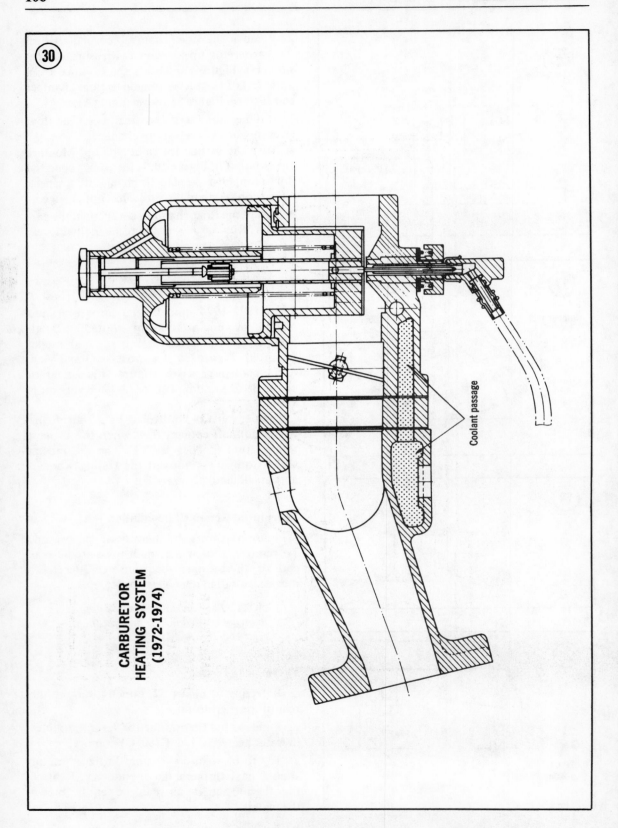

(30)

**CARBURETOR
HEATING SYSTEM
(1972-1974)**

Coolant passage

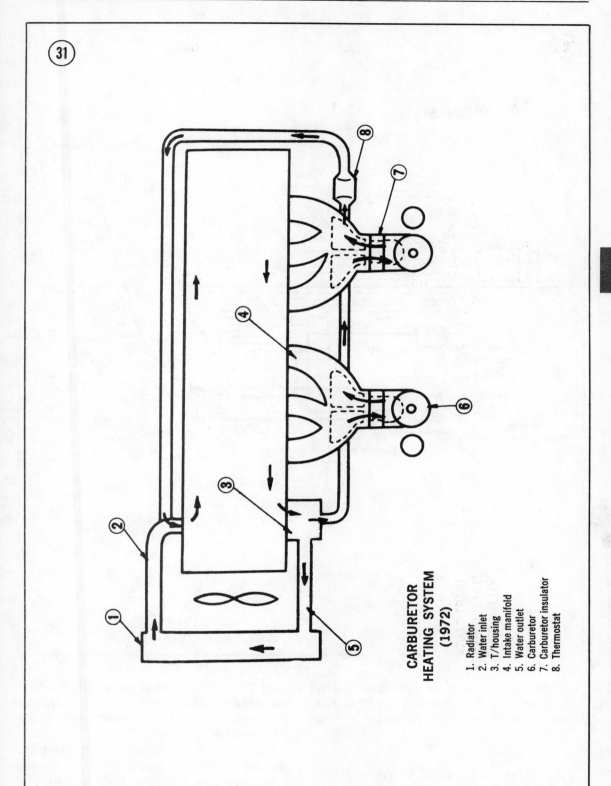

**CARBURETOR
HEATING SYSTEM
(1972)**

1. Radiator
2. Water inlet
3. T/housing
4. Intake manifold
5. Water outlet
6. Carburetor
7. Carburetor insulator
8. Thermostat

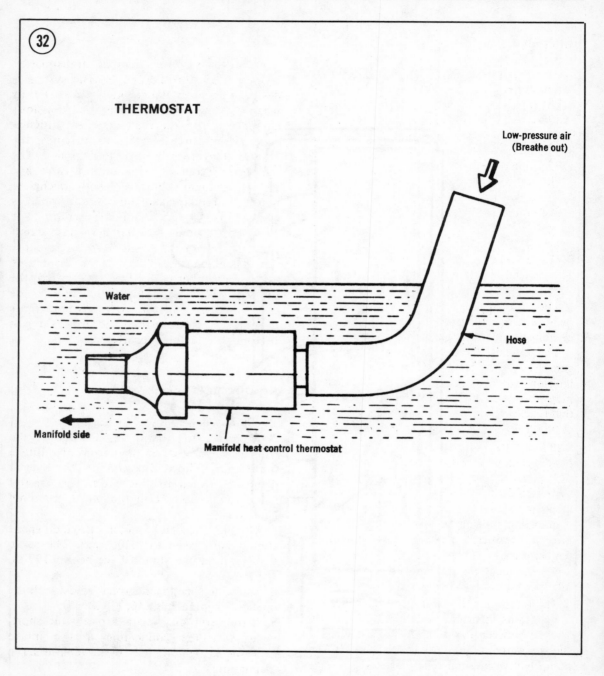

③2

THERMOSTAT

Low-pressure air
(Breathe out)

Water

Hose

Manifold side

Manifold heat control thermostat

4. Repeat the test with the thermostat in cold water. Air should pass through the thermostat easily. If not, replace the thermostat.

FUEL INJECTION SYSTEM

Bosch L-Jetronic electronic fuel injection is used on 280Z's. Unlike carburetors, which use engine vacuum to mix fuel and air, the fuel injection system forces fuel under pressure into the intake ports.

The fuel injection system is very complex. Diagnosis and repair should be left to a Datsun dealer or other mechanic familiar with the system. The following explanation should enable you to discuss the system intelligently with your mechanic.

Figure 33 is a schematic diagram of the Z system; **Figure 34** identifies individual components.

The injectors are solenoid valves. They open to admit fuel to the engine, or close to cut it off. Injector open time — and thus the amount of fuel delivered to the intake ports — is regulated by the control unit.

The control unit receives signals from several sources. The air flow meter indicates the quantity of intake air. The air temperature sensor indicates its temperature. The throttle valve switch shows throttle position. The water temperature switch indicates coolant temperature. The starting switch indicates whether or not the starter is operating.

The control unit uses the input signals to determine injector open time. It then sends an opening signal to each injector.

The electric current to open the injectors comes from the battery. It passes through the ignition switch, fuel injection relay, and dropping resistors. The resistors reduce the current that reaches the injectors.

When the engine is cold, the cold start valve supplies extra fuel to the intake manifold. To prevent engine flooding from repeated starter operation, the cold start valve is regulated by the thermotime switch. The switch sends an operating signal to the cold start valve during cold-engine starting. It discontinues the signal after a specified time, regardless of coolant temperature.

The air regulator admits extra air to increase idle speed during cold-engine running.

The fuel pump is a high-pressure vane type. It maintains sufficient fuel pressure so the difference between intake manifold vacuum and fuel pressure is 36.3 psi (2.55 kg/cm²). The pump has an internal relief valve which opens at 43-64 psi (3.0-4.5 kg/cm²).

The fuel damper supresses pulsation in the fuel as it emerges from the pump.

The pressure regulator maintains the correct difference between manifold vacuum and fuel pressure. When fuel pressure becomes excessive, the regulator routes the extra fuel back to the tank.

THROTTLE OPENER

All 240Z's, and manual transmission 260Z's, use a throttle opener. The system is designed to open the throttle valves slightly when the engine is decelerating. This allows air/fuel mixture into the engine, so sufficient combustion can take place to minimize the unburned hydrocarbons in the exhaust. The mechanism consists of a control valve and servo diaphragm (**Figure 35**), both attached to brackets on the intake manifold. The system is activated by intake manifold vacuum. The 1973-1974 models also use a vacuum cutoff solenoid. When car speed drops to 10 mph, the solenoid opens the servo diaphragm vacuum chamber to air. This ensures that the throttle will close completely. Neither the control valve nor the servo diaphragm is repairable. Replace them if they do not respond to adjustment procedures.

Adjustment (Through 1972)

1. Connect a tachometer to the engine.
2. Referring to **Figure 35**, disconnect the control valve vacuum line from the intake manifold. Then disconnect the servo diaphragm vacuum line from the control valve, and attach it to the intake manifold connections.
3. Check the tachometer. Engine speed should have risen to 1,400 rpm. The servo diaphragm stroke should have been 0.197 in. (5 mm).
4. If engine speed is incorrect, adjust with the opener adjusting screw (6, **Figure 35**).
5. If the servo diaphragm stroke is too short, make sure the connection to the intake manifold is tight. If it is tight, replace servo diaphragm.
6. Reconnect the servo diaphragm and control valve vacuum lines in their normal positions.
7. Move the throttle linkage by hand to increase engine speed to 2,000 rpm. Quickly release the throttle linkage and time the drop in engine speed. The drop from 2,000 to 1,000 rpm should take approximately 3 seconds.

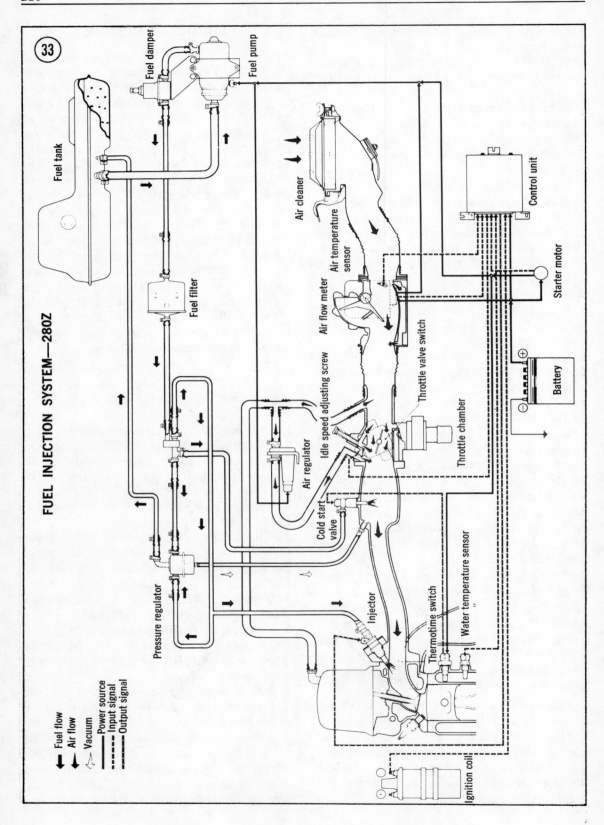

FUEL INJECTION SYSTEM—280Z

33

Fuel damper
Fuel pump
Fuel tank
Fuel filter
Air cleaner
Air temperature sensor
Air flow meter
Control unit
Throttle valve switch
Idle speed adjusting screw
Air regulator
Throttle chamber
Starter motor
Battery
Cold start valve
Pressure regulator
Injector
Thermotime switch
Water temperature sensor
Ignition coil

Fuel flow
Air flow
Vacuum
Power source
Input signal
Output signal

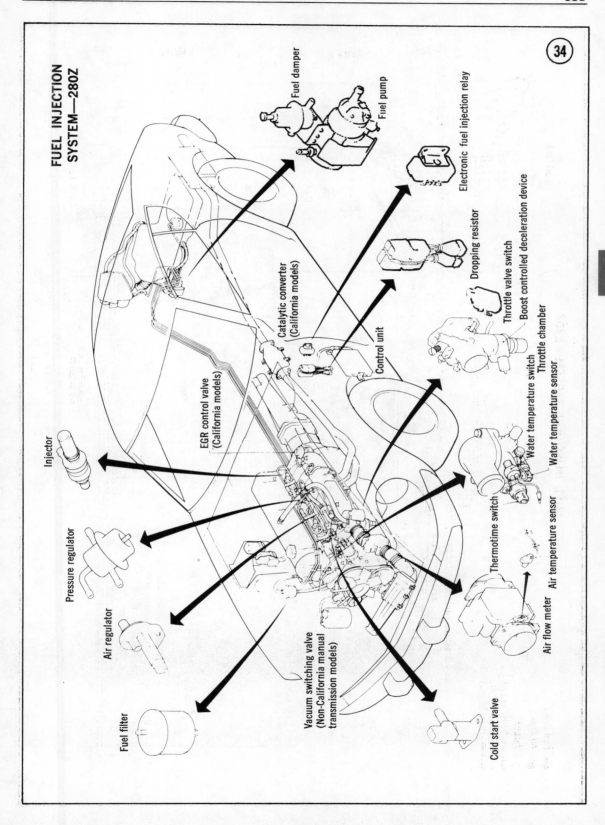

FUEL INJECTION SYSTEM—280Z

Fuel damper

Fuel pump

Electronic fuel injection relay

Dropping resistor

Throttle valve switch

Boost controlled deceleration device

Throttle chamber

Catalytic converter (California models)

Control unit

EGR control valve (California models)

Water temperature switch

Water temperature sensor

Injector

Thermotime switch

Air temperature sensor

Pressure regulator

Air regulator

Vacuum switching valve (Non-California manual transmission models)

Air flow meter

Cold start valve

Fuel filter

34

5

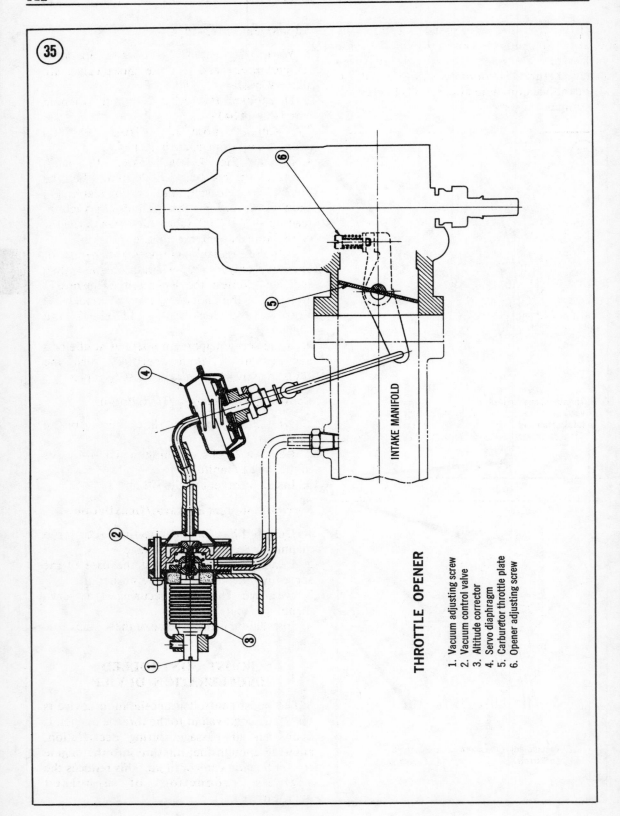

THROTTLE OPENER

1. Vacuum adjusting screw
2. Vacuum control valve
3. Altitude corrector
4. Servo diaphragm
5. Carburetor throttle plate
6. Opener adjusting screw

INTAKE MANIFOLD

8. If the drop in engine speed takes too long (6 seconds or more), loosen the control valve lock screw and turn the vacuum adjusting screw (**Figure 35**) counterclockwise to adjust. Turn the vacuum adjusting screw clockwise if the drop is too fast.

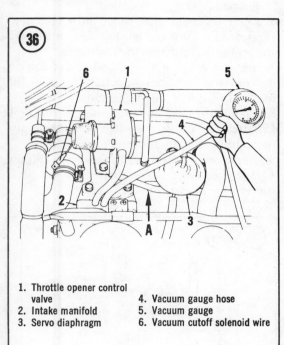

1. Throttle opener control valve
2. Intake manifold
3. Servo diaphragm
4. Vacuum gauge hose
5. Vacuum gauge
6. Vacuum cutoff solenoid wire

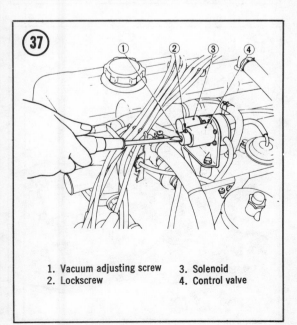

1. Vacuum adjusting screw
2. Lockscrew
3. Solenoid
4. Control valve

Adjustment (1973-1974)

1. Warm the engine to normal operating temperature. Make sure the choke valves are all the way open.
2. Disconnect the vacuum cutoff solenoid wire (**Figure 36**).
3. Disconnect hose (A, **Figure 36**), and connect a vacuum gauge in its place.
4. Moving the throttle linkage by hand, increase engine speed to 3,000 rpm. When the linkage is released, the servo diaphragm should operate for a few seconds at a vacuum reading of 17.7 in. (automatic transmission) or 18.5 in. (manual transmission).
5. If the servo diaphragm does not operate, or operates only at a vacuum higher than specified, loosen the lockscrew (**Figure 37**) and turn the adjusting screw clockwise. Tighten the lockscrew and check the adjustment.
6. If the servo diaphragm operates at idle or a vacuum lower than specified, turn the adjusting screw counterclockwise to adjust.

Control Valve Removal/Installation

1. Disconnect vacuum line from control valve.
2. Remove 2 bolts attaching the control valve to the intake manifold.
3. Install by reversing Steps 1 and 2.

Servo Diaphragm Removal/Installation

1. Detach the link connecting the servo diaphragm to the throttle linkage.
2. Remove the cotter pin at the base of the servo diaphragm and slide the washer off.
3. Remove the nut securing the servo diaphragm to its bracket.
4. Installation is the reverse of these steps.

BOOST CONTROLLED DECELERATION DEVICE

The boost controlled deceleration device is the 280Z's equivalent to the throttle opener. It opens an air passage during deceleration, allowing enough fuel mixture into the engine so combustion can continue. This reduces the engine's production of unburned hydrocarbons.

The BCDD is located at the base of the throttle chamber (**Figure 38**). A misadjusted BCDD can cause the throttle to hang open. Adjustment is a complicated procedure and seldom necessary. Leave the job to a Datsun dealer or other competent mechanic.

FUEL PUMP

The 240-260Z's use a mechanical fuel pump, driven by an eccentric lobe bolted to the front of the camshaft. The 260Z's also use an electric pump, mounted near the rear axle. The 280Z's use an electric pump only.

Fuel pump testing is covered in Chapter Two, under *Fuel System Troubleshooting*. This section covers fuel pump removal and installation.

Table 1 gives fuel pump specifications.

NOTE
The capacity test is not used in 280Z's. Instead, disconnect the wire from the starter "S" terminal. Have an assistant turn key to START and listen for the sound of the fuel pump. If you can't hear it, check the pump fuse and wiring. If these are O.K., replace the pump.

Removal/Installation (Mechanical Pump)

To remove, disconnect the inlet and outlet fuel lines from the pump. Then remove 2 nuts and one bolt securing the fuel pump to the cylinder head and lift it off (**Figure 39**). Install in the reverse order, using a new gasket.

Removal/Installation (260Z Electric Pump)

The pump is mounted near the rear axle, where the differential mounting member connects to the frame. **Figure 40** shows the installation.

1. Place a container beneath the pump to catch dripping gasoline. Disconnect the inlet and outlet hoses from the pump.
2. Disconnect the pump wires.
3. Remove 2 screws securing the pump to the bracket. Take the pump out.
4. Installation is the reverse of these steps.

Removal/Installation (280Z Electric Pump, 1975-1976)

1. Disconnect the negative cable from the battery.

2. Disconnect the wire running from the starter solenoid to starter. Leave the other solenoid wires connected.
3. Label and disconnect the fuel pump wires.
4. Remove 2 screws securing the cold start valve to the intake manifold. See **Figure 34**.
5. Reconnect the battery cable.
6. Place the cold start valve in a container (**Figure 41**). Turn the ignition key to START and let the fuel run into the container.
7. Securely block both front wheels so the car will not roll in either direction. Jack up the rear end and place it on jackstands.
8. Clamp the fuel line running to the tank (**Figure 42**). Place a container beneath the fuel pump, then disconnect both fuel lines.
9. Remove 2 bracket securing screws (**Figure 43**). Remove the bracket from the car, then remove the pump from the bracket.

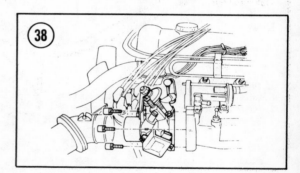

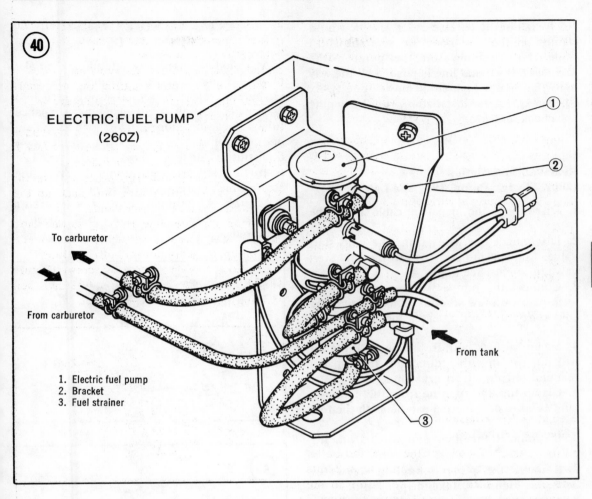

**ELECTRIC FUEL PUMP
(260Z)**

To carburetor

From carburetor

1. Electric fuel pump
2. Bracket
3. Fuel strainer

From tank

1

2

3

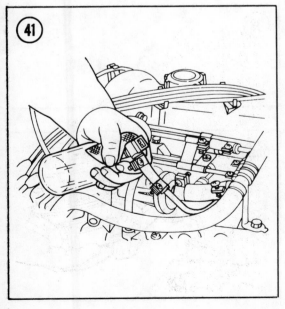

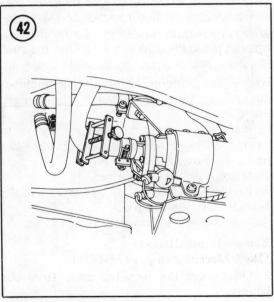

5

10. Install in the reverse order. Use new hose clamps on the fuel lines. Be sure the short rubber hose running from fuel pump to the fuel damper's metal line is pushed all the way onto the pump. Tighten clamps to one ft.-lb. (0.13 mkg). After installation, run the engine and check for leaks.

Removal/Installation
(280Z Electric Pump, 1977 and Later)

1. Disconnect the negative cable from the battery.
2. Disconnect the wires from the cold start valve. Connect jumper wires to the cold start valve terminals. See **Figure 44**.
3. Connect the jumper wires to the battery terminals for a few seconds. This operates the cold start valve and releases fuel pressure in the lines.
4. Securely block both front wheels so the car will not roll in either direction. Jack up the rear end and place it on jackstands.
5. Clamp the line running from fuel pump to tank (**Figure 45**). Place a pan beneath the fuel pump.
6. Disconnect the lines and wires from the pump.
7. Remove the pump mounting screws or bolts. See **Figure 46**. Take the pump out.
8. Installation is the reverse of removal. Use new hose clamps. Position the clamps so the rubber hoses protrude 1/8 in. (3 mm) past the edge of the clamps. When installing the fuel pump-to-fuel damper hose, make sure its ends are pushed against the pump and damper.

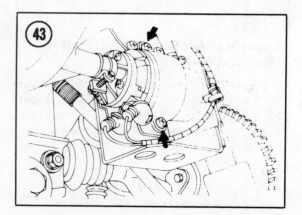

INTAKE AND EXHAUST MANIFOLDS

All models use cast aluminum intake manifolds and cast iron exhaust manifolds. Carburetor intake manifolds are divided into two major sections, connected by a balance tube. Fuel injection intake manifolds are one-piece units. All exhaust manifolds use a dual-outlet design. This lowers exhaust restriction and provides an inertia scavenging action which increases performance.

Figure 47 shows typical carburetor manifolds; **Figure 48** shows fuel injection manifolds.

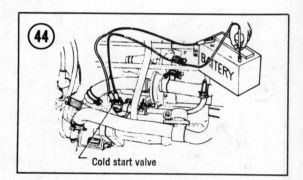
Cold start valve

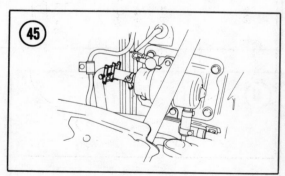

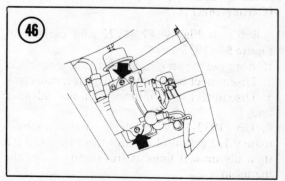

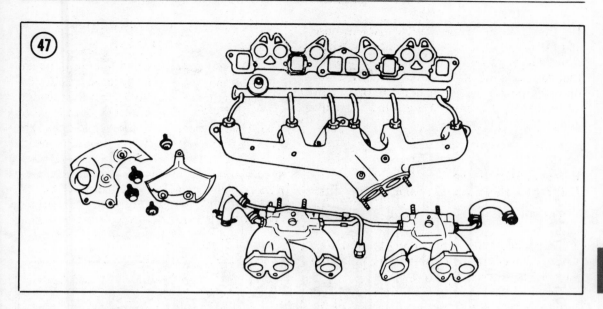

47

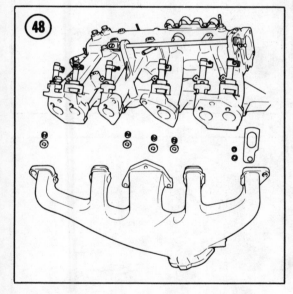

48

5

5. On 1973-1974 cars, disconnect the exhaust gas inlet tube from the rear of the balance tube.

6. Disconnect the short hose from the check valve (4, **Figure 49**; 1, **Figure 50**).

7. Disconnect the air pump outlet hose at the T-connection branching to the check valve and anti-backfire valve.

8. Disconnect the hose from the PCV valve (7, **Figure 49**).

9. Remove the bolts attaching the intake manifold to the cylinder head.

10. Lift the manifold off together with the carburetors.

11. Installation is the reverse of these steps. Connect all hoses as shown in **Figure 49** or **Figure 50**. Top up coolant on 1972-1974 models.

Intake Manifold Removal/Installation (Carburetors)

Refer to **Figure 49** (1972 and earlier) or **Figure 50** (1973-1974).

1. Remove the air cleaner as described earlier.

2. Disconnect the fuel line to each carburetor.

3. Disconnect distributor vacuum advance line.

4. On 1972-1974 models, drain approximately 1/2 gallon of coolant from the radiator, then disconnect lines at front and rear of the manifold.

Intake Manifold Removal/Installation (Fuel Injection)

Figure 51 shows the 1975-1976 vacuum lines and intake manifold connections. **Figure 52** shows the 1977 lines and connections. **Figure 53** shows the 1978 connections.

NOTE
Steps 1-6 apply to 1975-1976 models only.

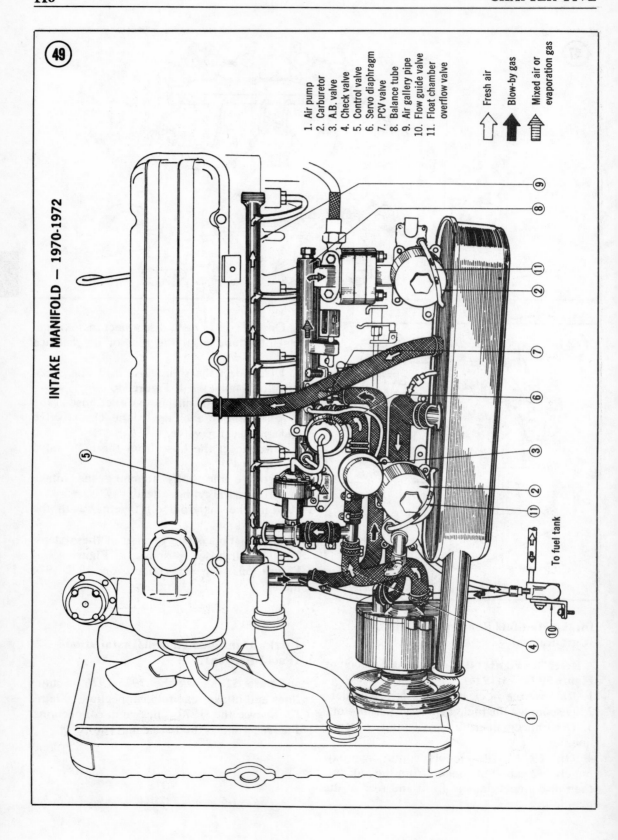

INTAKE MANIFOLD – 1970-1972

1. Air pump
2. Carburetor
3. A.B. valve
4. Check valve
5. Control valve
6. Servo diaphragm
7. PCV valve
8. Balance tube
9. Air gallery pipe
10. Flow guide valve
11. Float chamber overflow valve

⇧ Fresh air

⬆ Blow-by gas

⬆ Mixed air or evaporation gas

To fuel tank

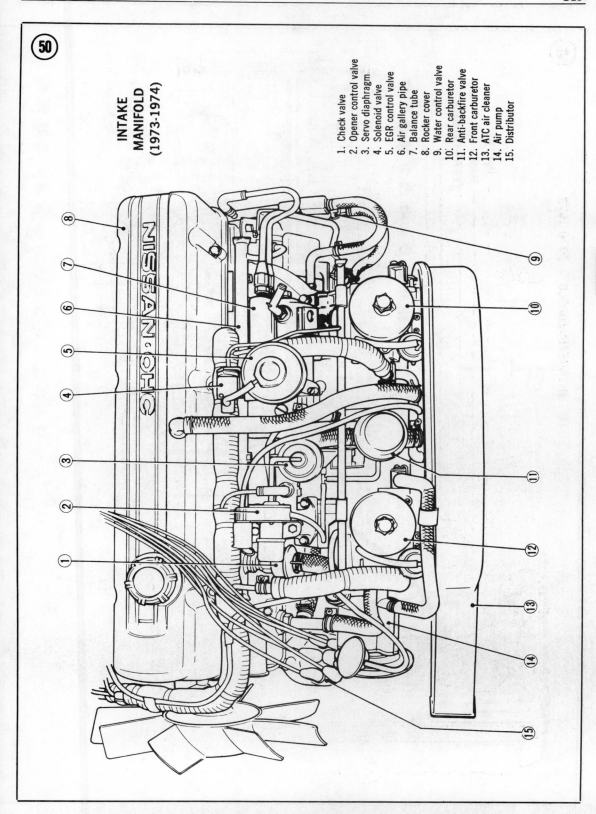

50

INTAKE MANIFOLD (1973-1974)

1. Check valve
2. Opener control valve
3. Servo diaphragm
4. Solenoid valve
5. EGR control valve
6. Air gallery pipe
7. Balance tube
8. Rocker cover
9. Water control valve
10. Rear carburetor
11. Anti-backfire valve
12. Front carburetor
13. ATC air cleaner
14. Air pump
15. Distributor

5

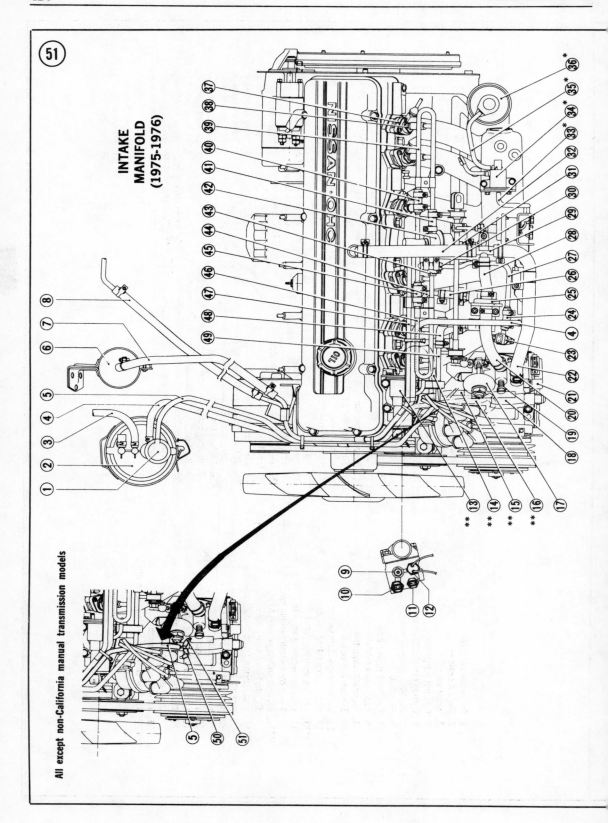

INTAKE MANIFOLD (1975-1976)

All except non-California manual transmission models

1. Purge control valve
2. Carbon canister
3. Vapor vent line
4. Canister purge line
5. Carbon canister to throttle chamber vacuum hose
6. Fuel filter
7. Fuel feed rubber hose
8. Fuel return rubber hose
9. Thermal transmitter
10. Thermotime switch
11. Water temperature sensor
12. Water temperature switch
**13. Vacuum switching valve
**14. Vacuum switching valve to 3-way connection vacuum hose
**15. Vacuum switching valve to distributor vacuum hose
**16. 3-way connector to throttle chamber vacuum hose
17. Anti-stall dashpot (manual transmission only)
18. Throttle chamber
19. Idle speed adjusting screw
20. Throttle chamber to air regulator rubber hose
21. Throttle valve switch
22. Throttle chamber to 3-way connector rubber hose

23. Cold start valve
24. Cold start valve to fuel pipe D rubber hose
25. Air regulator
26. Heater housing to water pipe rubber hose
27. Fuel pipe D
28. Air regulator to 3-way connector rubber hose
29. 3-way connector
30. Fuel pipe D to fuel pipe A rubber hose
31. Pressure regulator to intake manifold vacuum hose
32. 3-way connector to rocker cover rubber hose
*33. EGR solenoid valve to throttle chamber vacuum hose
*34. EGR solenoid valve
*35. EGR control valve to EGR solenoid valve vacuum hose
*36. EGR control valve
37. Injector holder
38. Injector
39. Fuel pipe C
40. Fuel pipe A to fuel pipe C rubber hose

41. Pressure regulator to fuel pipe C rubber hose
42. Pressure regulator
43. Pressure regulator to fuel pipe B rubber hose
44. Rubber hose to water pipe
45. Fuel pipe A to fuel pipe B rubber hose
46. Fuel pipe B
47. Fuel pipe A
48. Heater housing to water pipe rubber hose
49. Rubber hose to cylinder head water pipe
50. 3-way connector to distributor vacuum hose
51. 3-way connector to throttle chamber vacuum hose

*California models only
**Non-California manual transmission models only

5

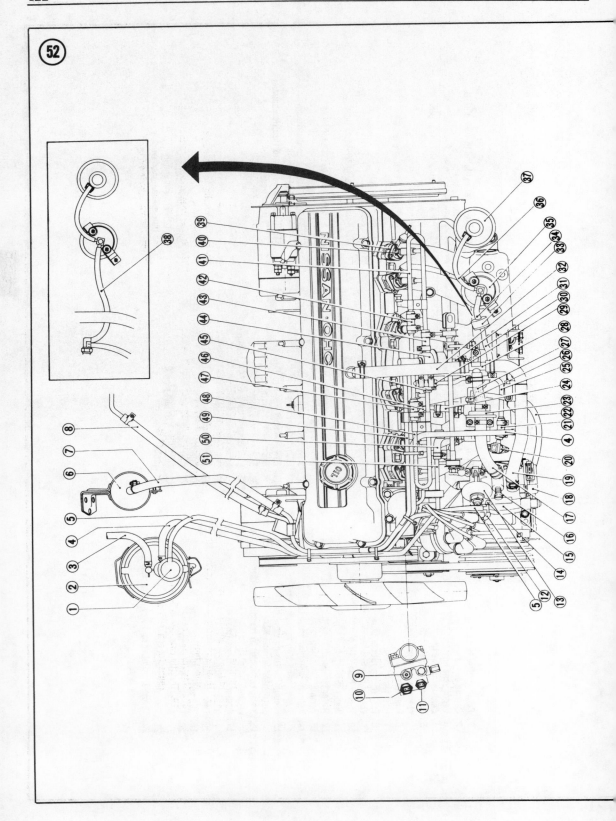

VACUUM LINES (1977)

1. Purge control valve
2. Carbon canister
3. Vapor vent line
4. Canister purge line
5. Carbon canister to 3-way connector vacuum hose
6. Fuel filter
7. Fuel feed rubber hose
8. Fuel return rubber hose
9. Thermal transmitter
10. Thermotime switch
11. Water temperature sensor
12. 3-way connector to distributor vacuum hose
13. Anti-stall dashpot (manual transmission only)
14. 3-way connector throttle chamber vacuum hose
15. Throttle chamber
16. Idle speed adjusting screw
17. Throttle chamber to air regulator rubber hose
18. Throttle valve switch
19. Throttle chamber to 3-way connector rubber hose
20. Cold start valve
21. Cold start valve to fuel pipe D rubber hose
22. Throttle chamber to thermal vacuum valve vacuum hose
23. Air regulator
24. Heater housing to water pipe rubber hose
25. Fuel pipe D
26. Thermal vacuum valve
27. Air regulator to 3-way connector rubber hose
28. 3-way connector
29. Fuel pipe D to fuel Pipe A rubber hose
30. Thermal vacuum valve to vacuum delay valve vacuum hose*
31. Pressure regulator to intake manifold vacuum hose
32. 3-way connector to rocker cover rubber hose
33. Vacuum delay valve*
34. Vacuum delay valve to BPT valve vacuum hose*
35. BPT valve
36. BPT valve to EGR control valve vacuum hose
37. EGR control valve
38. Thermal vacuum valve to BPT valve**
39. Injector holder
40. Injector
41. Fuel pipe C
42. Fuel pipe A to Fuel pipe C rubber hose
43. Pressure regulator to fuel pipe C rubber hose
44. Pressure regulator
45. Pressure regulator to fuel pipe B rubber hose
46. Rubber hose to water pipe
47. Fuel pipe A to fuel pipe B rubber hose
48. Fuel pipe B
49. Fuel pipe A
50. Heater housing to water pipe rubber hose
51. Rubber hose to cylinder head water pipe

*California models only
**Non-California models only

5

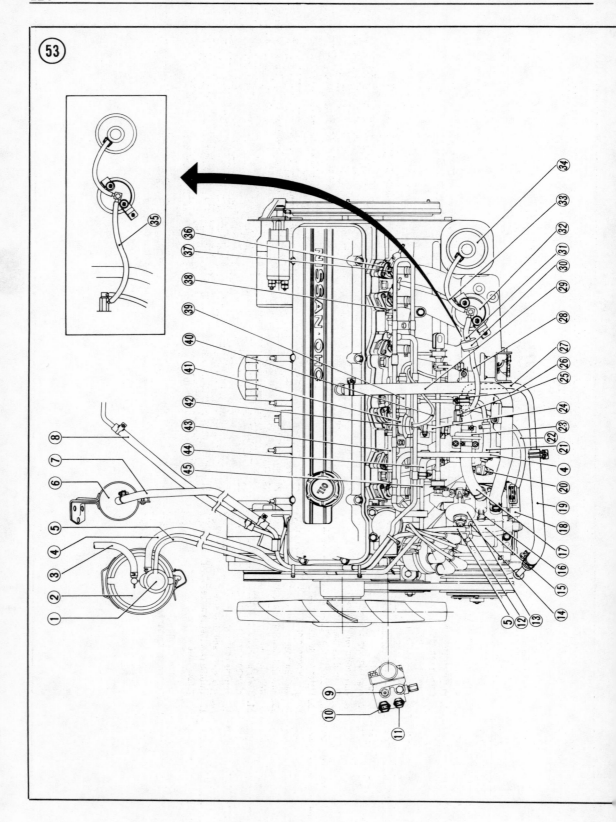

VACUUM LINES (1978)

1. Purge control valve
2. Carbon canister
3. Vapor vent line
4. Canister purge line
5. Carbon canister to 3-way connector vacuum hose
6. Fuel filter
7. Fuel feed rubber hose
8. Fuel return rubber hose
9. Thermal transmitter
10. Thermotime switch
11. Water temperature sensor
12. 3-way connector to distributor vacuum hose
13. Anti-stall dashpot (manual transmission only)
14. 3-way connector to throttle chamber vacuum hose
15. Throttle chamber
16. Idle speed adjusting screw
17. Throttle chamber to air regulator rubber hose

18. Throttle valve switch
19. Air duct to air regulator pipe rubber hose
20. Cold start valve
21. Cold start valve to fuel pipe rubber hose
22. Throttle chamber to thermal vacuum valve vacuum hose
23. Air regulator
24. Heater housing to water pipe rubber hose
25. Thermal vacuum valve
26. Air regulator to air regulator pipe rubber hose
27. Air regulator pipe
28. Thermal vacuum valve to vacuum delay valve vacuum hose*
29. Throttle chamber to rocker cover rubber hose
30. Vacuum delay valve*
31. Vacuum delay valve to BPT valve vacuum hose*

32. BPT valve
33. BPT valve to EGR control valve vacuum hose
34. EGR control valve
35. Thermal vacuum valve to BPT valve vacuum hose**
36. Injector holder
37. Injector
38. Fuel pipe
39. Fuel pipe to pressure regulator rubber hose
40. Pressure regulator to intake manifold vacuum hose
41. Pressure regulator
42. Rubber hose to thermostat housing water pipe
43. Pressure regulator to fuel pipe rubber hose
44. Heater housing to water pipe rubber hose
45. Rubber hose to cylinder head water pipe

*California models only
**Non-California models only

5

1. Disconnect negative cable from battery.

2. Disconnect the wire running from starter solenoid to starter. Leave the other wires connected.

3. Disconnect black wire from fuel pump.

4. Remove 2 screws securing the cold start valve to the intake manifold. See **Figure 34**.

5. Reconnect the battery cable.

6. Place the cold start valve in a container (**Figure 41**). Turn the ignition key to START and let the fuel run into the container.

NOTE
Steps 7-10 apply to 1977 and later models only.

7. Disconnect the negative cable from the battery.

8. Disconnect the wires from the cold start valve. Connect jumper wires to the cold start valve terminals. See **Figure 44**.

9. Connect the jumper wires to the battery terminals for a few seconds. This operates the cold start valve and releases fuel pressure in the lines.

10. Disconnect the hose from the cold start valve.

11. Remove the exhaust gas recirculation valve and vacuum switching valve (if so equipped). See **Figure 54**.

12. Disconnect the air flow meter from the air duct (**Figure 55**).

13. Disconnect the throttle linkage and injector wiring connectors. See **Figure 56**.

14. Disconnect the wires from throttle valve switch and boost controlled deceleration device solenoid. See **Figure 57**.

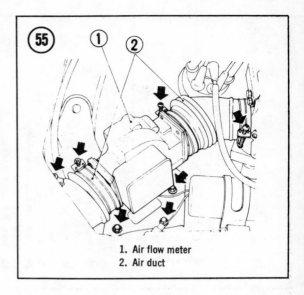

1. Air flow meter
2. Air duct

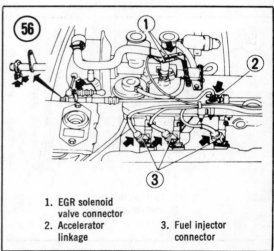

1. EGR solenoid valve connector
2. Accelerator linkage
3. Fuel injector connector

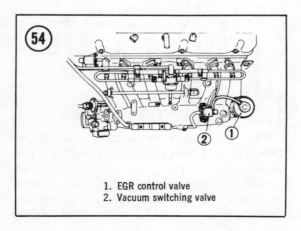

1. EGR control valve
2. Vacuum switching valve

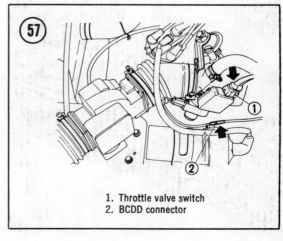

1. Throttle valve switch
2. BCDD connector

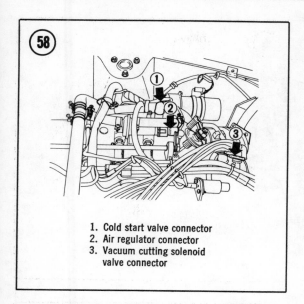

1. Cold start valve connector
2. Air regulator connector
3. Vacuum cutting solenoid
   valve connector

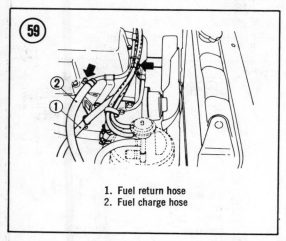

1. Fuel return hose
2. Fuel charge hose

15. Disconnect the wires from vacuum cutting solenoid (manual transmission only), air regulator, and cold start valve. See **Figure 58**.

16. Disconnect the fuel return and inlet lines (1 and 2, **Figure 59**).

17. Disconnect the PCV hose from the rocker cover (**Figure 60**).

18. Unbolt and remove the intake manifold together with its heat shield plate.

19. Install in the reverse order. Use a new manifold gasket without gasket sealer. Tighten small (M8) bolts to 10-13 ft.-lb. (1.4-1.8 mkg). Tighten large (M10) bolts to 25-36 ft.-lb. (3.5-5.0 mkg).

NOTE
*The M10 bolts come in 2 lengths. The shorter bolts go in the center holes (**Figure 61**). The longer bolts go in the outer holes.*

**Exhaust Manifold
Removal/Installation**

1. Remove the intake manifold as described earlier.

2. On carburetted cars, remove the exhaust manifold cover and heat shroud (if so equipped).

3. Disconnect the exhaust downpipe from the manifold.

4. Referring to **Figure 47** or **Figure 48**, remove the nuts and bolts attaching the exhaust manifold to the cylinder head.

5. Installation is the reverse of these steps. Use a new intake-exhaust manifold gasket. Do not use gasket sealer.

CAUTION
Do not remove the air injection tubing (if so equipped) from the exhaust manifold. Removal is very difficult without bending tubes.

AIR INJECTION SYSTEM

The air injection system, used on 240-260Z's, is designed to pump fresh air into each exhaust port, so combustion can continue for a longer time and reduce emissions. The system consists of an air pump, driven by the crankshaft pulley

5

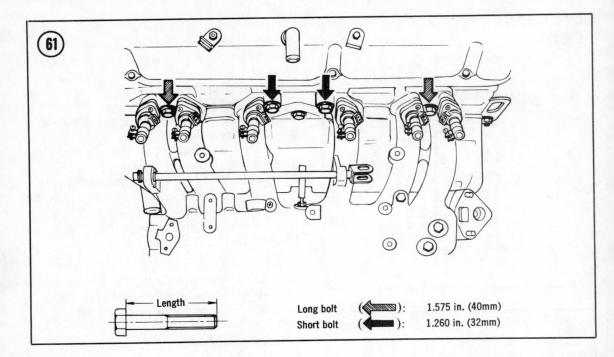

Length

| Long bolt | (⟸): | 1.575 in. (40mm) |
| Short bolt | (◄──): | 1.260 in. (32mm) |

through a belt, a check valve, tubing, hoses, and an anti-backfire valve. The air pump draws fresh air from the air cleaner and pumps it through a hose, the check valve, and tubing to the exhaust ports. The check valve prevents exhaust gas from flowing backward through the system. The anti-backfire valve lets air into the intake manifold just after the accelerator is let up. This leans the fuel mixture entering the engine, so it will not be rich enough to explode when it meets the fresh air entering the exhaust ports.

The check valve and anti-backfire valve are not repairable. Air pump repair requires several special tools, and should be left to a Datsun dealer or competent garage. **Figure 62** is a diagram of the air injection system.

Air Pump Removal/Installation

1. Disconnect the hoses from the air pump.
2. Remove the nut attaching the air pump to its adjusting bracket.
3. Remove the bolt attaching the air pump to its mounting bracket. Remove the air pump belt.
4. Lift the air pump up and out of the engine compartment.
5. Installation is the reverse of these steps.

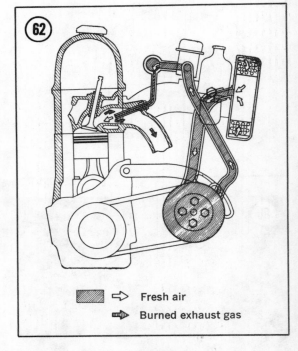

⟹ Fresh air

Burned exhaust gas

Anti-backfire Valve Replacement

If the anti-backfire valve is defective, the car will probably backfire severely. To replace the valve, disconnect the hoses and lift it out. Install a new valve in the reverse order.

Check Valve Replacement

1. Disconnect short air hose from check valve.
2. Carefully unscrew the check valve from the air injection tubing. Be careful not to bend the tubing.
3. Installation is the reverse of these steps. Tighten the check valve to 65-76 ft.-lb. (9.0-10.5 mkg).

Air Injection Tubing

Removal of the air injection tubing is very difficult without bending the tubing. Removal should not be attempted unless the tubes are damaged. To remove, disconnect the short air hose from the check valve. Then remove 6 nuts attaching the small injector tubes to the exhaust manifold. Install in the reverse order.

EXHAUST GAS RECIRCULATION SYSTEM

This system is used on all 1973-1976 California cars, and all models from 1977 on. It recycles part of the exhaust gas into the combustion chambers. This reduces combustion temperature, lowering the oxides of nitrogen in the exhaust.

On 1973-1974 models, the system should be inspected, and the EGR valve cleaned, every 12,000 miles. Regular maintenance is not required on later models. However, the system may need service if the engine idles roughly.

Inspection

Figure 63 shows the 1973-1974 system; **Figure 64** shows the 1975 and later system.

5

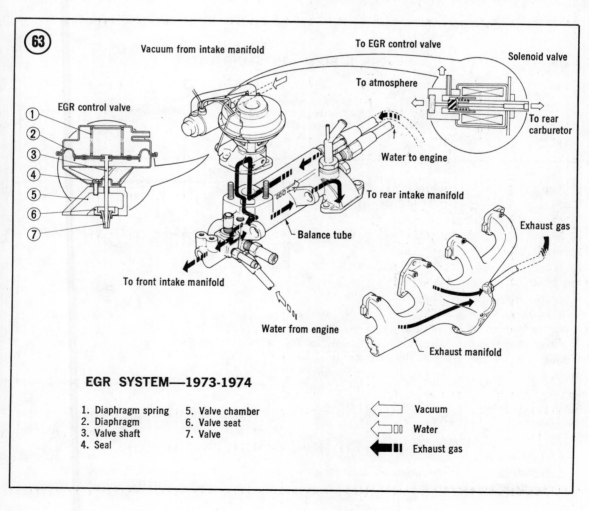

EGR SYSTEM—1973-1974

1. Diaphragm spring
2. Diaphragm
3. Valve shaft
4. Seal
5. Valve chamber
6. Valve seat
7. Valve

Vacuum
Water
Exhaust gas

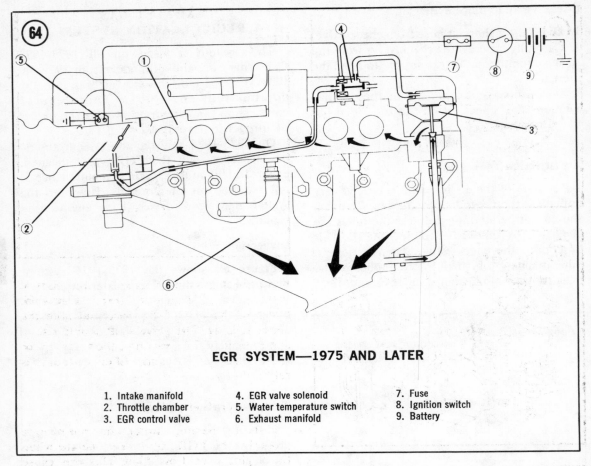

EGR SYSTEM—1975 AND LATER

1. Intake manifold
2. Throttle chamber
3. EGR control valve
4. EGR valve solenoid
5. Water temperature switch
6. Exhaust manifold
7. Fuse
8. Ignition switch
9. Battery

1. Replace cracked or worn hoses and tubes. Replace any parts showing obvious mechanical damage.

2. Make sure the solenoid valve wire is securely connected.

3. Warm the engine to normal operating temperature.

4. Increase engine speed to 3,000-3,500 rpm. The control valve shaft (visible inside the lower part of the valve) should rise.

5. Disconnect the solenoid valve wire. Connect it to the battery positive terminal with a jumper wire. Again, increase engine speed to 3,000-3,500 rpm. This time the control valve shaft should not rise. If it does, replace the solenoid valve.

WARNING
The control valve and surrounding area will be hot. Use a screwdriver or similar tool to perform the next step.

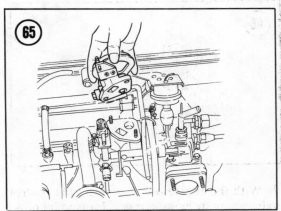

6. With the engine idling, reach into the control valve and push the diaphragm up. The idle should become unstable.

NOTE
Steps 7-9 apply to 1973-1974 models only.

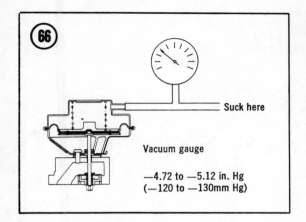

Suck here

Vacuum gauge

—4.72 to —5.12 in. Hg
(—120 to —130mm Hg)

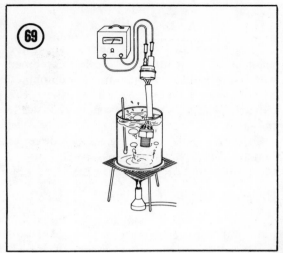

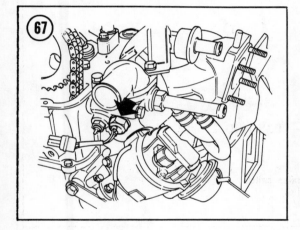

7. With the engine off, disconnect the control valve vacuum hose, remove 2 attaching nuts, and lift the control valve off the balance tube. See **Figure 65**.

8. Check the control valve for visible wear or damage. Clean the base of the valve with a wire brush and compressed air. Check the balance tube for excessive carbon buildup. If necessary, remove and clean the balance tube.

9. Connect a vacuum gauge to the control valve, using a T-fitting as shown in **Figure 66**. Suck on the end of the tube and note the gauge reading. The valve shaft should rise at approximately 5 in. vacuum, then stay up for more than 30 seconds after vacuum is released.

Temperature Switch Test

If the temperature switch does not operate properly, the EGR valve may operate when the engine is cold or idling. This may cause poor driveability or a rough idle. To test:

1. Drain approximately 1/2 gallon coolant from the engine, then remove the temperature switch. See **Figure 67** (1973-1974) or **Figure 68** (1975 and later).

2. Place the switch in water with a thermometer and connect an ohmmeter as shown (**Figure 69**).

3. On 1973-1974 cars, the ohmmeter should show infinite resistance (open switch) when water temperature is below 77° F (25° C). The ohmmeter reading should drop to zero at a temperature between 88-106° F (31-41° C). If not, replace the switch.

4. On 1975 and later models, the ohmmeter should show slight resistance (switch on) when water temperature is below 122° F (50° C). The switch should open (infinite resistance) between 135-145° F (57-63° C). It should stay open above 145° F. If not, replace the switch.

EXHAUST PIPE
AND MUFFLER

The Z exhaust system consists of three main units: front tube, pre-muffler combined with center tube, and main muffler combined with tailpipe. **Figure 70** shows the 240Z exhaust system. The 260Z system is basically the same.

California 280Z's use a catalytic converter (**Figure 71**). Non-California models use a pre-muffler instead. See **Figure 72**.

Removal/Installation

1. Prior to removal, soak all nuts, bolts, and pipe joints with penetrating oil such as WD-40.
2. Undo the necessary clamps and hanger brackets, referring to appropriate illustration.

> *NOTE*
> *260Z's use an injected sealer at the front end of the muffler (Figure 73). Tap the joint with a metal hammer, twist the muffler, then tap it off.*

3. Check removed parts for excessive rust, and for damage caused by bottoming the car. Check rubber mounts for melting, cracks, or deterioration. Replace as needed.
4. Install in the reverse order. On 260Z's, inject sealer into the muffler joint. Use a Datsun sealer kit as shown in **Figure 73**. Let the engine idle for 10 minutes to cure the sealer. Do not accelerate sharply for 20-30 minutes.

EVAPORATIVE EMISSION
CONTROL SYSTEM

The evaporative emission control system is designed to prevent gasoline vapor from escaping into the atmosphere. Gasoline fumes around the car may indicate a leaking vapor line. Fuel starvation or a deformed tank may indicate a clogged fuel filler cap. If any of these symptoms occur, have the system tested by a Datsun dealer or certified emission control station.

> *NOTE*
> *If fuel flow is inadequate, the fuel pump may be at fault. Test as described in Chapter Two.*

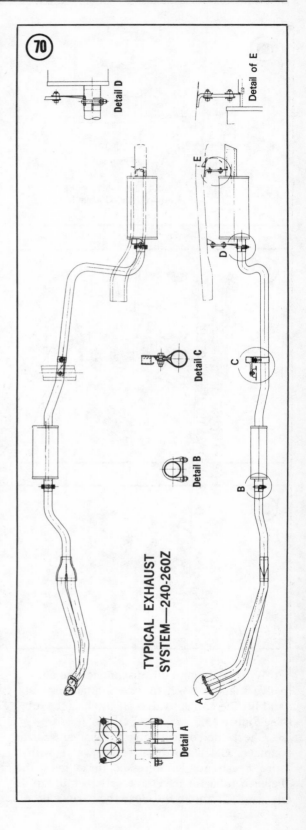

70

Detail D

Detail of E

E

D

Detail C

C

Detail B

B

Detail A

A

TYPICAL EXHAUST SYSTEM—240-260Z

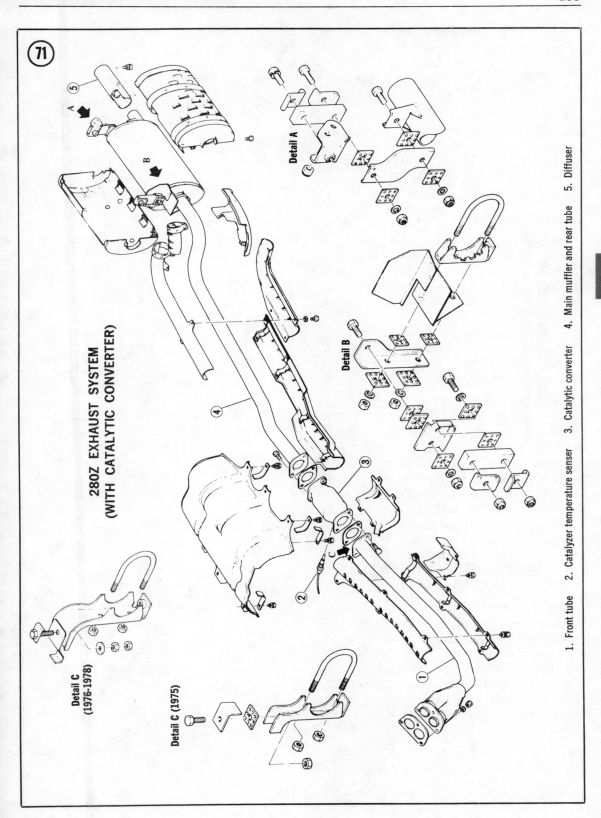

71

280Z EXHAUST SYSTEM
(WITH CATALYTIC CONVERTER)

Detail A

Detail B

Detail C
(1976-1978)

Detail C (1975)

5

1. Front tube   2. Catalyzer temperature senser   3. Catalytic converter   4. Main muffler and rear tube   5. Diffuser

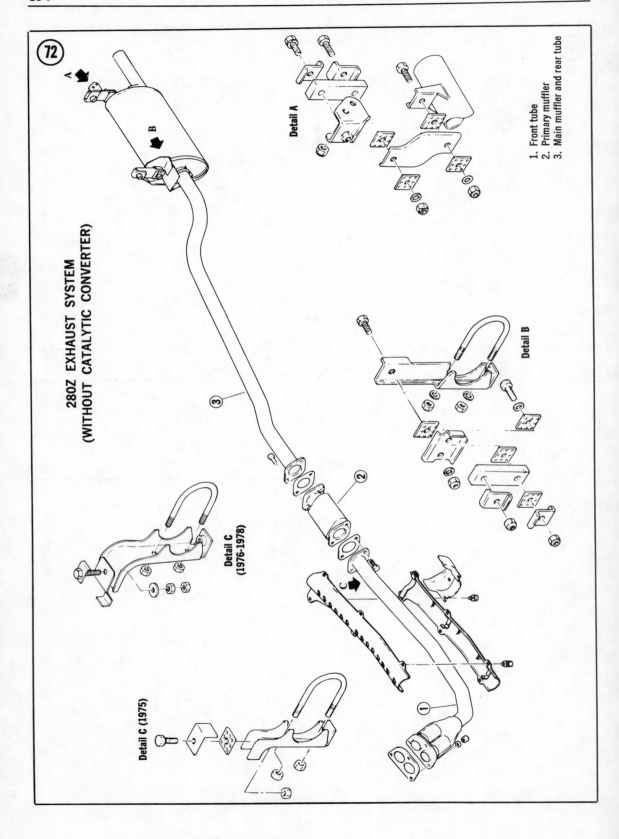

72

280Z EXHAUST SYSTEM (WITHOUT CATALYTIC CONVERTER)

Detail A

Detail B

Detail C (1976-1978)

Detail C (1975)

1. Front tube
2. Primary muffler
3. Main muffler and rear tube

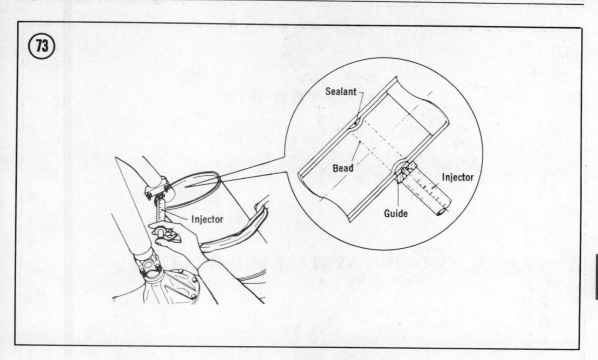

5

Table 1   FUEL PUMP SPECIFICATIONS

Mechanical pump pressure (240-260Z)	3.41-4.27 psi (0.24-0.30 kg/cm²)
Mechanical pump capacity (240-260Z)	$3\frac{3}{8}$ pt. (1,600cc) in one minute or less
Electric pump pressure (260Z only)	4.6 psi (0.32 kg/cm²)
Electric pump capacity (260Z only)	3 pt. (1,400cc) in one minute or less
Electric pump capacity (280Z only)	36.3 psi (2.55 kg/cm²)

CHAPTER SIX

COOLING SYSTEM AND HEATER

The cooling system uses a centrifugal water pump with a cast aluminum body to propel coolant through the engine and heating system. A pellet-type thermostat controls coolant flow. A down-flow radiator and temperature controlled viscous-hub fan cool the system. The 1976 and later cars use a coolant recovery system. A reservoir tank mounted on the radiator support catches any coolant overflow from the radiator. As coolant temperature drops, coolant is sucked from the reservoir tank back into the radiator.

The heater is a hot water type which circulates engine coolant through a small radiator behind the instrument panel. With the heating system turned off, the system can be used for fresh air ventilation.

This chapter includes service procedures for the thermostat, radiator, fan, water pump, and heater. Cooling system flushing and pressure checking procedures are described.

COOLING SYSTEM

All models come from the factory equipped with a 50/50 mixture of ethylene glycol-based anti-freeze and water. This protects the system from freezing to —31°F (—35°C). The system should be drained, flushed with clean water,

and refilled at intervals specified in Chapter Three. If desired, a chemical flushing agent may be used, following manufacturer's instructions, prior to the flushing method described here. However, make sure the flushing agent is compatible with the aluminum parts in the engine before using.

Flushing

Refer to **Figure 1** for this procedure.

1. Drain the cooling system by opening the drain tap on the lower right side of the radiator. Do not open the drain plug on the left side of the cylinder block.

2. Remove the radiator cap.

3. Set the heater control on the instrument panel to maximum.

4. Remove the thermostat as described under *Thermostat Removal and Testing* later in this chapter. Temporarily reinstall the housing without the thermostat.

5. Connect a water supply such as a garden hose to the thermostat housing. This does not have to be a positive fit, as long as most of the water enters the engine.

6. Turn the water on and flush for 3-5 minutes. Do not run the engine.

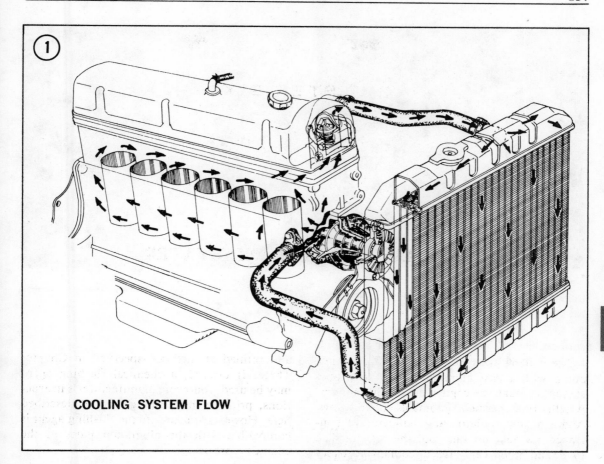

COOLING SYSTEM FLOW

6

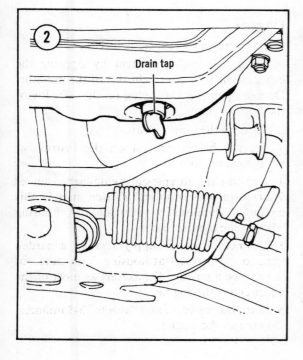

Drain tap

7. Turn off the water and reinstall thermostat.

8. Drain the entire system by opening the radiator drain tap (**Figure 2**) and removing the threaded plug on the left side of the cylinder block (**Figure 3**). Close the tap and put the plug back in after draining.

Refilling

1. Be sure all hoses are connected.

2. Set the heater control on the instrument panel to maximum.

3. Fill the system with a 50/50 mixture of ethylene glycol-based anti-freeze and water, even if you live in a climate which does not require this degree of freeze protection. The anti-freeze is a good corrosion inhibitor. Coolant capacity is given in **Table 1** (end of chapter). When the system is full, replace radiator cap.

4. Run the engine at a fast idle and recheck the coolant level in the radiator. Top up if more

than one inch below the filler neck. Also check the system for leaks.

5. After driving several miles, recheck the coolant level. It takes some time for all the air to be removed from the system.

THERMOSTAT

Opening and closing of the thermostat is controlled by a wax pellet which expands when heated and contracts when cooled. The pellet is connected through a piston to a valve. When the pellet expands, pressure is applied to a rubber diaphragm, forcing the valve open. As the pellet contracts, it allows a spring to close the valve.

Removal and Testing

1. Drain coolant by detaching upper radiator hose from the thermostat housing (**Figure 4**). This will allow a sufficient amount of coolant to escape.

2. Remove the thermostat housing and take out the thermostat (**Figure 5**).

3. Submerge the thermostat in water with a thermometer (**Figure 6**).

4. Heat the water until the thermostat valve just begins to open, then check the water temperature. Compare with specifications (end of chapter). If the valve opens at the wrong temperature or fails to open, replace the thermostat.

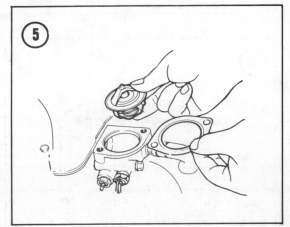

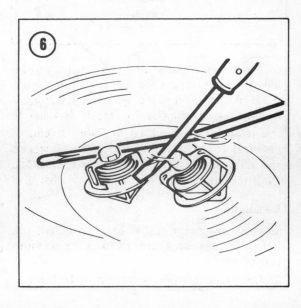

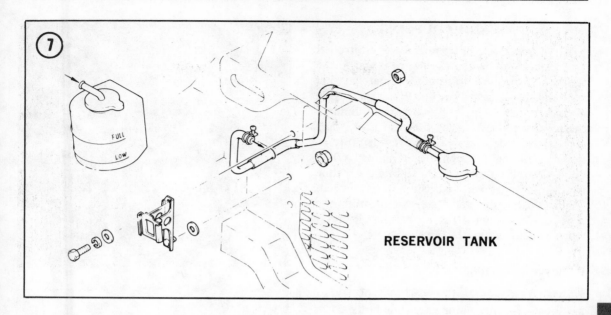

RESERVOIR TANK

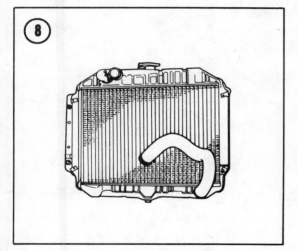

6

3. Install the thermostat housing, using a new gasket coated on both sides with gasket sealer.

4. Tighten the housing securing bolts.

RESERVOIR TANK

The reservoir tank (**Figure 7**) is used on 1976 and later models.

Removal/Installation

To remove the tank, disconnect its hose and slide it out of the bracket. To remove the bracket, undo 2 nuts and one bolt as shown. Install in the reverse order.

RADIATOR

Removal/Installation

1. Remove the radiator cap. Drain coolant by opening the tap on the bottom of the radiator.

2. Disconnect upper and lower radiator hoses.

3. On automatic transmission models, disconnect the torque converter oil cooler lines from the bottom of the radiator.

4. On air conditioned 260Z's, unbolt the lower half of the fan shroud from the radiator, then lower it out of the way.

5. Remove the radiator securing bolts. See **Figure 8**. Lift the radiator up and out.

6. Install by reversing Steps 1-5. After installation, run the engine and check for leaks.

5. Measure the maximum lift of the thermostat valve. To do this, mark a screwdriver at a point 0.315 in. (8mm) from the tip. The screwdriver is used as a measuring device. Heat the water to the temperature specified in **Table 1** (end of chapter) and measure the lift of the valve with the marked screwdriver. If the valve lift is less than 0.315 in. (8mm), replace the thermostat.

Installation

1. If a new thermostat is being installed, test before installation as described in the previous procedure.

2. Install the thermostat in the cylinder head.

FAN AND COUPLING

All models use a temperature controlled viscous-hub fan. When the engine is warm, the fan is kept turning up to approximately 2,500 rpm and then allowed to slip. When the engine is cold, the fan slips at 1,600 rpm. A bimetal thermostat in the fluid coupling opens or closes a slide valve, depending on the temperature of the air coming through the radiator. When open, the valve allows silicon oil into the torque transmitting groove and the fan is turned. When closed, the valve blocks oil from the groove. Centrifugal force moves the oil into a reserve chamber and the fan slips.

Removal/Installation

1. Remove the radiator as described earlier.

2. Loosen the alternator mounting bolts. Push the alternator toward the engine to loosen the fan belt. Take the belt off the water pump pulley.

3. Remove the pulley securing nuts (**Figure 9**). Remove the fan and pulley.

4. Install by reversing Steps 1 through 3. Adjust fan belt tension as described in Chapter Three.

WATER PUMP

A defective water pump is usually the problem when the engine overheats and no other cause can be found. A water pump will often warn of impending failure by making noise or leaking. If the pump is not working properly, it must be replaced. The water pump should never be disassembled, since there is considerable danger of cracking the aluminum pump body in the process.

Removal/Installation

1. Remove the radiator as described earlier.

2. Remove the fan belt, fan, and pulley.

3. Undo the water pump securing bolts and remove the pump (**Figure 10**).

> NOTE: *Inspect the pump after removal. If the vanes are badly corroded, replace the pump.*

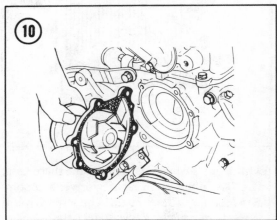

4. Installation is the reverse of these steps. Use a new gasket coated on both sides with gasket sealer.

HEATER

Figure 11 shows the 1970-1973 heater. **Figure 12** shows the 1974-1975 design. The 1976 and later versions are the same except for the water valve (**Figure 13**).

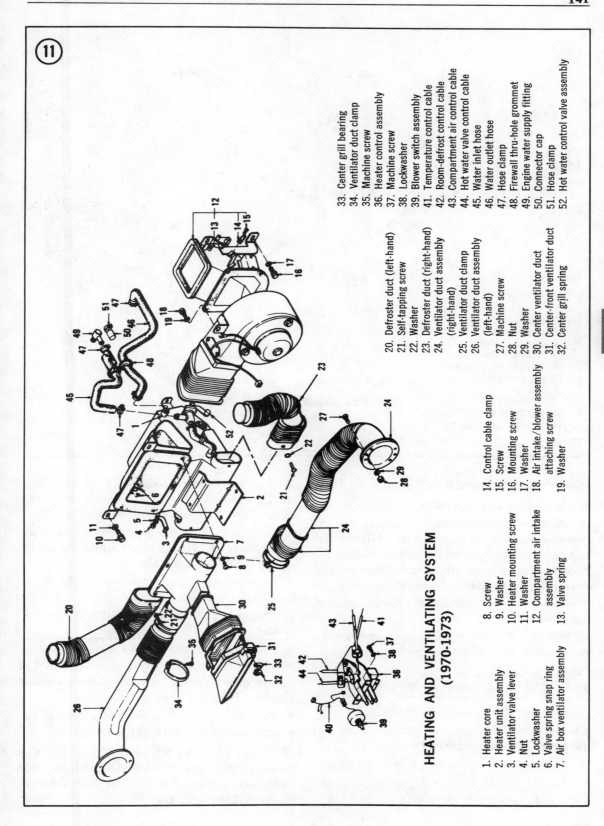

HEATING AND VENTILATING SYSTEM (1970-1973)

1. Heater core
2. Heater unit assembly
3. Ventilator valve lever
4. Nut
5. Lockwasher
6. Valve spring snap ring
7. Air box ventilator assembly
8. Screw
9. Washer
10. Heater mounting screw
11. Washer
12. Compartment air intake assembly
13. Valve spring
14. Control cable clamp
15. Screw
16. Mounting screw
17. Washer
18. Air intake/blower assembly attaching screw
19. Washer
20. Defroster duct (left-hand)
21. Self-tapping screw
22. Washer
23. Defroster duct (right-hand)
24. Ventilator duct assembly (right-hand)
25. Ventilator duct clamp
26. Ventilator duct assembly (left-hand)
27. Machine screw
28. Nut
29. Washer
30. Center ventilator duct
31. Center-front ventilator duct
32. Center grill spring
33. Center grill bearing
34. Ventilator duct clamp
35. Machine screw
36. Heater control assembly
37. Machine screw
38. Lockwasher
39. Blower switch assembly
40. Temperature control cable
41. Room-defrost control cable
42. Compartment air control cable
43. Hot water valve control cable
44. Hot water valve control cable
45. Water inlet hose
46. Water outlet hose
47. Hose clamp
48. Firewall thru-hole grommet
49. Engine water supply fitting
50. Connector cap
51. Hose clamp
52. Hot water control valve assembly

6

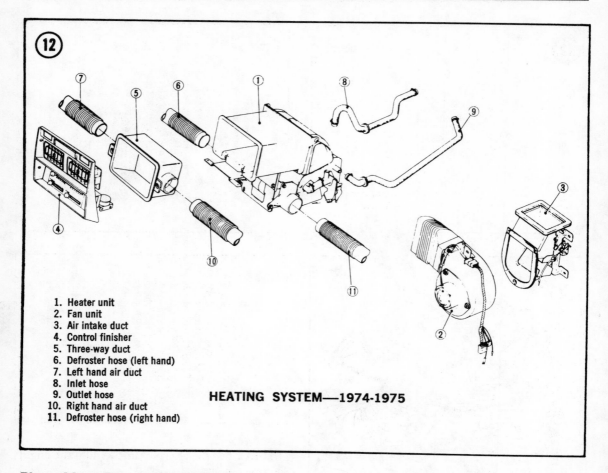

1. Heater unit
2. Fan unit
3. Air intake duct
4. Control finisher
5. Three-way duct
6. Defroster hose (left hand)
7. Left hand air duct
8. Inlet hose
9. Outlet hose
10. Right hand air duct
11. Defroster hose (right hand)

HEATING SYSTEM—1974-1975

Blower Motor Removal/Installation

1. Disconnect the positive battery cable.

2. On early cars, disconnect the red blower motor power wire at its connector. Loosen the top blower housing installation bolt to disconnect the black ground wire. Use a 10mm socket, universal, and extension to loosen the bolt.

3. On later cars, disconnect the motor wires at the connector.

4. Remove 3 bolts from the blower motor mounting flange. Withdraw the motor from the housing.

5. Installation is the reverse of these steps.

Control Assembly
Removal/Installation (1970-1973)

1. Disconnect the air vent cable at its terminal (1, **Figure 14**). Loosen the cable clamp (2, **Figure 14**) and detach the cable.

2. Disconnect the defroster cable at its terminal (3, **Figure 14**). Loosen the cable clamp (4, **Figure 14**) and detach the cable.

3. Disconnect the temperature control cable at its terminal (1, **Figure 15**). Loosen the cable clamp and detach the cable.

4. Separate the radio chassis from the floor brackets on both sides.

5. Disconnect all radio electrical and antenna connections.

6. Disconnect the blower switch electrical connector.

7. Remove 4 screws securing the console finisher to the instrument panel.

8. Pull the console finisher out far enough to expose the center heater duct. Disconnect the heater duct from its outlet.

9. Remove the map light lens and push the map light through the console finisher. Do not disconnect the map light wires.

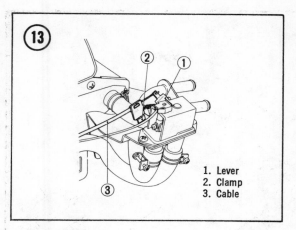

1. Lever
2. Clamp
3. Cable

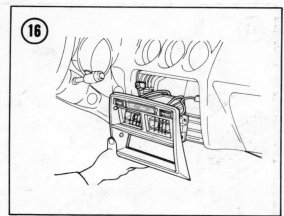

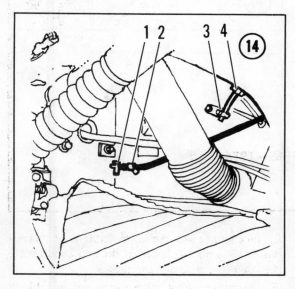

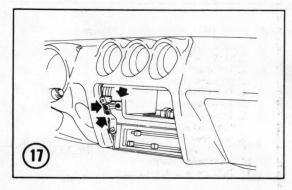

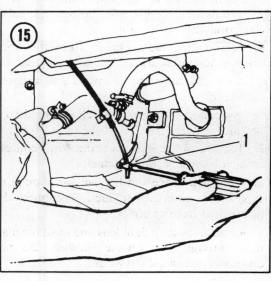

10. Remove the console finisher into the engine compartment.

11. Installation is the reverse of these steps.

Control Assembly
Removal/Installation (1974-1976)

1. Disconnect the negative cable from battery.

2. Drain the cooling system.

3. Remove the console.

4. Remove 4 screws securing the finisher panel. Pull the panel forward (**Figure 16**). Disconnect 2 wiring connectors and take panel out.

5. On 1974-1975 cars, remove 6 screws attaching the air duct to the instrument panel. See **Figure 17**. Disconnect the air intake hose from each side of the duct, then take the duct out.

6. Carefully note the positions of the following levers, then disconnect the cables from them:

   a. Intake door (**Figure 18**)

   b. 1974-1975 water valve (**Figure 19**)

   c. 1976 water valve (**Figure 20**)

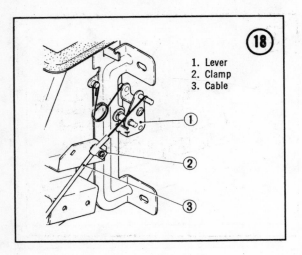

1. Lever
2. Clamp
3. Cable

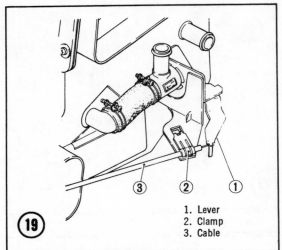

1. Lever
2. Clamp
3. Cable

   d. 1974-1975 mode door (**Figure 21**)

   e. 1976 mode door (**Figure 22**)

   f. Floor door (**Figure 23**)

> NOTE: *The levers on heater and control panel must be installed in the same relative positions.*

7. Remove the screws securing the control panel to instrument panel and heater.

8. Disconnect 2 control panel wiring connectors. The panel can then be removed.

9. Installation is the reverse of these steps. When connecting the cables, be sure the levers on the control panel and heater are positioned correctly.

Heating Unit Removal/Installation

1. Disconnect the negative cable from battery.

2. Completely drain the cooling system.

3. Remove the control assembly as described earlier. On 260-280Z's, remove the console.

> NOTE: *The next 3 steps apply to 240Z's only.*

4. Detach the left and right ventilator ducts from the ventilator.

5. Remove 6 screws from the ventilator. See **Figure 24**.

6. Remove the ventilator through the console finisher opening.

> NOTE: *The next steps apply to all models.*

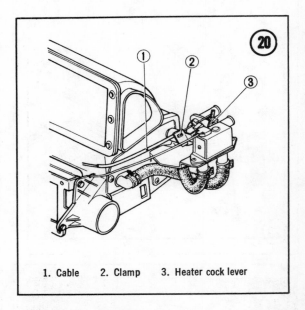

1. Cable   2. Clamp   3. Heater cock lever

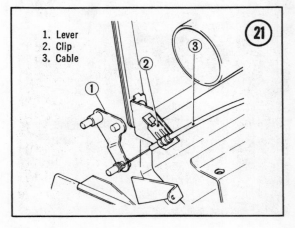

1. Lever
2. Clip
3. Cable

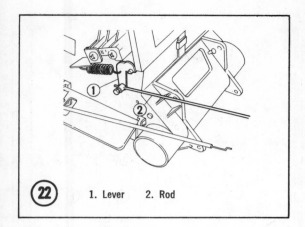

22

1. Lever   2. Rod

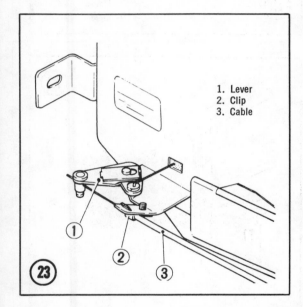

1. Lever
2. Clip
3. Cable

23

24

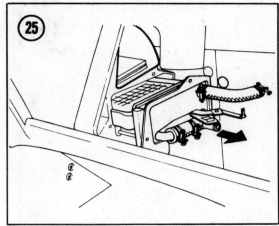

25

7. Detach both defroster ducts.

8. Place a plastic sheet on the car floor to catch any coolant remaining in heater hoses or core. Paint stores sell inexpensive plastic dropcloths which are suitable.

9. Disconnect the heater hoses from the right-hand side of the heater. **Figure 25** shows typical hoses.

10. Remove the heater attaching screws. See **Figure 26**.

11. Remove heater down and to the right.

12. Installation is the reverse of these steps.

AIR CONDITIONING

This section covers the maintenance and minor repairs that can prevent or correct most air conditioning problems. Major repairs require special training and tools, and should be left to a Datsun dealer or air conditioning shop.

SYSTEM OPERATION

A schematic of the air conditioning system is shown in **Figure 27**. These 5 basic components are common to all air conditioning systems:

    a. Compressor
    b. Condenser
    c. Receiver/drier
    d. Expansion valve
    e. Evaporator

6

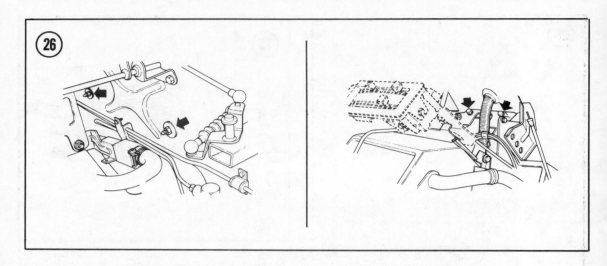

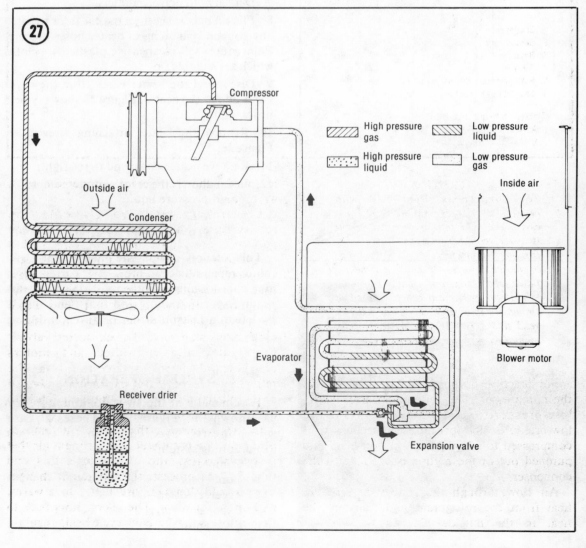

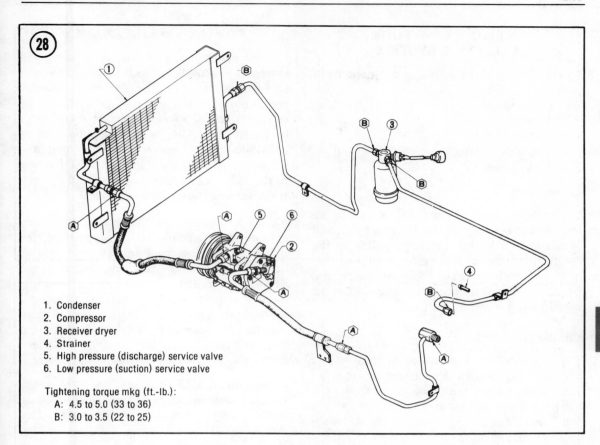

1. Condenser
2. Compressor
3. Receiver dryer
4. Strainer
5. High pressure (discharge) service valve
6. Low pressure (suction) service valve

Tightening torque mkg (ft.-lb.):
A: 4.5 to 5.0 (33 to 36)
B: 3.0 to 3.5 (22 to 25)

CAUTION

*The components, connected with high-pressure hoses and tubes, form a closed loop. The refrigerant in the system is under very high pressure. It can cause frostbite if it touches skin and blindness if it touches the eyes. If discharged near a flame, the refrigerant creates poisonous gas. If the refrigerant can is hooked up wrong, it can explode. For these reasons, **read this entire section** before working on the system.*

For practical purposes, the cycle begins at the compressor. The refrigerant, in a warm, low-pressure vapor state, enters the low-pressure side of the compressor. It is compressed to a high-pressure hot vapor and pumped out of the high-pressure side to the condenser.

Air flow through the condenser removes heat from the refrigerant and transfers the heat to the outside air. As the heat is removed, the refrigerant condenses to a warm, high-pressure liquid.

The refrigerant then flows to the receiver/drier where moisture is removed and impurities are filtered out. The refrigerant is stored in the receiver/drier until it is needed. The receiver/drier incorporates a sight glass that permits visual monitoring of the condition of the refrigerant as it flows. From the receiver/drier, the refrigerant then flows to the expansion valve. The expansion valve is thermostatically controlled and meters refrigerant to the evaporator. As the refrigerant leaves the expansion valve it changes from a warm, high-pressure liquid to a cold, low-pressure liquid.

In the evaporator, the refrigerant removes heat from the passenger compartment air that is blown across the evaporator's fins and tubes. In the process, the refrigerant changes from a cold, low-pressure liquid to a warm, high-pressure vapor. The vapor flows back to the compressor, where the cycle begins again.

6

GET TO KNOW YOUR VEHICLE'S SYSTEM

Locate each of the following components in turn:

a. Compressor
b. Condenser
c. Receiver/drier
d. Expansion valve
e. Evaporator

Compressor

The compressor (**Figure 28**) is located on the front of the engine, like the alternator, and is driven by a V-belt. The large pulley on the front of the compressor contains an electromagnetic clutch. This activates and operates the compressor when the air conditioning is switched on.

Condenser

The condenser is mounted in front of the radiator (**Figure 28**). Air passing through the fins and tubes removes heat from the refrigerant in the same manner it removes heat from the engine coolant as it passes through the radiator.

Receiver/Drier

The receiver/drier (**Figure 28**) is a small tank-like unit, usually mounted to one of the wheel wells. It incorporates a sight glass through which refrigerant flow can be seen. The refrigerant's appearance is used to troubleshoot the system.

Expansion Valve

The expansion valve (**Figure 29**) is located between the receiver/drier and the evaporator. It is mounted on the evaporator housing.

Evaporator

The evaporator (**Figure 27**) is located in the passenger compartment cooling unit, behind the instrument panel. Warm air is blown across the fins and tubes, where it is cooled and dried and then ducted into the passenger compartment.

ROUTINE MAINTENANCE

Basic maintenance of the air conditioning system is easy; at least once a month, even in cold weather, start your engine, turn on the air conditioner, and operate it at each of the control settings. Operate the air conditioner for about 10 minutes, with the engine running at 1,500 rpm. This will ensure that the compressor seal does not deform from sitting in the same position for a long period of time. If this occurs, the seal is likely to leak.

The efficiency of the air conditioning system also depends in great part on the efficiency of the cooling system. This is because heat from the condenser passes through the radiator. If the cooling system is dirty or low on coolant, it may be impossible to operate the air conditioner without overheating. Inspect the coolant. If necessary, flush and refill the cooling system as described under *Cooling System Flushing* in this chapter.

With an air hose and a soft brush, clean the radiator and condenser fins and tubes to remove bugs, leaves, and other imbedded debris.

Check drive belt tension as described under *Drive Belts*, Chapter Three.

If the condition of the cooling system thermostat is in doubt, test it as described under *Thermostat* in this chapter.

Once you are sure the cooling system is in good condition, the air conditioning system can be inspected.

Inspection

1. Clean all lines, fittings, and system components with solvent and a clean rag. Pay particular attention to the fittings; oily dirt around connections almost certainly indicates a leak. Oil from the compressor will migrate through the system to the leak. Carefully tighten the connection, but don't overtighten and strip the threads. If the leak persists, it will soon be apparent once again as oily dirt accumulates. Clean the sight glass with a clean, dry cloth.

2. Clean the condenser fins and tubes with a soft brush and an air hose, or with a high-pressure stream of water from a garden hose. Remove bugs, leaves, and other imbedded debris. Carefully straighten any bent fins with a screwdriver, taking care not to puncture or dent the tubes.

3. Start the engine and check the operation of the blower motor and the compressor clutch

by turning the controls on and off. If either the blower or the clutch fails to operate, shut off the engine and check the fuses and fusible links. If they are burned out, replace them. If the fuses are good, remove them and clean the fuse holder contacts. Then check the clutch and blower operation again.

Testing

1. Place the transmission in NEUTRAL. Set the parking brake.

2. Start the engine and run it at a fast idle.

3. Set the temperature control to its coldest setting and the blower to high. Allow the system to operate for 10 minutes with the doors and windows open. Then shut them and set the blower on its lowest setting.

4. Check air temperature at the outlet. It should be noticeably colder than the surrounding air. If not, the refrigerant level is probably low. Check the sight glass as described in the following step.

5. Run the engine at a fast idle and switch on the air conditioning. Look at the sight glass (**Figure 30**) and check for the following:

   a. Bubbles—the refrigerant level is low.

   b. Oily or cloudy—the system is contaminated. Have it serviced by a dealer or air conditioning shop.

   c. Clear glass—either there is enough refrigerant, too much, or the system is so close to empty it can't make bubbles. If there is no difference between the inlet and outlet air temperatures, the system is probably near empty. If the system does blow cold air, it either has the right amount of refrigerant, or too much. To tell which, turn off the air conditioner while watching the sight glass. If the refrigerant foams, then clears up, the amount is correct. If it doesn't foam, but stays clear, there is too much.

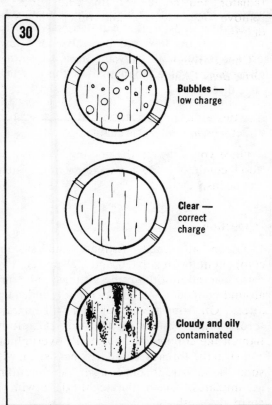

Bubbles —
low charge

Clear —
correct
charge

Cloudy and oily
contaminated

REFRIGERANT

The air conditioning system uses a refrigerant called dichlorodifluoromethane, or R-12.

WARNING
R-12 creates freezing temperatures when it evaporates. This can cause frostbite if it touches skin and blindness if it touches the eyes. If discharged near an open flame, R-12 creates poisonous gas. If the refrigerant can is hooked up to the pressure side of the compressor, it may explode. Always wear gloves and safety goggles when working with R-12.

Charging

This section applies to partially discharged or empty air conditioning systems. If a hose has been disconnected or any internal part of the system exposed to air, the system should be evacuated and recharged by a dealer or air conditioning shop. Recharge kits are available from auto parts stores. Be sure the kit includes a gauge set.

1. Carefully read and understand the gauge manufacturer's instructions before charging the system.
2. Place the refrigerant can in a pan of *warm* water, *not hot.*

WARNING
Water temperature must not exceed 40° C (104° F). If it does, the can may explode.

4. Turn the handle of the refrigerant can tap valve all the way counterclockwise to retract the needle.
5. Turn the disc on the can tap valve all the way counterclockwise. Install the valve on the can.
6. Connect the center hose to the can tap valve.
7. Make sure the gauge valves are closed.
8. Turn the can tap valve clockwise to make a hole in the can.
9. Turn the handle all the way counterclockwise to fill the center hose with air.
10. Slowly loosen the nut connecting the center hose to the gauge set, until hissing can be heard. Let this continue for a few seconds to purge air from the hose, then tighten the nut.

CAUTION
During the next steps, the refrigerant can must remain upright. If it is turned upside down, refrigerant will enter the system as a liquid, which may damage the compressor.

11. Open the low-pressure valve (**Figure 31**). Adjust the valve so the gauge reads no more than 2.8 kg/cm^2 (40 psi).

CAUTION
Leave the high-pressure valve closed at all times.

12. Run the engine at idle (below 1,500 rpm) and turn on the air conditioner. Let the system charge until the sight glass is free of air bubbles. See **Figure 30**.

NOTE
If the system is nearly empty, another can of refrigerant will be needed. Attach it as described in the following steps.

13. Close the low-pressure valve.
14. Remove the can tap valve and attach a new can. Don't make a hole in the new can yet.
15. Slightly loosen the can tap valve disc. Barely open the low-pressure valve for a few seconds to purge air from the hose. Close the low-pressure valve, then tighten the can tap valve disc.

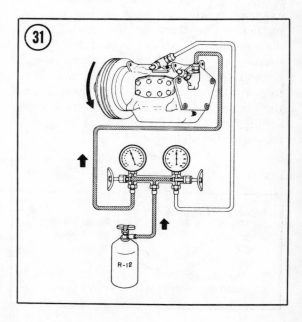

16. Turn the can tap valve handle clockwise to make a hole in the can. Let the system charge until the sight glass is free of air bubbles.

17. Once the system is fully charged, close the low-pressure valve.

18. Close the can tap valve. Very slowly loosen the charge line to allow any remaining refrigerant to escape.

WARNING
Wear gloves and safety goggles to prevent frostbite and blindness. Do not allow any open flame near the refrigerant or poisonous gas may be formed.

19. Turn off the engine. Cover the compressor service valve fittings with a shop rag, then quickly disconnect them.

20. Install the caps on the service valves.

TROUBLESHOOTING

If the air conditioner fails to blow cold air, the following steps will help locate the problem.

1. First, stop the car and look at the control settings. One of the most common air conditioning problems occurs when the temperature is set for maximum cold and the blower is set on low. This promotes ice buildup on the evaporator fins and tubes, particularly in humid weather. Eventually, the evaporator will ice over completely and restrict air flow. Turn the blower on high and place a hand over an air outlet. If the blower is running but there is little or no air flowing through the outlet, the evaporator is probably iced up. Leave the blower on high and turn the temperature control off or to its warmest setting, and wait. It will take 10-15 minutes for the ice to start melting.

2. If the blower is not running, the fuse or fusible link may be blown, there may be a loose wiring connection, or the motor may be burned out. First, check the fuse block for a blown or incorrectly seated fuse. Check for a burned out fusible link. Then check the wiring for loose connections.

3. Shut off the engine and inspect the compressor drive belt. If loose or worn, tighten or replace. See *Drive Belts*, Chapter Three.

4. Start the engine. Check the compressor clutch by turning the air conditioner on and off. If the clutch does not activate, its fuse or fusible link may be blown, or the evaporator temperature-limiting switches may be defective. If the fuse or fusible link is defective, replace it. If not, have the system checked by a Datsun dealer or air conditioning shop.

5. If the system checks out OK to this point, start the engine, turn on the air conditioner, and watch the refrigerant through the sight glass. If it fills with bubbles after a few seconds, the refrigerant level is low. If the sight glass is oily or cloudy, the system is contaminated and should be serviced by a shop as soon as possible. Corrosion and deterioration occur very quickly and if not taken care of at once will result in a very expensive repair job.

6. If the system still appears to be operating as it should but air flow into the passenger compartment is not cold, check the condenser and cooling system radiator for debris that could block air flow. Recheck the cooling system as described under *Inspection*.

7. If the preceding steps have not solved the problem, take the car to a dealer or air conditioning shop for service.

6

Table 1   COOLING SYSTEM SPECIFICATIONS

Approximate coolant capacity		Radiator cap working pressure	13 psi (0.9 kg/cm^2)
1970-1973	10 1/2 qt. (9.9 liters)	Thermostat opening temperature	
1974-1975	10 qt. (9.4 liters)	240Z	177-182°F (80.5-83.5°C)
1976	11 qt. (10.4 liters)	All others, standard	180°F (82°C)
1977-1978		All others, cold areas	190°F (88°C)
Manual transmission	10 7/8 qt. (10.3 liters)	All others, tropical areas	170°F (76.5°C)
Automatic transmission	10 5/8 qt. (10.1 liters)		

ELECTRICAL SYSTEM

All models use a 12-volt negative ground electrical system with a 3-phase alternator. This chapter includes service procedures for the battery, starter, charging system, lighting system, ignition system, fuses, instruments, and windshield wipers.

BATTERY

Care and Inspection

1. Disconnect both battery cables and remove the battery.

2. Clean the top of the battery with a baking soda and water solution. Scrub with a stiff bristle brush. Wipe battery clean with a cloth moistened in ammonia or baking soda solution.

> **CAUTION**
> *Keep cleaning solution out of battery cells or the electrolyte will be seriously weakened.*

3. Clean battery terminals with a stiff wire brush or one of the many tools made for this purpose.

4. Examine the battery and battery cables.

5. Install battery and reconnect battery cables.

6. Coat the battery connections with light mineral grease or Vaseline after tightening.

7. Check electrolyte level and top up with distilled water if necessary.

Testing

Hydrometer testing is a good way to check battery condition. Use a hydrometer with numbered graduations from 1.100-1.300 rather than one with just color-coded bands. To use the hydrometer, squeeze the rubber bulb, insert the tip in the cell, and release the bulb (**Figure 1**). Draw enough electrolyte to float the weighted float inside the hydrometer. Note the number in line with the surface of the electrolyte. This is the specific gravity of the cell. Return the electrolyte to the cell from which it came.

The specific gravity of the electrolyte in each battery cell is an excellent indicator of that cell's condition. A fully charged cell will read 1.26 at 68°F (20°C). If the cells test below 1.16, the battery must be recharged. In cold weather, recharge the battery if it tests below 1.22.

> **NOTE**
> *For every 10° F above 80° F (25° C) electrolyte temperature, add 0.004 to specific gravity reading. For every 10° below 80° F (25° C), subtract 0.004.*

> **CAUTION**
> *Battery electrolyte must be fully topped up and the battery cables disconnected before charging.*

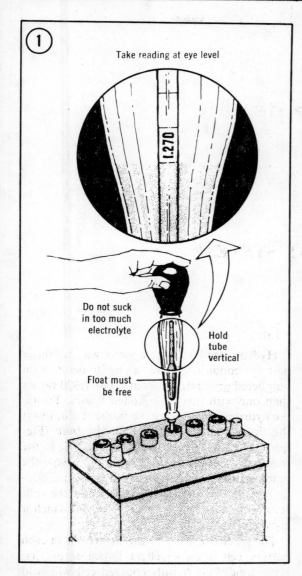

Take reading at eye level

1.270

Do not suck
in too much
electrolyte

Hold
tube
vertical

Float must
be free

ALTERNATOR

The alternator generates 3-phase alternating current in the armature coils. Silicon diodes act as one-way valves for the alternating current, letting only charging current through. In this manner, the AC is converted to DC. Models through 1972 use 6 removable diodes, mounted in positive and negative heat sinks. The 1973-1976 cars use a one-piece diode assembly. The 1970-1977 models have a mechanical regulator, mounted on the engine compartment sidewall. The 1978 cars use an integrated circuit regulator, mounted inside the alternator.

Alternator Output Testing (Through 1977)

This test requires a 30-volt voltmeter and a fully-charged battery.

1. Disconnect the alternator wires.

2. Connect the voltmeter between the alternator N terminal and ground. The voltmeter must indicate battery voltage.

3. Set up the test circuit shown in **Figure 2**.

4. Start the engine. Gradually increase engine speed to 1,100 rpm, then note the voltmeter reading.

CAUTION
*Do not run the engine at speeds above
1,100 rpm. Do not race the engine.*

The voltmeter should indicate 12.5 volts or more. If the reading is low, the alternator should be repaired or replaced.

7

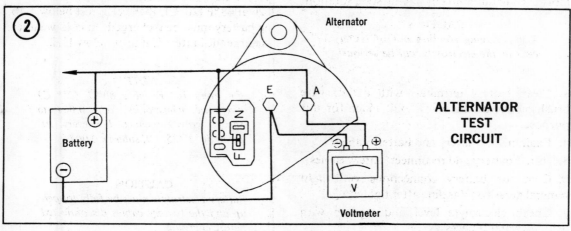

Alternator

E   A

Battery

Z

O O
F

+

−

V

**ALTERNATOR
TEST
CIRCUIT**

Voltmeter

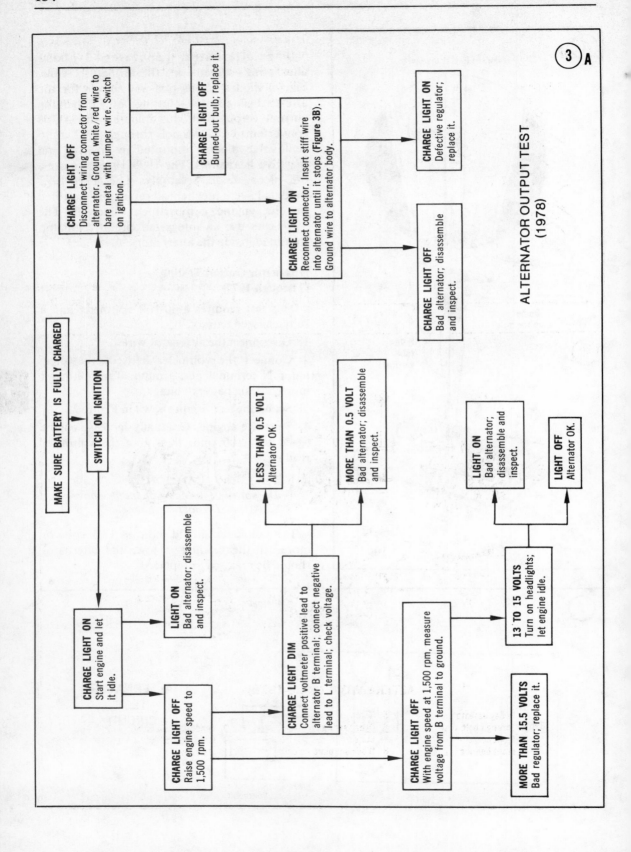

CHARGE LIGHT OFF
Disconnect wiring connector from alternator. Ground white/red wire to bare metal with jumper wire. Switch on ignition.

CHARGE LIGHT OFF
Burned-out bulb; replace it.

CHARGE LIGHT ON
Reconnect connector. Insert stiff wire into alternator until it stops (**Figure 3B**). Ground wire to alternator body.

CHARGE LIGHT ON
Defective regulator; replace it.

CHARGE LIGHT OFF
Bad alternator; disassemble and inspect.

ALTERNATOR OUTPUT TEST
(1978)

3 A

MAKE SURE BATTERY IS FULLY CHARGED

SWITCH ON IGNITION

LESS THAN 0.5 VOLT
Alternator OK.

MORE THAN 0.5 VOLT
Bad alternator; disassemble and inspect.

LIGHT ON
Bad alternator; disassemble and inspect.

LIGHT OFF
Alternator OK.

CHARGE LIGHT ON
Start engine and let it idle.

LIGHT ON
Bad alternator; disassemble and inspect.

CHARGE LIGHT DIM
Connect voltmeter positive lead to alternator B terminal; connect negative lead to L terminal; check voltage.

13 TO 15 VOLTS
Turn on headlights; let engine idle.

CHARGE LIGHT OFF
Raise engine speed to 1,500 rpm.

CHARGE LIGHT OFF
With engine speed at 1,500 rpm, measure voltage from B terminal to ground.

MORE THAN 15.5 VOLTS
Bad regulator; replace it.

Suitable wire

5. Connect an ohmmeter between the alternator E terminal (black wire) and F terminal (black/white wire). Resistance should be about 5-6 ohms. Resistance outside this range indicates problems in brushes or field coils. Disassemble and test the alternator as described later in this chapter.

Alternator Output Test (1978)

Refer to **Figures 3A and 3B** for this procedure.

Disassembly (1970-1977)

Refer to **Figure 4** (1970-1972) or **Figure 5** (1973-1977).

1. Unscrew 3 through bolts.

2. Separate the diode end (rear) housing from the drive end (front) housing by tapping the

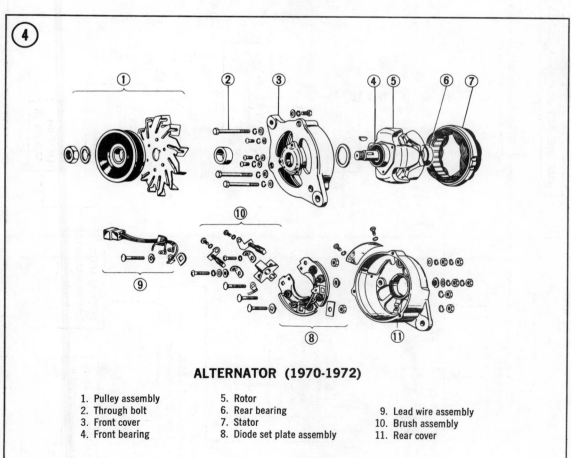

ALTERNATOR (1970-1972)

1. Pulley assembly
2. Through bolt
3. Front cover
4. Front bearing
5. Rotor
6. Rear bearing
7. Stator
8. Diode set plate assembly
9. Lead wire assembly
10. Brush assembly
11. Rear cover

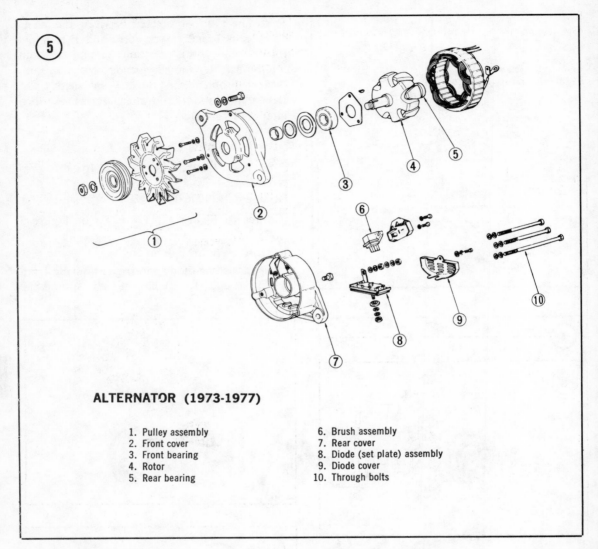

⑤

ALTERNATOR (1973-1977)

1. Pulley assembly
2. Front cover
3. Front bearing
4. Rotor
5. Rear bearing
6. Brush assembly
7. Rear cover
8. Diode (set plate) assembly
9. Diode cover
10. Through bolts

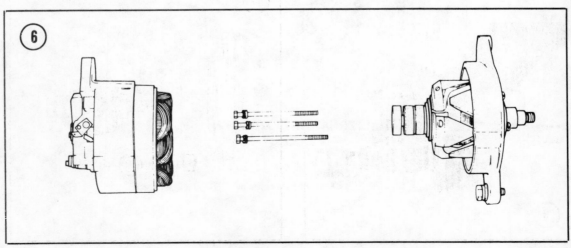

⑥

front housing lightly with a wooden mallet. **Figure 6** shows the through bolts and separated housings.

3. Place the drive end in a vise as shown in **Figure 7**. Remove the pulley nut.

CAUTION
Use a vise with wooden or copper jaws so the rotor won't be damaged.

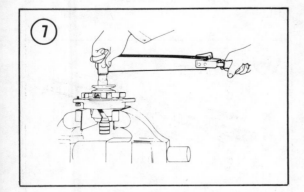

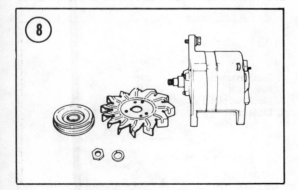

4. Take off the washers, pulley, fan, and spacer (**Figure 8**).

5. On early alternators, separate the rotor from the drive end housing. Hold the rotor and tap the housing lightly with a soft-faced mallet (**Figure 9**). Then remove 3 setscrews and take the bearing retainer out of the drive end housing (**Figure 10**).

6. On later models, remove the bearing retainer setscrews, then separate the rotor from the front housing. See **Figure 11**.

7. Examine the front and rear bearings. Spin them and check for noise, roughness, or excessive play. Leave the bearings in place if serviceable. If necessary, remove early type front

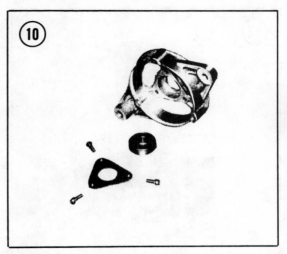

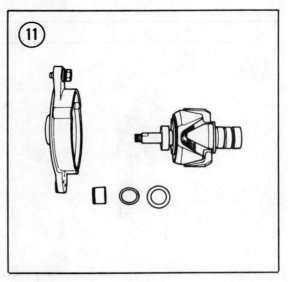

7

bearings with a press **(Figure 12)**. Remove late model bearings with a press **(Figure 13)** or gear puller **(Figure 14)**.

8. On early models, unsolder 3 coil lead wires from the negative diodes, then unsolder the wires from between the diodes **(Figure 15)**.

CAUTION
Excessive heat will destroy diodes. Use a 100-200 watt soldering iron for no more than 2 seconds at a time.

9. On later models, remove the diode cover screw and cover **(Figure 16)**. Unsolder 3 stator leads, remove the "A" terminal nut and diode attaching nut, then remove the diode assembly.

10. On early models, remove 2 setscrews and take off the brush cover **(Figure 17)**. Unsolder and disconnect the "N" terminal wire.

11. Separate the diode end (rear) housing from the stator.

12. On early models, remove the setscrews from the rear cover, then take out the heat sink and brush holder **(Figure 18)**. Be careful not to lose small parts such as screws, washers, and bushings.

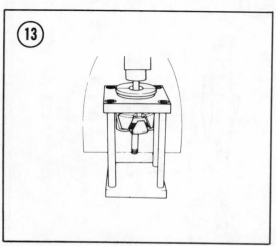

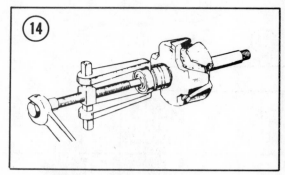

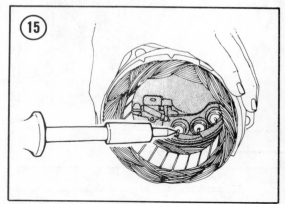

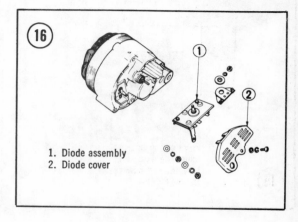

1. Diode assembly
2. Diode cover

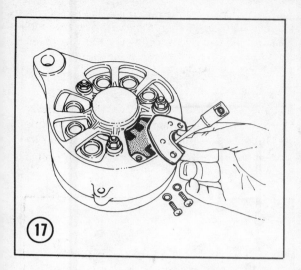

Figure 17

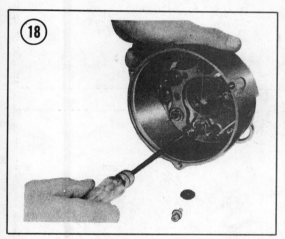

Figure 18

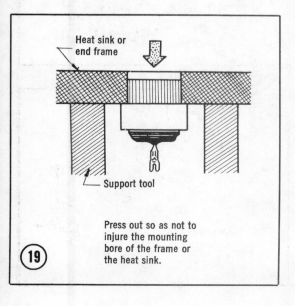

Press out so as not to
injure the mounting
bore of the frame or
the heat sink.

Figure 19

13. To disassemble the brush holder (early models), place the heat sink on a suitable support and press the diodes out (**Figure 19**).

CAUTION
Do not attempt to remove diodes with a hammer. The shock may damage all the diodes in the heat sink.

Disassembly (1978)

Refer to **Figure 20** for this procedure.

1. Remove 4 through bolts. Tap the front cover loose from the stator with a soft-faced mallet. See **Figure 21**.

2. Place the front cover in a soft-jawed vise. Remove the pulley nuts, then take off the fan and pulley. See **Figure 22**.

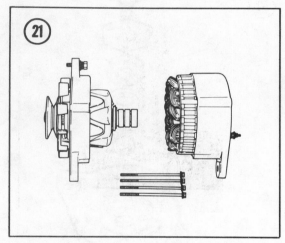

Figure 21

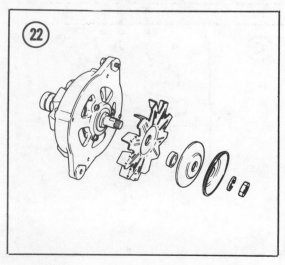

Figure 22

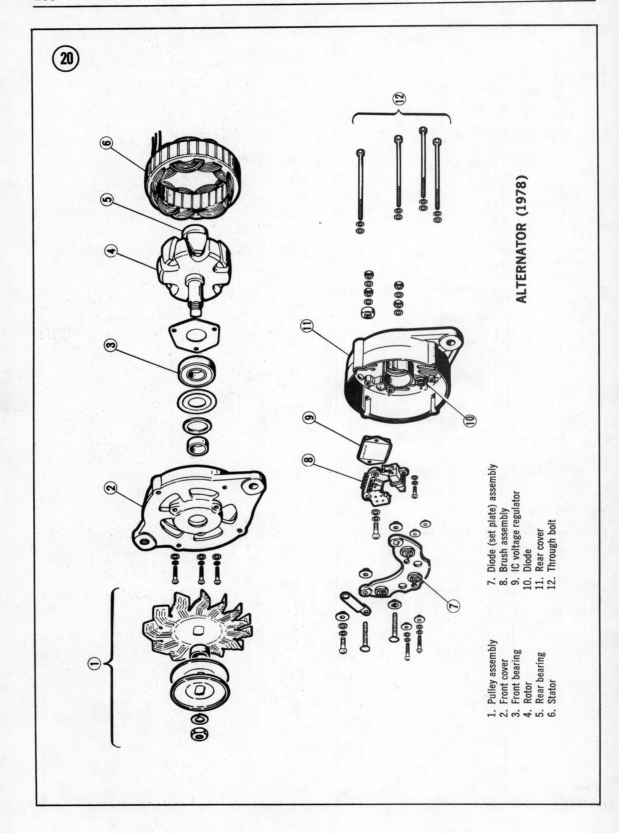

20

ALTERNATOR (1978)

1. Pulley assembly
2. Front cover
3. Front bearing
4. Rotor
5. Rear bearing
6. Stator
7. Diode (set plate) assembly
8. Brush assembly
9. IC voltage regulator
10. Diode
11. Rear cover
12. Through bolt

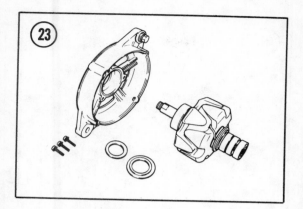

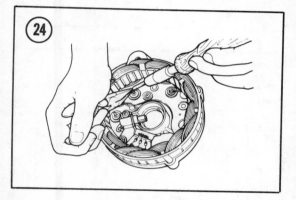

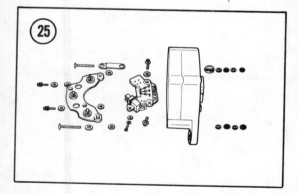

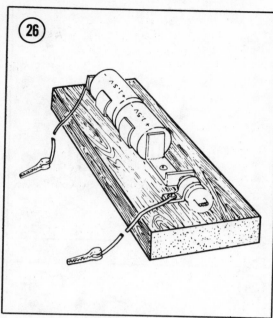

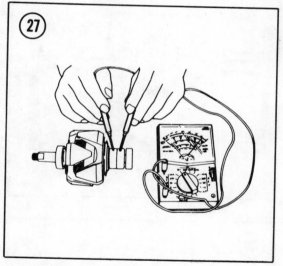

3. Remove 3 bearing retainer setscrews. Take the rotor out of the front cover. See **Figure 23**.

4. Remove the rotor bearing with a press (**Figure 13**) or gear puller (**Figure 14**).

5. Unsolder the stator coil lead wires from the terminals (**Figure 24**).

6. Separate the stator from the rear cover.

7. Unsolder the brush-to-diode wire at the brush assembly terminal.

8. Remove the brush assembly and diode holder. See **Figure 25**.

Alternator Inspection and Repair

For the following tests, make an ohmmeter or a small continuity tester like the one shown in **Figure 26**.

1. Test for rotor continuity by touching test leads to the rotor slip rings (**Figure 27**). The lamp should light if using the continuity tester. If using an ohmmeter, the resistance should be about 4.4 ohms. A reading of zero (lamp off) indicates a defective rotor, which must be replaced.

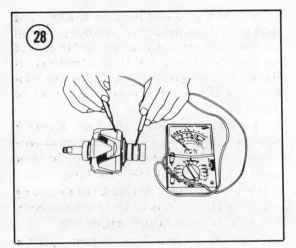

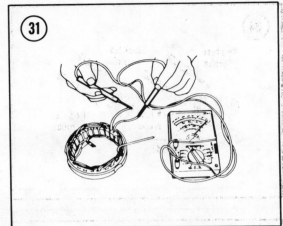

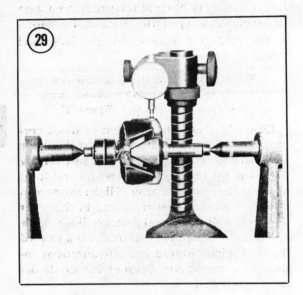

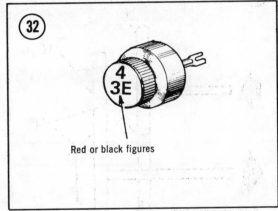

Red or black figures

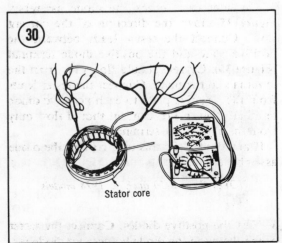

Stator core

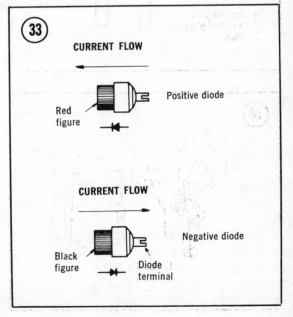

CURRENT FLOW

Positive diode

Red figure

CURRENT FLOW

Negative diode

Black figure

Diode terminal

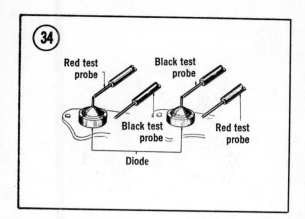

Red test probe

Black test probe

Black test probe

Red test probe

Diode

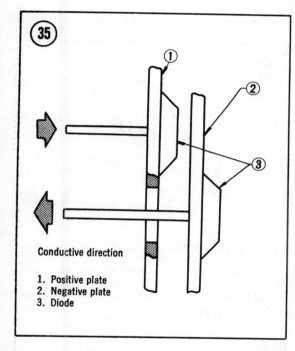

Conductive direction

1. Positive plate
2. Negative plate
3. Diode

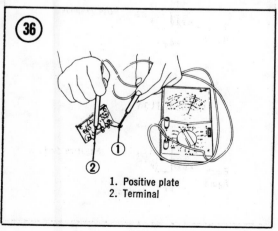

1. Positive plate
2. Terminal

2. Test for a grounded rotor by touching one test lead of the ohmmeter or continuity tester to the rotor core and the other test lead to each of the slip rings (**Figure 28**). If the ohmmeter indicates resistance or the lamp lights, the winding or a slip ring is grounded and must be replaced.

3. Check the rotor for eccentricity. Rotate it between accurate centers with a dial gauge connected as shown in **Figure 29**. Replace the rotor if eccentricity exceeds 0.004 in. (0.1mm).

4. If each lead wire of armature coil (including neutral wire) is not conductive with stator core, the condition is satisfactory (**Figure 30**).

5. Touch the test leads between pairs of stator leads (**Figure 31**). No continuity (test lamp stays out) indicates an open wire. Replace the stator.

6. On 1970-1972 models, test the individual diodes with an ohmmeter.

> *NOTE: Positive diodes are marked with red numbers; the negative diodes are marked with black numbers (**Figure 32**).*

Figure 33 shows the direction of diode current flow. Connect one test lead to the diode terminal and the other to the heat sink (**Figure 34**). Note the resistance. Reverse the test leads and note the resistance again. High resistance in one direction and low resistance in the other direction indicate a satisfactory diode. Low resistance in both directions indicates a shorted diode. High resistance in both directions indicates an open diode. Open or shorted diodes must be replaced.

7. On later cars, check the diode assembly. **Figure 35** shows the direction of the current flow. Connect the tester leads between the positive plate and the positive diode terminal (**Figure 36**). Current should flow only from the terminals to the plate. Connect the tester leads from the negative plate to each negative diode terminal (**Figure 37**). Current should flow only from the plate to the terminals.

If any diode fails this test, replace the diode assembly as a unit.

> *NOTE: Steps 8-10 apply to 1978 models only.*

8. Test the positive diodes. Connect the tester probes between the diode holder and diode ter-

7

minals (**Figure 38**). Current should flow only from the terminal to the holder. If current flows the other way, or not at all, replace the diode.

9. Test the negative diodes (**Figure 39**). Current should flow only from the rear cover to the diode terminal. If current flows the other way, or not at all, replace the diode.

10. Test the sub-diodes. Current should flow only in the direction shown in **Figure 40**. If current flows in the other direction, or not at all, unsolder the faulty diode and solder in a new one.

> **CAUTION**
> *When applying the soldering iron, grip the diode lead wire with needle-nosed pliers to absorb heat.*

11. Check the movement of the brushes in the holder. If the brushes do not move freely, clean the holder.

12. On early alternators, measure brush wear (**Figure 41**). If brushes are worn to less than 0.295 in. (7.5mm), replace them.

13. On later models, replace the brush assembly if the brushes are worn past the limit line. See **Figure 42** (1973-1977) or **Figure 43** (1978).

14. Check the brush spring pressure. Using a spring scale, press the brushes into the holder until they extend 0.039 in. (early models) or 0.079 in. (later type). See **Figure 44**. On early models, replace the springs if pressure is less than 7 oz. On the later type, replace the brush assembly if springs are weaker than 9 oz.

Alternator Assembly

Alternator assembly is the reverse of the disassembly procedure. When installing early model diodes, use a suitable support and drift as shown in **Figure 45**. The drift (A, **Figure 45**) should bear on the outer edge of the diode. Install the diodes with an arbor press so the "B" portion in **Figure 45** is contacting the heat sink.

> **CAUTION**
> *Use only resin core solder when assembling the alternator. Do not use acid core solder.*

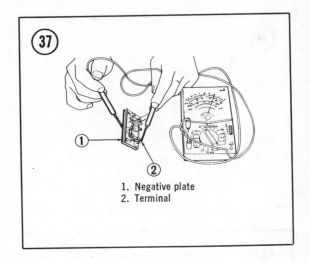

37

1. Negative plate
2. Terminal

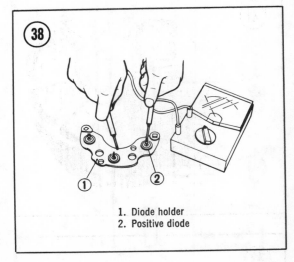

38

1. Diode holder
2. Positive diode

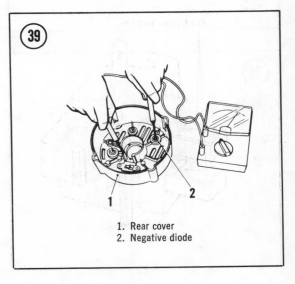

39

1. Rear cover
2. Negative diode

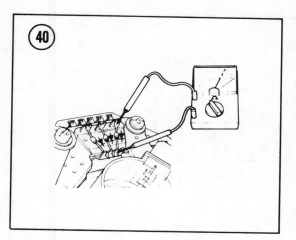

40

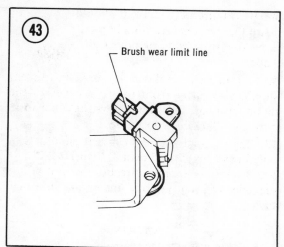

43

Brush wear limit line

41

BRUSH WEAR LIMIT

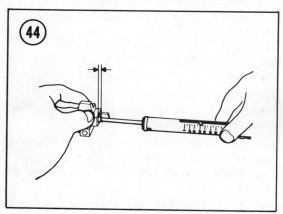

44

7

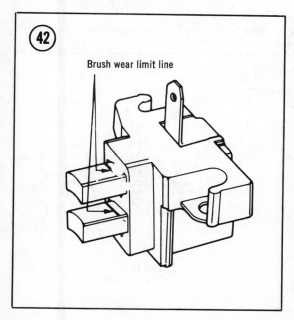

42

Brush wear limit line

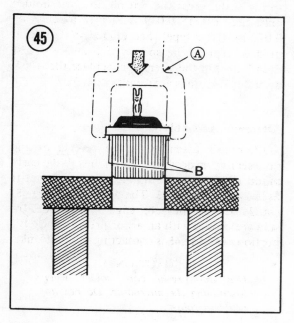

45

A

B

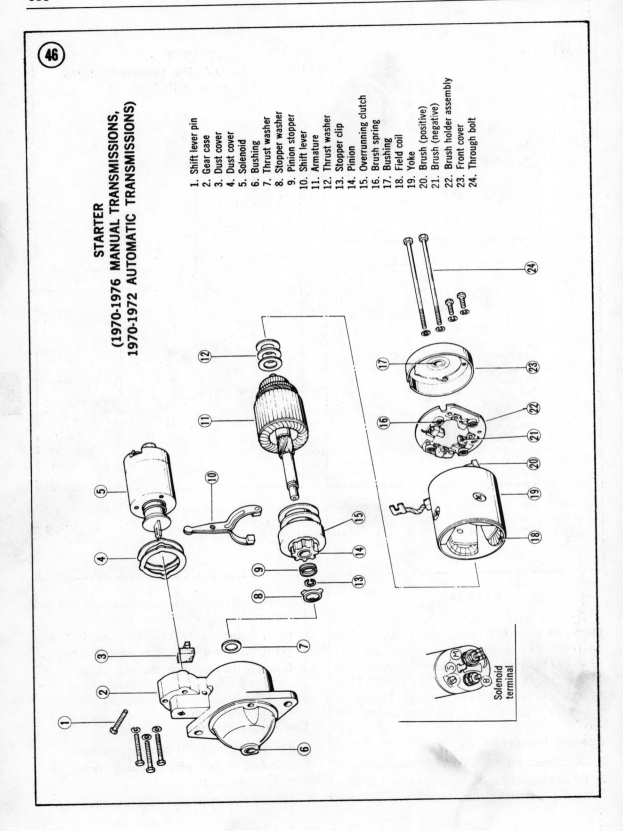

STARTER
(1970-1976 MANUAL TRANSMISSIONS,
1970-1972 AUTOMATIC TRANSMISSIONS)

1. Shift lever pin
2. Gear case
3. Dust cover
4. Dust cover
5. Solenoid
6. Bushing
7. Thrust washer
8. Stopper washer
9. Pinion stopper
10. Shift lever
11. Armature
12. Thrust washer
13. Stopper clip
14. Pinion
15. Overrunning clutch
16. Brush spring
17. Bushing
18. Field coil
19. Yoke
20. Brush (positive)
21. Brush (negative)
22. Brush holder assembly
23. Front cover
24. Through bolt

Solenoid terminal

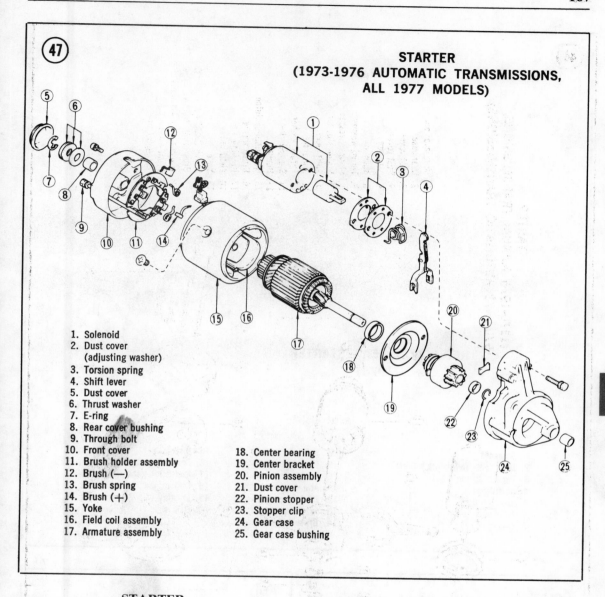

STARTER
(1973-1976 AUTOMATIC TRANSMISSIONS,
ALL 1977 MODELS)

1. Solenoid
2. Dust cover
   (adjusting washer)
3. Torsion spring
4. Shift lever
5. Dust cover
6. Thrust washer
7. E-ring
8. Rear cover bushing
9. Through bolt
10. Front cover
11. Brush holder assembly
12. Brush (—)
13. Brush spring
14. Brush (+)
15. Yoke
16. Field coil assembly
17. Armature assembly
18. Center bearing
19. Center bracket
20. Pinion assembly
21. Dust cover
22. Pinion stopper
23. Stopper clip
24. Gear case
25. Gear case bushing

STARTER

Three starter designs have been used. **Figure 46** shows the conventional design used on 1970-1976 manual transmission cars, and 1970-1972 automatics. **Figure 47** shows the conventional design used on 1973-1976 automatics, and all 1977 models. **Figure 48** shows the reduction gear starter used on 1978 cars.

Removal/Installation

1. Disconnect the negative cable from battery.

2. Disconnect one thick wire and one thin wire from the starter solenoid terminals. Do not disconnect the wire running from solenoid to starter body.

3. Remove the starter securing bolts. Pull the starter forward until it is clear, then lift it out.

4. Install in the reverse order.

Solenoid Replacement
(Conventional Starter)

1. Remove the starter as described earlier.

2. Disconnect the wire running from the solenoid to the starter.

3. Remove the solenoid attaching bolts.

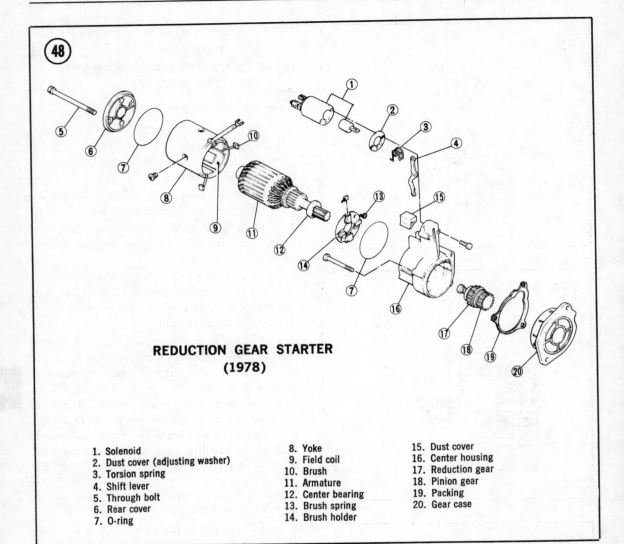

**REDUCTION GEAR STARTER
(1978)**

1. Solenoid
2. Dust cover (adjusting washer)
3. Torsion spring
4. Shift lever
5. Through bolt
6. Rear cover
7. O-ring

8. Yoke
9. Field coil
10. Brush
11. Armature
12. Center bearing
13. Brush spring
14. Brush holder

15. Dust cover
16. Center housing
17. Reduction gear
18. Pinion gear
19. Packing
20. Gear case

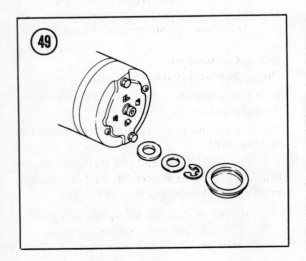

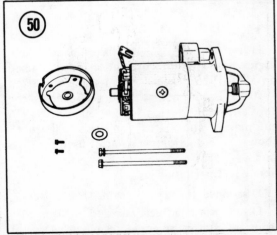

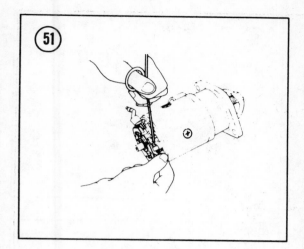

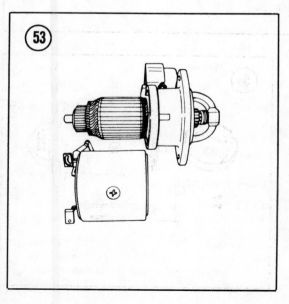

4. Unhook the solenoid plunger from the shift lever inside the starter. Lift the solenoid off.

5. Installation is the reverse of these steps.

**Brush Replacement
(Conventional Starter)**

1. Remove the starter as described earlier.

2. On late type starters, remove the dust cover, snap ring, and thrust washers from the starter's front end. See **Figure 49**.

3. Remove 2 through bolts and 2 setscrews. Take off the brush cover (**Figure 50**).

4. Make a wire hook and pull back the brush springs (**Figure 51**). Slide the brushes out of their slots.

5. Measure brush length. Minimum is 0.492 in. (12.5mm) on early starters; 0.47 in. (12mm) on late starters. Replace the brushes if any are shorter than the minimum.

6. Check brush movement in the slots. Clean the slots and brushes if the movement is not smooth. Examine brush springs. Replace if weak or damaged.

7. Check the brush holder for shorts to ground. Use an ohmmeter or a test lamp like the one shown in **Figure 26**. Touch one tester lead to the brush holder and the other to the positive (insulated) brush slots. See **Figure 52**. If the ohmmeter shows continuity (test lamp lights), a short circuit exists. Replace the insulator or brush holder.

8. Install brushes by reversing Steps 1-4.

CAUTION
Use resin core solder when resoldering brush leads. Do not use acid core solder.

**Brush Replacement
(Reduction Gear Starter)**

1. Remove the through bolts and front cover from the starter.

2. Separate the yoke from the center housing. See **Figure 53**.

3. Make a wire hook and pull back the positive brush springs. See **Figure 54**. Pull the positive brushes out of the slots.

NOTE: *The positive brushes are attached to the field coils, not to the brush holder.*

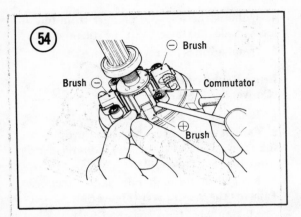

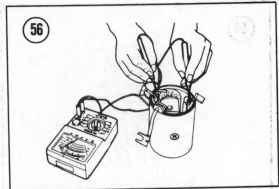

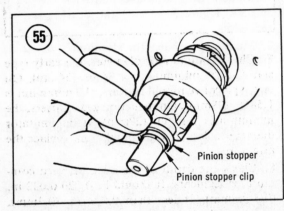

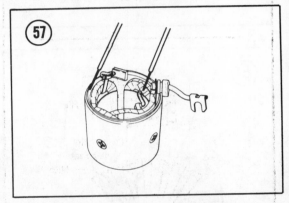

4. Slide the brush holder off of the commutator. Remove the negative brushes from their slots.

5. Measure brush length. Minimum length is 0.43 in. (11mm). Replace the brushes if any are shorter than the minimum.

6. Check brush movement in the slots. Clean the slots and brushes if movement is not smooth. Examine brush springs. Replace if weak or damaged.

7. Check the brush holder for shorts to ground. Use an ohmmeter or a self-powered test lamp like the one shown in **Figure 26**. Touch one probe to the brush holder, and the other to the positive (insulated) brush slots. If the ohmmeter shows continuity (or test lamp lights), replace the brush holder.

8. Install by reversing Steps 1-4.

Disassembly (Conventional Starter)

1. Remove the solenoid and brushes as described earlier.

2. Slide the yoke off the armature.

3. Push the pinion stopper toward the pinion (**Figure 55**). Remove the stopper clip, then the pinion stopper and pinion assembly (overrunning clutch).

Disassembly (Reduction Gear Starter)

1. Remove the solenoid and brushes as described earlier.

2. Take the armature out of the yoke.

3. Unbolt the center housing from the gear case.

4. Remove the reduction gear and pinion gear from the gear case.

Inspection (All Models)

1. Clean all parts with a lint-free cloth.

> CAUTION
> *Do not clean starter parts with solvent. Solvent will ruin the field coil insulation and melt the grease in the overrunning clutch.*

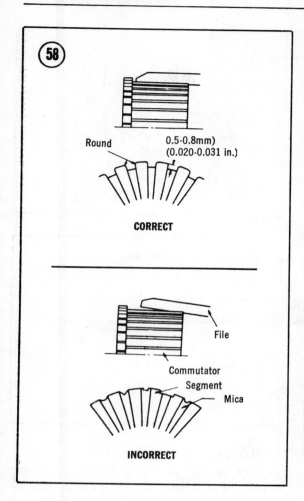

Round   0.5-0.8mm)
         (0.020-0.031 in.)

CORRECT

File

Commutator
Segment
Mica

INCORRECT

2. Check electrical terminals for visible wear or damage. Replace as needed.

3. Test field coils for continuity. Use an ohmmeter or a self-powered test lamp like the one shown in **Figure 26**. Connect one probe to the field coil positive terminal and the other to the positive brush leads (**Figure 56**). No reading on the ohmmeter (test lamp stays out) indicates an open field coil, which must be replaced.

4. Test for grounded field coils. Touch one test lead to the yoke and the other to the field coil positive terminal (**Figure 57**). Resistance (lamp lights) indicates a grounded field coil, which must be replaced.

5. Check the armature for visible damage such as burned windings or a worn shaft. Replace if these can be seen.

6. Inspect the commutator surface. If it is rough, sand lightly with 500 grit emery paper.

7. Check commutator diameter. On early type starters, the minimum is 1.34 in. (34mm). On late type conventional starters, the minimum is 1.54 in. (39mm). On reduction gear starters, the minimum is 1.14 in. (29mm). If commutator diameter is less than the minimum, replace the armature.

8. Check the depth of the mica between commutator segments. It should be 0.020-0.032 in. (0.5-0.8mm). If less than 0.008 in. (0.2mm), undercut the mica with a piece of hacksaw blade. **Figure 58** shows right and wrong ways to undercut the mica.

9. Inspect the soldered connections between the armature leads and commutator. Resolder loose connections with resin core solder.

10. Test for a grounded armature. Touch one test lead to the armature shaft and the other to each commutator segment in turn (**Figure 59**). If continuity occurs (tester lamp lights), the armature is grounded and must be replaced.

11. Check the armature winding for shorts. To check, use an armature tester (growler). Take this job to an automotive electrical shop if you don't have the tester.

12. Check the armature for opens. Usually these are indicated by burn marks on the commutator caused by brushes bridging the open circuit. Use an ohmmeter or continuity tester such as the one shown in **Figure 26**. Place the test leads on successive pairs of armature segments. If the ohmmeter shows no continuity (test lamp stays off), an open circuit exists.

7

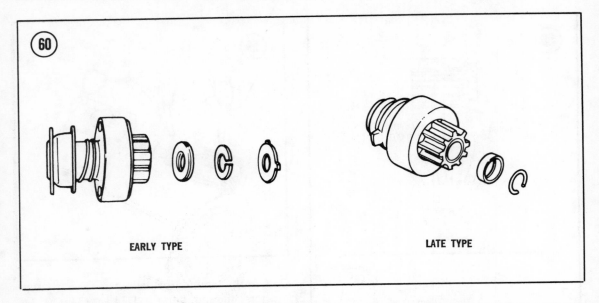

EARLY TYPE   **LATE TYPE**

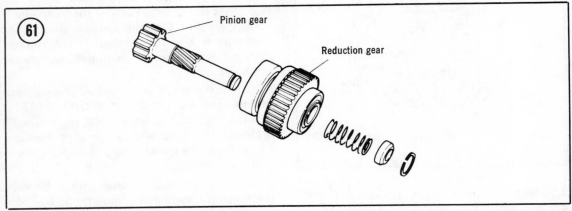

Pinion gear

Reduction gear

13. On conventional starters, inspect the overrunning clutch (**Figure 60**). The pinion gear should turn easily in one direction, and not at all in the other. If the overrunning clutch slips or drags, replace it. The pinion sleeve should slide easily along the armature shaft splines.

14. On reduction gear starters, inspect the pinion and reduction gear assembly (**Figure 61**). The pinion gear should slide freely along the armature shaft splines. The pinion gear shaft must slide freely through the reduction gear. If not, replace the pinion and reduction gear assembly.

15. On conventional starters, inspect the bushing at each end of the starter. If worn, tap them out with a suitable drift. Tap in new bushings with the same tool.

16. On reduction gear starters, inspect the ball bearing at each end of the starter. Replace if looseness or rough movement can be detected.

LIGHTING SYSTEM

Headlight Replacement

Figure 62 shows a typical headlight assembly.

1. Turn the steering wheel to the side away from the burned-out headlight.

2. Disconnect the negative cable from the battery.

3. Remove the inner fender protector (if so equipped).

4. Remove the headlight assembly from the body.

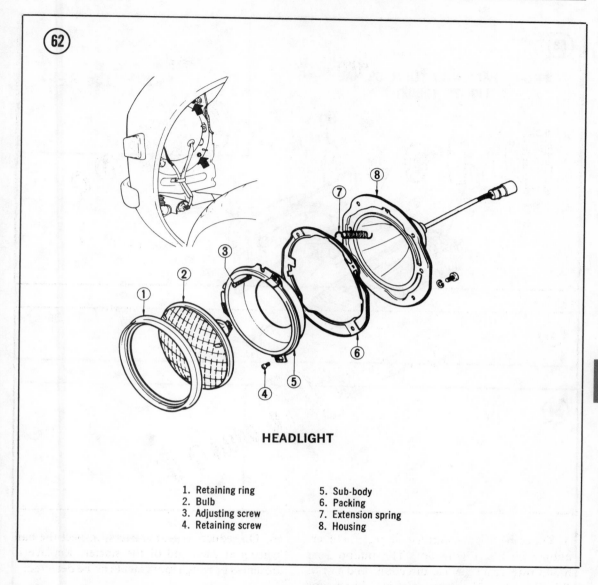

HEADLIGHT

1. Retaining ring
2. Bulb
3. Adjusting screw
4. Retaining screw
5. Sub-body
6. Packing
7. Extension spring
8. Housing

5. Loosen 3 screws securing the headlight retaining ring. Turn the ring counterclockwise and take it off.

6. Unplug the headlight bulb from the wiring connector and take it out.

7. Installation is the reverse of removal. Be sure the word TOP, molded in the lens, is up. If necessary, have headlights adjusted by a dealer or certified lamp adjusting station.

Front Parking/Turn Signal Lights

Front parking and turn signal lights are located under a common lens. **Figure 63**

shows the 280Z installation. All others are similar. To replace a bulb, remove the lens securing screws and take off the lens. Push the bulb into the socket and turn counter-clockwise to remove. Installation is the reverse of removal.

Side Marker Lights

Remove 2 lens securing screws and take off the lens. Push the bulb into its socket and turn counterclockwise to remove. Installation is the reverse of removal.

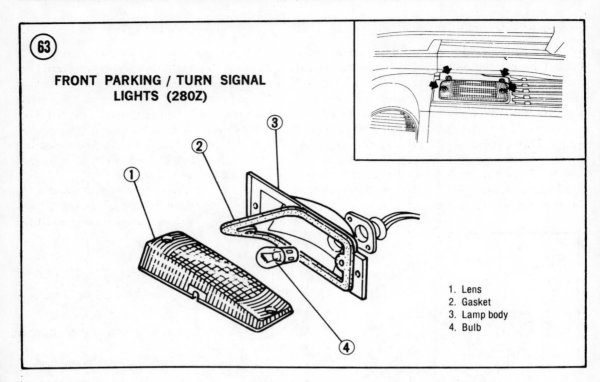

63

FRONT PARKING / TURN SIGNAL LIGHTS (280Z)

1. Lens
2. Gasket
3. Lamp body
4. Bulb

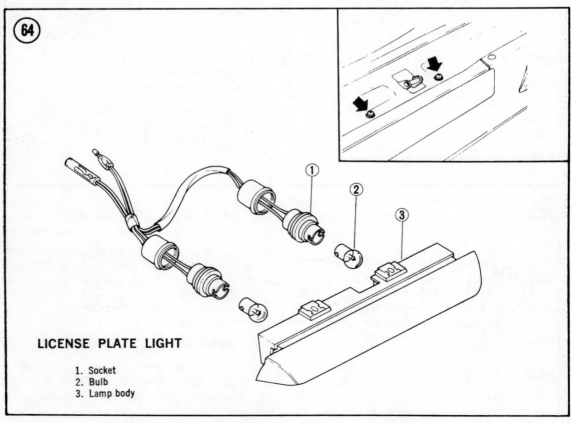

64

LICENSE PLATE LIGHT

1. Socket
2. Bulb
3. Lamp body

License Plate Light

240Z Bulb Replacement—Remove 3 screws and take off the light cover. Press the bulb into the socket and turn counterclockwise to remove. Installation is the reverse of removal.

260-280Z Bulb Replacement—Remove 2 screws securing the light body and take it out. See **Figure 64**. Turn the bulb socket counterclockwise and take it out of the lamp body. Push the bulb into the socket, turn counterclockwise, and take it out. Installation is the reverse of removal.

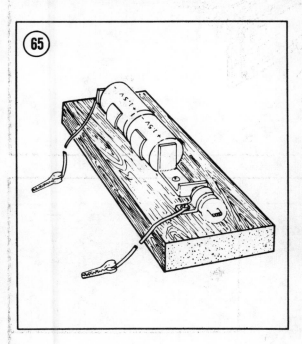

SWITCHES

Switches can be tested with an ohmmeter or a test lamp like the one shown in **Figure 65**. To test the 280Z left door switch, for example, refer to **Figure 66**. The continuity diagram shows that with the plunger out, there should not be continuity between any of the switch's wires. An ohmmeter connected between any of the wires should show infinite resistance (or a test lamp should stay out).

With the plunger in, there should be continuity between terminals 2 and 3, and terminals 1 and 4. **Figure 66** identifies terminal numbers.

Combination Switch Test

1. Disconnect the negative cable from the battery.

2. Remove the steering wheel and steering column shell.

3. Disconnect the switch wiring connectors.

4. Check for proper continuity in the different switch positions. For 1970-1976 Z's, see **Figure 67**; for 1977-1978 Z's, see **Figure 68**.

Combination Switch Removal/Installation

1. Perform Steps 1-3, *Combination Switch Test.*
2. Remove 2 screws and separate the switch halves. See **Figure 67** (1970-1976) or **Figure 68** (1977-1978).

7

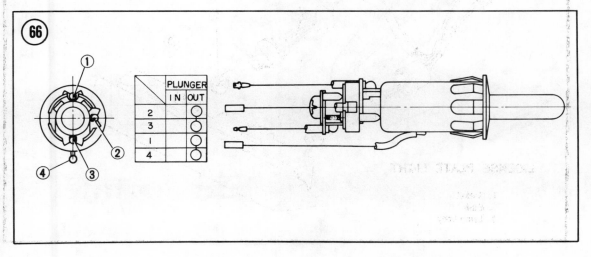

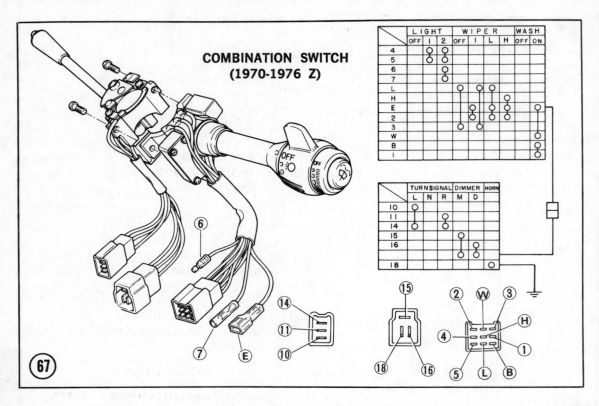

**COMBINATION SWITCH
(1970-1976 Z)**

	LIGHT			WIPER				WASH	
	OFF	1	2	OFF	I	L	H	OFF	ON
4		○	○						
5		○	○						
6			○						
7			○						
L					○	○	○		
H									
E						○	○	○	○
2					○	○		○	
3					○	○			
W									○
B									○
I									○

	TURNSIGNAL			DIMMER		HORN
	L	N	R	M	D	
10	○					
11				○		
14	○			○		
15					○	
16				○	○	
18						○

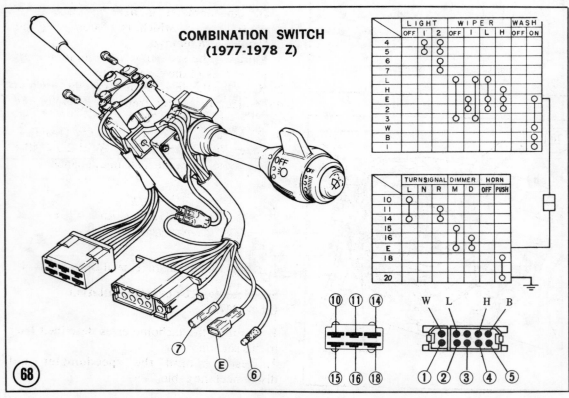

**COMBINATION SWITCH
(1977-1978 Z)**

	LIGHT			WIPER				WASH	
	OFF	1	2	OFF	I	L	H	OFF	ON
4		○	○						
5		○	○						
6			○						
7			○						
L					○	○	○		
H									
E						○	○	○	○
2					○	○		○	
3					○	○			
W									○
B									○
I									○

	TURNSIGNAL			DIMMER		HORN	
	L	N	R	M	D	OFF	PUSH
10	○						
11				○			
14	○			○			
15					○		
16				○	○		
E							
18						○	
20						○	

W L   H B

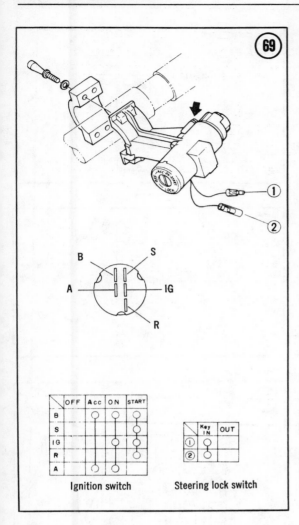

Ignition switch

Steering lock switch

Ignition Switch Test

1. Disconnect the negative cable from the battery.
2. Remove the steering wheel and steering column shell.
3. Disconnect the switch wires.
4. Check for proper continuity in the different switch positions. See **Figure 69**.

Ignition Switch Replacement

1. Perform Steps 1-3, *Ignition Switch Test*.
2. To replace the ignition part of the switch, remove its attaching screw and take it off.
3. To remove the seat belt part of the switch or the steering lock, drill out the self-shearing screws that secure the lock to the steering column. Then remove them with a screw extractor. Remove 2 plain screws (if used) and take the lock off the steering column.
4. Installation is the reverse of removal.

INSTRUMENTS

Speedometer Removal/Installation (240Z)

The speedometer is held in place by 2 brackets, one of which is shared with the tachometer. To remove:

1. Unscrew the speedometer cable union nut from the back of the speedometer.
2. Remove the instrument light sockets and disconnect the wires from the back of the speedometer (**Figure 70**).
3. Remove the bracket wing nuts (1 and 2, **Figure 70**) with pliers. Withdraw the speedometer from the instrument panel.

NOTE
The nuts will be easier to reach if heater air duct is removed first.

4. Installation is the reverse of these steps.

Speedometer Removal/Installation (260-280Z)

1. Remove the tachometer as described later in this section.
2. Reach behind the speedometer and disconnect the cable.

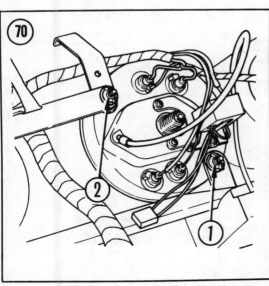

3. Reach through the tachometer hole. Remove the screw securing the tripmeter reset cable (**Figure 71**).

4. Remove attaching screws from the top and back of the speedometer. See **Figure 72** and **Figure 73**.

5. Disconnect the wiring connector shown in **Figure 73**. Pull the speedometer out, disconnect its main wiring connector, and remove the speedometer.

6. Installation is the reverse of these steps.

Tachometer Removal/Installation (240Z)

1. Disconnect the wiring connector and remove the bulb sockets from the back of the tachometer (**Figure 74**).

2. Remove the bracket wing nuts (1 and 2, **Figure 74**) with pliers. Withdraw the tachometer from the instrument panel.

Tachometer Removal/Installation (260-280Z)

1. Remove attaching screws at top and back of tachometer. See **Figures 75** and **76**.

2. Pull the tachometer out to expose the wiring connector. Detach the connector and remove the tachometer.

3. Installation is the reverse of these steps.

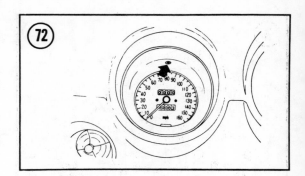

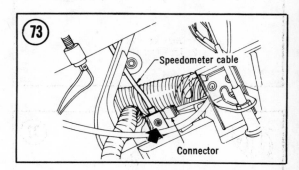

Speedometer cable

Connector

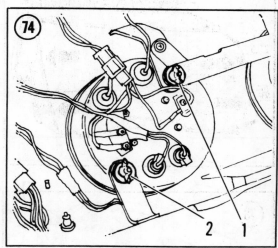

2   1

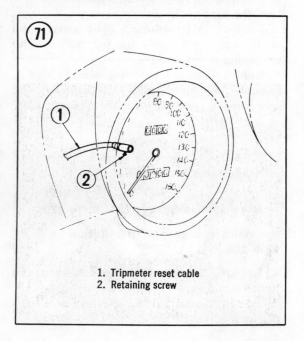

1. Tripmeter reset cable
2. Retaining screw

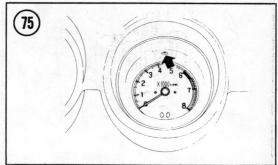

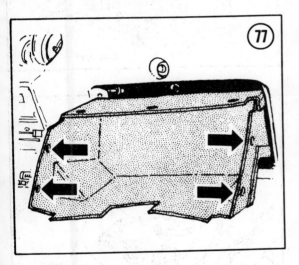

1. Steering shaft
2. Tachometer

Center Gauge Removal/Installation

Center gauges include a combined ammeter/fuel gauge (voltmeter/fuel gauge on 280Z's), combined oil pressure/temperature gauge, and clock. To remove:

1. On 240Z's, remove the glove compartment door and liner. Open the door and remove 3 screws from the hinge. Then remove 2 screws on each side of the liner. See **Figure 77**.

2. On 260-280Z's, remove 4 screws securing the center finisher panel. Pull the panel out (**Figure 78**), detach 2 wiring connectors, and remove the panel. Remove 3 screws from each side of the ventilator duct, detach the duct from the hoses, and take it out. See **Figure 79**.

3. On 240Z's, reach through the glove compartment opening. Detach gauge or clock wires. Remove the attaching screws (1 and 2, **Figure 80**). **Figure 80** shows the oil/water

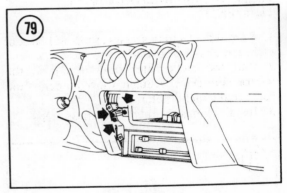

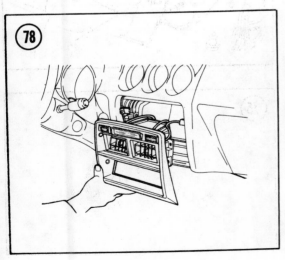

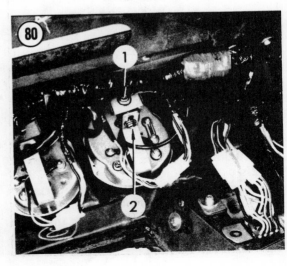

7

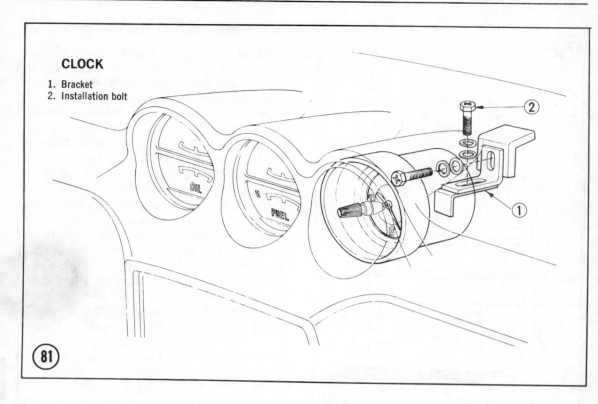

CLOCK

1. Bracket
2. Installation bolt

(81)

gauge screws. The amp/fuel gauge screws are similar. **Figure 81** shows the clock screws.

4. On 260Z's, remove the attaching screw beneath the gauge (**Figure 82**). Remove the gauge bracket, pull the gauge out, and detach its wiring connector.

5. Installation is the reverse of these steps.

FUSES AND FUSIBLE LINKS

The 240Z fuse block is located beneath the ashtray (**Figure 83**). Lift out the ashtray to gain access to the fuse block. Pull up on the knob to remove the fuse block cover.

On later models, the fuse block is located on the right side of the passenger footwell. **Figure 84** shows a typical installation.

The 240Z's use a fusible link in the white wire running from the starter solenoid. The 260Z's use 2 fusible links, mounted in a box on the right-hand engine compartment sidewall. See **Figure 85**. The 280Z's use 5 fusible links, 4 in boxes and one in the white wire running from the battery positive terminal. See **Figure 86**.

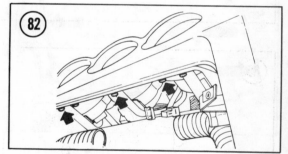

(82)

(83)

84 FUSE BOX

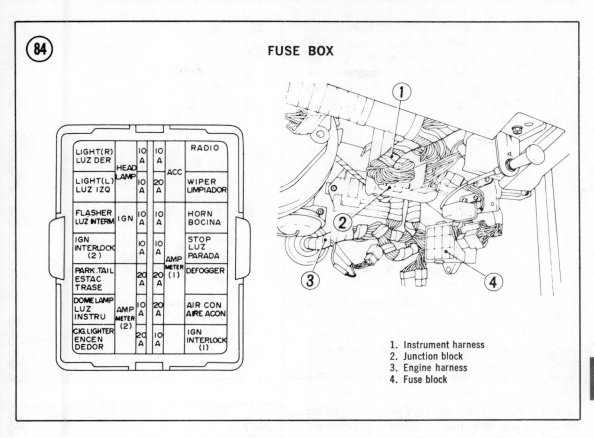

LIGHT(R) LUZ DER	HEAD LAMP	10 A	10 A	ACC	RADIO
LIGHT(L) LUZ IZQ		10 A	20 A		WIPER LIMPIADOR
FLASHER LUZ INTERM	IGN	10 A	10 A		HORN BOCINA
IGN INTERLOCK (2)		10 A	10 A	AMP METER (1)	STOP LUZ PARADA
PARK.TAIL ESTAC TRASE		20 A	20 A		DEFOGGER
DOME LAMP LUZ INSTRU	AMP METER (2)	10 A	20 A		AIR CON AIRE ACON
CIG.LIGHTER ENCEN DEDOR		20 A	10 A		IGN INTERLOCK (1)

1. Instrument harness
2. Junction block
3. Engine harness
4. Fuse block

7

85

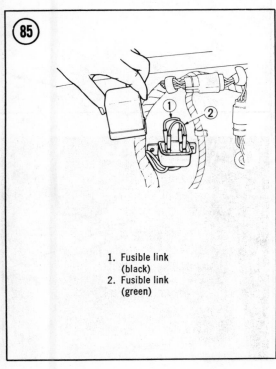

1. Fusible link (black)
2. Fusible link (green)

86

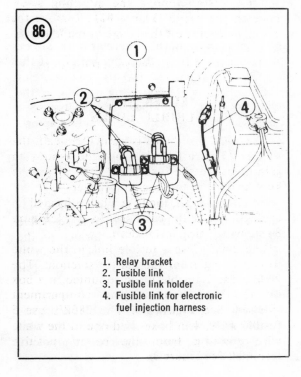

1. Relay bracket
2. Fusible link
3. Fusible link holder
4. Fusible link for electronic fuel injection harness

Whenever a fuse or fusible link blows, find out the cause before replacing. Usually the trouble is a short circuit in the wiring. This may be caused by worn-through insulation or a wire which works its way loose and shorts to ground. Carry several spare fuses in glove compartment.

> *CAUTION*
> *Never substitute tinfoil or wire for a fuse. An overload could cause a fire and complete loss of the car.*

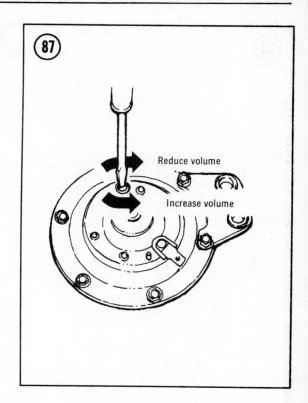

HORN

There are two horns, both located behind the radiator grille. One horn is high-pitched, the other is low-pitched. If the horns work, but are not loud enough, make sure the wire is making good contact and the horn is properly grounded. The 240Z horn volume can be adjusted by turning the screw at the back of the horn (**Figure 87**). Turn the screw clockwise to increase volume or counter-clockwise to decrease.

If only one horn works, check the wiring to the non-working horn. If neither horn works, check the horn fuse, then the battery. If the fuse and battery work properly, test the relay as described in the following section. If the relay is good, test the horn switch. See *Combination Switch Test* earlier in this chapter.

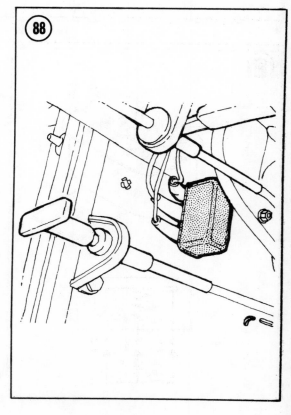

Horn Relay Test

1. Locate the horn relay. On early 240Z's, it is mounted above the hood release cable (**Figure 88**). On later Z's, it is located on the right side of the passenger footwell. It can be identified by its wire colors: green, green-black, and green-red.

2. Disconnect the negative cable from the battery. Disconnect the wires from the horn relay, remove its mounting screw, and take it out.

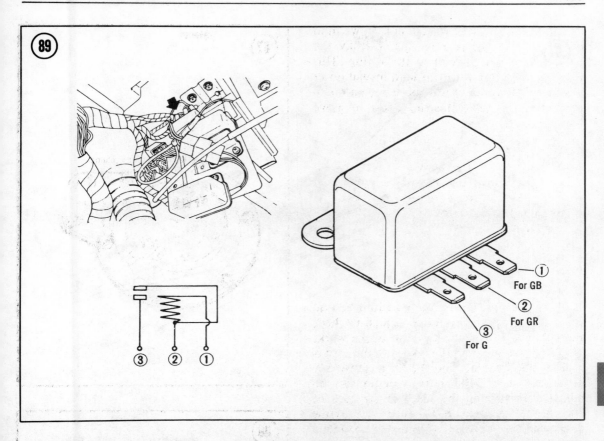

89

① For GB
② For GR
③ For G

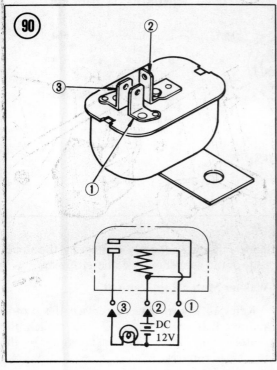

90

DC 12V

3. Connect battery between terminals 1 and 2 with short jumper wires. See **Figure 89** (early type) or **Figure 90** (late type).

4. Connect a voltmeter or 12-volt bulb between terminals 1 and 3. The voltmeter should show voltage, or test lamp should light, as long as the battery is connected to terminals 1 and 2.

WINDSHIELD WIPERS AND WASHERS

Wiper Motor Replacement

Refer to **Figure 91** for this procedure.

1. To gain access to the motor, remove both wiper arms together with the blades. Then remove the cowl top grille.

2. Disconnect wiper motor wiring connector.

3. Detach motor from wiper operating rod.

4. Remove 4 motor installation screws and lift the motor out.

7

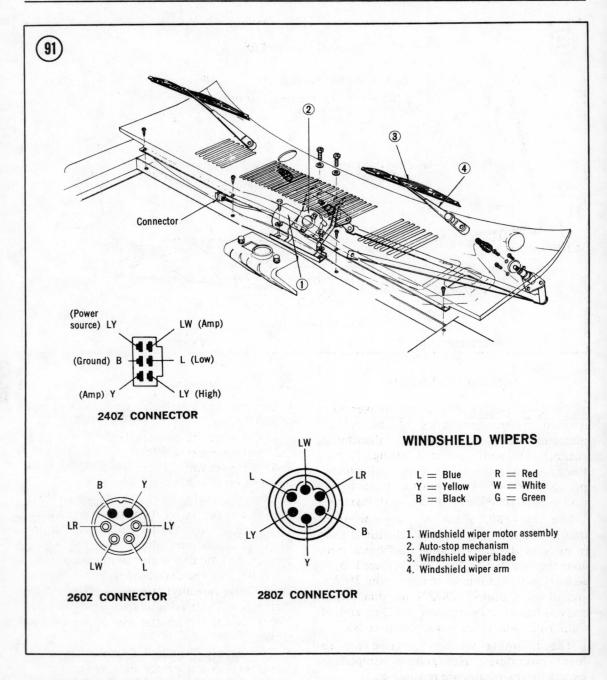

91

Connector

(Power source) LY — LW (Amp)

(Ground) B — L (Low)

(Amp) Y — LY (High)

240Z CONNECTOR

260Z CONNECTOR

B   Y

LR — LY

LW   L

280Z CONNECTOR

LW

L — LR

LY — B

Y

WINDSHIELD WIPERS

L = Blue   R = Red
Y = Yellow W = White
B = Black   G = Green

1. Windshield wiper motor assembly
2. Auto-stop mechanism
3. Windshield wiper blade
4. Windshield wiper arm

5. Installation is the reverse of these steps. Install the passenger side wiper arm so the blade is 5/16 in. (8 mm) from the base of the windshield at the bottom of its stroke. See **Figure 92**. Install the driver's side wiper arm so the blade is betweeen 19/32 and 1 7/8 in. (15-48 mm) from the left-hand edge of the windshield at the top of stroke. At rest, both blades should be lightly contacting the upper edge of the windshield weatherstripping.

Washer Motor Replacement

Refer to **Figure 93**. To replace the motor, simply disconnect its wires and detach the motor from the tank. Installation is the reverse of removal.

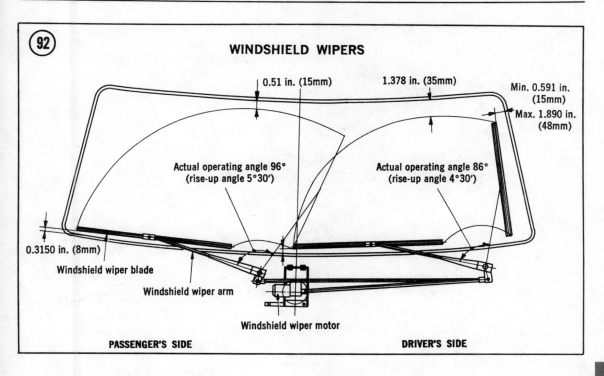

WINDSHIELD WIPERS

0.51 in. (15mm)   1.378 in. (35mm)

Min. 0.591 in. (15mm)
Max. 1.890 in. (48mm)

Actual operating angle 96° (rise-up angle 5°30′)

Actual operating angle 86° (rise-up angle 4°30′)

0.3150 in. (8mm)

Windshield wiper blade

Windshield wiper arm

Windshield wiper motor

PASSENGER'S SIDE   DRIVER'S SIDE

IGNITION SYSTEM

The 240Z uses a conventional breaker point ignition system comprising of the battery, ignition switch, ignition coil, distributor, spark plugs, and associated wiring. Manual transmission cars use one set of breaker points; 1971-1973 automatic transmission cars use two sets. **Figure 94** shows the systems.

The 260-280Z uses a pulse-controlled transistor ignition system. A reluctor is used in place of the conventional distributor cam, and the breaker points are replaced by a pickup coil. Automatic transmission 260Z's, and all non-California 280Z's, use dual pickup coils. Manual transmission 260Z's, and all California 280Z's, use single pickup coils.

The following sections describe replacement procedures. No ignition components except the distributor are repairable.

Although the distributor is repairable, very expensive test fixtures are required to set up the internal advance mechanisms. These mechanisms are vital to proper engine operation. Distributor overhaul should be left to a Datsun dealer or competent ignition specialist.

Distributor Removal

1. Remove the distributor cap clips and take off the cap.
2. Disconnect the primary lead wire(s) from the distributor terminal(s).
3. Disconnect the vacuum advance line from the vacuum advance unit.
4. Turn the engine over until No. 1 piston is at top dead center on its compression stroke. This occurs when the 0° timing mark at the front of the engine aligns with the timing pointer, and the distributor rotor points to No. 1 terminal in the distributor cap. Be sure to check rotor position as well as the timing marks, because the 0° mark also lines up when No. 1 cylinder is at the top of its exhaust stroke.
5. To simplify installation, make alignment marks on distributor body and engine.
6. Remove 2 distributor body setscrews. Lift the distributor out of the engine.

Distributor Installation

1. If the engine was turned over after distributor removal, place No. 1 piston at the top of its compression stroke. See *Removal*, Step 4.

7

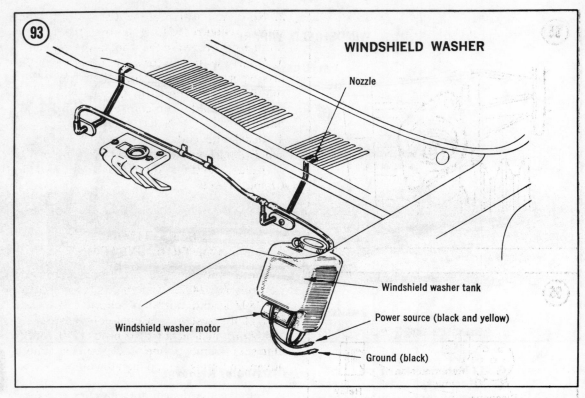

93

WINDSHIELD WASHER

Nozzle

Windshield washer tank

Power source (black and yellow)

Windshield washer motor

Ground (black)

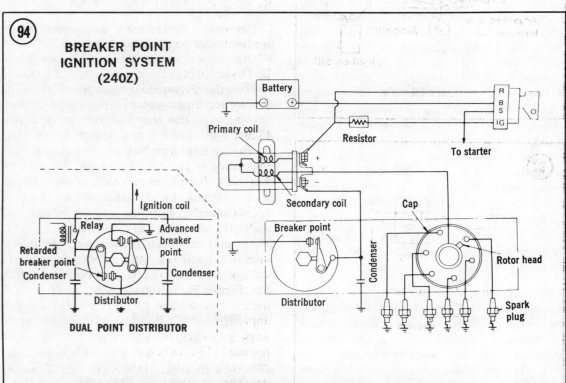

94

**BREAKER POINT
IGNITION SYSTEM
(240Z)**

Battery

Primary coil

Resistor

To starter

Secondary coil

Ignition coil

Relay

Advanced breaker point

Retarded breaker point

Condenser

Condenser

Distributor

DUAL POINT DISTRIBUTOR

Breaker point

Condenser

Distributor

Cap

Rotor head

Spark plug

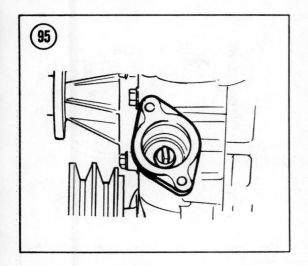

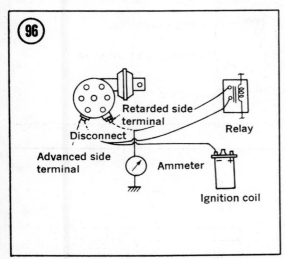

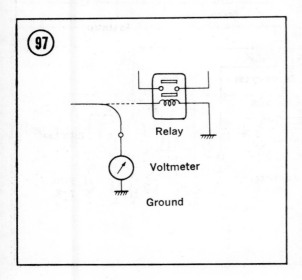

2. Note the position of the distributor driving spindle (**Figure 95**). Note that the spindle tooth is offset toward the front of the engine.

3. Insert the distributor so it engages with the driving spindle. Make sure the rotor points toward No. 1 terminal in the distributor cap. Align the marks on engine and distributor body.

4. Install the body setscrews and distributor cap. Connect primary lead(s) to distributor.

5. Adjust ignition timing as described in Chapter Three.

SPARK TIMING CONTROL SYSTEMS

These systems are used on automatic transmission 240Z's and 260Z's, as well as on all 280Z's sold outside California. The key part of the system is a dual-point distributor (240Z) or dual-pickup distributor (260-280Z). One set of points or one pickup coil has a more advanced timing setting than the other.

System Test (240Z)

Perform this test at a passenger compartment temperature above 52° F (11° C).

1. Disconnect the lead wires from the advanced and retarded terminals.

2. Connect an ammeter between the lead wire for the retarded terminal and ground. See **Figure 96**.

3. Turn the ignition key on, but do not start the engine.

4. Check that the temperature sensing switch is on. Check for an ammeter reading of approximately 3 amps.

5. If the ammeter indicates zero, check for loose relay terminals. If these are satisfactory, disconnect the relay lead wires and measure voltage between the terminals and ground. See **Figure 97**. If voltage is zero, the relay is defective and must be replaced. If voltage is approximately 12 volts, the temperature sensing switch is defective and must be replaced. The switch is mounted on the relay bracket on the right-hand side of the passenger footwell. See **Figure 98**.

Spark Timing Control System Testing (260Z)

1. Drain coolant below the level of the water temperature switch (**Figure 99**). Disconnect the switch wires, then unscrew the switch.
2. Connect an ohmmeter to the switch wires. Immerse the switch in water with a thermometer. See **Figure 100**.
3. With water temperature below 77° F, (25° C), the ohmmeter should show no continuity. The switch should come on (ohmmeter should show continuity) at a temperature between 88° F and 106° F (31-41° C). The switch should stay on above 106° F.

If the switch does not respond properly in Step 3, it must be replaced.

System Test (280Z)

1. Drain coolant below the temperature switch (**Figure 101**). Disconnect the switch wires and unscrew the switch.
2. Connect an ohmmeter to the switch wires (**Figure 102**). Immerse the switch in cool water with a thermometer as shown.
3. Warm the water and watch the ohmmeter. It should indicate zero at temperatures below 135° F (57° C).
4. Continue heating the water. The ohmmeter reading should change to infinity somewhere between 135-145° F (57-63° C). It should stay at infinity above 145° F (63° C).
5. If the switch fails either part of this test, replace it.

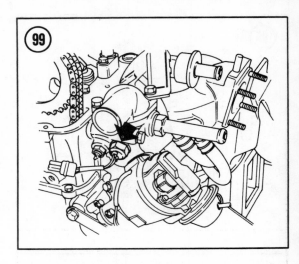

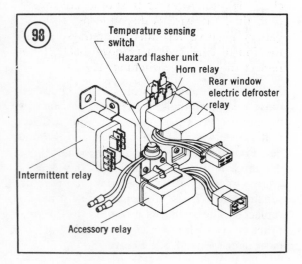

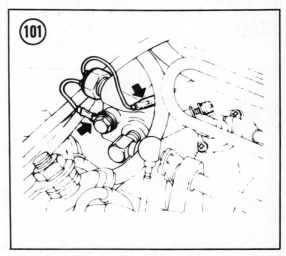

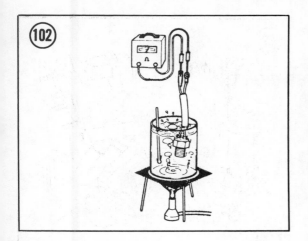

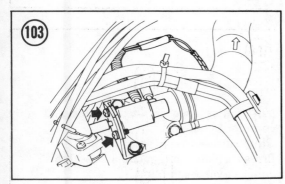

TRANSMISSION CONTROLLED VACUUM ADVANCE

This system is used on manual transmission 280Z's sold outside California. The system cuts off distributor vacuum advance in all gear positions except fourth. A vacuum switching valve, mounted in the distributor vacuum line, opens to atmosphere to cut off vacuum, or closes, permitting vacuum to advance ignition timing. The vacuum switching valve is controlled by a fourth gear switch, mounted on the right side of the transmission.

System Test

1. Make sure the vacuum switching valve hoses and wires are in good condition and properly connected. See **Figure 103**. Inspect the fourth gear switch wires (**Figure 104**).
2. Connect a timing light.
3. Run the engine at 3,200-3,500 rpm and note ignition timing.
4. Have an assistant move the shift lever through the gears. Timing with the car in fourth gear should be about 5° more advanced than in any of the other gears.
5. If the timing fails to advance, perform Steps 6 and 7.
6. Disconnect the white wire from the vacuum switching valve (**Figure 103**). Connect the valve end of the wire to the battery positive terminal.
7. Run the engine at 3,200-3,500 rpm and check ignition timing. It should advance 5° each time the wire is disconnected from the battery positive terminal. If it does, replace the fourth gear switch (**Figure 104**). If not, replace the vacuum switching valve.

7

CHAPTER EIGHT

CLUTCH

The Z uses a single dry-plate clutch with diaphragm spring. See **Figure 1**. Major components are the pressure plate, disc, release mechanism, and hydraulic linkage.

The pressure plate assembly consists of clutch cover, pressure plate, diaphragm spring, and wire rings.

The disc has friction material riveted to both sides. Coil springs are arranged in a link in the center of the disc to absorb shock and provide smooth clutch engagement. Engagement and disengagement are controlled by a release mechanism consisting of bearing, sleeve, and withdrawal lever. The release mechanism is in turn controlled by the hydraulic linkage, which transmits pedal pressure through the clutch master cylinder, hydraulic line, and operating cylinder. The operating cylinder pushrod moves the withdrawal lever.

This chapter includes service procedures for the clutch pedal, hydraulic linkage, release mechanism, pressure plate, and disc. Tightening torques are given in **Table 1** at end of chapter.

Clutch Part Names

Many clutch parts have two or more names. To prevent confusion, the following list gives part names used in this chapter and some common synonyms.

Clutch disc—driven plate
Pressure plate—pressure plate assembly, clutch cover assembly
Release bearing—throw-out bearing
Withdrawal lever—release lever, throw-out arm
Operating cylinder—slave cylinder

CLUTCH PEDAL

Adjustment

1. On early Z's without pedal stoppers, loosen the pushrod locknut (1, **Figure 2**). Rotate the pushrod to change its length, raising or lowering the pedal. Correct pedal pad height is 8 +/- 0.197 in. (202 +/- 5 mm). Tighten the locknut after adjusting.

2. On later Z's, back off the pedal stopper (3, **Figure 2**) until it is clear of the pedal. Loosen the locknut on the master cylinder pushrod. Rotate the pushrod to set pedal height at 8.9 in. (226 mm), then tighten the locknut. Turn the pedal stopper down, lowering pedal height to 8.78 in. (223 mm). Tighten the pedal stopper locknut. Pedal free-play should now be 0.04-0.20 in. (1.5 mm). If not, adjust by turning the master cylinder pushrod.

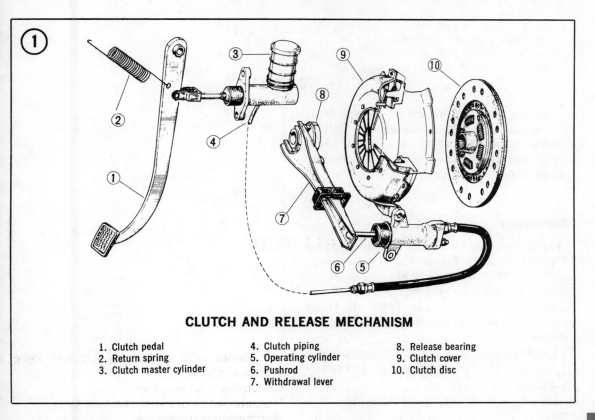

CLUTCH AND RELEASE MECHANISM

1. Clutch pedal
2. Return spring
3. Clutch master cylinder

4. Clutch piping
5. Operating cylinder
6. Pushrod
7. Withdrawal lever

8. Release bearing
9. Clutch cover
10. Clutch disc

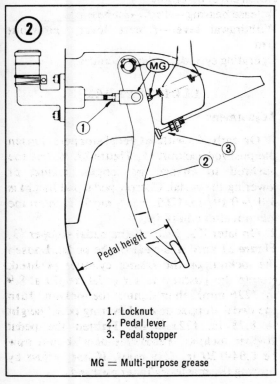

1. Locknut
2. Pedal lever
3. Pedal stopper

MG = Multi-purpose grease

Removal/Installation

Refer to **Figure 3**.
1. Before removing, measure pedal pad height from the floorboard.
2. Unhook the pedal return or assist spring.
3. Remove the clevis pin from the master cylinder pushrod. Separate the pushrod from the pedal.
4. Remove the pivot pin from the top of the pedal. Take the pivot pin out.
5. Installation is the reverse of these steps. Apply multipurpose grease to the friction points shown in **Figure 2**. Adjust pedal height as described earlier in this chapter.

CLUTCH MASTER CYLINDER

1. Remove the clevis pin securing the master cylinder pushrod to the clutch pedal.
2. With the container handy to catch dripping brake fluid, disconnect the hydraulic line from the master cylinder.

8

CAUTION
Hydraulic fluid will damage paint. Wipe up any spilled fluid immediately, then wash the area of the spill with soap and water.

3. Remove both master cylinder installation nuts (or bolts) and lift the cylinder out.

4. Install by reversing Steps 1-3. Adjust pedal height and bleed air out of the hydraulic system as described later in this chapter.

Disassembly

Figure 4 shows the master cylinder used on 1970-1975 models. **Figure 5** shows the design used from 1976 on. Overhaul procedures are basically the same for both types.

1. Remove the filler cap from the fluid reservoir. Drain hydraulic fluid from the cylinder.

2. Pull back dust cover and remove snap ring.

3. Take out the stopper, pushrod, and piston assembly.

4. On 1976 and later cars, take out the return spring.

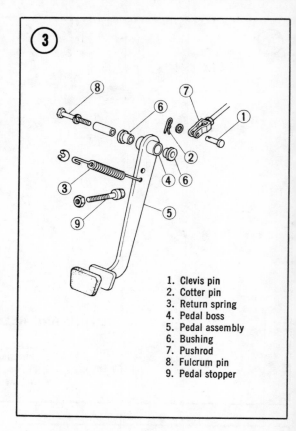

1. Clevis pin
2. Cotter pin
3. Return spring
4. Pedal boss
5. Pedal assembly
6. Bushing
7. Pushrod
8. Fulcrum pin
9. Pedal stopper

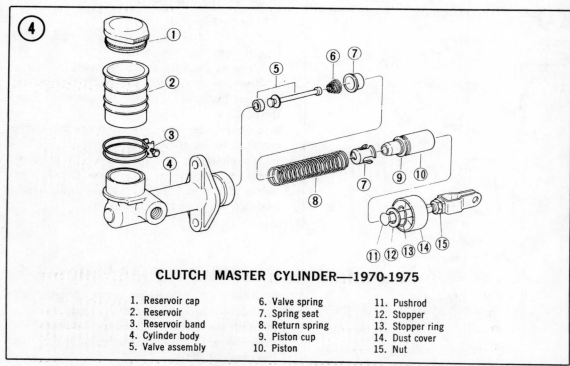

CLUTCH MASTER CYLINDER—1970-1975

1. Reservoir cap	6. Valve spring	11. Pushrod
2. Reservoir	7. Spring seat	12. Stopper
3. Reservoir band	8. Return spring	13. Stopper ring
4. Cylinder body	9. Piston cup	14. Dust cover
5. Valve assembly	10. Piston	15. Nut

NOTE

Do not remove the brake fluid reservoir unless absolutely necessary.

Inspection

1. Thoroughly clean all parts in brake fluid before inspection.
2. Check the piston for excessive or uneven wear, scoring, cracks, or corrosion. Replace the piston if any of these defects are found.
3. Check the cylinder bore for wear, cracks, scoring, or corrosion. Replace the cylinder if defects are visible.
4. As a final check on a suspect cylinder and piston, measure the outside diameter of the piston and the inside diameter of the cylinder. If the difference between these 2 figures exceeds 0.006 in. (0.15 mm), replace the master cylinder.

5. Inspect the dust cover for wear, cracks, or signs of deterioration. Replace if these are detected. Check the fluid reservoir, filler cap, and hydraulic line for wear or damage. Replace as needed.

NOTE

Replace piston cup whenever master cylinder is disassembled.

Assembly

1. Coat the cylinder bore with hydraulic fluid.
2. Install the piston return spring assembly.
3. Soak the piston cup with hydraulic fluid, then install it on the piston. The lip of the cup faces the front of the car when the cylinder is installed.
4. Coat the piston with hydraulic fluid and insert it in the cylinder. Be careful not to bend back the lip of the piston cup.

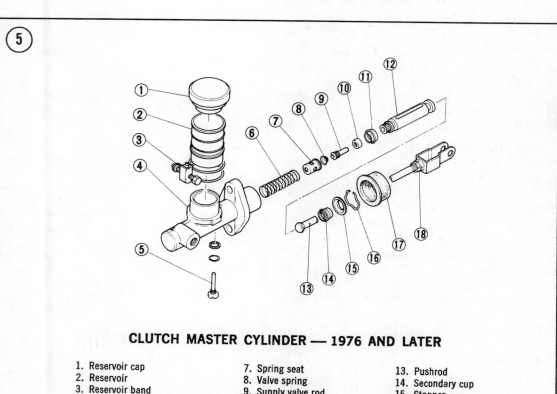

CLUTCH MASTER CYLINDER — 1976 AND LATER

1. Reservoir cap	7. Spring seat	13. Pushrod
2. Reservoir	8. Valve spring	14. Secondary cup
3. Reservoir band	9. Supply valve rod	15. Stopper
4. Cylinder body	10. Supply valve	16. Stopper ring
5. Supply valve stopper	11. Primary cup	17. Dust cover
6. Return spring	12. Piston	18. Locknut

5. Remove the dust cover on the pushrod. Insert the pushrod and stopper in the cylinder. Install the snap ring and push the lip of the dust cover over the cylinder.

CLUTCH OPERATING CYLINDER

Early cars use an adjustable operating cylinder, identified by its external return spring. Later cars use a non-adjustable cylinder with internal return spring.

Removal/Installation

1. On early models, unhook and remove the return spring (1, **Figure 6**). Loosen the pushrod locknut and detach the pushrod from the withdrawal lever.
2. With a container handy to catch dripping hydraulic fluid, disconnect the hydraulic line from the cylinder.
3. Remove 2 cylinder installation bolts and take the cylinder out.
4. Install by reversing Steps 1-3. Bleed the hydraulic system as described later in this chapter. On early cars, adjust withdrawal lever play as described later.

Disassembly and Inspection

Refer to **Figure 7** (early cars) or **Figure 8** (later cars).
1. Remove the dust cover.
2. Remove the snap ring, then take out the piston and cup. Discard the cup.
3. Remove internal return spring (later cars).
4. Clean all parts thoroughly in brake fluid.
5. Inspect the piston for excessive or uneven wear, scoring, cracks, or corrosion. Replace the piston if these conditions are found.
6. Inspect the cylinder bore for the defects described in Step 5. Replace the entire cylinder if any of these are found.

Assembly

Assembly is the reverse of the disassembly procedure, plus the following:
1. Soak the piston cup in brake fluid before installation. Make sure the lip of the cup faces into the cylinder when installing.
2. Coat the cylinder bore and piston with brake fluid before installing the piston.

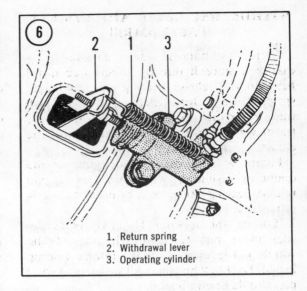

1. Return spring
2. Withdrawal lever
3. Operating cylinder

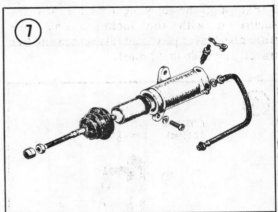

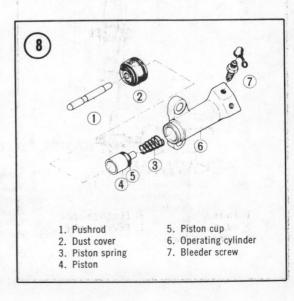

1. Pushrod
2. Dust cover
3. Piston spring
4. Piston
5. Piston cup
6. Operating cylinder
7. Bleeder screw

WITHDRAWAL LEVER ADJUSTMENT (EARLY CARS)

Correct withdrawal lever adjustment is essential, since it directly affects free travel between the release bearing and diaphragm spring fingers. Insufficient free travel will cause the clutch to slip, while excessive free travel will prevent full disengagement of the clutch.

Figure 9 is a cutaway side view of the operating cylinder, withdrawal lever, and release bearing. Refer to it as needed for this procedure.

1. Loosen the locknut (1) and rotate the adjustment nut (2) until the top of the withdrawal lever contacts the release bearing inside the clutch housing. All withdrawal lever play should be eliminated.

2. Back it off the adjusting nut 1 1/2 turns and secure it with the locknut. This sets withdrawal lever play (and release bearing free travel) at 0.0786 in. (2 mm).

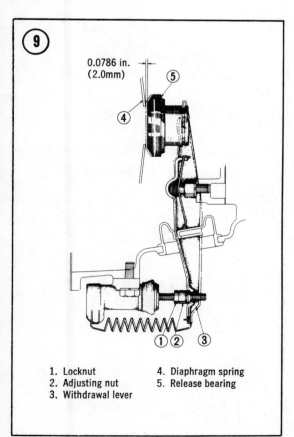

0.0786 in.
(2.0mm)

1. Locknut
2. Adjusting nut
3. Withdrawal lever
4. Diaphragm spring
5. Release bearing

BLEEDING THE CLUTCH

Bleeding air out of the clutch hydraulic system is necessary whenever air enters the system. This occurs when the hydraulic line is disconnected at either end. It can also result from a very low fluid level in the clutch master cylinder or from defective master or operating cylinders. Air in the system can make shifting gears extremely difficult.

NOTE
This procedure requires two people, one to operate the clutch pedal and the other to open and close the bleed valve.

1. Remove the bleed valve dust cap from the operating cylinder. Thoroughly clean the area around the bleed valve.

2. Attach a plastic tube to the bleed valve. Place the other end of the tube in a clear glass jar containing several inches of clean brake fluid.

NOTE
Do not allow the end of the tube to come out of the brake fluid during bleeding. If this happens, air may be sucked into the system, and the procedure will have to be repeated.

3. Top up the master cylinder reservoir with fluid.

4. Open the bleed valve approximately 3/4 turn.

5. Have an assistant depress the clutch pedal quickly. Close the bleed valve while the pedal is down. Let the pedal return slowly.

NOTE
Do not let the pedal up while the bleed valve is open.

6. Repeat Step 5 until the fluid entering the jar is free of air bubbles.

7. Depress the pedal and close the bleed valve. Remove tube and put dust cap on the valve.

CLUTCH REMOVAL

The engine and clutch housing must be separated to remove the clutch. This can be done either by removing the engine and

8

transmission and separating them (Chapter Four) or by removing only the transmission (Chapter Nine). The release mechanism is incorporated in the clutch housing (front of the transmission).

Once the engine and transmission have been separated, perform the following.

1. Mark the edges of the pressure plate and flywheel with a sharp punch so they may be reassembled in the same relative positions.

2. Remove the clutch cover bolts gradually in a diagonal pattern to prevent warping the pressure plate.

CLUTCH INSPECTION

Clutch Disc

Check the clutch disc for the following:

a. Oil or grease on the facings

b. Glazed facings

c. Warped facings

d. Loose or missing rivets

e. Facings worn to within 0.012 in. (0.3 mm) of the rivets. Measure facing depth with a vernier caliper as shown in **Figure 10**.

f. Broken springs

Small amounts of oil or grease may be cleaned from the disc with non-petroleum solvent, and the facings dressed with a wire brush. However, if the facings are soaked with

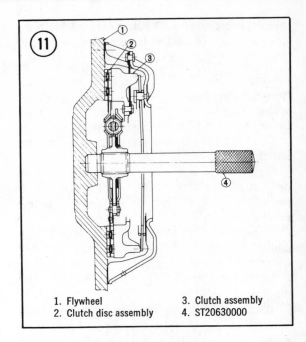

(11)

1. Flywheel	3. Clutch assembly
2. Clutch disc assembly	4. ST20630000

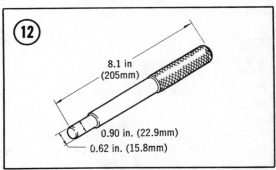

(12)

8.1 in (205mm)

0.90 in. (22.9mm)

0.62 in. (15.8mm)

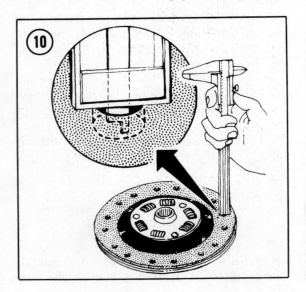

(10)

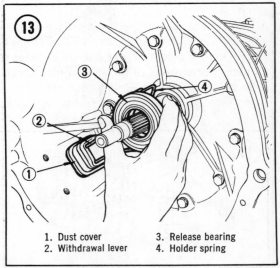

(13)

1. Dust cover	3. Release bearing
2. Withdrawal lever	4. Holder spring

oil or grease, or if any of the other defects are present, the disc must be replaced. It should also be replaced if the facings are worn and a new pressure plate is being installed.

Pressure Plate

Check the pressure plate for:
a. Scoring
b. Burn marks (blue-tinted areas)
c. Cracks
d. Broken or collapsed diaphragm spring

Replace the pressure plate if these are evident. If the clutch trouble still is not apparent, take the pressure plate and disc to a competent garage and have the disc checked for deflection, and the pressure plate checked for proper diaphragm spring height and runout. Do not attempt to readjust the fingers without proper tools and experience.

CLUTCH INSTALLATION

1. Be sure your hands are clean.
2. Inspect the disc facings, pressure plate, and flywheel to be sure they are free of oil, grease, or other foreign material.
3. Clean the clutch pilot bushing. On 240Z's, fill the bushing with multipurpose lithium grease. Later bushings do not require lubrication.
4. Place the clutch disc and pressure plate in position on the flywheel. The long side of the disc hub faces the rear of the car. Line up the punched alignment marks made during removal.
5. Center the disc and pressure plate with an aligning bar such as Datsun ST 20630000 (Kent-Moore J-26366). See **Figure 11**. **Figure 12** gives dimensions of the special tool in case it is not available. Aligning bars are sold at many foreign car parts stores. Some stores and

rental dealers also rent universal aligning bars. An old transmission input shaft also makes an excellent aligning bar.
6. Install the clutch cover bolts, tightening gradually in a diagonal pattern. Tighten to 12-15 ft.-lb. (1.6-2.1 mkg).

RELEASE MECHANISM

Removal

As with the clutch, release mechanism removal requires that the engine and transmission be separated first. The release mechanism is incorporated in the clutch housing, which is in turn attached to the front of the transmission. Either remove the engine and transmission as a unit and separate them (Chapter Four) or remove only the transmission (Chapter Nine).

Disassembly

1. Referring to **Figure 13**, remove the dust cover from the clutch housing.
2. On early cars, unhook the operating cylinder return spring from the withdrawal lever.
3. Remove the holder spring from the bearing sleeve. Separate withdrawal lever from sleeve.
4. Remove the release bearing and sleeve from the transmission input shaft. Remove the withdrawal lever from its ball pin.
5. Remove the release bearing from its sleeve with a puller (**Figure 14**). The bearing is a press fit on the sleeve.

Inspection

Check release mechanism for the following.
1. Wear at the contact point of the withdrawal lever and release bearing sleeve. Replace the sleeve if worn.
2. Grease leaking from the release bearing. Replace the bearing if this is evident.

> *CAUTION*
> *Do not clean the release bearing in solvent, since it is prelubricated at the factory. Clean with a lint-free cloth.*

3. A worn release bearing. To check, hold the inner race with fingers and rotate the outer

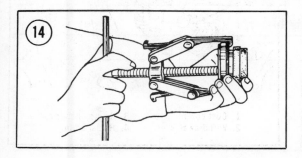

8

race while applying light pressure to it. If the bearing feels rough or makes noise, replace it.

Assembly

1. Press the release bearing onto the sleeve (**Figure 15**). When it is in place, rotate it to make sure it operates smoothly.

> *NOTE*
> *The press load must bear against the inner race only. If you don't have the equipment, take the job to a machine shop.*

2. Referring to **Figure 16**, apply a light coat of molybdenum disulfide grease to the following:

a. Withdrawal lever pivot point
b. Withdrawal lever tabs on the release bearing sleeve
c. Withdrawal lever fulcrum pin
d. Release bearing sliding surface on the transmission front cover

3. Fill the groove inside the bearing sleeve with molybdenum disulfide grease. See **Figure 17**.

4. Place the withdrawal lever in position over the transmission input shaft, with the operating cylinder end through the hole in the clutch housing.

5. Place the release bearing, together with its sleeve, in position on transmission input shaft.

6. Install the holder spring.

7. .Put dust cover back in clutch housing.

8. Attach the return spring to the end of the withdrawal lever (early cars).

9. Install the transmission, together with clutch housing, as described in Chapter Nine.

10. Bleed air from the clutch hydraulic system as described earlier in this chapter.

11. Check and adjust withdrawal lever and clutch pedal play as described earlier.

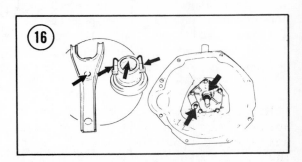

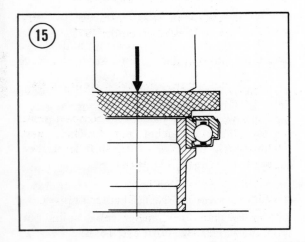

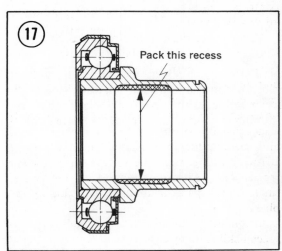

Pack this recess

Table 1   TIGHTENING TORQUES

	Ft.-lb.	Mkg
Clutch cover bolts	12-15	1.6-2.1
Master cylinder bolts/nuts	6-8	0.8-1.1
Operating cylinder bolts	18-22	2.5-3.0
Metal clutch line	11-13	1.5-1.8
Rubber clutch hose	12-15	1.6-2.1

CHAPTER NINE

TRANSMISSION

This chapter provides removal, overhaul, and installation procedures for the four-speed and five-speed manual transmissions used on the Z. It also includes testing and removal/installation procedures for the automatic transmission.

Manual transmission overhaul is not the best starting point for a beginning mechanic. However, it doesn't require special training, and the special tools shown in this chapter can easily be duplicated. Overhaul does require patience and the ability to concentrate. The work area must be very clean, free of distractions, and inaccessible to pets and small children. Before starting, read the procedure carefully. Obtain the necessary special tools or substitutes. Check parts availability with local suppliers.

Automatic transmission overhaul requires special skills, many expensive special tools, and extreme cleanliness. For these reasons, overhaul should be left to a Datsun dealer or other competent professional.

A few special tools are used in this chapter. All are available through your dealer. A few are manufactured by Kent-Moore Tool Division, 29784 Little Mack, Roseville, Michigan, 48066 and may be ordered direct from them.

The testing and adjustment procedures in this chapter will help you locate and solve many automatic transmission problems. The removal and installation procedures will help you reduce labor costs if major overhaul is necessary.

TRANSMISSION (F4W71A)

This transmission was installed in cars manufactured through September 1972.

Removal/Installation

1. Disconnect the negative cable from the battery.

2. Working in the passenger compartment, remove the self-locking nut, washer, and bushing from the base of the shift lever. See **Figure 1**. Lift the shift lever out.

3. Drain the transmission oil.

4. Remove the drive shaft (Chapter Twelve).

5. Unscrew the speedometer cable union nut from the transmission rear extension.

6. Remove the exhaust system (Chapter Five).

7. Remove the clutch operating cylinder (Chapter Eight).

8. Disconnect the electrical wires from the side of the transmission.

9. Remove the starter motor (Chapter Seven).

10. Place a jack beneath the transmission.

11. Remove the nut attaching the rear mount-

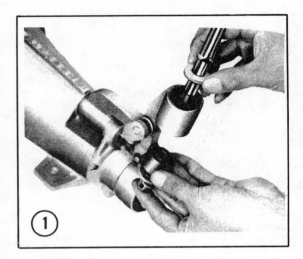

1. Rear engine mounting nut
2. Rear mounting member installation bolt

ing member to the transmission. Then remove 2 bolts attaching the mounting member to the car. See **Figure 2**.

12. Place a jack beneath the engine to support it. Use a block of wood between jack and oil pan so the pan won't collapse.

13. Unbolt the clutch housing from the engine (**Figure 3**).

14. Lower the jack beneath the transmission and move it rearward until the transmission separates from the engine. Take the transmission out from under the car.

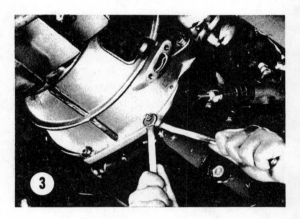

CAUTION
To prevent damage to the transmission's input shaft splines, never remove the transmission partway. Make sure the input shaft separates completely from the engine when removing the transmission.

15. Install in the reverse order. Tighten the transmission-to-engine bolts to 20-27 ft.-lb. (2.7-3.7 mkg). Fill the transmission with an oil recommended in Chapter Three. Capacity is 3-1/8 pt. (1.5 liters).

Disassembly

1. Thoroughly clean the outside of the transmission before disassembly.

2. Remove the dust cover from the clutch housing. Remove the release mechanism (Chapter Eight). **Figure 4** shows the dust cover and release mechanism.

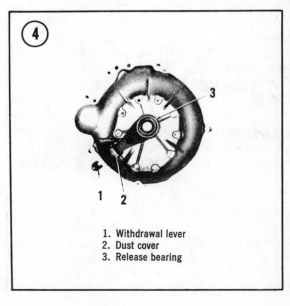

1. Withdrawal lever
2. Dust cover
3. Release bearing

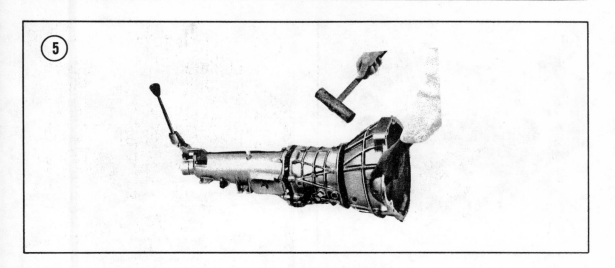

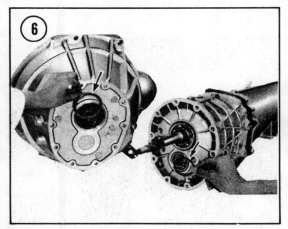

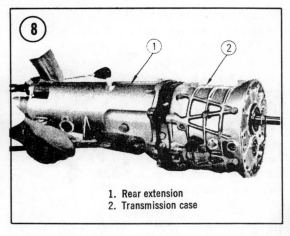

1. Rear extension
2. Transmission case

9

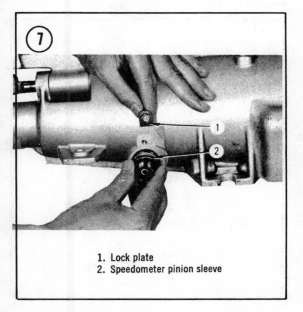

1. Lock plate
2. Speedometer pinion sleeve

3. Remove the back-up lamp switch from the right-hand side of the transmission case.

4. Remove the bolts attaching the clutch housing to the transmission case. Separate the clutch housing and transmission case by tapping with a wooden mallet (**Figure 5**). Remove the gasket between clutch housing and transmission case.

5. Remove the input shaft bearing spacer and countershaft bearing shim (**Figure 6**).

6. Remove the bolt from the speedometer pinion lock plate, then remove the speedometer pinion sleeve. See **Figure 7**.

7. Remove the pin attaching the shift lever bracket to the striking rod.

8. Remove the bolts attaching the rear extension to the transmission case. Separate the rear extension and transmission case by tapping with a wooden mallet (**Figure 8**).

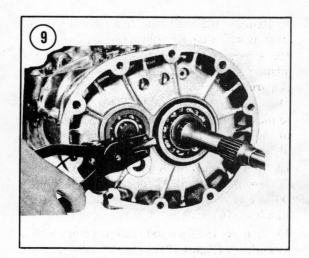

⑨

⑫

ST23500000

ST23810000

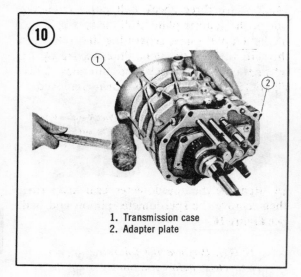

⑩

①
②

1. Transmission case
2. Adapter plate

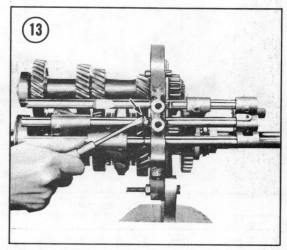

⑬

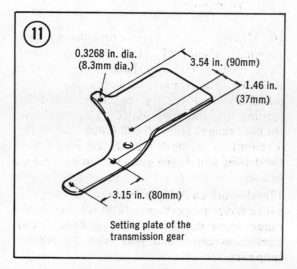

⑪

0.3268 in. dia.
(8.3mm dia.)

3.54 in. (90mm)

1.46 in.
(37mm)

3.15 in. (80mm)

Setting plate of the
transmission gear

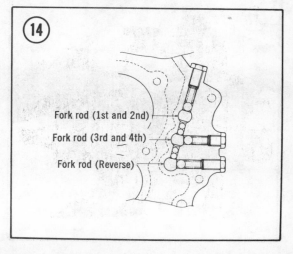

⑭

Fork rod (1st and 2nd)

Fork rod (3rd and 4th)

Fork rod (Reverse)

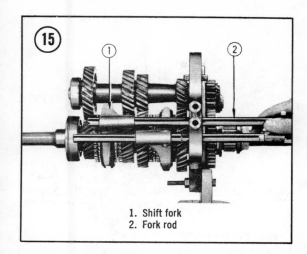

1. Shift fork
2. Fork rod

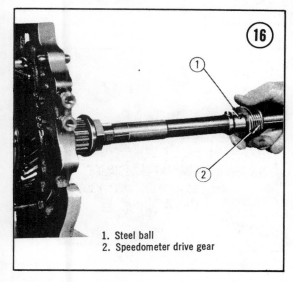

1. Steel ball
2. Speedometer drive gear

9. Remove the snap ring from the mainshaft bearing with snap ring pliers (**Figure 9**).

10. Separate the transmission case from the adapter plate by tapping with a wooden mallet (**Figure 10**).

11. Attach a support tool such as ST 23810000 to the adapter plate. **Figure 11** gives dimensions of the tool, which can be made from one-inch plywood.

12. Remove the retaining pins from reverse, first-second, and third-fourth gear fork rods (**Figure 12**). Use Datsun tool ST 23500000 or a standard pin punch.

13. Remove the fork rod retaining rings with a screwdriver (**Figure 13**).

14. Remove three check ball plugs from the side of the adapter plate. Pull the fork rods out of the adapter plate, separating the rods from the shift forks at the same time. **Figure 14** is a schematic of the check and interlock balls. **Figure 15** shows the fork rods being removed.

> NOTE: *Do not lose any check or interlock balls. Do not let the shifting forks fall when the shift rods are removed.*

15. Remove the speedometer gear snap ring, then remove the speedometer pinion and ball. See **Figure 16**.

> NOTE: *Perform the following inspection steps before continuing with the disassembly.*

16. Measure gear backlash with a dial gauge as shown in **Figure 17**. Hold the countershaft from turning with one hand and turn each mainshaft gear against the dial gauge as far as possible without turning the countershaft. The reading on the dial gauge (gear backlash) should range from 0.002-0.006 in. (0.05-0.15mm). If backlash exceeds this range, both the driving and driven gears should be replaced as a set.

17. Measure end play of the reverse idler gear with a feeler gauge (**Figure 18**). End play should range from 0.002-0.014 in. (0.05-0.35mm). Correct excessive end play with an oversize snap ring.

9

REVERSE IDLER GEAR

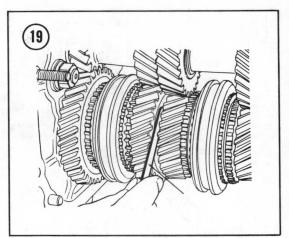

18. Measure end play between individual gears with a feeler gauge (**Figure 19**). End play should range from 0.005-0.008 in. (0.12-0.19mm). Correct excessive end play with an oversize snap ring.

NOTE: *Continue with disassembly as follows:*

19. Unbend the mainshaft lockwasher. Loosen the mainshaft nut (**Figure 20**), then remove the mainshaft lockwasher, thrust washer, reverse hub, and reverse gear.

20. Remove the snap ring from the counter reverse gear, then remove the gear (**Figure 21**).

21. Remove the snap ring from the reverse idler gear (next to the counter reverse gear), then remove the reverse idler gear together with its thrust washer and needle bearing.

22. Tie one end of a piece of wire around the countershaft. Tie the other end to some point above the countershaft so the countershaft will not fall to the ground during the next step.

23. Refer to **Figures 22 and 23** for this step. Tap the rear end of the mainshaft forward (**Figure 22**). This will separate the input (main drive) shaft and mainshaft (**Figure 23**), as well as separating the countershaft from the adapter plate. After the mainshaft and input shaft have been separated, tap the mainshaft the rest of the way out of the adapter plate.

24. Remove the reverse idler shaft setscrew (1, **Figure 24**). Remove the nut, lockwasher, and

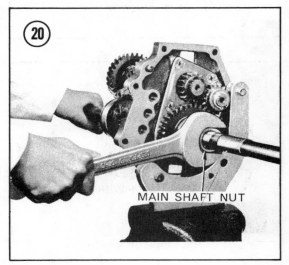

MAIN SHAFT NUT

COUNTER REVERSE GEAR

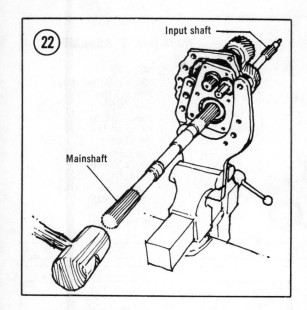

Input shaft

Mainshaft

(22)

(23)

MAIN DRIVE SHAFT

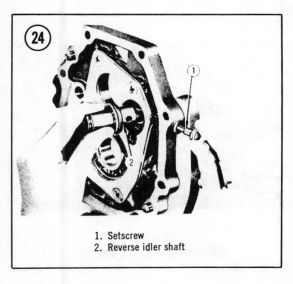

(24)

1. Setscrew
2. Reverse idler shaft

plain washer from the front end of the reverse idler shaft. Then remove the shaft (2, **Figure 24**) from the adapter plate.

> NOTE: *The reverse idler shaft cannot be removed unless the setscrew is removed first.*

25. Remove the six Phillips machine screws that attach the bearing retainer plate to the adapter plate. These screws have been locked in place by hitting the heads with a hammer and punch, so an impact screwdriver will be necessary to remove them.

26. Remove the mainshaft rear bearing from the adapter plate.

27. Referring to **Figure 25**, remove the following parts in order from the front end of the mainshaft: Snap ring, third-fourth gear synchronizer assembly, third gear, and needle bearing.

28. Again referring to **Figure 25**, remove the following parts in order from the rear end of the mainshaft: Thrust washer, steel ball, first gear, needle bearing, first gear bushing, first-second gear synchronizer assembly, second gear, and needle bearing.

29. Referring to **Figure 26**, remove the snap ring and input shaft bearing spacer from the input shaft.

30. Remove the input shaft bearing from the input shaft with a press and a support such as Datsun ST 30030000 (Kent-Moore J-25733). See **Figure 27**. This can be done by an automotive machine shop if you do not have the equipment.

31. Referring to **Figure 28**, remove the snap ring from each end of the countershaft. Remove the bearing from each end of the countershaft with a press and holder as shown in **Figure 29**.

32. Remove the countershaft drive gear and countershaft third gear in the same manner as the bearings. Use a suitable drift with the press. Once the gears are off, remove the Woodruff keys from the countershaft.

33. Remove the snap ring and striking rod pin (**Figure 30**). Remove the control arm pin and separate the control arm from the control lever.

9

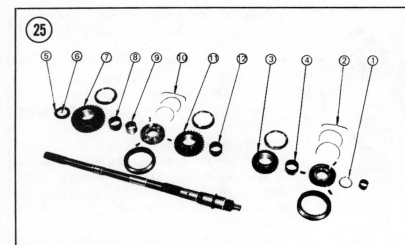

MAINSHAFT ASSEMBLY

1. Snap ring
2. Synchronizer assembly (3rd and 4th)
3. Third gear
4. Needle bearing
5. Thrust washer
6. Steel ball
7. First gear
8. Needle bearing
9. First gear bushing
10. Synchronizer assembly (1st and 2nd)
11. Second gear
12. Needle bearing

Inspection

1. Thoroughly clean all parts in solvent. Remove all traces of old gasket and sealer. Inspect all parts while cleaning and replace any with obvious wear or damage.

2. Check the transmission case and rear extension for cracks. Check all gasket surfaces for gouges or roughness which could cause an oil leak. Replace if these conditions are found.

3. Inspect bearings for wear and damage. Hold the outer race with one hand and rotate the inner race with the other. See **Figure 31**. Listen for noise or roughness. Replace any suspect bearings.

4. Check the bushing and oil seal at the back of the rear extension. Replace the bushing if worn unevenly. Replace the oil seal if the lip is worn or damaged.

5. Inspect the shafts for bending, twisting, or damaged splines. **Figure 32** shows examples of defective splines.

6. Inspect all gears for chipped, broken, or badly worn teeth. Replace any gears with these conditions.

7. Place each balk ring on its gear cone. Measure the gap between the balk ring and the small teeth on the gear. See **Figure 33**. If the gap is smaller than specified, replace the balk ring.

8. Check the clutch housing oil seal for wear or damage. Replace the oil seal if there is any doubt about its condition.

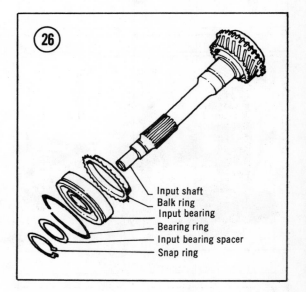

Input shaft
Balk ring
Input bearing
Bearing ring
Input bearing spacer
Snap ring

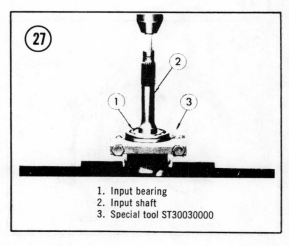

1. Input bearing
2. Input shaft
3. Special tool ST30030000

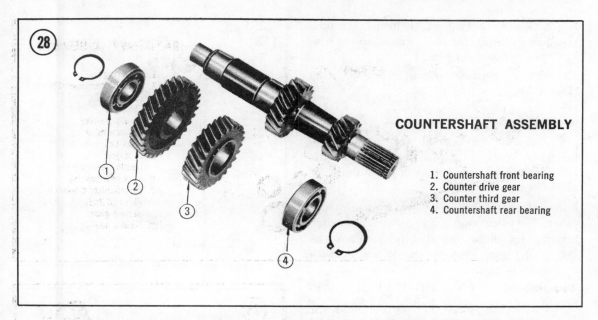

COUNTERSHAFT ASSEMBLY

1. Countershaft front bearing
2. Counter drive gear
3. Counter third gear
4. Countershaft rear bearing

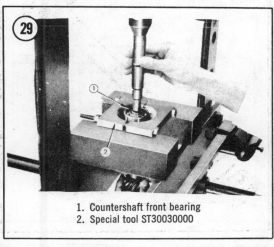

1. Countershaft front bearing
2. Special tool ST30030000

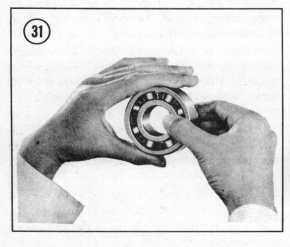

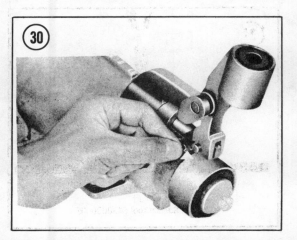

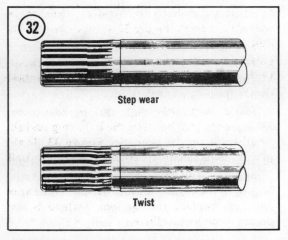

Step wear

Twist

9

9. Check the rubber insulator in the transmission rear mounting member. Replace if the rubber is cracked or deteriorated.

10. Replace speedometer pinion sleeve O-ring (**Figure 34**).

Assembly

Cleanliness is essential for transmission assembly. Work in a dust-free area and handle parts with clean bare hands only. Do not wear gloves or use rags.

1. Install the O-ring in the transmission front cover. The front cover is a press fit in the clutch housing. Install the oil seal in the front cover as shown in **Figure 35**. Coat the oil seal lip with multipurpose grease.

2. Install the rear extension oil seal as shown in **Figure 36**. Use a suitable drift.

3. Clean all gear components in solvent and blow dry with compressed air.

4. Assemble the first-second and third-fourth gear synchronizer mechanisms. Install a spread spring on each side of the synchronizer (**Figure 37**). Make sure the gaps of the front-side spring and rear-side spring are not directly opposite each other.

5. Referring to **Figures 25 and 38**, install the following parts in order from the rear end of the mainshaft: needle bearing, second gear, balk ring, first-second synchronizer, balk ring, first gear bushing, needle bearing, first gear, steel ball, and thrust washer.

> NOTE: *Figure 39 shows the correct installation direction for both synchronizers.*

6. Install the mainshaft rear bearing with a hollow drift such as Datsun ST 23800000 (Kent-Moore J-25691-01). See **Figure 40**. **Figure 41** shows dimensions of the drift.

7. Install the countershaft rear bearing in the adapter plate.

8. Insert the mainshaft through the front side of the adapter plate. Tap the mainshaft far enough into the adapter plate so the snap ring groove in the mainshaft bearing just comes out on the rear side of the adapter plate. See **Figure 42**. Use a Datsun "B" drift ST 30600000

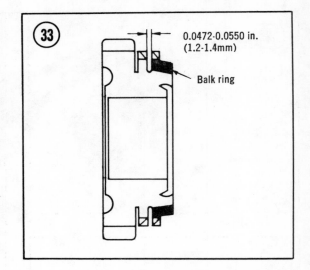

(33) 0.0472-0.0550 in. (1.2-1.4mm)

Balk ring

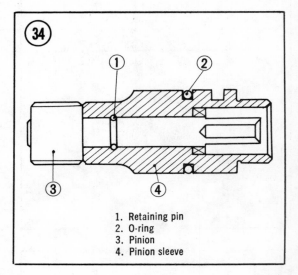

(34)

1. Retaining pin
2. O-ring
3. Pinion
4. Pinion sleeve

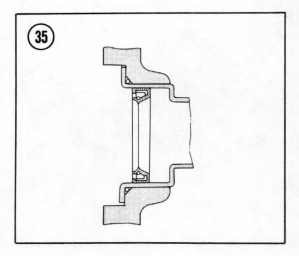

(35)

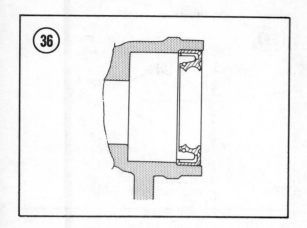

36

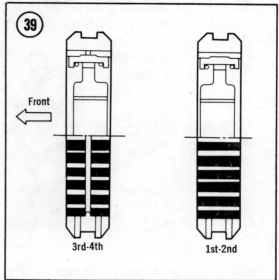

39

Front

3rd-4th   1st-2nd

37

1. Spread spring
2. Shifting insert

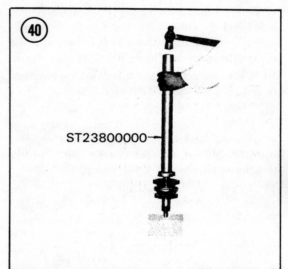

40

ST23800000

9

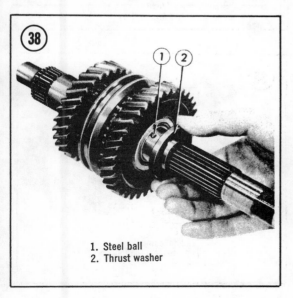

38

1. Steel ball
2. Thrust washer

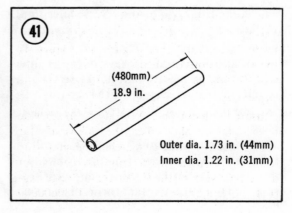

41

(480mm)
18.9 in.

Outer dia. 1.73 in. (44mm)
Inner dia. 1.22 in. (31mm)

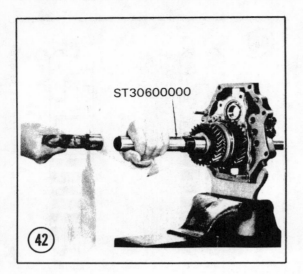

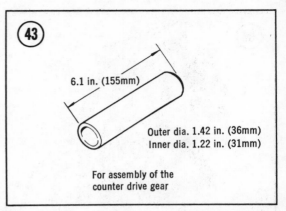

6.1 in. (155mm)

Outer dia. 1.42 in. (36mm)
Inner dia. 1.22 in. (31mm)

For assembly of the
counter drive gear

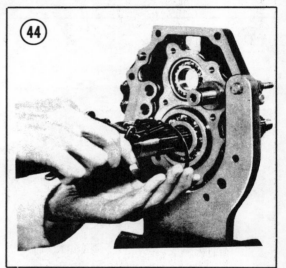

(Kent-Moore J-25863-01) or equivalent. **Figure 43** gives dimensions of the drift.

9. Install the snap ring on the mainshaft rear bearing (**Figure 44**). The snap ring must be tight against the adapter plate. If it is not, tap the mainshaft from the rear side until it is.

10. Place the countershaft bearing ring against the rear side of the countershaft bearing.

11. Install the bearing retainer plate on the adapter plate. Tighten the six machine screws to 9-13 foot-pounds (1.2-1.8 mkg). After tightening, hit each screw head at two points with a punch to lock the screw. See **Figure 45**.

12. Insert the reverse idler shaft into the adapter plate from the rear side (**Figure 46**). Coat the setscrew threads with Loctite. Install the setscrew, make sure it locks the reverse idler shaft in place, then tighten to 9-13 foot-pounds (1.2-1.8 mkg).

13. Install the lockwasher, plain washer, and nut on the front end of the reverse idler shaft. Tighten the nut to 44-58 foot-pounds (6-8 mkg).

14. Install the Woodruff keys in the countershaft. Press the countershaft third gear onto the countershaft and secure it with a snap ring.

15. Install the countershaft in the adapter plate.

16. Referring to **Figures 25 and 47**, install the following parts in order from the front end of the mainshaft: needle bearing, third gear, balk ring, and third-fourth gear synchronizer.

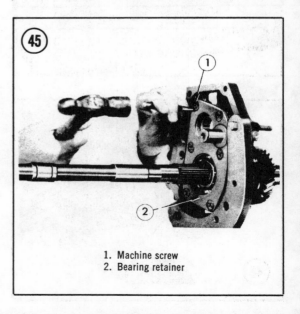

1. Machine screw
2. Bearing retainer

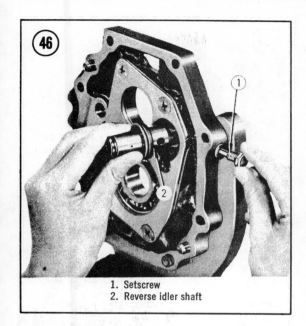

1. Setscrew
2. Reverse idler shaft

SYNCHRONIZER ASSEMBLY
(3RD & 4TH)

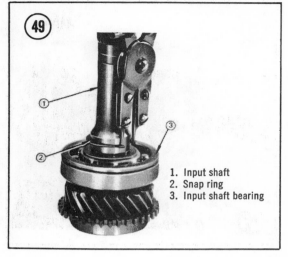

1. Input shaft
2. Snap ring
3. Input shaft bearing

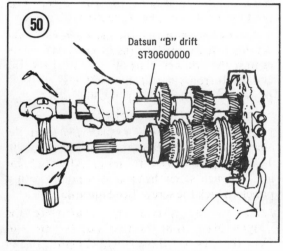

Datsun "B" drift
ST30600000

9

17. Install a snap ring on the front end of the mainshaft (**Figure 48**). Snap rings are available in five thicknesses, ranging from 0.056-0.064 in. (1.425-1.625mm).

18. Press the input shaft bearing onto the input shaft and install a snap ring (**Figure 49**). The groove in the bearing outer race goes toward the front of the shaft. Snap rings are available in five thicknesses, ranging from 0.071-0.082 in. (1.80-2.08mm).

19. Place the needle bearing inside the rear end of the input shaft. Mesh the input shaft gear with the countershaft drive gear, then install them simultaneously on the mainshaft and countershaft. See **Figure 50**. Make sure the key slot in the countershaft drive gear lines up with

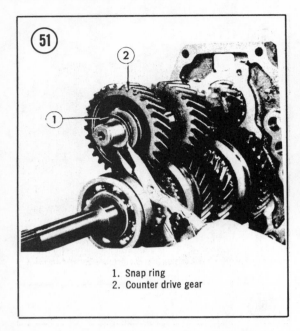

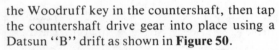

1. Snap ring
2. Counter drive gear

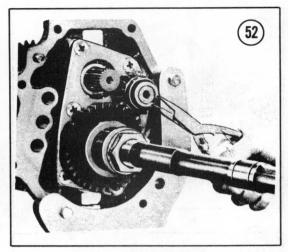

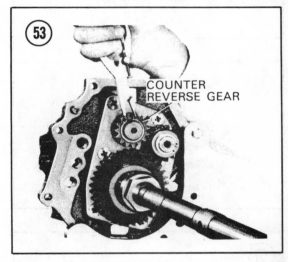

COUNTER
REVERSE GEAR

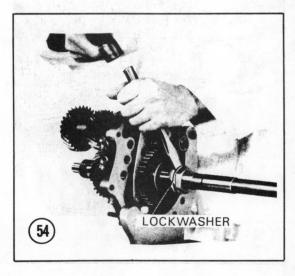

LOCKWASHER

the Woodruff key in the countershaft, then tap the countershaft drive gear into place using a Datsun "B" drift as shown in **Figure 50**.

> CAUTION
> *Have someone hold the rear end of the countershaft to prevent damage to the countershaft bearing.*

20. Once the countershaft drive gear is installed, secure it with a snap ring **(Figure 51)**.

21. Install the following parts in order on the rear end of the mainshaft: reverse hub, reverse gear, thrust washer, lockwasher, and mainshaft nut. Do not tighten the mainshaft nut yet.

22. Coat the reverse idler shaft with gear oil, then install the following from the rear side: needle bearing, reverse idler gear, and thrust washer. Secure with a snap ring as shown in **Figure 52**.

23. Install the counter reverse gear on the rear side of the countershaft and secure with a snap ring **(Figure 53)**. Snap rings are available in five thicknesses, ranging from 0.043-0.059 in (1.1-1.5mm).

24. Intermesh the first-second gear synchronizer with reverse gear. Tighten the mainshaft nut to 130-152 foot-pounds (18-21 mkg). Bend the lockwasher against the mainshaft nut as shown in **Figure 54**.

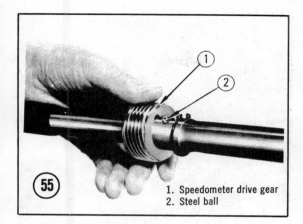

55
1. Speedometer drive gear
2. Steel ball

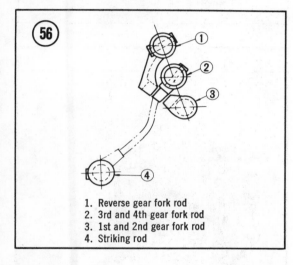

56
1. Reverse gear fork rod
2. 3rd and 4th gear fork rod
3. 1st and 2nd gear fork rod
4. Striking rod

57
1. Check ball plug
2. Check ball spring
3. Check ball

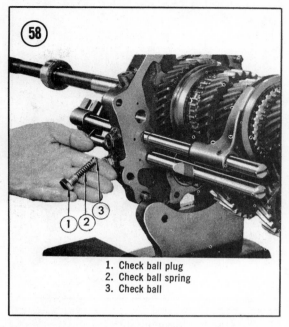

58
1. Check ball plug
2. Check ball spring
3. Check ball

25. Install a snap ring, steel ball, speedometer drive gear, and second snap ring onto the mainshaft. See **Figure 55**. Snap rings are available in five thicknesses, ranging from 0.043-0.059 in. (1.1-1.5mm).

26. Remove the gear assembly from the support tool, turn it over (so the countershaft is on the bottom), and reinstall it in the support tool.

27. Place the reverse shift fork over reverse gear. Insert the reverse gear fork rod through the reverse shift fork and adapter plate. **Figure 56** is an end view of the fork rods.

28. Install the reverse fork rod check ball, spring, and plug in the side of the adapter plate (**Figure 57**). Use Loctite on the plug threads.

29. Tap the retaining pin into the reverse shift fork and fork rod.

30. Drop 2 interlock balls in on top of the reverse check ball (the one installed in Step 28).

31. Referring to **Figure 58**, place the third-fourth gear shift fork in the groove in the third-fourth gear synchronizer. Insert the third-fourth gear shift rod through the shift fork and adapter plate. Install the check ball, spring, and plug as shown in the figure. Use Loctite on the plug threads.

NOTE: *The third-fourth gear check ball plug is shorter than the other two plugs.*

9

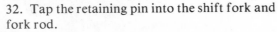

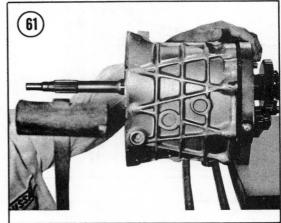

32. Tap the retaining pin into the shift fork and fork rod.

33. Drop 2 interlock balls in on top of the third-fourth gear check ball (the one installed in Step 31).

34. Place the first-second gear shift fork in the groove in the first-second gear synchronizer. Install the first-second gear fork rod through the adapter plate and shift fork. Install the check ball, spring, and plug. Use Loctite on the plug threads.

35. Tighten all 3 check ball plugs to 16-22 foot-pounds (2.2-3.0 mkg).

36. Tap the retaining pin into the first-second gear shift fork and fork rod. See **Figure 59**.

37. Install the retaining ring on each fork rod. See **Figure 60**.

38. Coat all friction points with gear oil. Mesh the synchronizers with each gear and make sure they work smoothly. Make sure the gears mesh smoothly with each other.

39. Install the transmission case on the adapter plate (**Figure 61**). Use a new gasket coated on both sides with gasket sealer.

40. Install the front countershaft bearing in the transmission case as shown in **Figure 62**. Use a Datsun "C" drift ST 22360000 (Kent-Moore J-25679-01) and a hammer as shown. **Figure 63** gives dimensions of the drift.

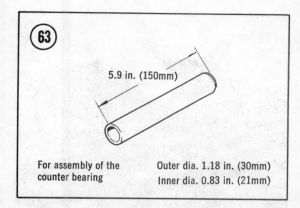

For assembly of the counter bearing

Outer dia. 1.18 in. (30mm)
Inner dia. 0.83 in. (21mm)

5.9 in. (150mm)

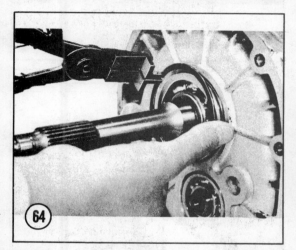

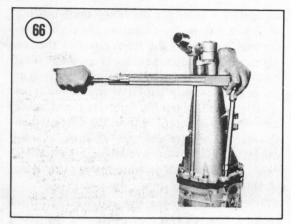

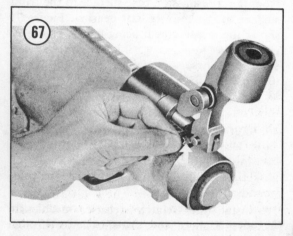

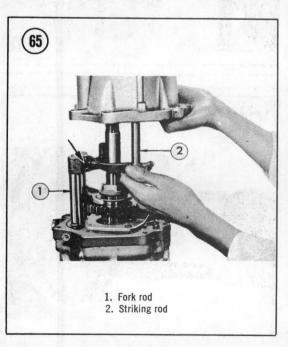

1. Fork rod
2. Striking rod

41. Install the bearing ring in the input shaft bearing groove (**Figure 64**).

42. Coat the adapter plate-to-rear extension gasket on both sides with gasket sealer. Position the gasket on the rear side of the adapter plate.

43. Line up the fork rods and striking rod, then install the rear extension. Refer to **Figures 65 and 66**.

CAUTION
Do not let the rear end of the mainshaft damage the rear extension oil seal.

44. Insert the pivot pin through the striking rod and shift lever bracket. Secure the pin with a retaining ring. See **Figure 67**.

45. Install the control arm pin and its plain washers, thrust washer, and control spring. Secure the control arm pin with a retaining pin as shown in **Figure 68**.

9

46. Select a shim for the input shaft bearing. To select a shim, first measure the depth from the rear surface of the front cover to the rear surface of the clutch housing (**Figure 69**). Then measure the distance that the input shaft bearing protrudes from the front end of the transmission case (**Figure 70**). Subtract the measurement shown in **Figure 70** from the measurement shown in **Figure 69** to determine shim thickness. Shims are available in two thicknesses: 0.055 in. (1.4mm) and 0.063 in. (1.6mm).

47. Select a shim for the countershaft front bearing. To select a shim, measure the depth from the transmission case surface to the front surface of the countershaft bearing. **Figure 71** shows the measurement being taken. **Figure 72** is a cross-sectional view. Shims are available in seven thicknesses, ranging from 0.0157 in. (0.4mm) to 0.0394 in. (1mm).

48. Once the shims have been selected, place them on their bearings.

49. Bolt the clutch housing to the transmission case. Use a new transmission case-to-clutch housing gasket, coated on both sides with gasket sealer. Tighten the bolts to 11-16 footpounds (1.5-2.2 mkg).

50. Install the clutch release mechanism (Chapter Eight). Move the shift lever through the gears, and make sure the transmission operates smoothly in each gear.

TRANSMISSION (F4W71B)

This four-speed transmission was standard equipment on all Z's manufactured after September, 1972.

Removal/Installation

1. Disconnect the negative cable from the battery.

2. Disconnect the throttle linkage from the firewall.

3. Remove the starter (Chapter Seven).

4. Remove the center console.

5. Make sure the transmission is in neutral. Remove the snap ring from the shift lever pin (**Figure 73**), then lift the shift lever out.

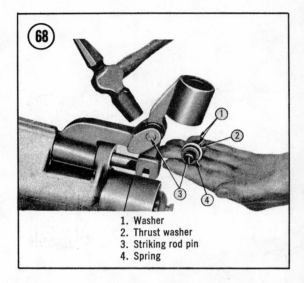

1. Washer
2. Thrust washer
3. Striking rod pin
4. Spring

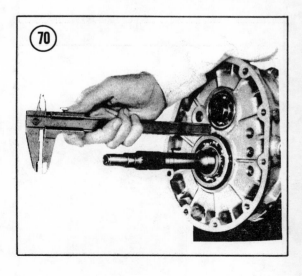

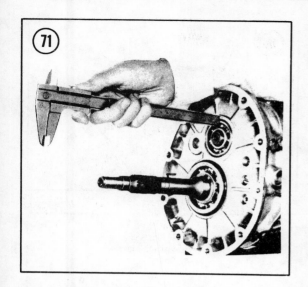

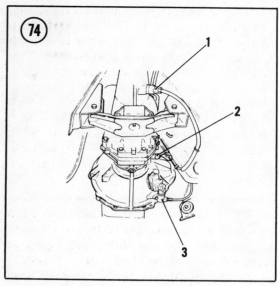

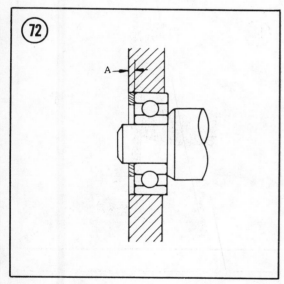

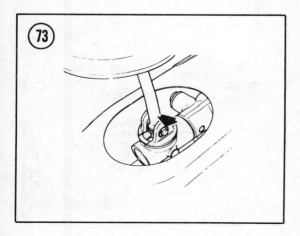

6. Jack up all 4 corners of the car and place it on jackstands.

7. Disconnect the exhaust pipe from the manifold. Unbolt the exhaust pipe bracket from the transmission rear extension. Tie the pipe up with wire.

8. Remove the drive shaft (Chapter Twelve).

9. Unscrew the speedometer cable union nut (1, **Figure 74**). Disconnect the back-up light switch wires (2), and remove the clutch operating cylinder (3).

10. If equipped with a catalytic converter, unbolt the converter's heat shield from the body and let it rest on the exhaust pipe.

11. Drain the transmission oil.

12. Place a jack beneath the oil pan. Use a block of wood between the jack and oil pan so the oil pan won't collapse.

13. Place a jack beneath the transmission. Unbolt the mounting member from the transmission, then from the car's frame.

14. Unbolt the transmission from the engine. Lower the jacks beneath engine and transmission. Remove the transmission downward and to the rear.

CAUTION
Do not remove the transmission partway, or its weight will hang on the input shaft. This could damage the input shaft and its bearing.

9

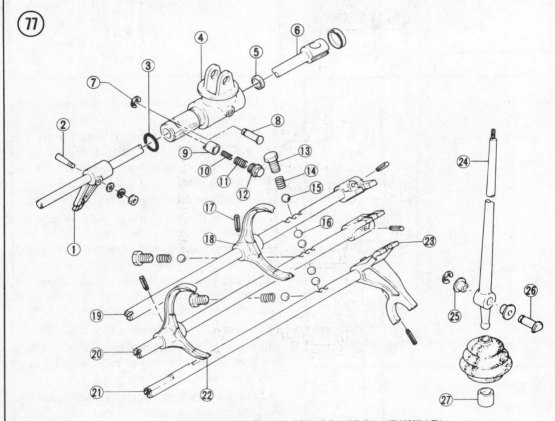

TRANSMISSION SHIFT CONTROL (F4W71B)

1. Striking lever	10. Return spring	19. 1st and 2nd fork rod
2. Lock pin	11. Reverse check spring	20. 3rd and 4th fork rod
3. O-ring	12. Return spring plug	21. Reverse fork rod
4. Striking guide	13. Check ball plug	22. 3rd and 4th shift fork
5. Oil seal	14. Check spring	23. Reverse shift fork
6. Striking rod	15. Check ball	24. Control lever
7. E-ring	16. Interlock ball	25. Control lever bushing
8. Stopper guide pin	17. Retaining pin	26. Control lever pin
9. Return spring plunger	18. 1st and 2nd shift fork	27. Control lever bushing

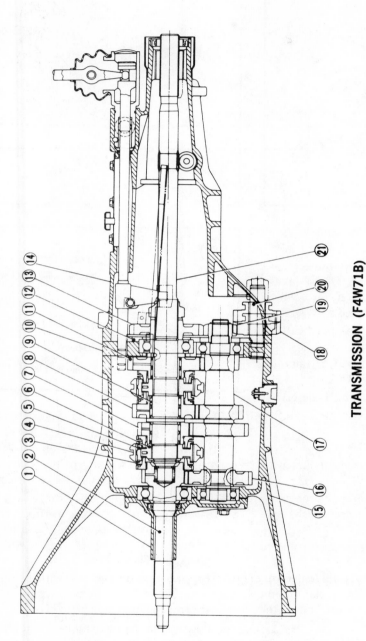

TRANSMISSION (F4W71B)

1. Front cover
2. Input gear
3. Balk ring
4. Coupling sleeve
5. Shifting insert
6. Synchronizer hub, 3rd and 4th
7. 3rd main gear
8. 2nd main gear
9. Needle bearing
10. Adapter plate
11. 1st main gear
12. Bearing retainer
13. Reverse main gear
14. Rear extension housing
15. Transmission case
16. Counter drive gear
17. Counter gear
18. Reverse idler gear
19. Reverse counter gear
20. Reverse idler shaft
21. Mainshaft

9

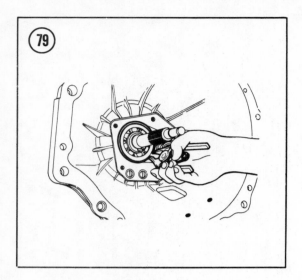

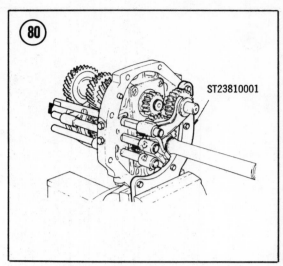

ST23810001

15. Installation is the reverse of removal, plus the following.

   a. Apply a *thin* coat of multipurpose grease to the input shaft splines. Excess grease will spin off onto the clutch disc, which may then have to be replaced.

   b. Tighten nuts and bolts to specifications (**Table 1**, end of chapter).

   c. Fill the transmission with an oil recommended in Chapter Three.

   d. If necessary, bleed the clutch as described in Chapter Eight.

Disassembly

1. Clean the outside of the transmission with solvent.

2. Remove the dust cover from the clutch housing. Remove the clutch release mechanism (Chapter Eight).

3. Unscrew the back-up lamp switch from the side of the transmission.

4. Make sure the transmission is still in neutral. Remove the speedometer pinion clamp bolt from the rear extension, then take the speedometer pinion out.

5. Remove the snap ring and pin from the striking rod. See **Figure 75**.

6. Unscrew the return spring plug (**Figure 76**).

7. Take out the reverse check spring, return spring, and return spring plunger. See **Figure 77**.

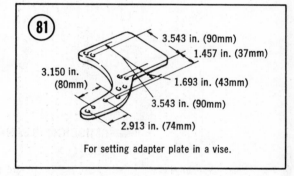

3.543 in. (90mm)
1.457 in. (37mm)
3.150 in. (80mm)
1.693 in. (43mm)
3.543 in. (90mm)
2.913 in. (74mm)

For setting adapter plate in a vise.

8. Turn the striking guide (4, **Figure 77**) counterclockwise (viewed from rear of transmission). Referring to **Figure 78**, unbolt the rear extension from the adapter plate and transmission case. Tap the extension loose with a soft-faced mallet, then remove it.

9. Unbolt the front cover from the transmission case. Remove the input shaft bearing shim, then remove the bearing snap ring with snap ring pliers. See **Figure 79**.

10. Tap the transmission case with a soft-faced mallet to free it from the adapter plate. Then take the transmission case off.

11. Position the gear assembly in a holding fixture such as Datsun tool ST23810001 (**Figure 80**). **Figure 81** gives dimensions of the tool, which can easily be made from plywood.

   NOTE: *Figure 82 is an exploded view of the gear assembly. Refer to it as needed for the following steps.*

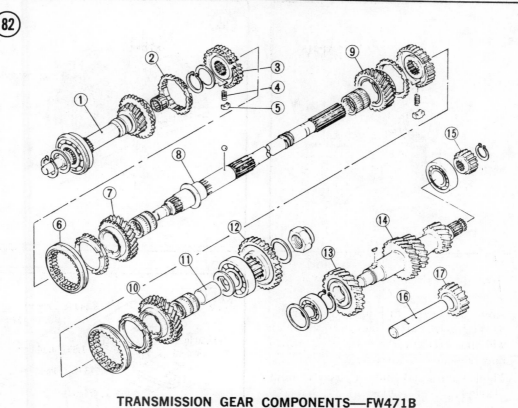

TRANSMISSION GEAR COMPONENTS—FW471B

1. Main drive gear	7. 3rd main gear	13. Counter drive gear
2. Balk ring	8. Mainshaft	14. Countershaft
3. Synchronizer hub, 3rd and 4th	9. 2nd main gear	15. Reverse counter gear
4. Shifting insert spring	10. 1st main gear	16. Reverse idler shaft
5. Shifting insert	11. 1st gear spacer	17. Reverse idler gear
6. Coupling sleeve	12. Reverse main gear	

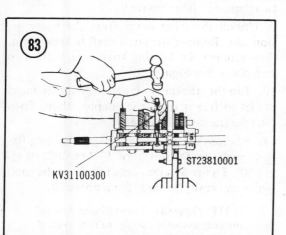

KV31100300
ST23810001

12. Drive the roll pins out of the shift forks and rods. Use Datsun tool KV31100300 or Kent-Moore J-25689-A (**Figure 83**) or an ordinary pin punch.

13. Remove all 3 check ball plugs. **Figure 84** is a cross-section view of the adapter plate which shows the check ball plugs, check and interlock balls, and shift fork rods.

14. Tap the shift fork rods out of the adapter plate, then remove the check and interlock balls.

NOTE: *Perform the following inspection steps before continuing with disassembly.*

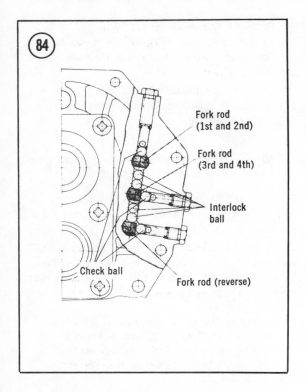

Fork rod
(1st and 2nd)

Fork rod
(3rd and 4th)

Interlock
ball

Check ball

Fork rod (reverse)

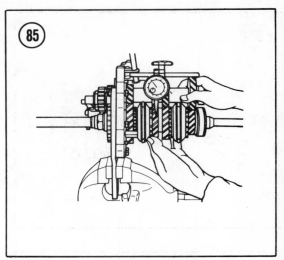

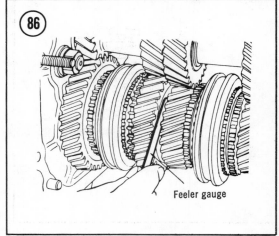

Feeler gauge

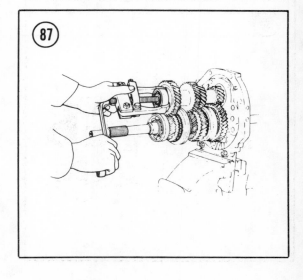

15. Measure gear backlash with a dial gauge as shown in **Figure 85**. Hold the countershaft from turning with one hand and turn each mainshaft gear as far as possible against the dial gauge without turning the countershaft. The reading on the dial gauge should be 0.002-0.004 in. (0.05-0.10mm) on the input shaft gear, and 0.002-0.008 in. (0.05-0.20mm) on all others. If backlash is excessive, replace driving and driven gears as a set.

16. Measure gear end play with a feeler gauge (**Figure 86**). It should be 0.013-0.015 in. (0.32-0.39mm) for first gear; 0.005-0.007 in. (0.12-0.19mm) for second gear; 0.005-0.014 in. (0.13-0.37mm) for third gear; and 0.0004-0.0079 in. (0.01-0.20mm) for countershaft reverse gear. Excessive end play can be corrected with oversize snap rings. The mainshaft thrust washers should also be checked closely for wear.

NOTE: *Continue with disassembly as follows.*

17. Engage 2 gears at once. To do this, slide each synchronizer sleeve over the small teeth on one of the gears next to it. This locks the mainshaft and gears so they won't turn.

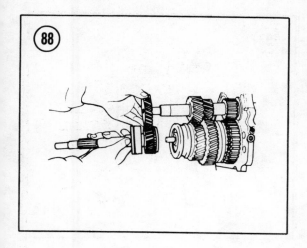

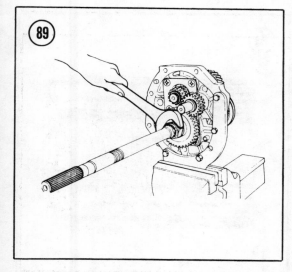

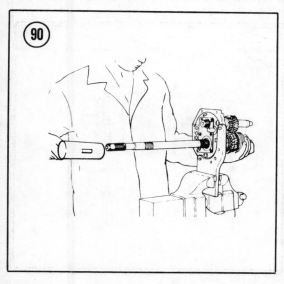

18. Remove the countershaft gear front bearing with a gear puller (**Figure 87**). Gear pullers can be rented from tool rental outlets and some auto parts stores.

19. Pull off the countershaft drive gear with a gear puller. Remove the input shaft at the same time. See **Figure 88**.

CAUTION
Do not let the needle roller bearing fall out of the input shaft onto the floor.

20. Remove the snap ring, thrust washer, third-fourth gear synchronizer, and third gear from the front end of the mainshaft.

21. Carefully file away the lip of the mainshaft nut where it is punched into the mainshaft. Remove the nut with a 1½ in. (38mm) box wrench and throw it away. See **Figure 89**.

NOTE: *The nut is tightened to 101-123 ft.-lb. (14-17 mkg). If you don't have the correct wrench, take the gear assembly to a Datsun dealer to have the nut removed.*

22. Remove the snap ring from the rear end of the countershaft, then remove the countershaft reverse gear.

23. Tap the mainshaft with a soft-faced mallet to free it (**Figure 90**). Then remove the mainshaft and countershaft from the adapter plate.

24. Remove 6 machine screws securing the bearing retainer to the adapter plate. These screws have been punched in place, so an impact screwdriver is necessary to remove them.

25. Remove the reverse idler shaft and mainshaft bearing from the adapter plate.

26. Remove the thrust washer, its steel ball, first gear, and first gear's needle bearing from the rear end of the mainshaft.

27. Have the first gear bushing, first-second gear synchronizer, and second gear pressed off the mainshaft by a machine shop.

Inspection

1. Thoroughly clean all parts in solvent. Remove all traces of old gasket and sealer. Inspect all parts while cleaning and replace any with obvious wear or damage.

9

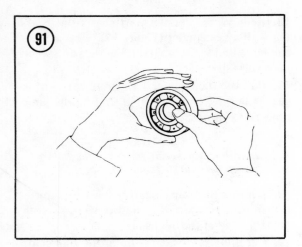

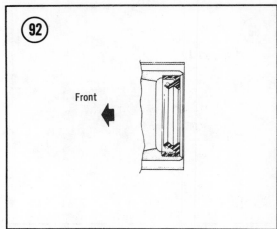

Front

2. Check the transmission case and rear extension for cracks. Check all gasket surfaces for gouges or roughness which could cause an oil leak. Replace if these conditions are found.

3. Check all bearings for wear or damage. Hold the outer race with one hand and rotate the inner race with the other. See **Figure 91**. Check for noise, roughness, and wear. Replace any suspect bearings.

> NOTE: *If the input shaft bearing or countershaft bearing needs to be replaced, have the old one pressed off and a new one pressed on by a machine shop.*

4. Since needle roller bearing wear is hard to see, the needle roller bearings should be replaced whenever transmission is overhauled.

5. Inspect the bushing at the back of the rear extension. If worn or damaged, the rear extension must be replaced.

6. Carefully pry the oil seal out of the rear extension. Tap in a new one. Use a block of wood to spread the hammer's force, so the seal won't tilt sideways and jam. Coat the seal lip and rear extension bushing with gear oil.

> NOTE: *The lip of the seal faces into the transmission. See Figure 92.*

7. Replace the front cover oil seal in the same manner as the rear extension oil seal.

8. Check the mainshaft for bending, twisting, cracks, or other damage. Check the splines for the types of wear and damage shown in **Fig-**

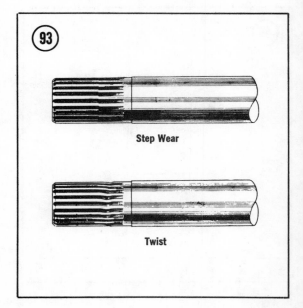

Step Wear

Twist

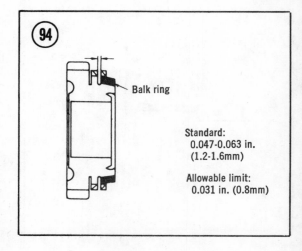

Balk ring

Standard:
0.047-0.063 in.
(1.2-1.6mm)

Allowable limit:
0.031 in. (0.8mm)

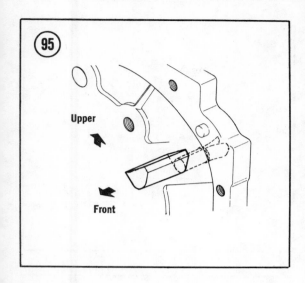

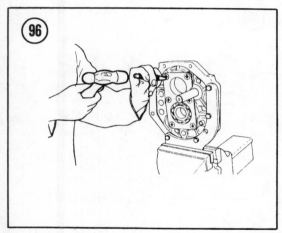

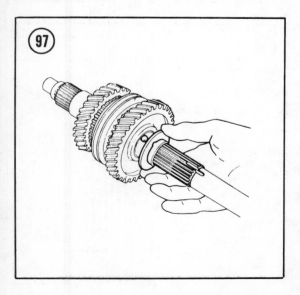

ure 93. Replace if any of these conditions is found.

9. Check gears for chipped, broken, or badly worn teeth. Replace gears with these conditions.

10. Slip a balk ring onto the cones of first, second, third, and input shaft gears. Measure the gap between balk ring and the small teeth on the gear (**Figure 94**). Normal gap is 0.047-0.063 in. (1.2-1.6mm). Minimum is 0.031 in. (0.8mm). If the gap is less than the minimum, replace the balk ring.

Assembly

Transmission assembly should be done in a dust-free area.

> NOTE: *Dip each bearing, gear, and synchronizer in new gear oil just before installing.*

1. If the oil gutter was removed from the adapter plate, install it as shown in **Figure 95**.

2. If the mainshaft bearing was removed from the adapter plate, tap it into position with a soft-faced mallet.

3. Install the reverse idler shaft in the adapter plate. Make sure the cutout in the shaft faces toward the center of the adapter plate.

4. Install the adapter plate. Make sure the cutout in the reverse idler shaft lines up with the adapter plate. Tighten the adapter plate screws to 14-18 ft.-lb. (1.9-2.5 mkg). Stake each screw at 2 points with a hammer and punch. See **Figure 96**.

5. Install the following parts in order from the rear end of the mainshaft: Needle bearing, second gear, balk ring, first-second gear synchronizer, balk ring, first gear bushing, needle bearing, and first gear.

6. Coat the steel ball with grease and install it next to first gear (**Figure 97**). Slip the thrust washer over it.

7. Have the mainshaft pressed into the adapter plate by a machine shop. A support tool such as KV31100400 (**Figure 98**) is necessary to prevent damage to the adapter plate.

8. Install new Woodruff keys in the countershaft gear. Tap the keys in gently with a soft-faced hammer.

9

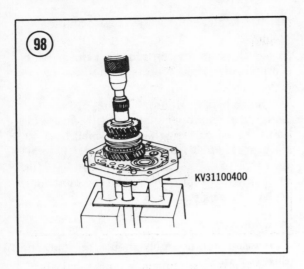

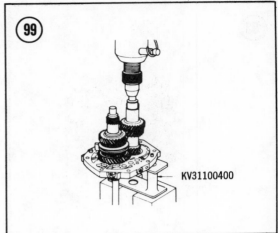

9. Have the countershaft gear pressed into the adapter plate by a machine shop. See **Figure 99**.

10. Install the following parts in order from the front end of the mainshaft: needle bearing, third gear, balk ring, and third-fourth gear synchronizer.

> NOTE: *The third-fourth gear synchronizer hub is offset toward the rear of the mainshaft (Figure 100). The first-second synchronizer hub is not offset.*

11. Place a thrust washer against the synchronizer, then secure it with a snap ring. Use the thickest snap ring that will fit in the groove. Snap rings are available in thicknesses of 0.055 in. (1.4mm), 0.059 in. (1.5mm), and 0.063 in. (1.6mm).

12. Place a balk ring on the third-fourth gear synchronizer.

13. Place the input shaft pilot bearing on the end of the mainshaft.

14. Mesh the countershaft drive gear with the input shaft gear. Position the gears as shown in **Figure 101**, and press the countershaft drive gear onto the countershaft. At the same time, guide the input shaft onto the mainshaft.

15. Secure the countershaft drive gear with the thickest snap ring that will fit in the groove (**Figure 102**). See Step 11 for available thicknesses.

16. Press the countershaft front bearing onto the countershaft, next to the countershaft drive gear.

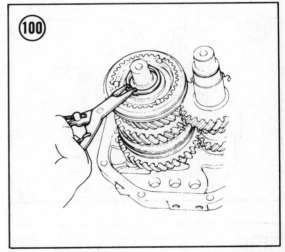

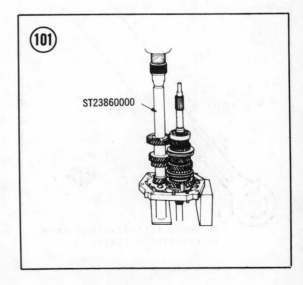

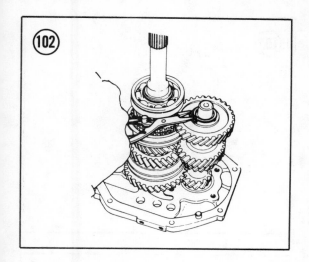

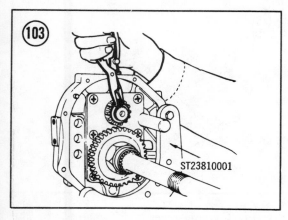

ST23810001

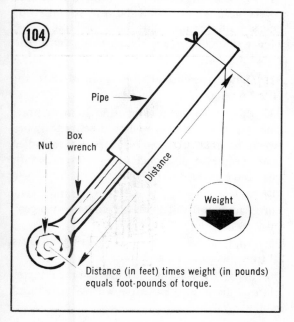

Pipe

Box wrench

Nut

Distance

Weight

Distance (in feet) times weight (in pounds) equals foot-pounds of torque.

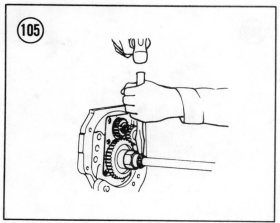

17. Install reverse main gear on the mainshaft. Install the plain washer next to the gear, then install the mainshaft nut. Don't torque the nut yet.

18. Install countershaft reverse gear on the rear end of the countershaft. Secure with the thickest snap ring that will fit in the groove (**Figure 103**). See Step 11 for available thicknesses.

19. Install reverse idler gear on the reverse idler shaft.

20. Slide the third-fourth gear synchronizer sleeve over the small teeth on third gear. Slide the first-second synchronizer sleeve over the small teeth on first or second gear. This engages 2 gears at once, so the mainshaft won't turn.

21. Tighten the mainshaft nut to 101-123 ft.-lb. (14-17 mkg). If you are near a Datsun dealer, the easiest way to do this is to take the gear assembly to the dealer and have the nut tightened. If not, you will need a 1 ½ in. (38mm) box wrench and a piece of pipe large enough to fit over it. The pipe should be about 3 ft. long.

To tighten, place the box wrench over the nut, and slip the pipe over the wrench. Measure 2 ft. out from the center of the mainshaft, and mark this point on the pipe. See **Figure 104**. Hang a 55 lb. weight on the pipe at this point, and let it turn the wrench as far as it will go. The distance (2 ft.) times the weight (55 lb.) equals 110 ft.-lb. of torque. This is within the specified range of 101-123 ft.-lb.

22. Once the mainshaft nut is tightened, punch its lip into the groove in the mainshaft. See **Figure 105**.

9

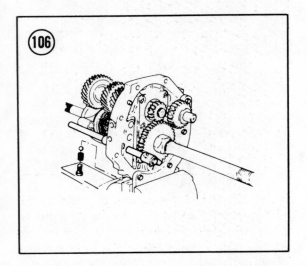

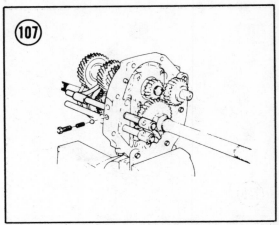

23. Place the first-second gear shifting fork in its groove on the first-second gear synchronizer. This is the synchronizer closest to the adapter plate.

> NOTE: *The first-second and third-fourth gear shifting forks are interchangeable. The first-second gear fork is installed with its longer leg toward the countershaft gear.*

24. Place the third-fourth gear shifting fork on the third-fourth gear synchronizer sleeve. The longer leg faces away from the countershaft gear.

25. Slide the first-second gear shift rod through the adapter plate into the first-second gear shifting fork. Secure the rod to the fork with a new roll pin.

26. Coat the threads of the longest check ball plug with gasket sealer. Install a check ball, spring, and the plug in the adapter plate. See **Figure 106**.

27. Install 2 interlock balls in the adapter plate, on top of the first-second shift rod. See **Figure 84**.

28. Slide the third-fourth gear shift rod through the adapter plate into the third-fourth gear shifting fork. Secure with a new roll pin.

29. Apply gasket sealer to the threads of one of the check ball plugs. Install a check ball, spring, and the plug. See **Figure 107**.

30. Install 2 more interlock balls in the adapter plate **(Figure 84)**.

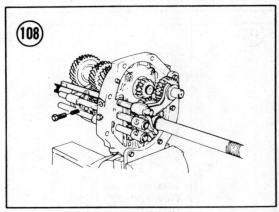

31. Position the reverse shifting fork on the reverse idler gear. Install the reverse shift rod, check ball, spring, and check ball plug. See **Figure 108**. Once again, use gasket sealer on the plug threads.

32. Tighten the check ball plugs to 14-18 ft.-lb. (1.9-2.5 mkg).

33. Make sure the transmission is in neutral. The synchronizer sleeves should be midway between the small teeth on the gears. Reverse idler gear should be disengaged from reverse main gear and counter reverse gear.

34. Make sure all bearings, gears, synchronizers, and shift rods are coated with gear oil.

35. Apply gasket sealer to the mating surfaces of transmission case and adapter plate.

36. Install the transmission case on the adapter plate. Tap it into position with a soft-faced mallet.

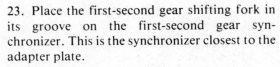

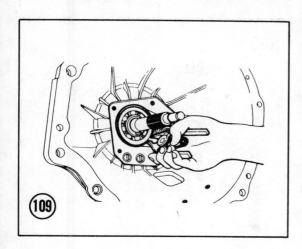

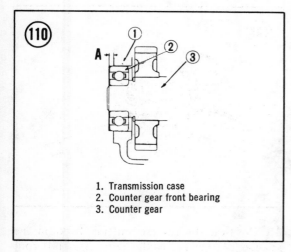

1. Transmission case
2. Counter gear front bearing
3. Counter gear

Table 2   SHIM SIZES

Bearing Protrusion		Shim Thickness	
Inches	mm	Inches	mm
0.115-0.118	2.92-3.01	0.024	0.6
0.119-0.122	3.02-3.11	0.020	0.5
0.123-0.126	3.12-3.21	0.016	0.4
0.127-0.130	3.22-3.31	0.012	0.3
0.131-0.134	3.32-3.41	0.008	0.2
0.135-0.138	3.42-3.51	0.004	0.1

with gasket sealer. Smear gasket sealer on the bolt threads. Tighten the front cover bolts to 12-15 ft.-lb. (1.6-2.1 mkg).

43. Install the speedometer pinion in the rear extension.

44. Coat the threads of the back-up lamp switch with gasket sealer. Install the switch and tighten to 14-22 ft.-lb. (2-3 mkg).

45. Install the clutch release mechanism (Chapter Eight).

46. Temporarily install the shift lever. Move it through the gear positions. Turn the input shaft at each position and make sure the mainshaft turns smoothly. In neutral, it should be possible to hold the mainshaft still while turning the input shaft.

47. Install the drain plug. Use gel-type gasket sealer on the plug threads.

37. Make sure the mainshaft and input shaft rotate freely. Secure the input shaft bearing with a snap ring (**Figure 109**).

38. Apply gasket sealer to the mating surfaces of adapter plate and rear extension. Install the rear extension on the adapter plate. Make sure the striking lever engages the shift rod brackets.

39. Tighten the rear extension bolts to 12-15 ft.-lb. (1.6-2.1 mkg).

40. Select a shim for the countershaft front bearing. Measure bearing protrusion from the front of the transmission case (distance "A," **Figure 110**), and select a shim according to **Table 2**.

41. Stick the shim to the front cover with multipurpose grease.

42. Install the front cover on the transmission case. Use a new gasket, coated on both sides

TRANSMISSION (FS5W71B)

This is the five-speed version of the F4W71B transmission. It was a factory option on 1977-1978 280Z's. The transmission is very similar to the F4W71B. The following section covers the differences. Any information not included will be found in the F4W71B section preceding this section.

Figure 111 shows the transmission case. **Figure 112** shows the shift mechanism. **Figure 113** shows the gear assembly.

Gear Disassembly

1. Before disassembling, check gear end play and backlash. Refer to *Transmission (F4W71B) Disassembly* earlier in this chapter. Specifica-

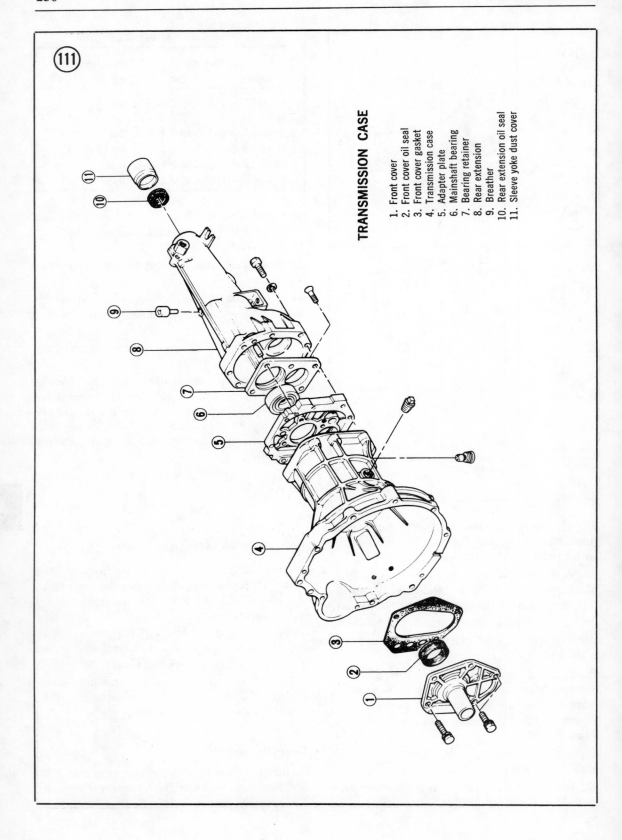

TRANSMISSION CASE

1. Front cover
2. Front cover oil seal
3. Front cover gasket
4. Transmission case
5. Adapter plate
6. Mainshaft bearing
7. Bearing retainer
8. Rear extension
9. Breather
10. Rear extension oil seal
11. Sleeve yoke dust cover

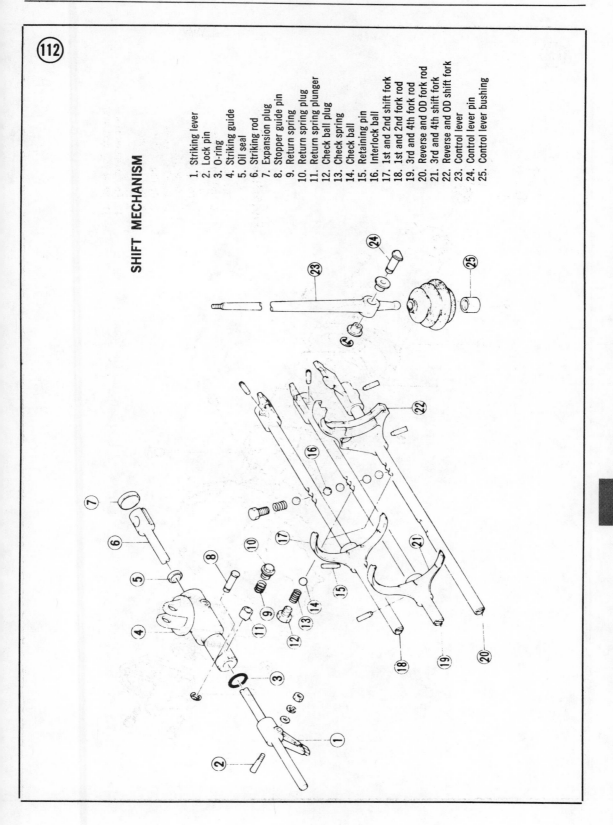

SHIFT MECHANISM

1. Striking lever
2. Lock pin
3. O-ring
4. Striking guide
5. Oil seal
6. Striking rod
7. Expansion plug
8. Stopper guide pin
9. Return spring plug
10. Return spring
11. Return spring plunger
12. Check ball plug
13. Check spring
14. Check ball
15. Retaining pin
16. Interlock ball
17. 1st and 2nd shift fork
18. 1st and 2nd fork rod
19. 3rd and 4th fork rod
20. Reverse and OD fork rod
21. 3rd and 4th shift fork
22. Reverse and OD shift fork
23. Control lever
24. Control lever pin
25. Control lever bushing

9

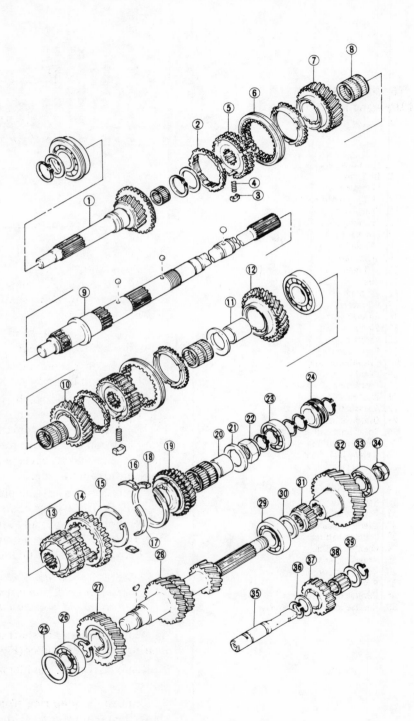

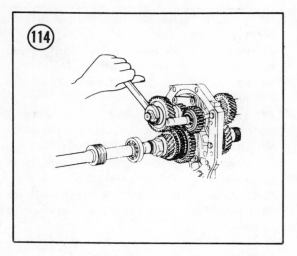

TRANSMISSION GEAR COMPONENTS—FSW71B

1. Main drive gear
2. Balk ring
3. Shifting insert
4. Shifting insert spring
5. Synchronizer hub
6. Coupling sleeve
7. 3rd main gear
8. Needle bearing
9. Mainshaft
10. 2nd main gear
11. Bushing
12. 1st main gear
13. OD-reverse synchronizer hub
14. Reverse gear
15. Circlip
16. Thrust block
17. Brake band
18. Synchronizer ring
19. Overdrive main gear
20. Overdrive gear bushing
21. Washer
22. Mainshaft nut
23. Overdrive mainshaft bearing
24. Speedometer drive gear
25. Countershaft front bearing shim
26. Countershaft front bearing
27. Countershaft drive gear
28. Countershaft
29. Countershaft bearing
30. Reverse counter gear spacer
31. Reverse counter gear
32. Overdrive counter gear
33. Countershaft rear bearing
34. Countershaft nut
35. Reverse idler shaft
36. Reverse idler thrust washer
37. Reverse idler gear
38. Reverse idler gear bearing
39. Reverse idler thrust washer

tions are the same, with 2 exceptions: fifth gear end play is 0.005-0.007 in. (0.12-0.19mm); and reverse idler gear end play is 0.002-0.020 in. (0.05-0.50mm). Countershaft reverse gear end play is not measured.

2. Remove the front bearing and snap ring from the countershaft gear.

3. Remove the countershaft drive gear and input shaft simultaneously.

4. Slide the third-fourth gear synchronizer sleeve over the small teeth on third gear. Slide the first-second synchronizer sleeve over the small teeth on one of the gears next to it. This engages 2 gears at once, which prevents the mainshaft from turning.

5. Carefully file away the punched portions of the mainshaft nut and countershaft gear nut. Loosen both nuts with a 1½ in. (38mm) wrench (**Figure 114**). Take the countershaft gear nut off. Leave the mainshaft nut on for now.

NOTE: *If you don't have the correct wrench, take the gear assembly to a Datsun dealer and have the nut removed.*

6. Remove the countershaft overdrive gear and bearing with a gear puller (**Figure 115**).

7. Remove reverse countershaft gear and its spacer.

8. Remove the snap ring from the reverse idler shaft, then remove reverse idler gear.

9. Remove a snap ring, the speedometer drive gear, and 2 more snap rings from the rear end of the mainshaft.

9

10. Have the mainshaft rear bearing pressed off by a machine shop.

11. Remove the following parts in order from the rear end of the mainshaft: nut, thrust washer, reverse main gear, overdrive synchronizer, and overdrive (fifth) gear.

12. Tap the mainshaft loose from the adapter plate with a soft-face mallet. Remove the mainshaft and countershaft simultaneously.

13. Remove the following parts in order from the front end of the mainshaft: snap ring, thrust washer, balk ring, third-fourth gear synchronizer, balk ring, third gear, and needle bearing.

Gear Assembly

Assembly is the reverse of disassembly, plus the following.

1. Dip all gears, bearings, and synchronizers in new gear oil before installing.

2. Assemble the overdrive gear (fifth gear) and its synchronizer as shown in **Figure 116**.

3. Assemble the reverse idler gear and shaft as shown in **Figure 117**.

4. Tighten the countershaft and mainshaft locknuts. Refer to Step 21, *Transmission (F4W71B) Assembly*, for the correct method. Since specified torque for the countershaft nut is 72-94 ft.-lb. (10-13 mkg), use a 45 lb. weight.

This will give a torque of 90 ft.-lb., which is within the specified range.

5. After tightening the nuts, stake them in place with a hammer and punch. See **Figure 118**.

TRANSMISSION (3N71B)

This automatic transmission has been optional for all model years since 1972. This section provides testing, removal, and installation procedures.

Checking Procedures

1. With the car on a level surface, start the engine and let it run for approximately 10

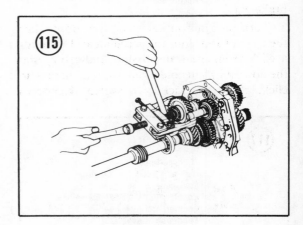

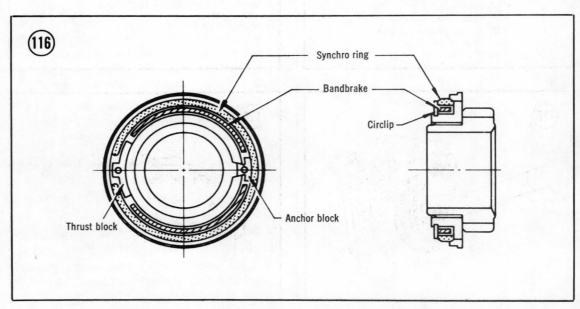

minutes to warm the transmission fluid to 122-176°F (50-80°C). Apply the brakes and move the shift lever through all gear positions to P. Check the transmission fluid level on the dipstick. If necessary, top up to the "F" line, using Dexron type automatic transmission fluid. Do not use Type F or Type A fluid.

CAUTION
Do not fill the transmission past the "F" line. Overfilling will cause the fluid to foam, resulting in wear and damage.

Inspect the fluid on the dipstick. Clean transmission fluid is a transparent red. If the fluid has deteriorated to a varnish-like condition, it may cause the control valve to stick. If it is black, it may indicate a burned clutch or brake band.

2. Turn the ignition key to ON (but don't start the engine) and floor the accelerator. Listen for a click from the transmission, indicating that the downshift solenoid is working. If there is no click, check the kickdown switch, kickdown

solenoid, and the wiring between them. See **Figure 119**.

If the solenoid is defective, drain approximately 2⅛ pints (1 liter) of fluid from the transmission, unscrew the solenoid, and install a new one. **Figure 120** shows the solenoid.

3. Move the selector lever through the gears, feeling for the detents in the lever positioning plate. Make sure the selector lever pointer indicates the correct gear at each lever position.

4. Check that the starter operates only in N and P. Make sure the back-up light operates only in R. If a problem is detected, adjust the starter inhibitor switch as described later.

5. Check idle speed as described in Chapter Three, *Tune-Up* section. Adjust if necessary.

6. With the engine idling and the brakes applied, move the selector lever through the gears. The shift into gear should be noticeable, but not excessively harsh.

7. With the engine idling, let off the brakes and check for excessive creeping in 1, 2, D, and R.

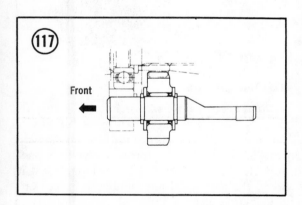

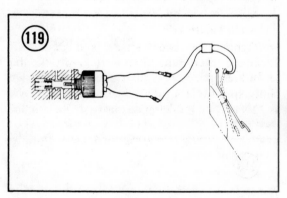

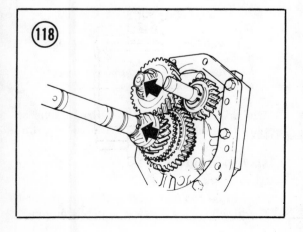

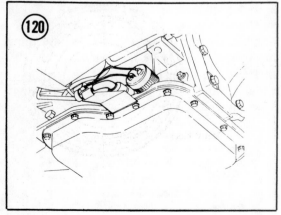

Table 3   AUTOMATIC TRANSMISSION LINE PRESSURE

	Psi	Kg/cm²
Drive and first		
1972-1977	43-57	3-4
1978	46-54	3.2-3.8
Second		
1972-1974	85-171	6-12
1975-1976	107-199	7.5-14.0
1977 and later	112-196	7.9-13.8
Reverse		
1972-1974	43-78	3.0-5.5
1975-1977	43-107	3.0-7.5
1978	74-101	5.2-7.1

Stall Test

The stall test is combined with line pressure tests to isolate various problems. The tests require a tachometer and an oil pressure gauge. Connect the tachometer to the engine and connect the pressure gauge to the transmission as shown in **Figure 121**.

1. With the selector level in P, run the engine at 1,200 rpm for several minutes to warm the transmission fluid to 140-212°F (60-100°C).

2. While the fluid is warming, mark the tachometer face with small pieces of tape. On 240 and 260Z's, place the marks at 2,150 and 2,350 rpm. On 280Z's, place the marks at 2,100 and 2,400 rpm. The tachometer must be read very quickly during this test, and the marks will make it easier.

3. Place the tachometer and oil pressure gauge where they can easily be seen from the driver's seat.

4. Block all 4 wheels so the car can't roll in either direction.

5. Place the selector level in D. Compare idling line pressure with **Table 3**.

6. Press the accelerator slowly to the floor. Quickly note the rpm reading when engine speed levels off.

CAUTION
Do not run the engine at full load for more than five seconds. The transmission fluid heats very rapidly during this test, and severe damage could result from excessive full-load running.

7. Place the selector lever in N. Run the engine at 1,200 rpm for at least one minute to let the transmission fluid cool.

8. Repeat the line pressure check and stall speed check in 2 and R. Compare results with **Table 3**.

CAUTION
Between each stage of the test, run the engine at 1,200 rpm in N for at least one minute. This is necessary to cool the transmission fluid.

Test Interpretation

1. *Stall speed within specifications* — This indicates that the engine is delivering full power and the control elements of the transmission are working properly. The torque converter's one-way clutch could possibly be sticking, but if it were, the car would not be able to exceed approximately 50 mph.

CAUTION
If the torque converter's one-way clutch is sticking, the transmission fluid will heat up excessively. The car should not be driven more than absolutely necessary until it can be repaired.

2. *Stall speed too high in all gears* — One or more of the clutches in the transmission is slipping.

3. *Stall speed too high in D, 2 and 1* — The rear clutch is slipping.

4. *Stall speed too high in D and 2, normal in 1* — Torque converter one-way clutch is slipping.

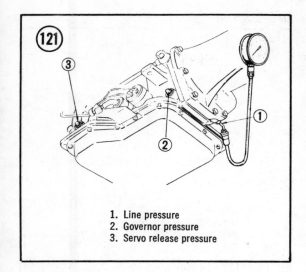

1. Line pressure
2. Governor pressure
3. Servo release pressure

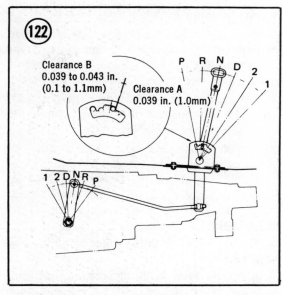

5. *Stall speed too high in R only* — Either the front clutch or the low and reverse brake is slipping. This problem can be isolated further in the road test, described later in this chapter.

6. *Stall speed too low* — Either the engine is not delivering full power, or the torque converter one-way clutch is slipping. This can be further isolated in the road test.

7. *Line pressure too low in all ranges* — This could indicate a worn oil pump, oil pressure leakage in the oil pump, valve body, or case, or a sticking regulator valve.

8. *Line pressure normal in D, 2, and 1, low in R* — This indicates an oil leak in the low and reverse brake circuit.

9. *Line pressure normal in R, low in 1, 2, and D* — This indicates an oil leak in the rear clutch and governor.

Road Test

1. If the stall speed was excessive in R only, determine the cause by accelerating, then letting up on the accelerator, while the selector lever is in 1. If the engine slows the car (compression braking), the front clutch is slipping. If there is no engine braking effect, the low and reverse brake is slipping.

2. If the stall speed was too low, isolate the cause by checking the acceleration. Accelerate to a speed over 30 mph. If acceleration is poor to 30 mph and improves about that speed, the torque converter one-way clutch is slipping. If

acceleration does not improve above 30 mph, the engine is not delivering full power and may need a tune-up.

3. While driving at approximately 31 mph, let up the accelerator and pull the selector into 1. The transmission should downshift into second, then into first.

4. While driving at approximately 31 mph, pull the selector lever into 2 without letting up the accelerator. The transmission should shift into second gear. Once in second gear, it should not shift up or down.

5. Park the car on a slope. Apply the brakes and shift to P. Let off the brakes and make sure the transmission holds the car. Check with the car facing up and down the hill.

Linkage Adjustment

1. Move the selector lever back and forth from 1 to P several times. A slight click should be heard and felt at each gear position.

2. Place the selector lever in N. Detach the selector lever from the linkage. See **Figure 122**.

3. Working beneath the car, make sure the range select lever on the side of the transmission is in the N position. This occurs when the slot in the manual shaft, to which the lever is attached, is vertical.

4. Make sure the selector lever inside the car is in N, then reconnect the linkage.

9

Starter Inhibitor Switch

If the starter operates in any gear other than N or P, or if the reverse light lights in any gear other than R, check the linkage. If the linkage is adjusted correctly, check the inhibitor switch.

1. Detach the range select lever (9, **Figure 123**) from the transmission shift linkage. Move the range select lever to the N position.

2. Attach a continuity tester (such as an ohm-meter or self-powered test lamp) to the black-and-yellow inhibitor switch wires. The tester should indicate continuity (the lamp should light) while the range select lever is within 3° of the N position.

3. Repeat Step 2 with the range select lever in the P position.

4. Move the lever to the R position, and connect the tester to the red and red-and-black wires on the inhibitor switch. Again, the tester should indicate continuity in a 3° range on either side of the R position.

5. If the tester shows continuity when the lever is obviously more than 3° away from the N, R, or P positions in Steps 2, 3, or 4, adjust the inhibitor switch. To do this, first move the range select lever to the N position. Then remove the lever retaining nut (6, **Figure 123**), 2 inhibitor switch installation bolts, and the machine screw under the switch. Align the machine screw hole with the pinhole in the manual shaft. Check the alignment by inserting a piece of wire ⅟₁₆ in. (1.5mm) thick through the 2 holes. Then install the switch bolts, pull out the wire and install the machine screw. Install the nut on the manual shaft and recheck the switch as described in Steps 2, 3, and 4.

6. If the tester still indicates continuity when the lever is moved from the N, R, or P positions, replace the inhibitor switch.

Transmission Removal/Installation

1. Drain the transmission fluid.

2. Jack up the car on both ends and place it on jackstands.

3. Disconnect one cable from the battery.

4. Disconnect and remove the front section of the exhaust system.

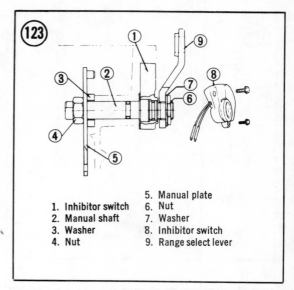

1. Inhibitor switch
2. Manual shaft
3. Washer
4. Nut
5. Manual plate
6. Nut
7. Washer
8. Inhibitor switch
9. Range select lever

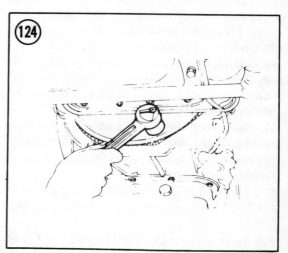

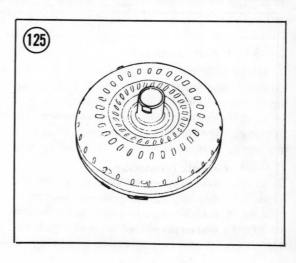

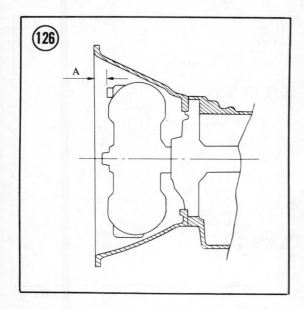

5. Disconnect the wires from the starter inhibitor switch and kickdown solenoid.

6. Disconnect the vacuum line from the vacuum diaphragm (located next to the kickdown solenoid). Disconnect the transmission oil cooler lines.

7. Disconnect the shift linkage from the transmission.

8. Disconnect the speedometer cable from the rear extension.

9. Remove the drive shaft (Chapter Twelve).

10. Place a jack beneath the engine to support it. Use a block of wood between the jack and the oil pan.

11. Remove the cover from the torque converter housing. Remove 4 bolts attaching the torque converter to the drive plate. See **Figure 124**.

> NOTE: *Mark the torque converter and drive plate so they can be reassembled in the same relative positions.*

12. Remove the starter (Chapter Six).

13. Place a jack beneath the transmission to support it. Remove 2 bolts attaching the rear mounting member to the transmission, then detach the mounting member from the car.

14. Remove bolts attaching the transmission to the engine.

15. Lower the jack beneath the transmission gradually and remove the transmission toward the rear of the car.

16. Installation is the reverse of these steps. If the torque converter has been separated from the transmission, be sure to align the notch shown in **Figure 125** with the corresponding notch in the transmission oil pump. Also, be sure dimension ''A'' in **Figure 126** is 0.846 in. (21.5mm).

9

Table 1   **TIGHTENING TORQUES**

	Ft.-lb.	Mkg
Manual transmission		
Transmission to engine		
F4W71A	20-27	2.7-3.7
F4W71B, FS5W71B	32-43	4.3-5.9
Mounting insulator to transmission	23-31	3.2-4.3
Bracket to mounting insulator	23-31	3.2-4.3
Bracket to car frame	23-31	3.2-4.3
Automatic Transmission		
Transmission to engine	29-36	4.0-5.0
Mounting insulator to transmission	23-31	3.2-4.3
Bracket to mounting insulator	23-31	3.2-4.3
Bracket to car frame	23-31	3.2-4.3

CHAPTER TEN

BRAKES

The Z uses disc brakes on the front and drum brakes at the rear. All brakes are self-adjusting. A vacuum booster reduces braking effort, and a proportioning valve prevents premature rear wheel lockup. The handbrake is a mechanical type, operating the rear brakes through a front rod and two rear cables.

FRONT BRAKES

Figure 1 shows the brake assembly.

Pad Replacement

When the pads are worn to 0.079 in. (2mm) they should be replaced. Inspect the pads for wear from the direction shown in **Figure 2**.

1. Loosen the front wheel nuts, jack up the front end of the car, place it on jackstands, and remove the front wheels.

2. Referring to **Figure 2**, remove the clips (1), retaining pins (2), anti-squeal springs (3), and pads (4). The pads are removed together with the anti-squeal shims.

3. Inspect the pads for wear and for damage caused by overheating. Check for grease, oil, or hydraulic fluid on the friction material. If the pads are only slightly oily or greasy, and not excessively worn, they can be cleaned in non-petroleum solvent and reused. If they are saturated with oil or grease, wet with hydraulic fluid, or damaged from overheating, replace the pads. Always replace the pads in full sets.

4. Carefully clean out the space which holds the brake pads. Inspect the cylinders. If there is any dirt in the cylinders, recondition the caliper unit as described later. The caliper must also be overhauled if hydraulic fluid has been leaking past the piston seals.

5. Clean the calipers, pad retaining clips, pins, anti-squeal springs, and anti-squeal shims in suitable solvent.

6. Place rags beneath the master cylinder in case it overflows. Open the caliper bleed valves to let hydraulic fluid escape. Press the pistons into the cylinders far enough to install the pads. Close the bleed valves.

> ### CAUTION
> *Do not push the pistons in past the piston seals. If they are pushed too far, the pistons will catch on the seals. The caliper will then have to be removed and disassembled to get the pistons out.*

7. Apply brake grease to the friction points shown in **Figure 3**.

> ### CAUTION
> *Do not let brake grease touch the pad friction material.*

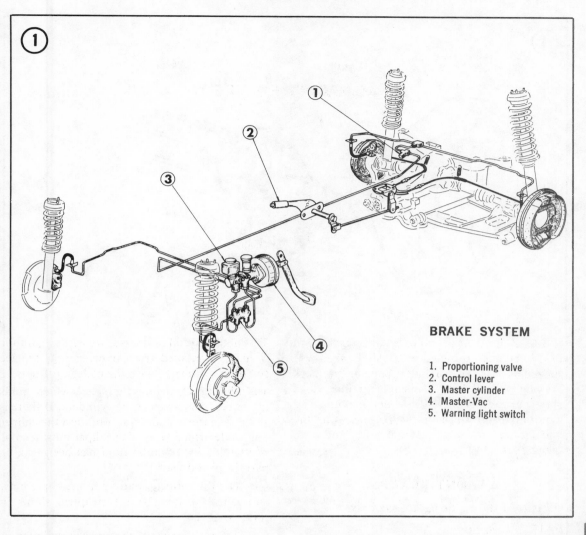

BRAKE SYSTEM

1. Proportioning valve
2. Control lever
3. Master cylinder
4. Master-Vac
5. Warning light switch

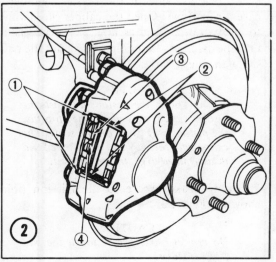

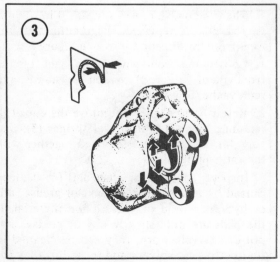

10

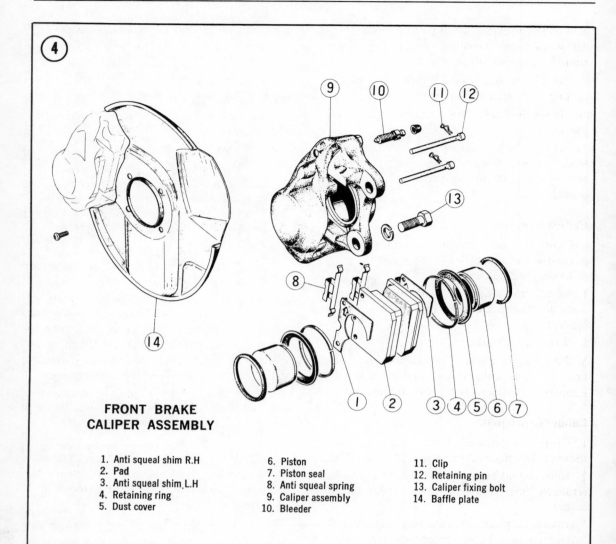

**FRONT BRAKE
CALIPER ASSEMBLY**

1. Anti squeal shim R.H
2. Pad
3. Anti squeal shim L.H
4. Retaining ring
5. Dust cover

6. Piston
7. Piston seal
8. Anti squeal spring
9. Caliper assembly
10. Bleeder

11. Clip
12. Retaining pin
13. Caliper fixing bolt
14. Baffle plate

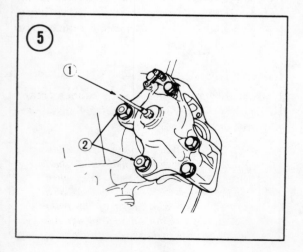

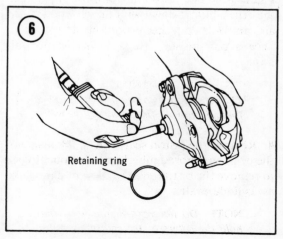

Retaining ring

8. Install the pads and anti-squeal shims. The arrow marks on the shims point in the forward rotating direction of the wheel.

9. Install the anti-squeal springs and pad retaining pins. Secure the pins with the clips.

10. Press the brake pedal several times to seat the pads.

11. Drive the car enough to make sure the brakes work properly and that no air has entered the hydraulic system. Bleed the brakes if necessary.

Caliper Removal

Figure 4 is an exploded view of the caliper assembly for one wheel. Refer to it for the following procedures.

1. Inspect the calipers. If hydraulic fluid leaks from the piston area, the piston seals must be replaced.

2. Remove the brake pads as described earlier.

3. Referring to **Figure 5**, disconnect the brake line (1) and caliper installation bolts (2). Remove the caliper assembly from the car.

Caliper Disassembly

1. Clean the outside of the caliper assembly thoroughly before taking it apart.

2. Referring to **Figure 4**, remove the dust cover retaining rings and dust covers from the cylinders.

3. Insert a piece of plywood between the caliper pistons. Blow compressed air into the brake hose hole to push the pistons out. See **Figure 6**. If one piston moves more easily than the other, hold it down with the plywood so the air can force the other piston out. If you don't have a compressor, use a service station air hose.

WARNING
The pistons may come out with extreme force. Keep your fingers out of the way.

4. Remove the piston seals. Clean the inside of the cylinders thoroughly. Use only your fingers to remove the piston seals to prevent damage to the cylinder walls.

NOTE: *Do not remove the bolts that hold the halves of the caliper assembly*

together. If hydraulic fluid is leaking from between the caliper halves, the entire caliper must be replaced.

Caliper Inspection and Repair

1. Thoroughly clean all parts in alcohol or brake fluid before inspection.

CAUTION
Never allow brake fluid to come in contact with brake pads. Brake fluid will ruin the pads, and they will have to be replaced. Do not clean rubber parts in solvent as this will cause them to deteriorate.

2. Inspect the pads as described earlier under *Pad Replacement*.

3. Check the cylinder walls for wear or damage. If these conditions are apparent, replace the caliper. The caliper must also be replaced is the cylinder walls are rough or excessively corroded. Slight amounts of corrosion or dirt can be removed with fine emery paper.

4. Inspect the pistons for uneven or excessive wear, damage, scoring, or corrosion. Replace the piston if these are evident.

NOTE: *The piston friction surfaces are plated. Therefore, the pistons cannot be cleaned with emery paper. If the pistons cannot be cleaned with chrome cleaner and a rag, replace them.*

5. As a final check on suspect pistons and cylinder walls, measure the inside diameter of the cylinders and the outside diameter of the pistons. If the difference between these figures is greater than 0.006 in. (0.15mm), replace both cylinder and piston.

Caliper Assembly

1. Coat new piston seals with rubber grease. Using only your fingers, carefully install the piston seals in the cylinders.

NOTE: *Never reuse a piston seal. In addition to preventing hydraulic fluid leaks, the seals retract the pistons when the brake pedal is let up. They are also critical to self-adjustment of the front brakes. Very minor damage or age deterioration can make the seals useless.*

10

2. Coat the cylinder bores and piston friction surfaces with brake fluid. Install the dust covers on the pistons. Insert pistons into cylinders. Secure dust covers with their retaining rings.

Caliper Installation

Caliper installation is the reverse of the removal procedure, plus the following steps.

1. Tighten caliper mounting bolts and brake lines to specifications (**Table 1**, end of chapter).

2. Bleed the brakes as described under *Brake Bleeding* in this chapter.

Adjustment

The front brakes are adjusted automatically by the piston seals. Therefore, no adjustment procedure is necessary or provided. When the brake pedal is pressed, the pistons are forced against the pads, which in turn are forced against the discs. When the pedal is let up, the elasticity of the piston seals pulls the pistons back into the cylinders (**Figure 7**). As the pads wear, the pistons must extend farther to press the pads against the disc. The longer stroke causes the piston to slip on the seal and not return as far into the cylinder. In this manner, the proper pad-to-disc clearance is maintained.

Disc Inspection

1. Loosen the front wheel nuts, jack up the front of the car, place it on jackstands and remove the front wheel(s).

2. Remove the caliper assembly as described earlier in this chapter.

3. Check wheel bearing adjustment as described in Chapter Eleven.

4. With a dial gauge contacting the center of the disc's swept area (**Figure 8**), rotate the disc one full turn and measure runout. If it exceeds specifications (**Table 1**, end of chapter), the disc can be trued on a lathe. However, the disc must not be cut thinner than 0.413 in. (10.5mm). If it would have to be cut thinner than this to straighten it, the disc must be replaced.

5. Measure parallelism around the circumference of the disc. Use a micrometer contacting the center of the disc's swept area (**Figure 9**) and rotate the disc one full turn. The

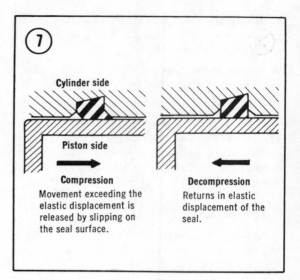

Compression
Movement exceeding the elastic displacement is released by slipping on the seal surface.

Decompression
Returns in elastic displacement of the seal.

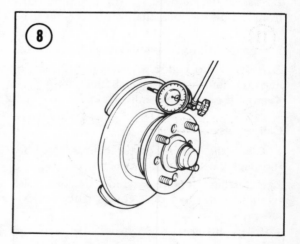

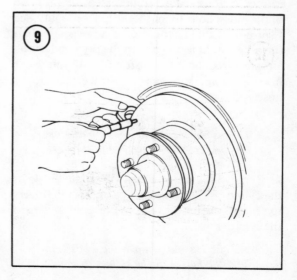

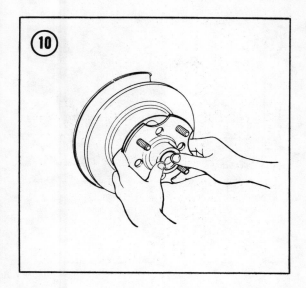

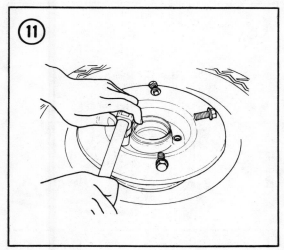

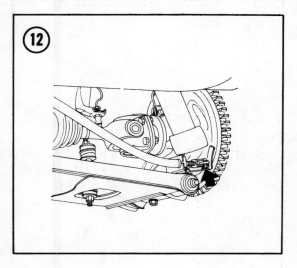

variation in thickness around the disc should be within 0.0012 in. (0.03mm) if the disc is new. Maximum permissible thickness variation is 0.0028 in. (0.07mm). If the variation exceeds this limit, have the disc turned to correct it. However, the disc must not be cut any thinner than 0.413 in. (10.5mm).

6. Using the micrometer, measure the thickness of the disc at several points around the circumference and at varying distances from the center. Normal disc thickness is 0.492 in. (12.5mm). If the disc is thinner than 0.413 in. (10.5mm), replace it.

Disc Removal/Installation

1. Loosen the front wheel nuts, jack up the car, place it on jackstands, and remove front wheels.

2. Remove caliper assembly, described earlier.

3. Remove the wheel bearing grease cap and locknut as described in Chapter Eleven.

4. Remove the brake disc together with the wheel hub (**Figure 10**).

5. Remove 4 bolts and separate the brake disc from the hub (**Figure 11**).

6. Bolt the disc to the hub. Tighten the bolts to 28-38 ft.-lb. (3.9-5.3 mkg).

7. Pack the wheel bearings with grease as described in Chapter Eleven.

8. Install the hub and brake disc on the bearing spindle. Adjust the bearing preload as described in Chapter Eleven.

9. Install the caliper assembly.

10. Install the front wheels, lower the car, and bleed brakes as described later in this chapter.

REAR BRAKES (1970-1976)

Drum Removal

1. Loosen the rear wheel nuts, jack up the car, place it on jackstands, and remove rear wheels.

2. If the brake shoes are not against the drum, simply pull it off. If the drum is difficult to remove, perform the next steps.

3. Remove the clevis pin (**Figure 12**) from the handbrake operating arm and disconnect the handbrake cable.

10

4. Remove the brake drum adjusting hole plug (**Figure 13**).

5. Insert a screwdriver in the adjusting hole and push the self-adjuster away from the adjusting wheel (**Figure 14**).

6. Turn the adjusting wheel downward with the screwdriver to loosen the brake shoes. Pull the drum off.

Drum Inspection

1. Clean the drum thoroughly in solvent before inspection.

2. Check for visible scoring, excessive or uneven wear, or corrosion. If you have a micrometer, measure the drum for wear and out-of-roundness. If you do not have a micrometer, this measurement can be done by a dealer or automotive machine shop. Maximum permissible out-of-roundness is 0.002 in. (0.05mm). If the drum is out-of-round or otherwise defective, it can be turned on a lathe to correct it. However, the inside diameter of the drum must not exceed 9.055 in. (230mm). If turning the drum would require that it be cut to more than this figure, it must be replaced.

Shoe Inspection

1. Remove the brake drum as described earlier.

2. Inspect the lining material on the brake shoes. Make sure it is not cracked, unevenly worn, or separated from the shoes. If linings are only slightly oily or greasy, and not excessively worn, they can be cleaned in non-petroleum solvent and reused. If the linings are saturated with oil or grease, or contaminated with brake fluid, they must be replaced. The linings must also be replaced if they are worn thinner than 1/18 in. (1.5mm).

Shoe Removal

Refer to **Figure 15** for this procedure.

1. Remove the anti-rattle pins. To remove, twist the pins with pliers until they fit through the slots in the retaining collars. Collect the pins, retaining collars, springs, and spring washers.

2. Pull the brake shoes off together with the return springs.

3. Separate return springs from brake shoes.

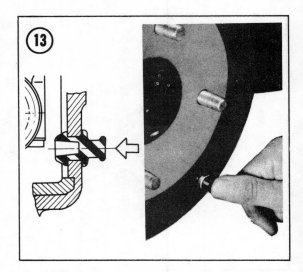

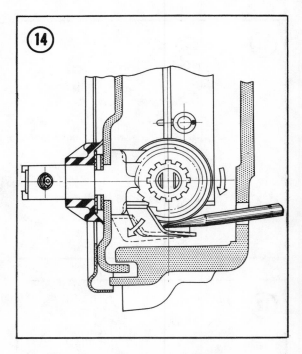

Wheel Cylinder Removal/Installation

1. Remove the wheel(s), brake drum, and brake shoes as described earlier.

2. Referring to **Figure 16**, disconnect the brake line (1), remove the dust cover (2), and slide out the front half of the retaining shim (3).

3. Remove the rear half of the retaining shim and take the wheel cylinder out.

4. Install by reversing Steps 1-3. Bleed the brakes after installation.

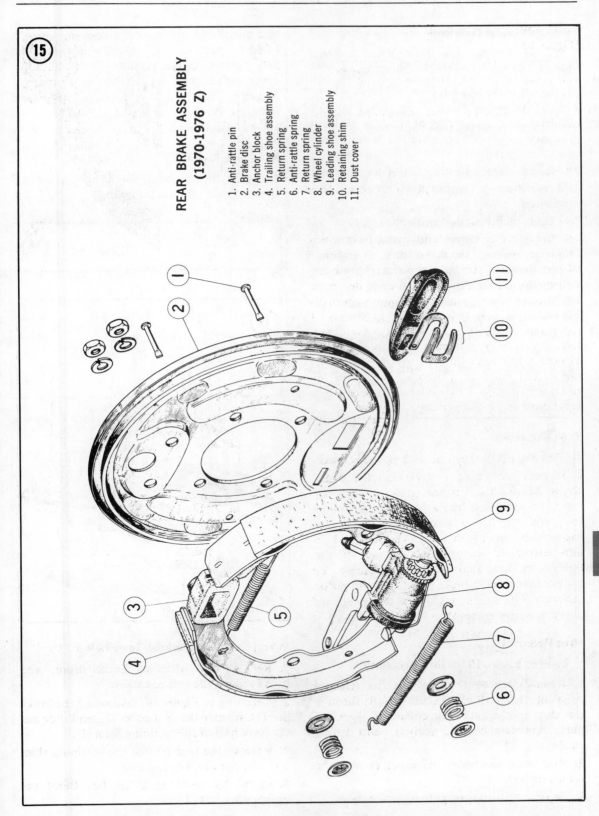

(15)

REAR BRAKE ASSEMBLY (1970-1976 Z)

1. Anti-rattle pin
2. Brake disc
3. Anchor block
4. Trailing shoe assembly
5. Return spring
6. Anti-rattle spring
7. Return spring
8. Wheel cylinder
9. Leading shoe assembly
10. Retaining shim
11. Dust cover

10

Wheel Cylinder Overhaul

Figure 17 shows a 240Z wheel cylinder. **Figure 18** shows the 260-280Z design.

1. Clean the cylinder thoroughly in alcohol before taking it apart.

2. Remove the snap ring or clip ring. Take off the cust cover, then remove the piston, piston cup, and spring.

3. Remove the adjusting wheel together with the adjusting screw. Separate the screw from the wheel.

4. Clean all metal parts in alcohol.

5. Inspect the piston and cylinder bore for scoring, cracks, corrosion, dirt, or excessive wear. Replace cylinder and piston if these conditions are detected.

6. Inspect the adjusting wheel and lever. Replace if wear or damage is visible.

7. Check the return springs for wear, damage, or signs of weakness. Replace if required.

8. Coat the cylinder bore with brake fluid. Install the spring in the wheel cylinder. Coat a new piston cup with rubber grease and install it in the cylinder. Coat the piston with brake fluid and insert it in the cylinder. Install the dust cover and secure it with the circlip. Grease the adjusting wheel and screw at the points marked in **Figure 19**, then install them. Install the bleed valve and dust cover.

Shoe Installation

1. Apply brake grease to the metal-to-metal friction points shown in **Figure 20**.

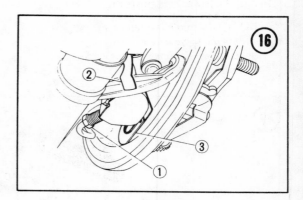

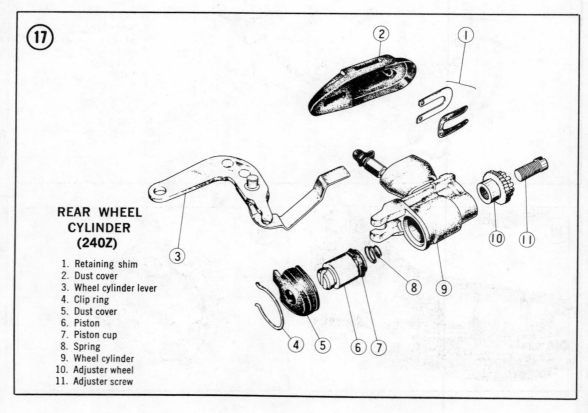

REAR WHEEL CYLINDER (240Z)

1. Retaining shim
2. Dust cover
3. Wheel cylinder lever
4. Clip ring
5. Dust cover
6. Piston
7. Piston cup
8. Spring
9. Wheel cylinder
10. Adjuster wheel
11. Adjuster screw

CAUTION
Do not use ordinary multipurpose grease. Do not let grease touch the brake linings.

2. Hook the upper return spring to both brake shoes.

3. Place the upper ends of the brake shoes in their slots in the anchor block (3, **Figure 15**).

4. Spread apart the lower ends of the brake shoes and place them in their slots in the wheel cylinder.

5. Install the lower return spring.

NOTE: *Although the return springs are almost the same length, they are not interchangeable.* **Figure 21** *shows the different shapes of springs.*

6. Install the anti-rattle pins. Place the washers and springs over the anti-rattle pins and secure them with the retaining collars.

Drum Installation

1. Place the brake drum in position over the rear wheel studs.

2. Insert a screwdriver in the brake adjusting hole and turn the adjusting wheel upward until brake shoes are lightly in contact with the drum.

3. Connect the handbrake cable to the wheel cylinder lever.

4. Pull the handbrake lever several times. This will automatically adjust the rear brakes. Continue pulling the handbrake lever until clicks

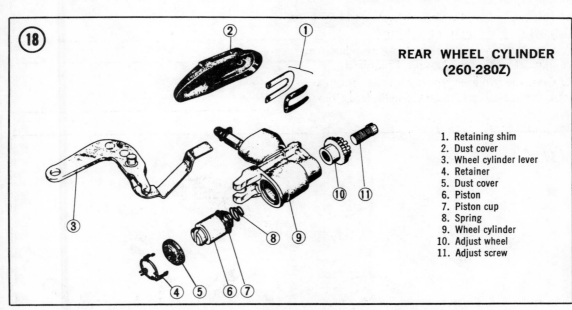

REAR WHEEL CYLINDER (260-280Z)

1. Retaining shim
2. Dust cover
3. Wheel cylinder lever
4. Retainer
5. Dust cover
6. Piston
7. Piston cup
8. Spring
9. Wheel cylinder
10. Adjust wheel
11. Adjust screw

10

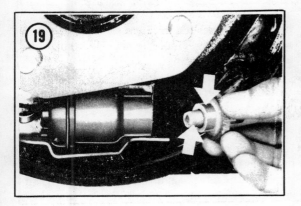

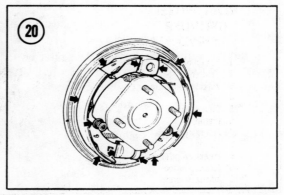

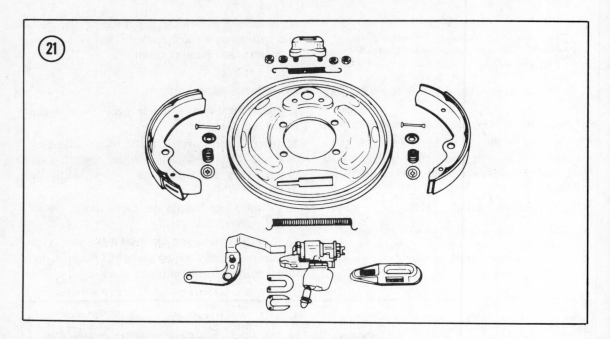

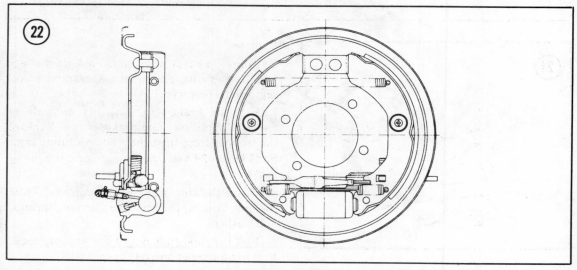

can no longer be heard from the adjusting wheel on the rear wheel cylinder.

5. Install the adjusting hole plug. Push hard on the center of the plug and make sure the lip is inserted all the way into the wheel cylinder.

6. Install the rear wheels and lower the car.

Backing Plate Removal/Installation

This procedure is rarely necessary for brake service. However, should backing plate removal be required, remove the rear wheel bearing as described in Chapter Twelve. Then remove 4 nuts attaching the backing plate to the wheel bearing housing.

Install in the reverse order. Tighten the nuts to 20-27 ft.-lb. (2.7-3.7 mkg).

REAR BRAKES (1977-1978 Z)

The rear brakes are similar to earlier models, but use bolt-on wheel cylinders and a redesigned adjuster mechanism. **Figure 22** is an assembled view; **Figure 23** is an exploded view.

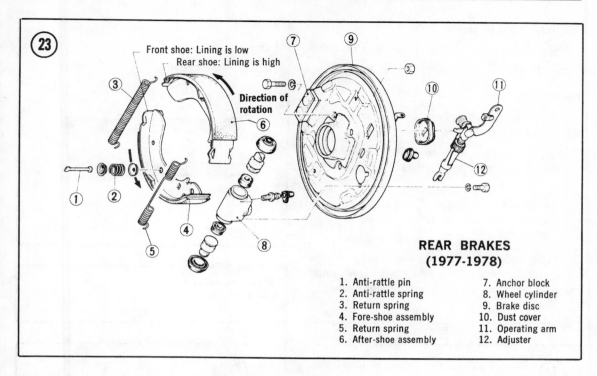

REAR BRAKES (1977-1978)

1. Anti-rattle pin
2. Anti-rattle spring
3. Return spring
4. Fore-shoe assembly
5. Return spring
6. After-shoe assembly
7. Anchor block
8. Wheel cylinder
9. Brake disc
10. Dust cover
11. Operating arm
12. Adjuster

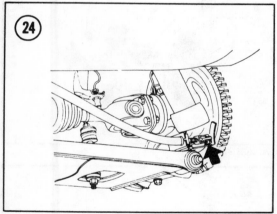

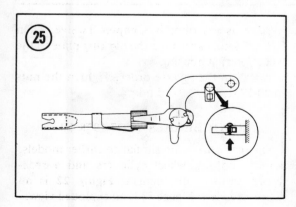

Removal

1. Loosen the rear wheel nuts, jack up the rear end of the car, place it on jackstands, and remove the rear wheels.

2. Pull the brake drum off. If difficult to remove, apply the handbrake firmly. Remove the stopper from the handbrake operating arm. See **Figures 24 and 25.** Then release the handbrake.

3. Grasp the anti-rattle pins with pliers. Twist the pins ¼ turn, then remove the pins, springs, and washers.

4. Pull the shoe ends out of the anchor block. Remove the shoes and return springs.

5. Disconnect the handbrake adjuster from the operating arm. Take the adjuster out.

> NOTE: *Left and right adjusters are not interchangeable.*

6. If wheel cylinder overhaul is planned, disconnect and plug the wheel cylinder brake line. The factory recommends brake line wrench GG94310000 (**Figure 26**). Do not use an adjustable wrench.

7. Remove 2 bolts and take the wheel cylinder out.

10

Inspection and Repair

This is the same as for 1970-1976 models, described earlier in this chapter.

Installation

Installation is the reverse of removal, plus the following:

1. Apply *small* amounts of brake grease to the friction points shown in **Figures 27, 28, and 29**.

> CAUTION
> *Do not use ordinary multipurpose grease. Do not let grease touch the brake linings.*

2. After installation, adjust the brakes. To do this, pull and release the handbrake lever until no more clicks are heard from the rear wheels.

MASTER CYLINDER

All models use tandem (dual piston) master cylinders with a 7/8 in. (22.22 mm) bore.

Datsuns are equipped in production with either Nabco or Tokico master cylinders. The brand name is molded in the cylinder body or fluid reservoir caps. Repair kits for the two brands are not interchangeable. When you buy a repair kit, make sure you get the same brand as your master cylinder.

Removal/Installation

1. Disconnect the brake lines from the master cylinder.

> CAUTION
> *Place rags or a container beneath the master cylinder to keep brake fluid off the paint.*

2. Remove 2 master cylinder installation nuts (**Figure 30**). Separate the master cylinder from the vacuum booster and lift it out.
3. Install by reversing Steps 1 and 2. Fill the fluid reservoirs with brake fluid marked DOT 3 or DOT 4, then bleed the brakes.

Disassembly

Refer to the following exploded views:
Early 240Z — **Figure 31**.

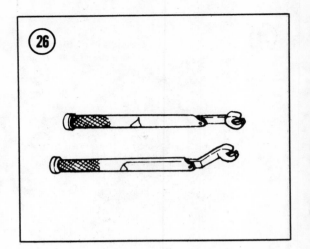

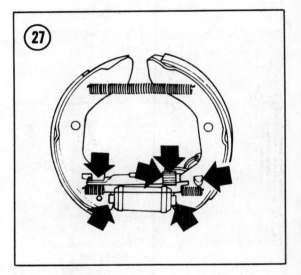

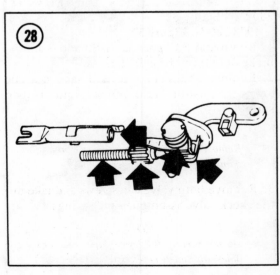

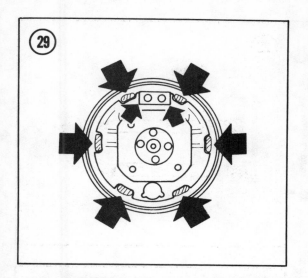

Late 240Z, all 260Z's and 1975-1977 280Z's—**Figure 32**.

1978 280Z—**Figure 33**.

1. Remove the stopper screw(s) and drain the brake fluid from the cylinder.

2. Remove the snap ring and take out the stopper, piston assemblies, and return spring(s).

> *CAUTION*
> *Remove the piston carefully to prevent damaging its friction surface.*

3. Remove both valve cap screws and take out the check valve assemblies and springs.

> *NOTE*
> *Do not remove the brake fluid reservoirs unless absolutely necessary.*

Inspection

1. Thoroughly clean all metal parts in alcohol before inspection. Discard the piston cups, check valves, and valve packing rings.

2. Check the cylinder bore and piston for excessive or uneven wear, scoring, or corrosion. Wear is excessive if clearance between the cylinder wall and pistons exceeds 0.006 in. (0.15 mm). Replace cylinder and piston if these conditions are evident.

3. Check the cylinder springs for wear, damage, or weakness. Replace as needed.

4. Inspect the bleed valves, stopper screws, check valve cap screws, and fluid reservoirs for wear or damage. Replace as needed.

Assembly

Assembly is the reverse of the disassembly procedure, plus the following steps.

1. Coat the cylinder bore and pistons with brake fluid before assembly.

2. Lightly coat all internal rubber parts with rubber grease before installation.

> *CAUTION*
> *Do not scratch the master cylinder bore or pistons when installing.*

3. Tighten the stopper screws and check valves to specifications (end of chapter).

4. After installation, bleed the brakes and check for brake fluid leaks.

5. Check pedal pad height and adjust if necessary. See the *Brake Pedal* section of this chapter.

VACUUM BOOSTER

All models use a Bendix Master-Vac brake booster. All except the 280Z 2 + 2 use a 7.5 in. diaphragm. The 280Z 2 + 2 uses a 9 in. diaphragm. Although the shape and size of some parts differ slightly, overhaul procedures are the same for both types.

The factory recommends overhauling 240Z and 260Z brake boosters every two years. At two-year intervals, an "A" repair kit (**Figure 34**) should be installed. At four-year intervals, a "B" repair kit (**Figure 35**) should be installed. Regular overhaul of 280Z brake boosters is not called for.

10

MASTER CYLINDER (EARLY 240Z)

1. Reservoir cap
2. Brake oil reservoir
3. Brake oil reservoir
4. Brake master cylinder
5. Piston assembly (A)
6. Piston cup
7. Cylinder spring
8. Primary piston cup
9. Piston assembly (B)
10. Secondary piston cup
11. Stopper
12. Snap ring
13. Valve spring
14. Check valve assembly
15. Check valve assembly
16. Packing
17. Valve cap screw
18. Stopper bolt
19. Stopper bolt
20. Bleeder

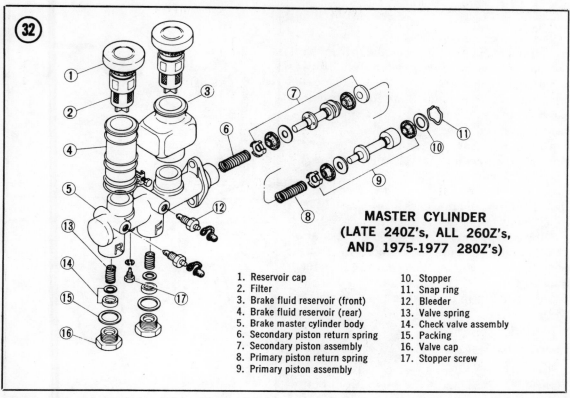

**MASTER CYLINDER
(LATE 240Z's, ALL 260Z's,
AND 1975-1977 280Z's)**

1. Reservoir cap
2. Filter
3. Brake fluid reservoir (front)
4. Brake fluid reservoir (rear)
5. Brake master cylinder body
6. Secondary piston return spring
7. Secondary piston assembly
8. Primary piston return spring
9. Primary piston assembly
10. Stopper
11. Snap ring
12. Bleeder
13. Valve spring
14. Check valve assembly
15. Packing
16. Valve cap
17. Stopper screw

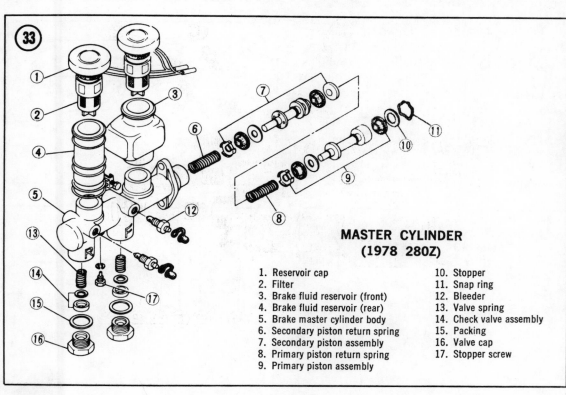

**MASTER CYLINDER
(1978 280Z)**

1. Reservoir cap
2. Filter
3. Brake fluid reservoir (front)
4. Brake fluid reservoir (rear)
5. Brake master cylinder body
6. Secondary piston return spring
7. Secondary piston assembly
8. Primary piston return spring
9. Primary piston assembly
10. Stopper
11. Snap ring
12. Bleeder
13. Valve spring
14. Check valve assembly
15. Packing
16. Valve cap
17. Stopper screw

10

Vacuum Check

This procedure is designed to uncover problems which can be attributed either to the vacuum booster or to the check valve. If this test indicates a problem, perform the next procedure (*Check Valve Test*) to determine whether the cause is the check valve or vacuum booster.

1. Connect a vacuum gauge in the line between the vacuum booster and the check valve. See **Figure 36**.

2. Run the engine, increasing the speed until the vacuum reading reaches approximately 20 in. (500 mm).

3. Shut off the engine and watch the vacuum gauge. If the pressure drops more than one inch (25 mm) within 15 seconds, either the check valve or the vacuum booster is defective. Perform the next test to help isolate the cause.

Check Valve Test

1. Remove the check valve clip (arrow, **Figure 37**). Disconnect the hoses from both ends of the check valve and take it out.

2. Apply soap solution to the Master-Vac end of the check valve. See **Figure 38**. Blow through the other end of the valve. If bubbles form on the Master-Vac end (indicating air has passed through the valve), replace the valve.

3. Apply soap solution to the manifold end of the check valve and blow through the Master-Vac end. If you cannot blow air through the valve, replace it.

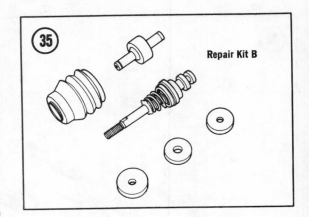

Repair Kit B

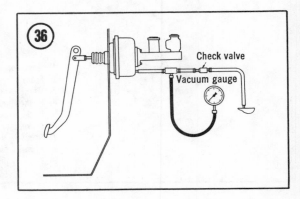

Check valve
Vacuum gauge

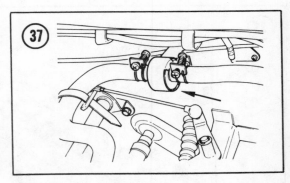

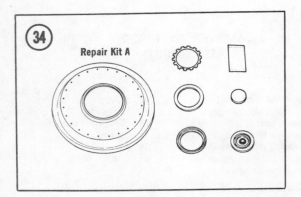

Repair Kit A

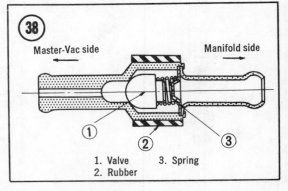

Master-Vac side — Manifold side

1. Valve   3. Spring
2. Rubber

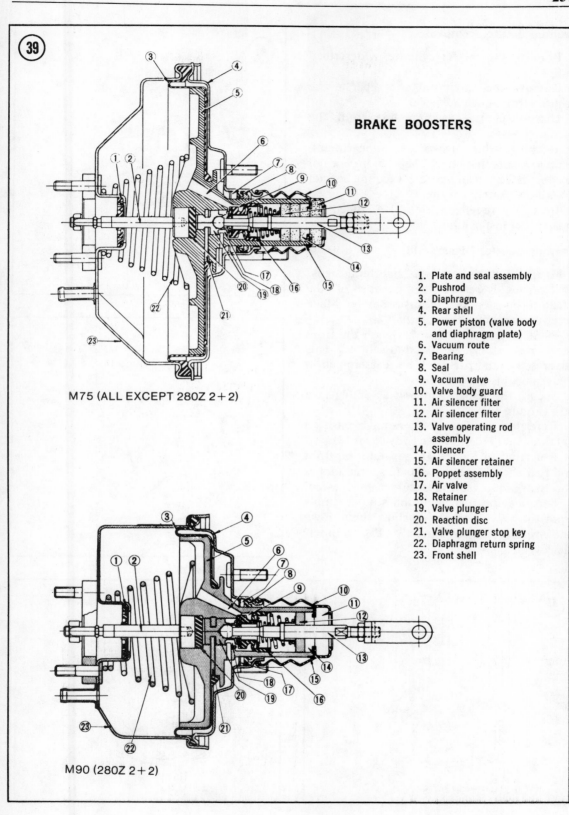

39

BRAKE BOOSTERS

M75 (ALL EXCEPT 280Z 2+2)

M90 (280Z 2+2)

1. Plate and seal assembly
2. Pushrod
3. Diaphragm
4. Rear shell
5. Power piston (valve body and diaphragm plate)
6. Vacuum route
7. Bearing
8. Seal
9. Vacuum valve
10. Valve body guard
11. Air silencer filter
12. Air silencer filter
13. Valve operating rod assembly
14. Silencer
15. Air silencer retainer
16. Poppet assembly
17. Air valve
18. Retainer
19. Valve plunger
20. Reaction disc
21. Valve plunger stop key
22. Diaphragm return spring
23. Front shell

10

Vacuum Booster Removal

1. Remove the master cylinder as described earlier.
2. Remove the clevis pin and separate the pushrod from the brake pedal.
3. Disconnect the vacuum line from the vacuum booster.
4. Working in the passenger compartment, remove 4 nuts that attach the vacuum booster to the firewall. Remove the vacuum booster toward the front of the car.
5. Install by reversing Steps 1-4. Bleed the brakes after installation.

Vacuum Booster Disassembly

Figure 39 shows both brake booster designs.
1. Thoroughly clean the outside of the vacuum booster before disassembly. Make sure your working area is *clean*.
2. Paint or scribe mating marks on the front shell, rear shell, and stud assembly. This ensures that the parts will be reassembled in their same relative positions.
3. Secure the flange and bolt assembly in a vise (**Figure 40**).
4. Referring to **Figure 40**, remove pushrod (1), locknut (2), and valve body cover (3).
5. Referring to **Figure 41**, separate the front and rear shells. Use the Datsun special tool as shown or improvise a substitute from plywood.
6. Separate the rear shell and stud assembly from the valve body by pushing them down and rotating approximately 17° counterclockwise.

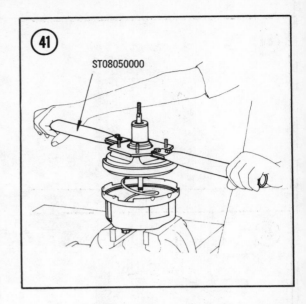

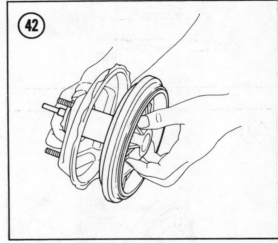

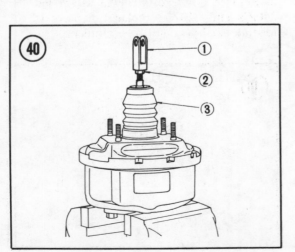

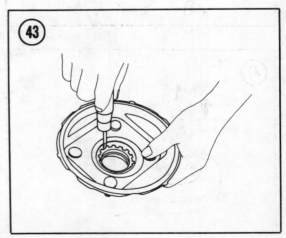

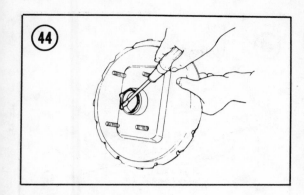

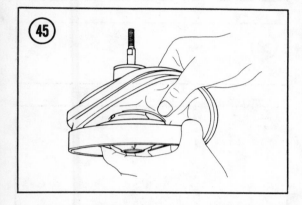

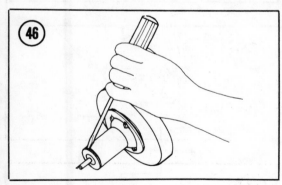

7. Remove pushrod from diaphragm plate.

8. Detach the valve body and diaphragm from the rear shell and stud assembly (**Figure 42**). The vacuum booster is now separated into 3 subassemblies: rear seal and shell assembly; diaphragm plate assembly; front shell and stud assembly.

9. If necessary, remove the rear seal and bearing retainer with a screwdriver. See **Figure 43** (M75) or **Figure 44** (M90). Take out the bearing and seal.

10. Pull the diaphragm out of its groove in the diaphragm plate (**Figure 45**).

11. Remove the air silencer retainer with a screwdriver (**Figure 46**).

CAUTION
Don't use a hammer to tap loose the air silencer retainer. The plastic housing can easily be chipped.

12. Press in the valve operating rod and shake out the stop key (**Figure 47**). Then pull the valve operating rod, together with the air silencer filter, up and out of the body.

13. Push reaction disc out through valve body.

14. Referring to **Figure 48**, remove 2 nuts (1) and the flange (2). Then remove the plate and seal assembly from beneath the flange.

Inspection

1. Check the valve poppet for wear and damage. Replace the valve operating rod (contained in repair kit ''B'') if anything is wrong with the poppet.

2. Replace other components as needed. On 240Z's and 260Z's, replace all parts in the repair kit at 2-year and 4-year intervals.

10

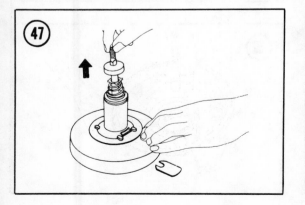

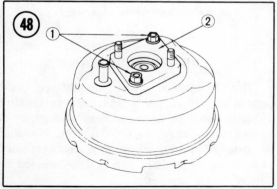

Vacuum Booster
Assembly and Adjustment

Assembly is the reverse of the disassembly procedure, plus the following.

1. Using silicone grease contained in the repair kits, apply a light coat to the following:

   a. On the seal (8, **Figure 39**), the lip, and the face contacting the rear shell

   b. The lip of the valve poppet

   c. Both faces of the reaction disc

   d. The edge of the diaphragm where it makes contact with the front and rear shells

   e. The surfaces on the plate and seal assembly (1, **Figure 39**) that contact the front shell and pushrod

   f. The pushrod surface (2, **Figure 39**) that contacts diaphragm plate (5, **Figure 39**)

2. When inserting the valve operating rod in the valve body, be sure the rod goes straight in and is not tilted to either side. When the rod is in, press it down against its spring and insert the stop key. See **Figure 49**.

3. When installing the bearing and seal retainer on the rear shell, use a drift like the one shown in **Figure 50**.

4. After the vacuum booster is assembled, adjust pushrod length (dimension B, **Figure 51**). Loosen the locknut and turn the pushrod as shown in **Figure 52**. Dimension B on 240Z's and 260Z's is 0.137-0.157 in. (3.5-4.0 mm). On 280Z's, dimension B is 0.384-0.394 in. (9.75-10.0 mm).

> *CAUTION*
> *Make this adjustment with the pushrod pointing up, or the reaction disc may fall out of place. If this happens, the booster will have to be disassembled to put the reaction disc back where it belongs.*

BRAKE BLEEDING

The hydraulic system should be bled whenever air enters it and reduces braking effectiveness. If the pedal feels spongy, or if pedal travel increases considerably, bleeding is usually required. Bleeding is also necessary whenever a hydraulic line is disconnected or the system is repaired.

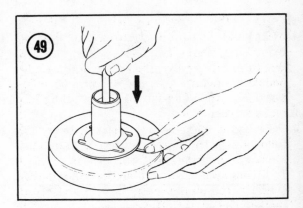

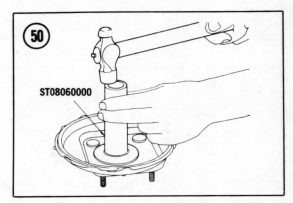

ST08060000

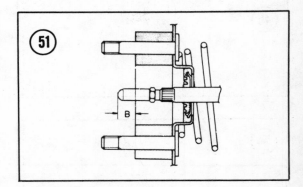

B

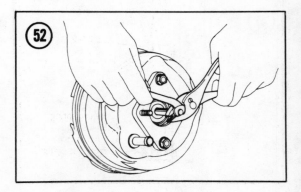

Since this procedure requires handling brake fluid, be careful not to get any fluid on brake pads, shoes, drums, or discs. Clean all dirt from bleed valves before beginning. Two people are required, one to operate the brake pedal and the other to open and close the bleed valves.

Bleeding should be conducted in the following order: master cylinder, right rear, left rear, right front, left front.

1. Clean away any dirt around the master cylinder. Top up the reservoir with brake fluid marked DOT 3 or DOT 4.

2. Attach a plastic tube to the bleed valve. Dip the end of the tube in a jar containing several inches of clean brake fluid.

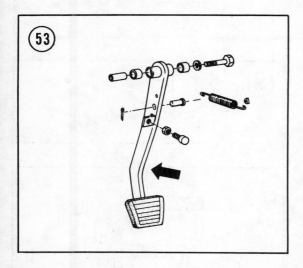

NOTE
Do not allow the end of the tube to come out of the brake fluid during bleeding. This could allow air into the system, requiring that the bleeding procedure be done over.

3. Press the brake pedal as far as it will go, 2 or 3 times, then hold it down.

4. With the brake pedal down, open the bleed valve until the pedal goes to the floor, then close the bleed valve. Do not let the pedal up until the bleed valve is closed.

5. Let the pedal back up slowly.

6. Repeat Steps 3-5 until the fluid entering the jar is free of air bubbles.

7. Repeat the process for the other bleed valves.

NOTE
Keep an eye on the brake fluid in the master cylinder throughout the bleeding process. If the reservoirs are allowed to become empty, air will enter the hydraulic system and the bleeding procedure will have to be repeated.

BRAKE PEDAL

Adjustment

1. Measure brake pedal height from the floor. On all Z's, it should be 8 in. (203 mm).

2. If necessary, change pedal height. On 1970-1976 models, this is done by rotating the pedal stopper (**Figure 53**). On later models, it is done by rotating the stoplight switch (4, **Figure 54**).

3. If necessary, adjust pedal pushrod length. To do this, loosen the pushrod locknut. Rotate the pushrod to change its length, then tighten the locknut.

Removal/Installation

1. Referring to **Figure 54**, remove the pedal return spring (1).

2. Remove the clevis pin (2) from the brake pedal pushrod. Separate the pedal from the pushrod.

3. Remove the pedal fulcrum pin (3) and take the pedal out.

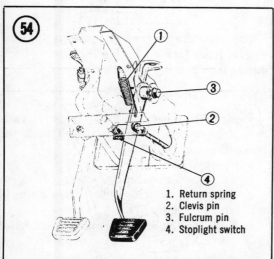

1. Return spring
2. Clevis pin
3. Fulcrum pin
4. Stoplight switch

10

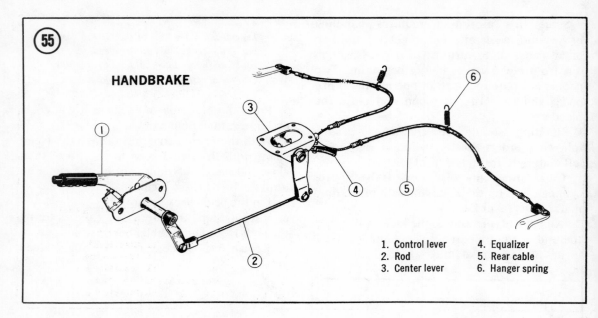

HANDBRAKE

1. Control lever   4. Equalizer
2. Rod   5. Rear cable
3. Center lever   6. Hanger spring

4. Installation is the reverse of removal. Apply multipurpose grease to points 2 and 3 (clevis pin and fulcrum pin). Tighten the fulcrum pin nut to 25-29 ft.-lb. (3.5-4.0 mkg).

HANDBRAKE

The handbrake operates the rear wheels through a rod and two cables. **Figure 55** shows the system.

Adjustment

1. Let off the handbrake lever. Check that the handbrake operating arms (at the rear wheel cylinders) release all the way.
2. Turn the adjusting nut on the handbrake rod (1, **Figure 56**) to eliminate any play in the handbrake linkage.

BRAKE LINES, WARNING SWITCH, AND PROPORTIONING VALVE

The hydraulic system is separated into two circuits, one operating the front wheels and the other operating the rear wheels. If one circuit fails, the other will keep working.

On 1970-1977 models, a pressure switch activates an instrument panel warning light if pressure in either circuit drops severely. On 1978 models, level indicators in the master cylinder activate the light if brake fluid level drops below a safe minimum.

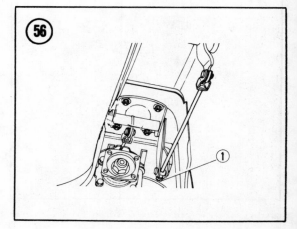

The proportioning valve prevents the rear wheels from locking before the front wheels during hard braking.

Brake Line Inspection

Figure 57 shows the brake lines on early cars. Later versions are similar. Check the brake lines for the following.
  a. Cracks or wear
  b. Leakage at connections
  c. Warped or twisted rubber brake hoses (4 and 14, **Figure 57**)
  d. Sufficient clearance between brake hoses and other parts of the car to prevent wear and damage to the hoses

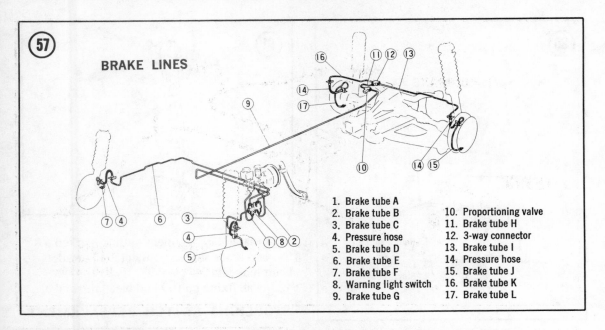

57 BRAKE LINES

1. Brake tube A
2. Brake tube B
3. Brake tube C
4. Pressure hose
5. Brake tube D
6. Brake tube E
7. Brake tube F
8. Warning light switch
9. Brake tube G
10. Proportioning valve
11. Brake tube H
12. 3-way connector
13. Brake tube I
14. Pressure hose
15. Brake tube J
16. Brake tube K
17. Brake tube L

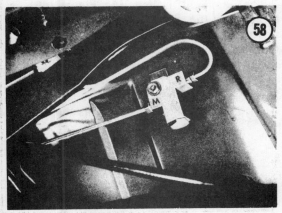

Warning Light Switch Replacement

The warning light switch must be replaced if defective. Do not attempt to repair it. Refer to **Figure 57**.
1. Disconnect the warning light wire.
2. Disconnect the brake lines.
3. Remove fixing bolt and take out switch.
4. Installation is the reverse of removal. Bleed the brakes after installation.

Proportioning Valve Testing

To test, drive the car at a speed in excess of 31 mph (50 kph). Brake hard enough to lock the wheels *slightly*. If the front wheels lock before or at the same time as the rear wheels, the valve is working properly. If the rear wheels lock first, the valve is defective and must be replaced.

CAUTION
Do not lock the wheels completely when braking, or the tires will be flat-spotted.

Proportioning Valve Replacement

Figure 58 shows the early type proportioning valve, mounted in the brake line above the rear suspension. **Figure 59** shows the later design, mounted on the firewall near master cylinder.

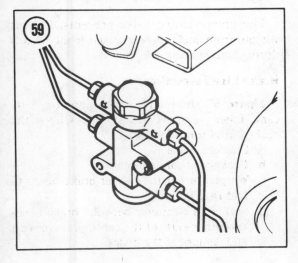

10

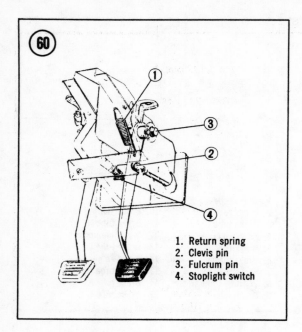

1. Return spring
2. Clevis pin
3. Fulcrum pin
4. Stoplight switch

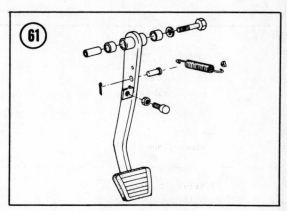

1. Disconnect the brake lines, remove the fixing bolt(s), and take the valve out.

2. On early cars, install the new valve so the side marked "M" is connected to the brake line running to the front of the car. The side marked "R" connects to the line running to the rear brakes.

3. On later cars, connect outlets marked "R" to rear brake lines; connect "F" outlets to front brake lines.

4. Install fixing bolt(s) and bleed the brakes.

STOPLIGHT SWITCH REPLACEMENT

The stoplight switch (4, **Figure 60**) is located on the pedal bracket. To replace it, unscrew the switch and screw in a new one. On cars with pedal stoppers (**Figure 61**), screw the switch in until its threaded portion is flush with the pedal bracket. On cars without pedal stoppers, adjust brake pedal height as described under *Brake Pedal* in this chapter.

Table 1 BRAKE SPECIFICATIONS

Master cylinder	
Inside diameter	7/8 in. (22.22 mm)
Maximum clearance,	
piston to cylinder bore	0.006 in. (0.15 mm)
Calipers	
Inside diameter	2 1/8 in. (53.98 mm)
Wheel cylinders	
Inside diameter	7/8 in. (22.22 mm)
Maximum clearance,	
piston to cylinder bore	0.006 in. (0.15 mm)
Discs	
Outer diameter	10.67 in. (271 mm)
Minimum thickness	0.413 in. (10.5 mm)
Drums	
Inside diameter, maximum	9.055 in. (230 mm)
Out-of-round, maximum	0.002 in. (0.05 mm)
Linings	
Minimum thickness (pads)	0.08 in. (2 mm)
Minimum thickness (shoes)	1/16 in. (1.5 mm)

Table 2 TIGHTENING TORQUES

	Ft.-lb.	Mkg
Disc installation bolts	28-38	3.9-5.3
Caliper installation bolts	53-72	7.3-9.9
Rear backing plate nuts	20-27	2.7-3.7
Anchor block nuts (1970-1976)	10-13	1.4-1.8
Wheel cylinder bolts (1977-1978)	4 1/2-6	0.6-0.8
Master cylinder nuts	6-8	0.8-1.1
Brake booster nuts	6-8	0.8-1.1
Metal brake lines	11-13	1.5-1.8
Rubber brake hoses	12-14	1.7-2.0

10

FRONT SUSPENSION, WHEEL BEARINGS AND STEERING

All models use a MacPherson strut front suspension. The shock absorbers and springs are combined into a single unit, with the bearing spindles permanently attached to the bottom. The struts are attached to the wheel wells at the top. At the bottom, the struts are secured through ball-joints to the transverse links. The front-rear movements of the tranverse links are controlled by compression rods. A sway bar connects the transverse links. **Figure 1** shows the front suspension. Rack-and-pinion steering is used on all Z's.

This chapter includes service procedures for the front suspension, wheel bearings, steering wheel and column, and steering gear. Specifications and tightening torques are listed in **Table 1** and **Table 2** at the end of the chapter.

A few special tools are used in this chapter. All are available through your dealer. A few are manufactured by Kent-Moore Tool Division, 29784 Little Mack, Roseville, Michigan, 48066 and may be ordered direct from them.

WHEEL ALIGNMENT

Several front suspension angles affect the running and steering of the front wheels.

These angles must be properly aligned to prevent excessive tire wear, as well as to maintain directional stablity and ease of steering. These angles are:
- a. Caster
- b. Camber
- c. Toe-in
- d. Steering axis inclination
- e. Steering angle

Caster, camber, and steering axis inclination are built-in and cannot be adjusted. These angles are measured to check for bent suspension parts. Steering angle is not adjustable, and may indicate an incorrectly assembled rack-and-pinion mechanism if it is incorrect. Toe-in, however, can easily be adjusted.

Pre-alignment Check

The steering and various suspension angles are affected by several factors. Perform the following steps before checking or adjustment.

1. Check tire pressure and wear. See *Tire Wear Analysis*, Chapter Two.

2. Check play in front wheel bearings. Adjust if necessary, using procedures described later in this chapter.

3. Check play in ball-joints. See Chapter Two.

4. Check for broken springs.
5. Remove any excessive load.
6. Check shock absorbers.
7. Check rack-and-pinion mechanism (or linkage) and tie rods for looseness.
8. Check wheel balance.
9. Check rear suspension for looseness.

Front tire wear patterns can indicate several alignment problems. These problems are discussed and illustrated under *Tire Wear Analysis*, Chapter Two.

Caster and Camber

Caster is the inclination of the angle from the vertical through the ball-joints. Positive caster shifts the wheel forward; negative caster shifts the wheel rearward. Caster causes the wheels to return to a straight ahead position after a turn. It also prevents the wheels from wandering due to wind, potholes, or uneven road surfaces.

Camber is the inclination of the wheel from vertical. With positive camber, the top of the tire leans outward. With negative camber, the top of the tire leans inward.

Toe-in

When a car moves forward, the front wheels tend to point outward. Because of this, the wheels are pointed straight ahead or slightly inward when the car is at rest. The distance between tire tread centers (A, **Figure 2**) is the same as or slightly less than distance B.
1. Park the car on a level, smooth surface with the wheels pointing straight ahead.
2. Mark the center of the tread at the front and rear of each tire.
3. Measure the distance between forward chalk marks (A, **Figure 2**). Use 2 pieces of telescoping aluminum tubing. Telescope the tubing so each end contacts a chalk mark. Using a sharp scribe, mark the small diameter tubing exactly where it enters the large tube.

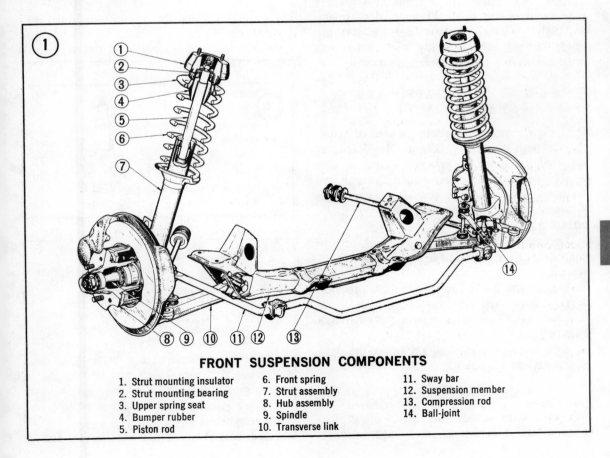

11

FRONT SUSPENSION COMPONENTS

1. Strut mounting insulator
2. Strut mounting bearing
3. Upper spring seat
4. Bumper rubber
5. Piston rod
6. Front spring
7. Strut assembly
8. Hub assembly
9. Spindle
10. Transverse link
11. Sway bar
12. Suspension member
13. Compression rod
14. Ball-joint

4. Measure between the rear chalk marks with the telescoping tubes. Make another mark on the small tube where it enters the large one. The distance between the 2 scribe marks is toe-in.

If toe-in is incorrect, loosen the tie rod locknuts at both wheels. See **Figure 3**. Rotate the tie rods to increase or reduce toe-in as needed.

> *NOTE*
> *Tie rod lengths should be equal after adjustment.*

Steering Axis Inclination

Steering axis inclination is the inward or outward lean of the front suspension. It is not adjustable.

Steering Angle

When a car turns, the inside wheel makes a smaller circle than the outside wheel. Because of this, the inside wheel turns at a greater angle than the outside wheel. Setting toe-in correctly should produce correct steering angle. If not, the steering rack-and-pinion mechanism may be assembled incorrectly.

FRONT SHOCK ABSORBER REPLACEMENT

The front shock absorbers are located inside the suspension struts (**Figure 4**). Replacement of the shock absorbers requires several expensive tools. However, much expense can be saved by removing the strut assemblies yourself and taking them to a dealer for shock absorber replacement.

1. Loosen the front wheel nuts, jack up the car, place it on jackstands, and remove front wheels.
2. Detach the brake lines from their brackets on the struts (**Figure 5**).
3. Unbolt the knuckle arm from the strut. See **Figure 6**.
4. Remove 3 nuts securing the top of the strut to the wheel well. See **Figure 7**.

> *WARNING*
> ***Do not*** *remove the center nut from the top of the strut. This could allow the coil spring to fly out and cause serious injury.*

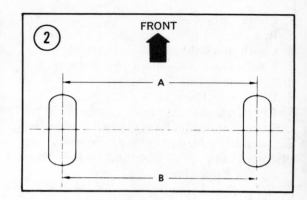

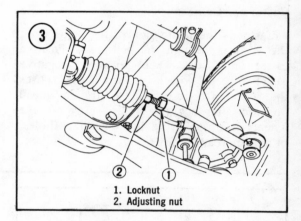

1. Locknut
2. Adjusting nut

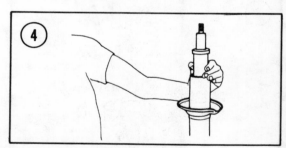

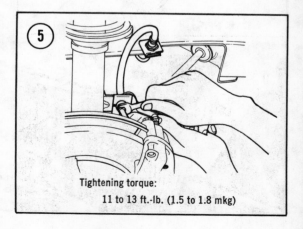

Tightening torque:
11 to 13 ft.-lb. (1.5 to 1.8 mkg)

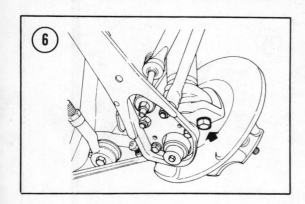

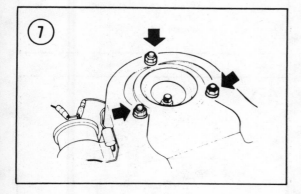

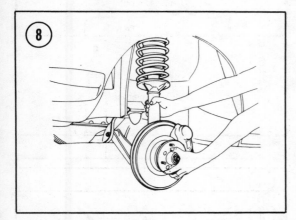

5. Pry the knuckle arm downward away from the strut with a strong steel bar.

6. Take the strut out. See **Figure 8**.

7. Have new shock absorbers installed in the struts by a Datsun dealer.

8. Install by reversing Steps 1-6. Tighten all fasteners to torque specifications (**Table 2**, end of chapter). Bleed the brakes as described under *Brake Bleeding*, Chapter Ten.

COIL SPRING REPLACEMENT

The coil spring is part of the strut assembly. To replace the spring, follow the shock absorber procedure. Since the procedure requires special tools, it is best to remove the strut yourself and let a dealer install a new spring. Then install the strut using the same procedure.

SWAY BAR

Removal/Installation

1. Raise the car on jackstands and remove both front wheels.

2. Remove the splash panel from under the front of the car.

3. Check for a white paint mark on the sway bar next to the frame bracket. See **Figure 9**. If there is no mark, make your own. This is necessary to center the bar properly during installation.

4. Unbolt the sway bar brackets from the frame. Unbolt the sway bar end bushings from the transverse links, then take the bar out.

5. Inspect the rubber mounting bushings for wear, cracks, or deterioration. Replace as needed.

6. Installation is the reverse of removal. Be sure the bar is centered before tightening the frame bracket bolts. Tighten all bolts to specifications (**Table 2**, end of chapter).

COMPRESSION ROD

This rod controls front-to-rear movements of the transverse links. The rod runs from the transverse link backward to the frame. Since forward movement of the car places the rod under compression, it is called a compression rod.

11

Removal/Installation

1. Jack up the front end of the car and place it on jackstands.

2. Unbolt the rod from the frame and transverse link, then take it out. See **Figure 10**.

3. Inspect the rubber bushings for wear, cracks, or deterioration. Replace as needed.

4. Position the rod and bushings in the frame. Do not tighten the nut yet.

5. Bolt the rod to the transverse link. Tighten bolts to specifications (**Table 2**, end of chapter).

6. Tighten rod-to-frame nut to specifications. Lower the car.

TRANSVERSE LINKS
AND BALL-JOINTS

Removal

1. Loosen the front wheel nuts, jack up the car, place it on jackstands, and remove front wheels.

2. Detach the stablilizer bar and compression rod from the transverse link as described earlier.

3. Detach the tie rod from the knuckle arm. See **Figure 11**. Use a puller such as HT72520000 (**Figure 12**) or a fork-type separator (**Figure 13**). These are available from rental dealers.

4. Remove the knuckle arm bolts (**Figure 14**). This separates the knuckle arm, ball-joint, and transverse link outer end from the strut assembly.

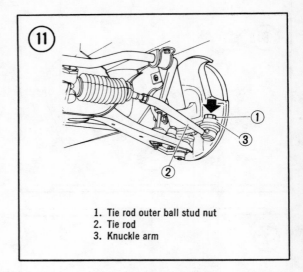

1. Tie rod outer ball stud nut
2. Tie rod
3. Knuckle arm

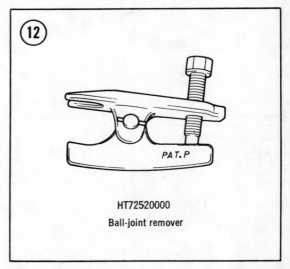

HT72520000
Ball-joint remover

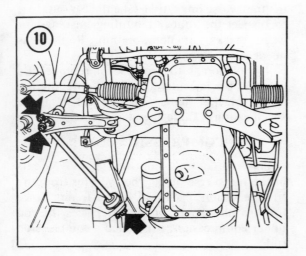

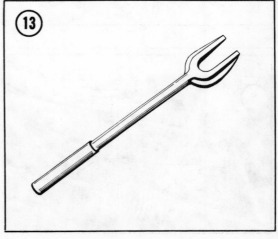

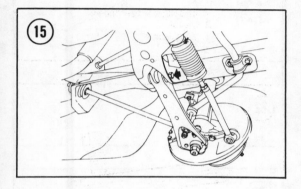

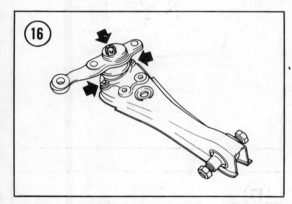

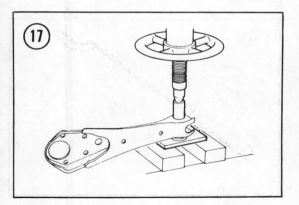

5. Unbolt the transverse link inner end from the suspension crossmember. See **Figure 15**.

6. Take the transverse link out, together with the knuckle arm.

Disassembly

1. Place the transverse link in a vise and remove the cotter pin from the knuckle arm nut. See **Figure 16**. Remove the nut and lift the knuckle arm off the ball-joint.

2. Remove the bolts attaching the ball-joint to the transverse link, then lift the ball-joint off.

Inspection

1. Throughly clean all parts in solvent before inspection.

2. Check the knuckle arm for wear, cracks, and other visible defects. Replace the knuckle arm if defects are found.

3. Check the transverse link bushing for melted or cracked rubber. If the bushing is defective, press it out with a press, drift, and support tool. See **Figure 17**. Press in a new bushing with the same tools. When installed, the bushing should be flush with the transverse link. See **Figure 18**.

> *NOTE*
> *Apply soap solution to the bushing hole in the transverse link before installation. If you do not have the special tools or an acceptable substitute, the pressing operation can be performed by a machine shop.*

11

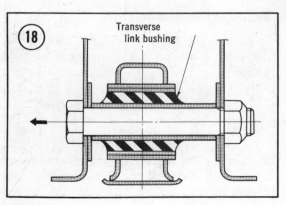

Transverse link bushing

4. Inspect the ball-joint for looseness, damage, or cracks. Check the dust cover and replace the ball-joint if the rubber is cracked or shows signs of deterioration.

Assembly

1. Be sure all parts are clean.
2. Install the ball-joint on the transverse link. Tighten the installation bolts to specifications (**Table 2**, end of chapter).
3. Install the knuckle arm on the ball-joint (**Figure 19**). Tighten the nut to specifications and secure with a cotter pin.

Installation

1. Thoroughly clean the strut assembly around the area where it attaches to the knuckle arm.
2. Bolt the knuckle arm to the strut. Tighten the bolts to specifications.
3. Attach the inner end of the transverse link to the suspension crossmember. Tighten the bolt slightly.

> *NOTE*
> *Install the bolt so the head is toward the front of the car, and the nut toward the rear.*

4. Attach the stablilizer bar and connecting rod to the transverse link.
5. Install the wheels and lower the car.
6. Tighten the transverse link bolt to specifications (**Table 2**, end of chapter). This is done with the car carrying the standard load (2 passengers weighing 150 lb. each).

CROSSMEMBER

Removal/Installation

1. Loosen the front wheel nuts, jack up the car, place it on jackstands, and remove front wheels.

> *NOTE*
> *Locate the jackstands as shown in **Figure 20** to ensure that they will not be in the way during this procedure.*

2. Remove the transverse link mounting bolt from each side of the crossmember. See **Figure 15**.

3. Unbolt the steering gear housing as described in this chapter.
4. Loosen the motor mount nuts shown in **Figure 21**. Do not remove them yet.
5. Attach a hoist to the engine. Use the hoist to remove all weight from the motor mounts. Then remove the nuts and bolts shown in **Figure 21**. Do not detach the mounts from the engine.

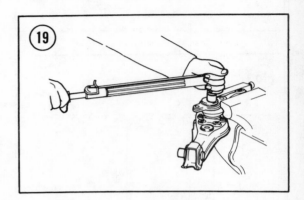

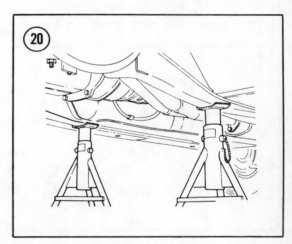

NOTE

Use a hoist which can be locked in one position, and which is capable of supporting the engine for an extended length of time. Hydraulic hoists, available from tool rental dealers, are ideal for this.

6. Remove the crossmember-to-frame bolts (**Figure 22**) and lower the crossmember clear of the car.

NOTE

This is a good time to inspect the rubber motor mount insulators, which were removed with the crossmember. Replace the insulators if the rubber shows signs of deterioration or damage.

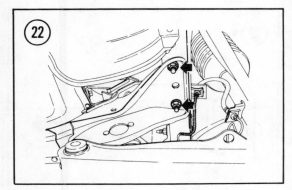

7. Install by reversing Steps 1-6. Tighten the crossmember-to-frame bolts and motor mount bolts to specifications (**Table 2**, end of chapter). Install the transverse link-to-crossmember bolts so the bolt heads are toward the front of the car. Tighten slightly. Lower the car. Tighten to specifications with the car carrying the standard load (2 passengers weighing 150 lb. each).

WHEEL BEARINGS

Figure 23 shows the front wheel bearings and related parts on one side of the car.

Removal

1. Loosen the front wheel nuts, jack up the front of the car, place it on jackstands, and remove the front wheels.

2. Remove the brake caliper (Chapter Ten).

3. Remove the grease cap from the wheel hub (**Figure 24**). Tap lightly with a mallet to free cap.

4. Remove the cotter pin from the wheel bearing locknut, then remove the nut.

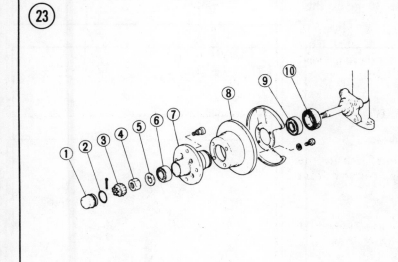

FRONT WHEEL BEARINGS

1. Hub cap
2. O-ring
3. Adjusting cap
4. Wheel bearing nut
5. Wheel bearing washer
6. Outer wheel bearing
7. Wheel hub
8. Disc brake rotor
9. Inner wheel bearing
10. Grease seal

11

5. Pull the wheel hub and brake disc off the bearing spindle (**Figure 25**). The bearings and washer will come off together with the hub.

Disassembly

1. Using 2 grooves inside the hub, tap out the bearing outer races with a suitable drift (**Figure 26**).
2. If necessary, remove 4 bolts to separate the brake disc from the hub (**Figure 27**).

> *NOTE*
> *The brake disc and hub need not be separated unless one or the other is to be replaced.*

Inspection

1. Thoroughly clean wheel bearings in solvent.
2. Inspect inner and outer races and rollers for rust, galling, and the bluish tint that indicates overheating. Rotate the bearings and check for roughness and excessive noise. Compare the races and rollers to the defective bearing parts shown in **Figure 28**. Replace any bearings with similar defects.

Installation

1. Install the bearing outer races with a hammer and drift such as Datsun ST 35300000 (**Figure 29**). **Figure 30** gives the dimensions of the drift.

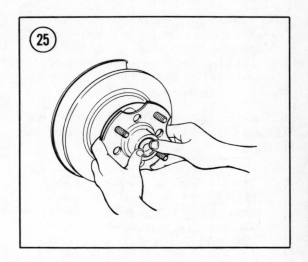

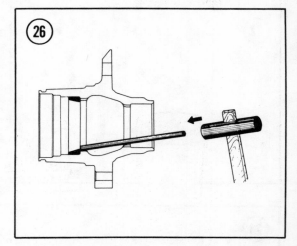

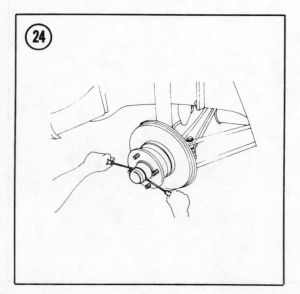

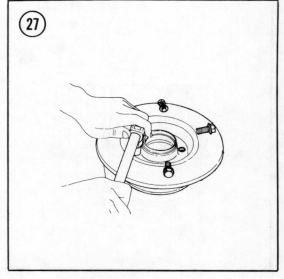

WHEEL BEARING WEAR

Inner race flaking

Roller flaking

Chipped inner race

Chipped roller

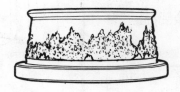

Recess on inner race

Recess on outer race

Recess on roller

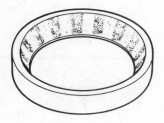

Rust on outer race

11

2. If the disc was removed from the hub, reinstall it. Make sure the disc-to-hub mating surfaces are perfectly clean. Tighten the disc-to-hub bolts in a cross pattern, in several stages. This will make sure disc and hub align correctly. Tighten to 28-38 ft.-lb. (3.9-5.3 mkg).

3. Fill the hub and grease cap to the points shown in **Figure 31** with wheel bearing grease.

4. Fill the spacer between the grease seal lips with grease (**Figure 32**).

5. Work as much grease as possible between the wheel bearing rollers (**Figure 33**).

6. Apply a light coat of grease to the bearing spindle, locknut, and bearing washer.

7. Install the wheel bearing and grease seal in the hub.

8. Assemble the brake disc and hub.

9. Install the hub on the bearing spindle.

Adjustment

1. Tighten the wheel bearing locknut to 18-22 ft.-lb. (2.5-3.0 mkg). See **Figure 34**.

2. Turn the hub several turns in both directions to seat the bearing. Retighten to 18-22 ft.-lb. (2.5-3.0 mkg).

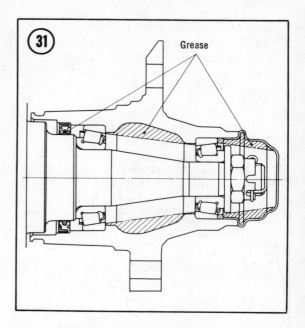

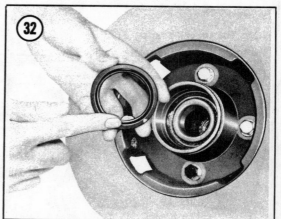

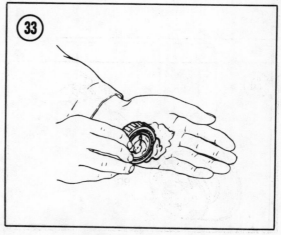

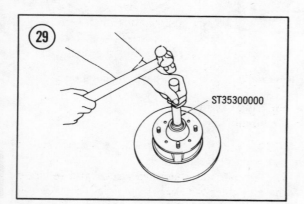

ST35300000

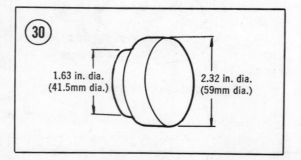

1.63 in. dia. (41.5mm dia.)   2.32 in. dia. (59mm dia.)

3. Back off the wheel bearing locknut 60° to line up the locknut notches with the cotter pin hole in the bearing spindle. See **Figure 35**. If the notches do not line up with the hole, the nut may be loosened 15°.

> *CAUTION*
> *Do not loosen more than specified.*

4. Attach a spring scale to one of the wheel lugs (**Figure 36**). Measure the amount of pull necessary to rotate the hub. The pull should range from 1.5-3.3 lb. (new bearings) or 0.4-1.8 lb. (used bearings).

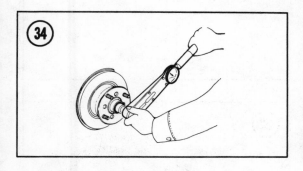

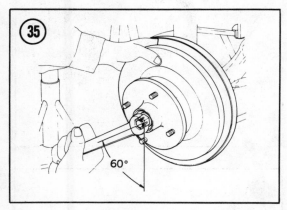

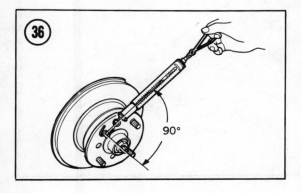

5. Grasp the hub firmly in both hands and try to shake it up, down, and sideways. There should be no play in the bearing.

6. If all the adjustments are within specifications, secure the locknut with a cotter pin and install the grease cap.

7. Install the brake caliper (Chapter Ten) and wheel. Lower the car and bleed the brakes.

STEERING

Figure 37 shows the steering system.

Steering Wheel
Removal/Installation

1. Turn the steering wheel to the straight ahead position.

2. On 240Z's, pull the horn button off. On 260Z's and 280Z's, press the button down, turn counterclockwise, and lift off.

3. Remove steering wheel nut (**Figure 38**).

4. Remove the steering wheel from the column. If necessary, use a puller like the one shown in **Figure 39**. Do not use a knock-off type puller. Do not allow the wheels to turn while the steering wheel is removed.

5. Install by reversing Steps 1-4. Be sure the steering wheel is on straight, not rotated right or left. Tighten steering wheel nut to specifications (**Table 2**, end of chapter).

Steering Column
Removal/Installation

1. Remove the steering wheel as described in the previous procedure.

2. Remove the attaching screws and separate the upper and lower halves of the steering column shell (**Figure 40**). Remove 2 screws and take off the turn signal-lighting switch.

3. Make alignment marks on the rubber coupling clamp and lower column splines. Then remove the column clamp bolt. See **Figure 41**.

> *NOTE*
> *The bolt fits into a notch in the lower column, so it must be removed, not just loosened.*

11

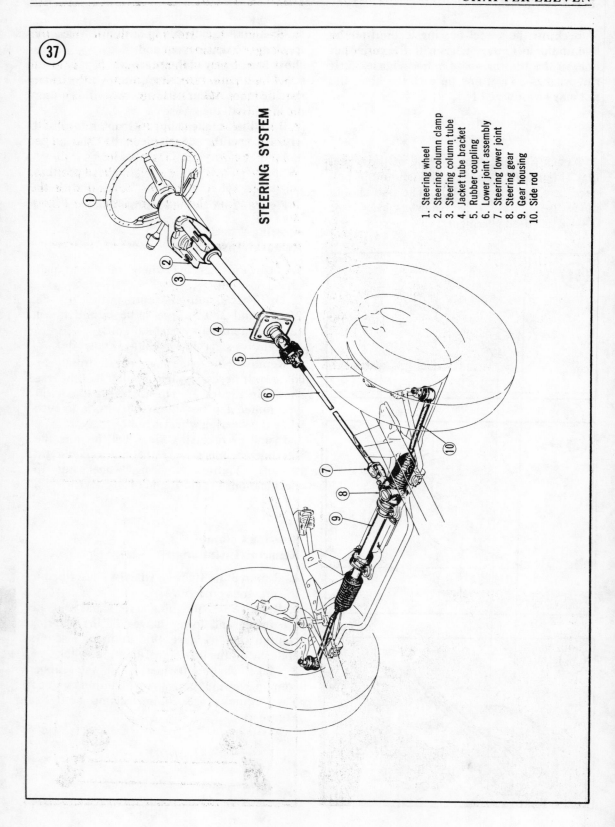

37

STEERING SYSTEM

1. Steering wheel
2. Steering column clamp
3. Steering column tube
4. Jacket tube bracket
5. Rubber coupling
6. Lower joint assembly
7. Steering lower joint
8. Steering gear
9. Gear housing
10. Side rod

4. Remove 4 screws securing the steering column grommet to the floor. See **Figure 42**.
5. Detach the steering column clamp from the dash. See **Figure 43**.

NOTE
Some early models use 4 bolts.

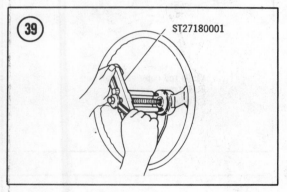

ST27180001

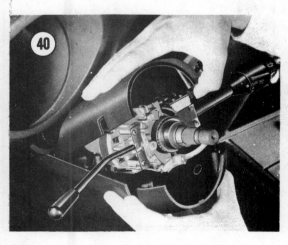

6. Remove the steering column into the passenger compartment.
7. If the lower column must be removed (rack-and-pinion steering), remove the clamp bolt (**Figure 44**). The lower column can then be lifted out.
8. Installation is the reverse of removal. On rack-and-pinion steering, install the upper column before installing the lower column. With the wheels in the straight ahead position, align the slit in the lower column with the punch mark in the upper column. See **Figure 45**.

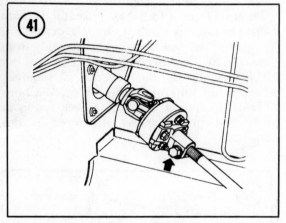

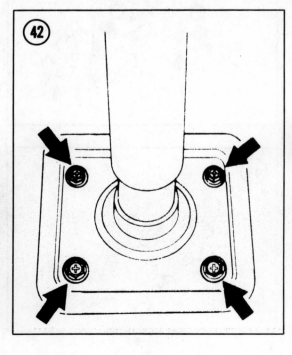

11

Rack-and-Pinion Removal/Installation

1. Loosen the front wheel nuts, jack up the car, place it on jackstands, and remove front wheels.

2. Disconnect the lower joint assembly from the steering column (**Figure 41**).

3. Remove the clamp bolt from the lower joint assembly (**Figure 44**). Detach the lower joint assembly from the pinion.

4. Remove the splash panel from under the front of the car.

5. Disconnect the tie rods from the knuckle arms (**Figure 46**). Use a puller such as Datsun tool HT72520000 (Kent-Moore J-25730-A) (**Figure 47**) or a fork-type separator (**Figure 48**). These are available from rental dealers.

6. Unbolt the rack-and-pinion assembly from the crossmember. See **Figure 49**.

7. Installation is the reverse of removal. Tighten all nuts and bolts to specifications (**Table 2**, end of chapter). Check toe-in as described under *Wheel Alignment* in this chapter.

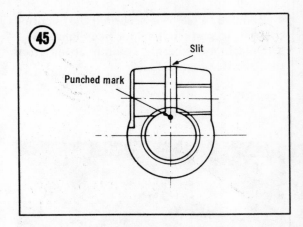

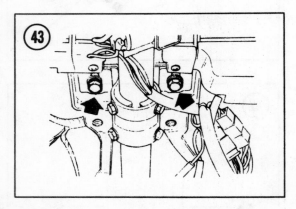

1. Tie rod outer ball stud nut
2. Tie rod
3. Knuckle arm

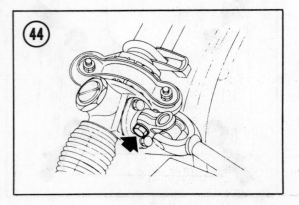

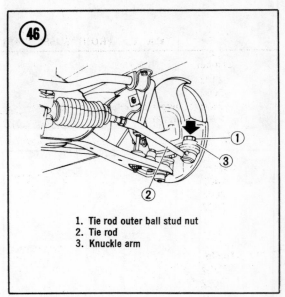

HT72520000

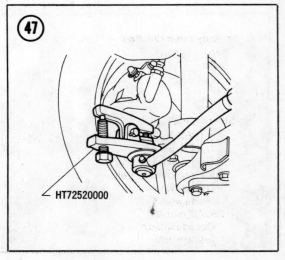

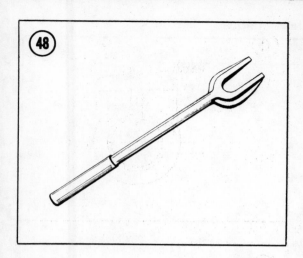

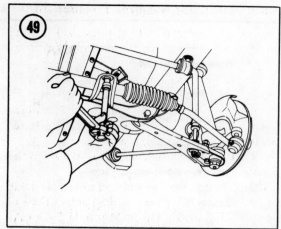

Table 1   FRONT SUSPENSION AND STEERING SPECIFICATIONS

Camber
240Z	50' ± 45'
260Z	46' ± 45'
280Z (standard model)	18' to 1° 48'
280Z (2 plus 2)	21' to 1° 51'

Caster
240Z	2° 55' ± 45'
260Z	2° 54' ± 45'
280Z	2° 33' to 3° 33'

Toe-In
240Z	1/16 to 7/32 in. (1.59-5.56mm)
260Z	0.079-0.197 in. (2-5mm)
280Z	0-1/8 in. (0-3mm)

Steering axis inclination
240Z and 260Z	12° 10' ± 30'
280Z	11° 14' to 12° 44'

Steering angle
240Z, 260Z	
Outside wheel	31° 42' ± 30'
Inside wheel	33° ± 30'
280Z (standard model)	
Outside wheel	32° 6' to 34° 6'
Inside wheel	33° 54' to 34° 54'
280Z (2 plus 2)	
Outside wheel	34° 24' to 36° 24'
Inside wheel	36° 18' to 37° 18'

Table 2 TIGHTENING TORQUES

	ft.-lb.	mkg
Wheel bearing locknut	18-22	2.5-3.0
Strut-to-body nuts	18-25	2.5-3.5
Knuckle arm-to-strut bolts	53-72	7.3-10.0
Ball-joint nut	40-54	5.5-7.5
Transverse link-to-ball-joint bolts		
240Z	35-46	4.9-6.3
260Z	44-51	6.1-7.1
280Z	14-18	1.9-2.5
Transverse link-to-crossmember bolts		
240Z	80-94	11-13
260Z, 280Z	80-101	11-14
Compression rod-to-transverse link bolts		
240Z	36-45	5.0-6.2
260Z, 280Z	44-51	6.1-7.1
Compression rod-to-frame nuts	33-40	4.5-5.5
Stabilizer bushing to transverse link nuts		
240Z	14-19	1.9-2.6
260Z, 280Z	9-20	1.2-2.7
Stabilizer bushing-to-stabilizer nuts	9-20	1.2-2.7
Stabilizer-to-frame bolts	14-18	1.9-2.5
Crossmember-to-frame bolts		
240Z	30-36	4-5
260Z, 280Z	33-36	4.5-5.0
Crossmember to motor mounts		
240Z	12-19	1.6-2.6
260Z, 280Z	12-15	1.6-2.1
Rack-and-pinion steering		
240Z	16-22	2.2-3.0
260Z	19-22	2.6-3.0
280Z (bolt to welded nut)	19-22	2.6-3.0
280Z (locknut)	22-25	3.0-3.5
Tie-rod end stud nuts	40-55	5.5-7.6

Table 2   TIGHTENING TORQUES (continued)

	Ft.-lb.	Mkg
Steering wheel nut		
240Z,	29-36	4-5
260Z, 280Z	36-51	5-7
Lower column-to-upper column clamp bolt (rack-and-pinion)		
240Z	11-13	1.5-1.8
260Z, 280Z	17-20	2.3-2.7
Lower column-to-pinion clamp bolt (rack-and-pinion)	29-36	4-5
Stub shaft-to-coupling clamp bolt	24-28	3.3-3.9

11

CHAPTER TWELVE

REAR SUSPENSION, DIFFERENTIAL
AND DRIVE SHAFT

All models use a strut-type independent suspension at the rear with lower transverse links. At the top, the struts are attached to the body by nuts. At the bottom, the struts are permanently attached to the axle housing.

Power is transmitted from the drive shaft to the differential, and from the differential to the axle shafts. The axle shafts turn the spindles, which turn the wheels.

This chapter includes service procedures for the rear suspension, axle shafts, wheel bearings, drive shaft, and differential. Tightening torques are listed in **Table 1** at the end of the chapter.

Figure 1 shows the Z rear suspension.

DIFFERENTIAL

This section provides removal, installation, and inspection procedures for the differential. Actual differential repair, however, requires professional skills and many expensive special tools. Repair should be left to a dealer or other competent shop. Inspection procedures in this section will tell you if repairs are necessary.

Removal/Installation

1. Securely block both front wheels so the car will not roll in either direction.

2. Jack up the rear of the car and place it on jackstands.

3. Remove the main muffler (Chapter Five, *Exhaust System* section).

4. Remove 4 bolts securing the drive shaft to the differential (**Figure 2**).

REAR SUSPENSION

1. Differential
2. Differential case mount rear member
3. Differential case mount rear insulator
4. Strut assembly
5. Link mount brace
6. Spindle
7. Axle shaft
8. Transverse link
9. Differential link mount front member
10. Differential case mount front insulator

12

5. Loosen both of the inner front transverse link bolts (**Figure 3**).

6. Unbolt each axle shaft from its spindle flange (**Figure 4**).

7. Unbolt the axle shafts from the differential. The axle shafts may be flange types with 4 bolts (**Figure 5**) or spline types with single bolts (**Figure 6**).

8. Place a jack beneath the differential to support it.

9. Remove 2 nuts from the differential rear mounting member (arrows, **Figure 7**).

10. Remove 4 bolts from the differential front mounting member (**Figure 8**).

11. Lower the jack until the differential is clear of the car, then take it out.

12. Installation is the reverse of removal. Fill with an oil recommended in Chapter Three if the differential was drained.

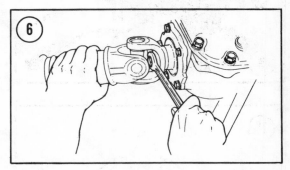

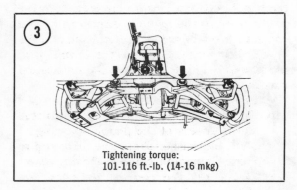

Tightening torque:
101-116 ft.-lb. (14-16 mkg)

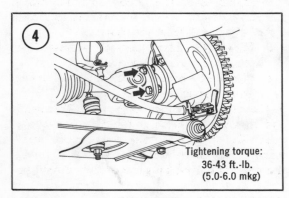

Tightening torque:
36-43 ft.-lb.
(5.0-6.0 mkg)

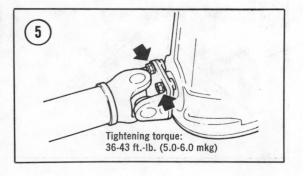

Tightening torque:
36-43 ft.-lb. (5.0-6.0 mkg)

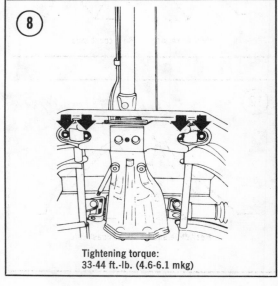

Tightening torque:
33-44 ft.-lb. (4.6-6.1 mkg)

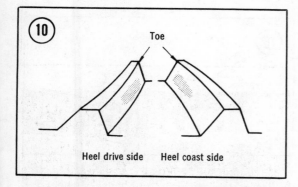

Heel drive side   Heel coast side

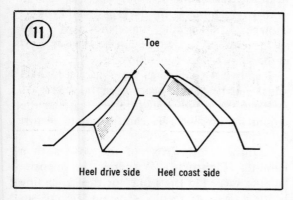

Heel drive side   Heel coast side

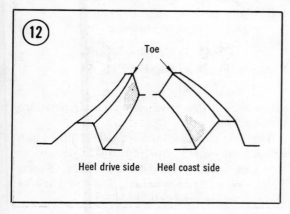

Heel drive side   Heel coast side

Inspection (All Models)

1. Drain gear oil from the differential.
2. Place the differential on a workbench and remove the inspection cover (**Figure 9**).

> *NOTE*
> ***Figure 9*** *shows the differential mounted on a special Datsun work stand. This stand is not needed for inspection.*

3. Look for visible wear or damage and check the gears for chipped or missing teeth.
4. Check the tooth contact pattern of the pinion and ring gear. To do this, apply a thin, even coat of red lead oxide to 4 or 5 ring gear teeth at 2 or 3 positions on the gear. Turn the gear several turns in both directions so the contact pattern of the teeth is pressed into the coat of lead oxide. Compare the contact with the following figures to determine differential condition.

    a. **Figure 10**—Correct contact pattern.
    b. **Figure 11**—Heel contact. Indicates that the thickness of the pinion adjusting shim and washer should be increased to move the pinion closer to the ring gear.
    c. **Figure 12**—Toe contact. Indicates that thickness of the pinion adjusting shim and washer should be reduced to move pinion away from the ring gear.
    d. **Figure 13**—Flank contact. Adjusted in the same manner as toe contact.
    e. **Figure 14**—Face contact. Adjusted in the same manner as heel contact.

5. Connect a dial gauge as shown in **Figure 15** and measure backlash of the pinion and ring gear. To measure, hold the pinion from turning and move the ring gear while noting the reading on the gauge. Backlash should be

12

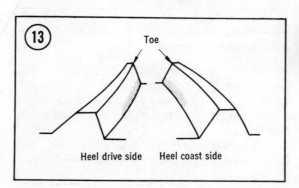

Heel drive side   Heel coast side

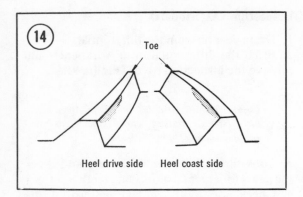

Toe

Heel drive side   Heel coast side

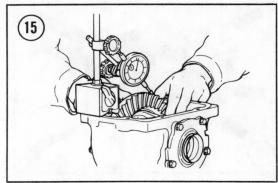

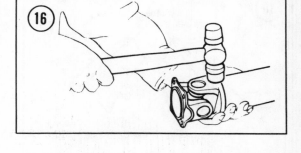

within 0.004-0.008 in. (0.2-0.2 mm). Backlash above or below this range requires disassembly and adjustment of the differential.

DRIVE SHAFT

The drive shaft is a 2-joint type with sliding splines at the front end.

Removal/Installation

1. Securely block the front wheels so the car will not roll in either direction. Jack up the rear of the car and place it on jackstands.
2. Remove the pre-muffler or catalytic converter (Chapter Five).
3. Remove 4 bolts to disconnect the drive shaft from the differential flange (**Figure 2**).
4. Slide the drive shaft rearward out of the transmission.

CAUTION
Do not drop the drive shaft, since it may be bent or thrown out of balance.

5. Install by reversing Steps 1-5. Take care not to damage the transmission rear oil seal when installing.

Universal Joint Disassembly/Assembly

The factory recommends against disassembling 240Z and 260Z U-joints, since the drive shaft is balanced as a unit. The U-joints should be disassembled only to replace worn bearings.

The 280Z drive shafts cannot be disassembled. If U-joints are worn, the drive shaft must be replaced as a unit.

1. Before taking the assembly apart, check for factory match marks on the crosses and yokes. If these are not visible, make your own marks so the crosses and yokes can be reassembled in the same relative positions.
2. Remove 4 snap rings from each universal joint. Snap rings hold bearings in the yokes.
3. Place the drive shaft in a vise as near the U-joint as possible. Be careful not to distort the shaft.
4. Lightly tap the base of the yoke with a hammer (**Figure 16**). Withdraw the opposite bearing race. Do the same for the remaining bearing races. Carefully separate the crosses and yokes.
5. Assemble in the reverse order. Apply grease liberally to the bearings and races.

AXLE SHAFTS

The axle shafts must be replaced as assemblies if defective, since repair parts are not available.

The axle shafts should be disassembled and lubricated with multipurpose grease at intervals specified in Chapter Three. **Figure 17** shows a flange-type axle shaft; **Figure 18** shows a spline-type axle shaft.

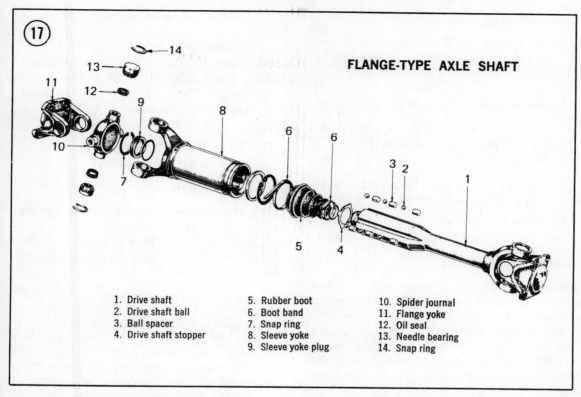

FLANGE-TYPE AXLE SHAFT

1. Drive shaft	5. Rubber boot	10. Spider journal
2. Drive shaft ball	6. Boot band	11. Flange yoke
3. Ball spacer	7. Snap ring	12. Oil seal
4. Drive shaft stopper	8. Sleeve yoke	13. Needle bearing
	9. Sleeve yoke plug	14. Snap ring

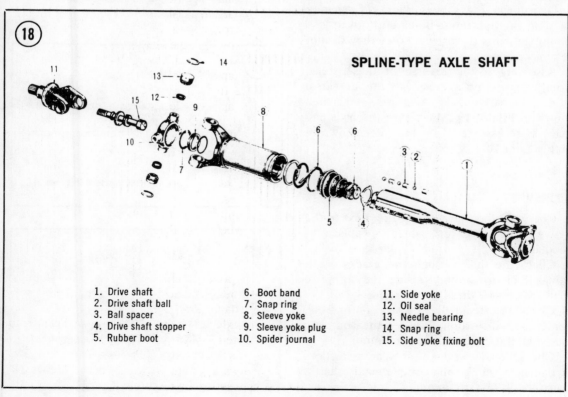

SPLINE-TYPE AXLE SHAFT

1. Drive shaft	6. Boot band	11. Side yoke
2. Drive shaft ball	7. Snap ring	12. Oil seal
3. Ball spacer	8. Sleeve yoke	13. Needle bearing
4. Drive shaft stopper	9. Sleeve yoke plug	14. Snap ring
5. Rubber boot	10. Spider journal	15. Side yoke fixing bolt

12

Removal/Installation

1. Securely block the front wheels so the car will not roll in either direction. Jack up the rear of the car and place it on jackstands.
2. Unbolt the axle shaft from bearing spindle and differential. Take shaft out from under car.

CAUTION
The axle shaft is easily damaged if it is dropped.

3. Install in the reverse order. Tighten all installation bolts to specifications (end of chapter).

Disassembly/Assembly

1. Disassemble and inspect the universal joints in same manner as drive shaft universal joints.
2. Referring to **Figure 17** or **18**, remove the snap ring (7) from the sleeve yoke plug (9).
3. Compress the axle shaft and remove the snap ring from the stopper (4). Remove the stopper.
4. Disconnect the rubber boot and separate the axle shaft sections. Be careful not to lose any of the balls or spacers, since they cannot be replaced.
5. Assembly is the reverse of these steps. Apply multipurpose grease to the universal joints and ball splines. Also grease the area shown in **Figure 19**. Make sure the balls and spacers are assembled in the order shown in **Figure 17** or **18**.

Inspection

1. Check the boot and the O-ring next to the sleeve yoke plug for damage. Replace as needed.
2. Check the shaft for bending, cracks, wear, damage, or distortion. Replace the complete shaft assembly if these are detected.
3. Check the steel balls and spacers for wear, damage, or distortion. Replace the complete axle shaft if these conditions are found.
4. Check the sleeve yoke for wear, distortion, or damage. Replace the complete axle shaft if these conditions are found.

5. Check the universal joints for wear or damage. The axle shaft assembly must be replaced if defects are found.
6. Place the axle shaft in a soft-jawed vise and connect a dial gauge as shown in **Figure 20**. Fully compress the axle shaft and measure play. Maximum permissible is 0.004 in. (0.1 mm).

WHEEL BEARINGS AND SPINDLES

Removal/Installation

1. Securely block the front wheels so the car will not roll in either direction.
2. Loosen the rear wheel nuts, jack up the rear end of the car, place it on jackstands, and remove the car wheels.

WARNING
*This procedure requires undoing wheel bearing locknuts, which are torqued to 181-239 ft.-lb. Make sure the front wheels are **securely** blocked, and use good quality jackstands, located as shown in **Figure 21**. Otherwise, the force required to undo the nuts could knock the car off the jackstands.*

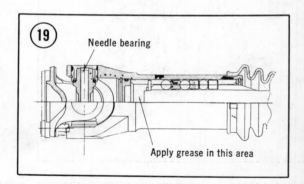

19   Needle bearing

Apply grease in this area

20

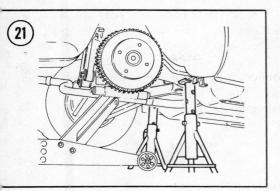

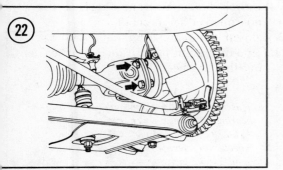

3. Detach the axle shaft from the spindle companion flange (**Figure 22**). Lower the axle shaft out of the way.

4. Remove the wheel bearing locknut with a socket and long breaker bar (**Figure 23**). Hold the wheel from turning with a slide hammer adapter (ST 07640000) and a metal bar. **Figure 24** shows dimensions of the adapter.

NOTE
*The nut is locked by bending the lip against the spindle threads at 2 points with a drift (**Figure 25**). Do not attempt to bend the lip away from the threads or otherwise unlock the nut before removing it. Simply undo it.*

5. Remove the spindle with the slide hammer and slide hammer adapter (**Figure 26**). If these tools are not available, drive the spindle out from the inside. Use a soft metal drift.

6. Remove the spacer and companion flange from the bearing housing.

7. Take out the inner wheel bearing and oil seal.

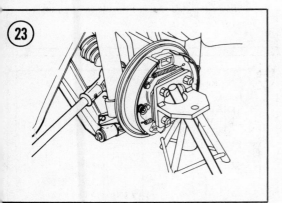

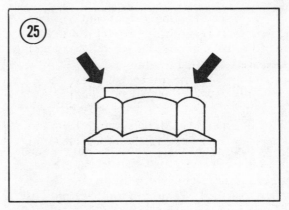

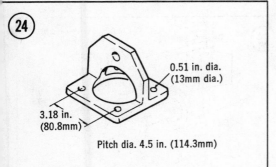

0.51 in. dia.
(13mm dia.)

3.18 in.
(80.8mm)

Pitch dia. 4.5 in. (114.3mm)

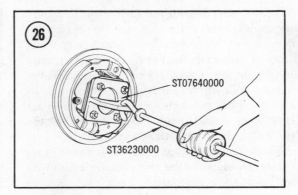

ST07640000

ST36230000

12

8. Press the outer wheel bearing off the spindle (**Figure 27**).

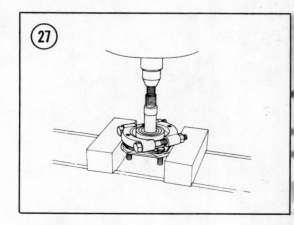

> *NOTE*
> *Have the bearing pressed off by a dealer or automotive machine shop if you do not have the necessary equipment.*

Inspection

1. Clean all parts thoroughly in solvent before inspection.
2. Check the bearings for play and wear by holding the inner race with fingers and rotating the outer race. Check bearing friction surfaces for wear, chips, scoring, signs of seizure, and the bluish tint that indicates overheating. Replace any bearings with these defects.
3. Check bearing oil seals for wear and distortion. Replace as needed.
4. Check the ends of the bearing spacer. Replace spacers showing signs of compression, distortion, or wear.
5. Check the bearing spindles for signs of wear or damage. Replace if these conditions are evident.

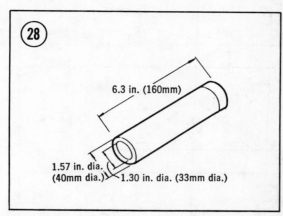

Assembly and Installation

Assembly and installation are the reverse of the removal and disassembly procedures, plus the following steps.

1. Outer wheel bearings are equipped with an oil seal on one side. When pressing an outer bearing onto the spindle, make sure the oil seal will face outward (toward the wheel) when installed. To install the bearing, use bearing drift Datsun ST 37780000 (Kent-Moore J-25863-01). **Figure 28** shows the dimensions of the drift.
2. If new bearing spacers are being used, select a spacer according to the marks shown in **Figure 29**. Bearing housings are marked "A," "B," and "C" at the point shown in the figure. The correct size spacer for each housing is marked with the same letter as the housing at the point shown in the figure.
3. Before installing the spindle, apply multipurpose grease to the points marked with an asterisk in **Figure 30**. Pack each bearing

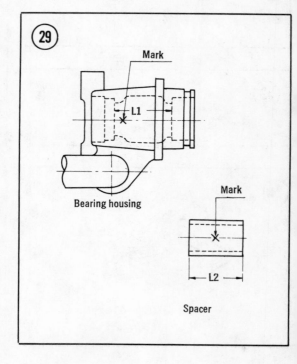

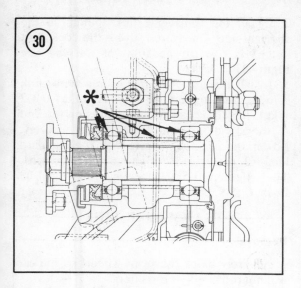

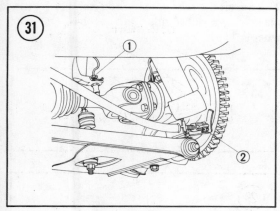

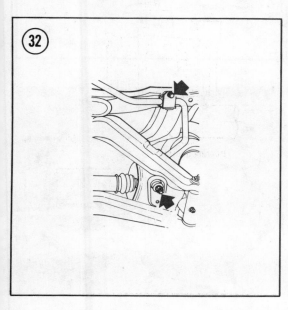

with grease, working as much as possible into the space between balls and races.

4. After the spindle and bearings are installed in the housing, tighten the wheel bearing locknut to 181-239 ft.-lb. (25-33 mkg). This should result in spindle end play of 0-0.006 in. (0-0.15 mm). Turn the spindle with a spring scale attached to one of the lug nut studs. Force required to turn the spindle should be 28 oz. (790 grams) or less. If necessary, tighten or loosen the bearing locknut to adjust. However, tightness of the nut must remain between 181-239 ft.-lb. (25-33 mkg).

5. After tightening the locknut, bend the lip into the spindle threads at 2 points with a drift (**Figure 25**).

REAR SHOCK ABSORBER REPLACEMENT

The rear shock absorbers are part of the suspension strut. Replacement of the shock absorbers requires several special tools. However, much expense can be saved by removing the struts yourself as described later in this chapter and taking them to a dealer for shock absorber replacement.

REAR SPRING REPLACEMENT

Like the shock absorbers, the rear springs are part of the strut assemblies. Replacement of the springs requires a special Datsun coil spring compressor or similar tool. If you do not have such a tool, remove the struts as described in the following procedure, then take them to a Datsun dealer for spring replacement.

STRUT REMOVAL

1. Securely block the front wheels so the car will not roll in either direction.

2. Loosen the rear wheel nuts, jack up the rear of the the car, place it on jackstands, and remove the rear wheels.

3. Detach brake line and handbrake cable (1 and 2, **Figure 31**).

4. On 260Z's and 280Z's, detach the stabilizer bar from the transverse link. See **Figure 32**.

5. Remove lock bolt and self-locking nuts (1 and 2, **Figure 33**) from the transverse link.

12

6. Withdraw the spindle from the transverse link (**Figure 34**).

7. Disconnect the axle shaft from the bearing spindle companion flange (**Figure 35**).

8. Place a jack beneath the strut assembly to support it. Working inside the car, remove 3 self-locking nuts from the top of the strut (inset, **Figure 36**).

> *WARNING*
> *Do not remove the center nut at the top of the strut. This could allow the coil spring to fly out and cause serious injury.*

9. Slowly lower the jack until the strut is clear of the car.

STRUT INSTALLATION

Installation is the reverse of the removal procedure, plus the following steps.

1. Use new self-locking nuts.

2. Install the transverse link spindle so the shorter side (measured from the lock bolt notch) is toward the front of the car. See **Figure 37**.

3. Install the lock bolt in the transverse link spindle and tighten to 7-9 ft.-lb. (1.0-1.2 mkg). Install new self-locking nuts on the end of the spindle, but do not tighten securely. Lower the car and load it with the standard load (2 passengers weighing 150 lb. each). Then tighten the self-locking nuts to 54-69 ft.-lb. (7.5-9.5 mkg).

TRANSVERSE LINK

Removal

1. Securely block the front wheels so the car will not roll in either direction.

2. Loosen the rear wheel nuts, jack up the car, place it on jackstands, and remove the rear wheels.

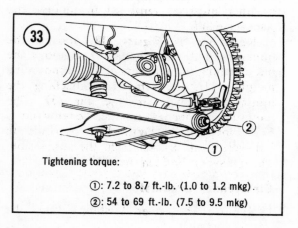

Tightening torque:

①: 7.2 to 8.7 ft.-lb. (1.0 to 1.2 mkg)
②: 54 to 69 ft.-lb. (7.5 to 9.5 mkg)

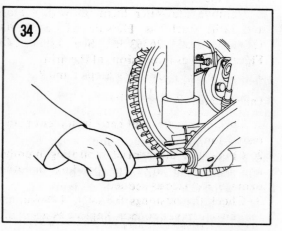

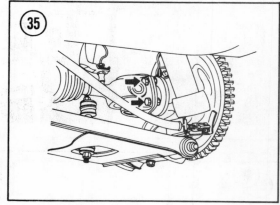

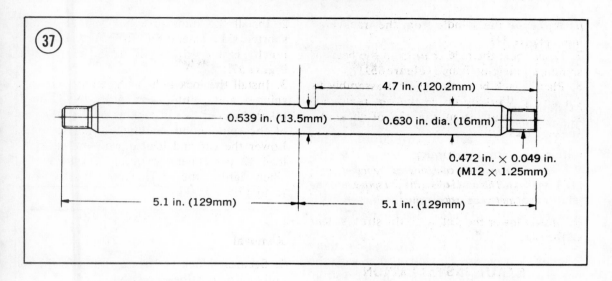

4.7 in. (120.2mm)

0.539 in. (13.5mm)   0.630 in. dia. (16mm)

0.472 in. × 0.049 in.
(M12 × 1.25mm)

5.1 in. (129mm)   5.1 in. (129mm)

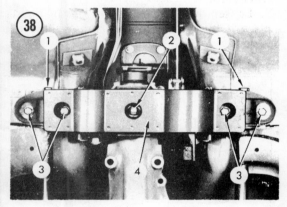

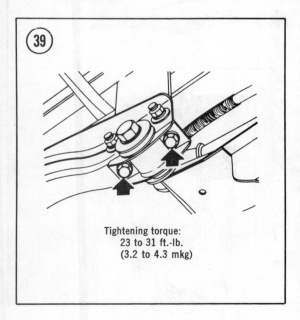

Tightening torque:
23 to 31 ft.-lb.
(3.2 to 4.3 mkg)

3. Separate the strut and transverse link. See Steps 4-6 of *Strut Removal*.

4. Place a jack beneath the differential to support it. The differential front mounting member must be removed to remove the transverse link.

5. Referring to **Figure 38**, loosen the transverse link inner bolts (1). Remove the nut attaching the differential to the mounting member (2), then the nuts attaching the mounting member to the car (3). The mounting member (4) can then be removed.

6. Remove 2 bolts (**Figure 39**) to separate the transverse link bracket from the suspension. The transverse link can then be removed.

Disassembly/Assembly

1. Remove the inner bushings from the transverse link.

2. Remove the outer bushings with a press and drift such as Datsun ST 38800000 (Kent-Moore J-26363-B). See **Figure 40**. **Figure 41** gives dimensions of the drift.

3. Assemble by reversing Steps 1 and 2.

Inspection

1. Thoroughly clean all parts in solvent before inspection.

2. Check the differential mounting member and transverse links for bending or other damage. Replace as needed.

3. Check the bushings for wear, damage, and melted or cracked rubber. Replace as needed.

12

Installation

Installation is the reverse of the removal procedure, plus the following steps.

1. Use new self-locking nuts.

2. Make sure the inner front transverse link bushings are aligned with the differential front mounting member as shown in **Figure 42**.

3. Install the rubber insulator in the differential front mounting member so the ''F'' mark faces the front of the car.

4. Install the transverse link spindle so the shorter side (measured from the lock bolt) is toward the front of the car. See **Figure 37**.

5. Install the transverse link inner bolts and outer self-locking nuts and tighten them slightly. Lower the car and load it with the standard load (2 passengers weighing 150 lb. each). Then tighten the transverse link inner bolts to 101-116 ft.-lb. (14-16 mkg) and the outer self-locking nuts to 54-69 ft.-lb. (7.5-9.5 mkg).

SWAY BAR

A rear sway bar is used on all models except the 240Z.

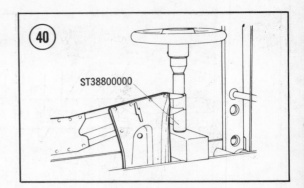

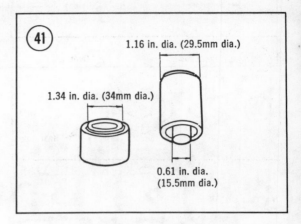

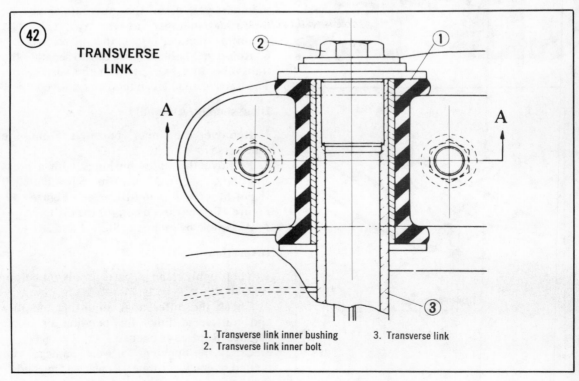

TRANSVERSE
LINK

1. Transverse link inner bushing
2. Transverse link inner bolt
3. Transverse link

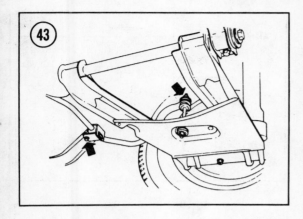

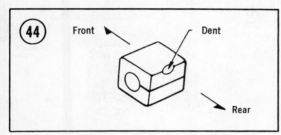

Removal/Installation

1. Loosen the rear wheel nuts, jack up the rear end of the car, place it on jackstands, and remove the rear wheels.

2. Remove the main muffler (Chapter Five).

3. Place a jack beneath the outer end of each transverse link and raise it slightly. This will relieve downward pressure on sway bar ends.

4. Remove the stabilizer end nuts, then the bracket bolts. See **Figure 43**.

5. Check the sway bar for bending or cracks. Check rubber bushings for wear, damage, or deterioration. Replace as needed.

6. Install in the reverse order. Tighten end nuts to 9-12 ft.-lb. (1.2-1.7 mkg). Tighten bracket bolts to 7-9 ft.-lb. (1.0-1.2 mkg).

NOTE
*Be sure the notch in each sway bar-to-frame bushing faces up and to the rear. See **Figure 44**.*

Table is on the following page.

12

Table 1   TIGHTENING TORQUES

	Ft.-lb.	Mkg
Drive shaft to differential		
240Z-260Z	18-23	2.5-3.2
280Z	29-33	4.0-4.5
Differential-to-rear mounting member nuts		
1970-1976	54-69	7.5-9.5
1977-1978 manual	54-69	7.5-9.5
1977-1978 automatic	43-51	6-7
Inspection cover bolts		
1970-1974	14-19	1.9-2.6
1975-1976	12-17	1.6-2.4
1977-1978 manual	12-17	1.6-2.4
1977-1978 automatic	14-18	1.9-2.5
Axle shaft outer end bolts	36-43	5-6
Axle shaft inner end bolts		
240Z, 1975-1976 280Z	36-43	5-6
260Z	23-31	3.2-4.3
1977-1978 280Z manual	36-43	5-6
1977-1978 280Z automatic	23-31	3.2-4.3
Brake backing plate bolts	20-27	2.7-3.7
Wheel nuts	58-65	8-9
Rear link mounting bracket bolts	23-31	3.2-4.3
Differential front mounting member bolts		
240Z	23-31	3.2-4.3
260Z	22-33	3.0-4.6
280Z	33-44	4.6-6.1
Differential front mount-to-insulator nuts	23-31	3.2-4.3
Differential-to-rear mounting member nuts		
1977-1978 automatic	43-51	6-7
All others	54-69	7.5-9.5
Rear wheel bearing locknuts	181-239	25-33

INDEX

13

1970-1972 240Z
(PART I)

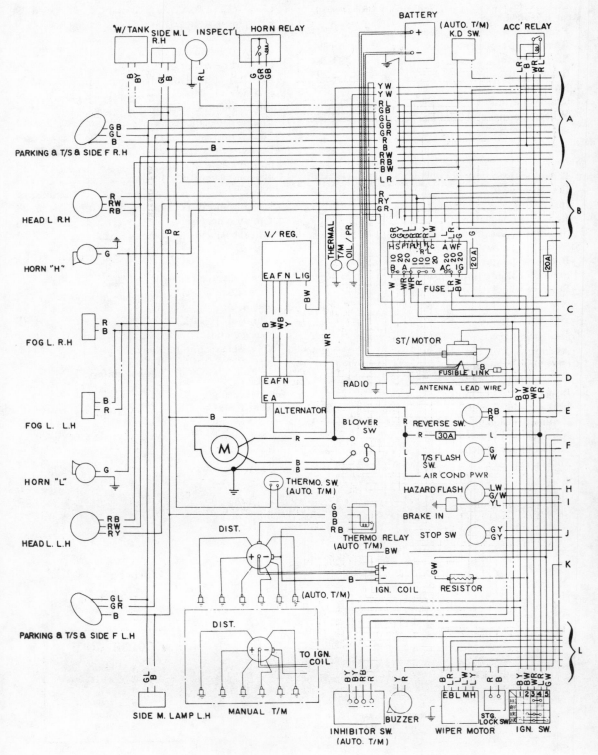

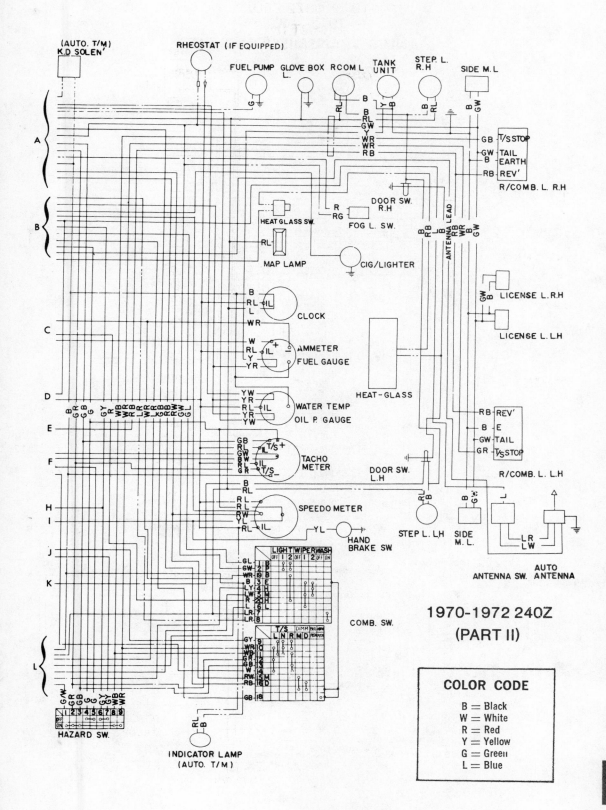

1970-1972 240Z
(PART II)

COLOR CODE

B = Black
W = White
R = Red
Y = Yellow
G = Green
L = Blue

14

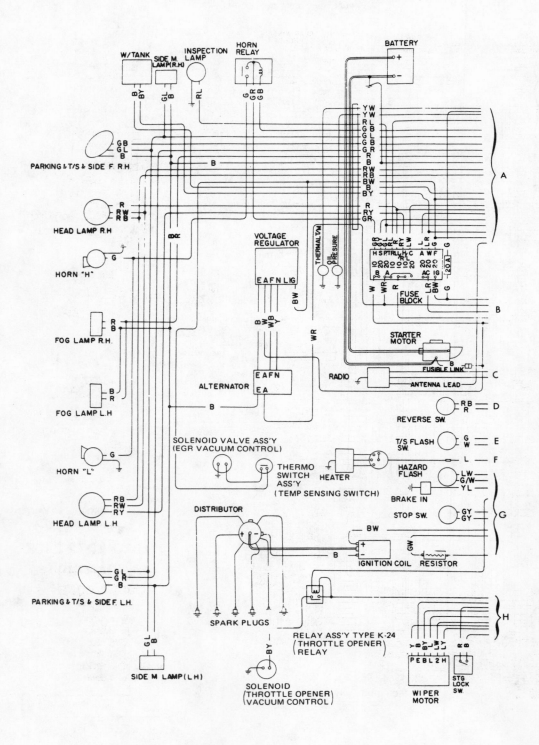

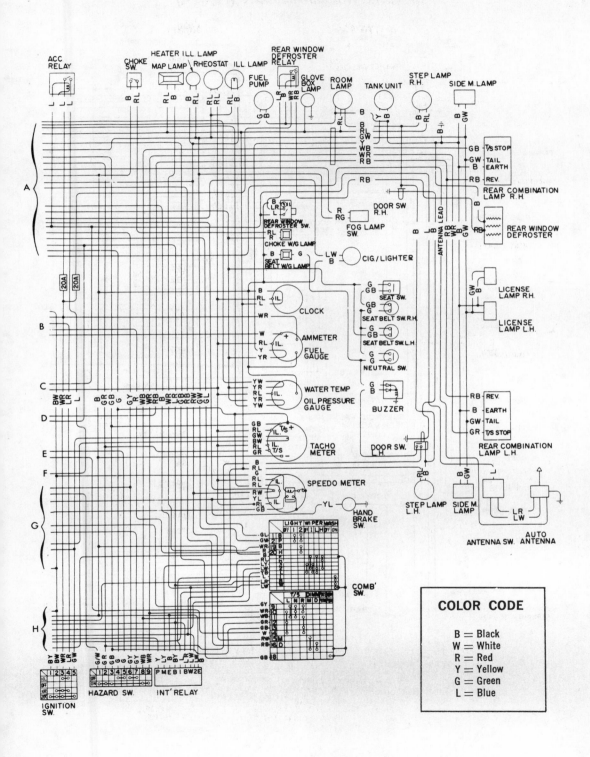

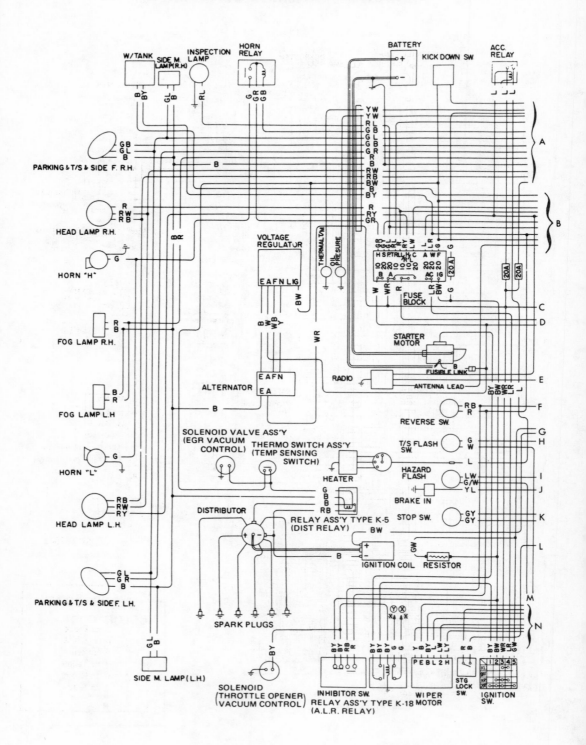

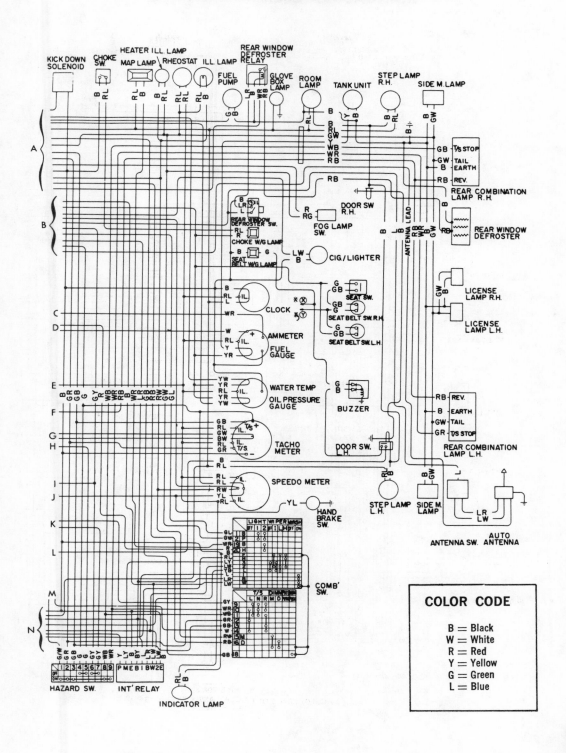

1974 260Z
MANUAL TRANSMISSION (PART I)

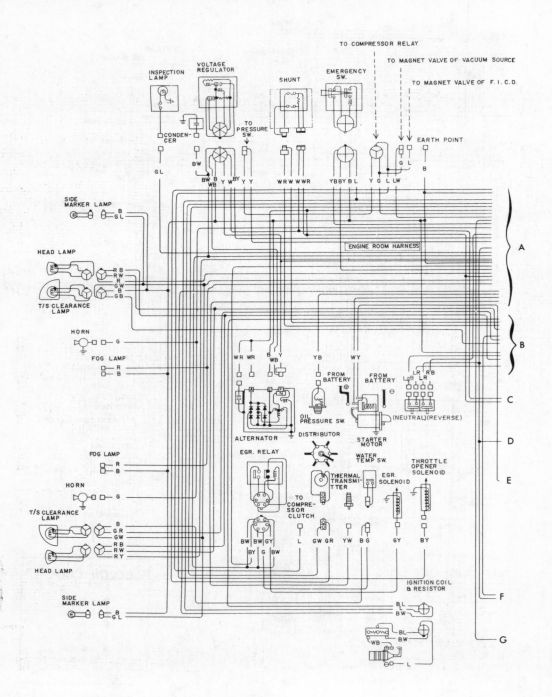

1974 260Z
MANUAL TRANSMISSION (PART II)

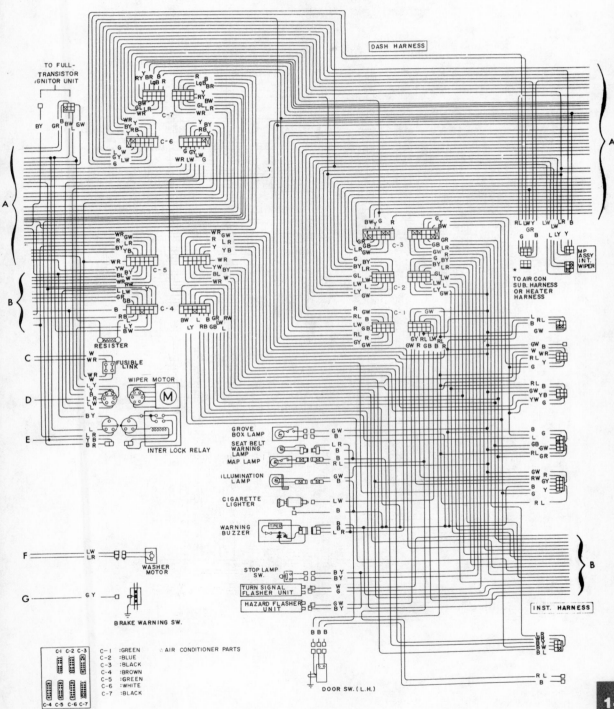

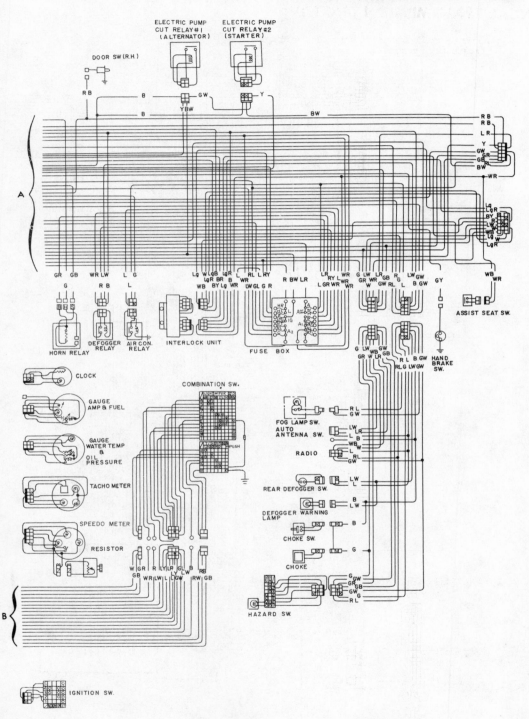

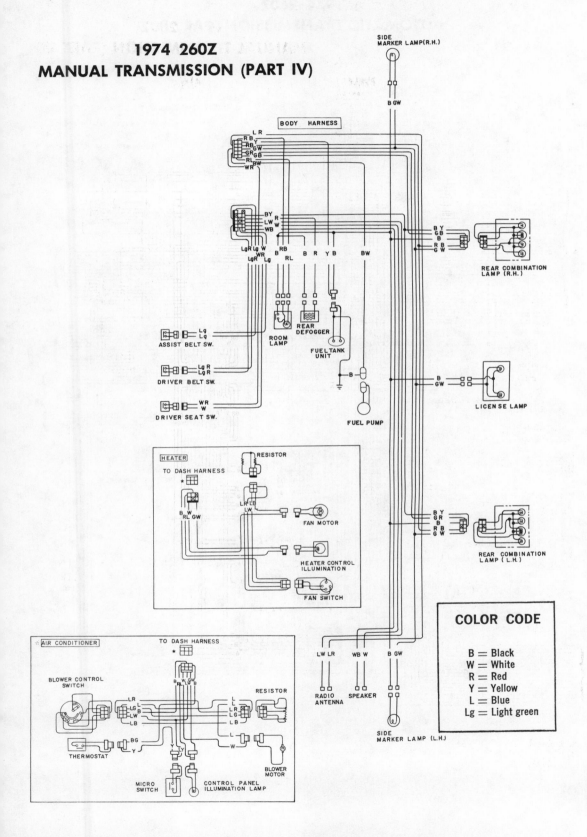

1974 260Z
MANUAL TRANSMISSION (PART IV)

SIDE MARKER LAMP(R.H.)

B GW

BODY HARNESS

REAR COMBINATION LAMP (R.H.)

ASSIST BELT SW.

DRIVER BELT SW.

DRIVER SEAT SW.

ROOM LAMP

REAR DEFOGGER

FUEL TANK UNIT

FUEL PUMP

LICENSE LAMP

HEATER

TO DASH HARNESS

RESISTOR

FAN MOTOR

HEATER CONTROL ILLUMINATION

FAN SWITCH

REAR COMBINATION LAMP (L.H.)

AIR CONDITIONER

TO DASH HARNESS

BLOWER CONTROL SWITCH

RESISTOR

THERMOSTAT

BLOWER MOTOR

MICRO SWITCH

CONTROL PANEL ILLUMINATION LAMP

RADIO ANTENNA

SPEAKER

SIDE MARKER LAMP (L.H.)

COLOR CODE

B = Black
W = White
R = Red
Y = Yellow
L = Blue
Lg = Light green

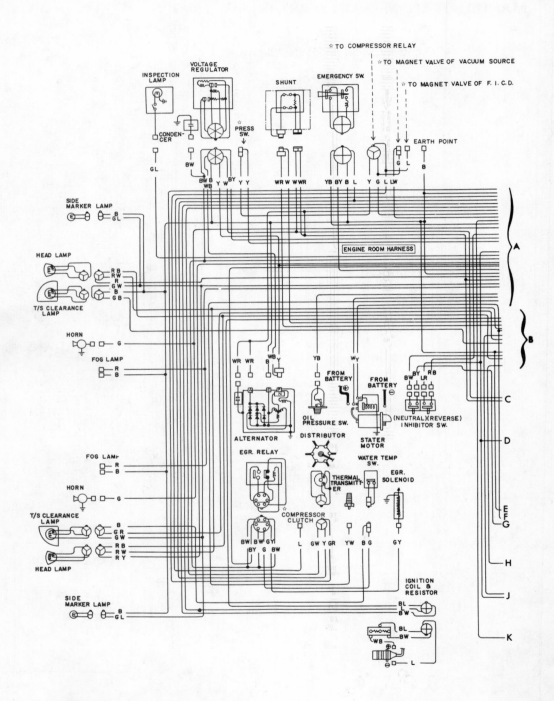

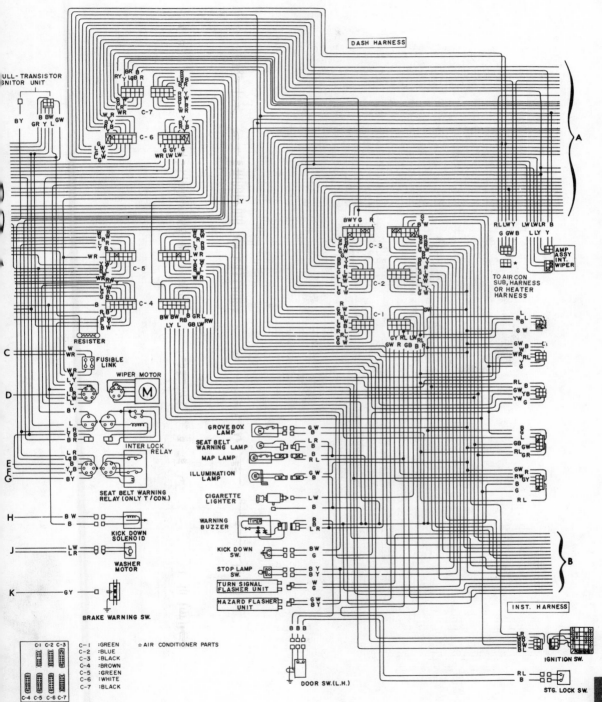

14

1974 260Z
AUTOMATIC TRANSMISSION (PART III)

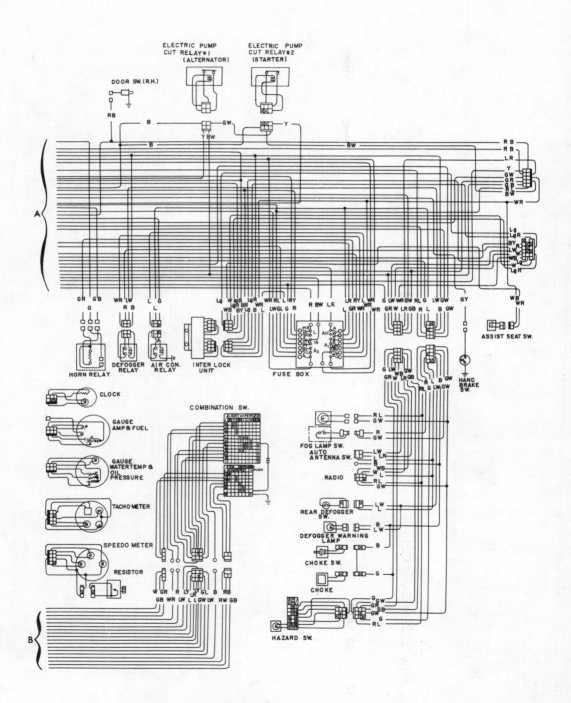

1974 260Z
AUTOMATIC TRANSMISSION (PART IV)

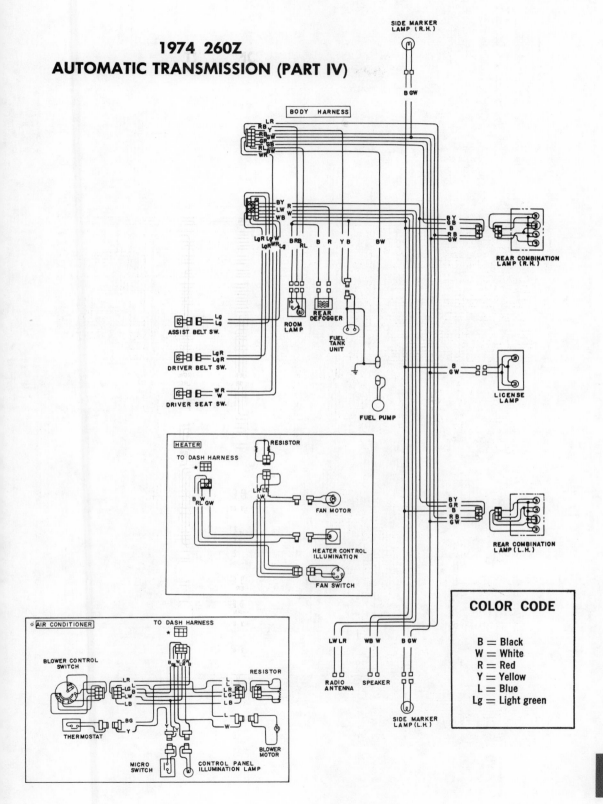

SIDE MARKER LAMP (R.H.)

BODY HARNESS

COLOR CODE

B = Black
W = White
R = Red
Y = Yellow
L = Blue
Lg = Light green

ASSIST BELT SW.

DRIVER BELT SW.

DRIVER SEAT SW.

ROOM LAMP

REAR DEFOGGER

FUEL TANK UNIT

FUEL PUMP

REAR COMBINATION LAMP (R.H.)

LICENSE LAMP

REAR COMBINATION LAMP (L.H.)

HEATER
TO DASH HARNESS

RESISTOR

FAN MOTOR

HEATER CONTROL ILLUMINATION

FAN SWITCH

RADIO ANTENNA

SPEAKER

SIDE MARKER LAMP (L.H.)

AIR CONDITIONER
TO DASH HARNESS

BLOWER CONTROL SWITCH

THERMOSTAT

MICRO SWITCH

CONTROL PANEL ILLUMINATION LAMP

BLOWER MOTOR

RESISTOR

14

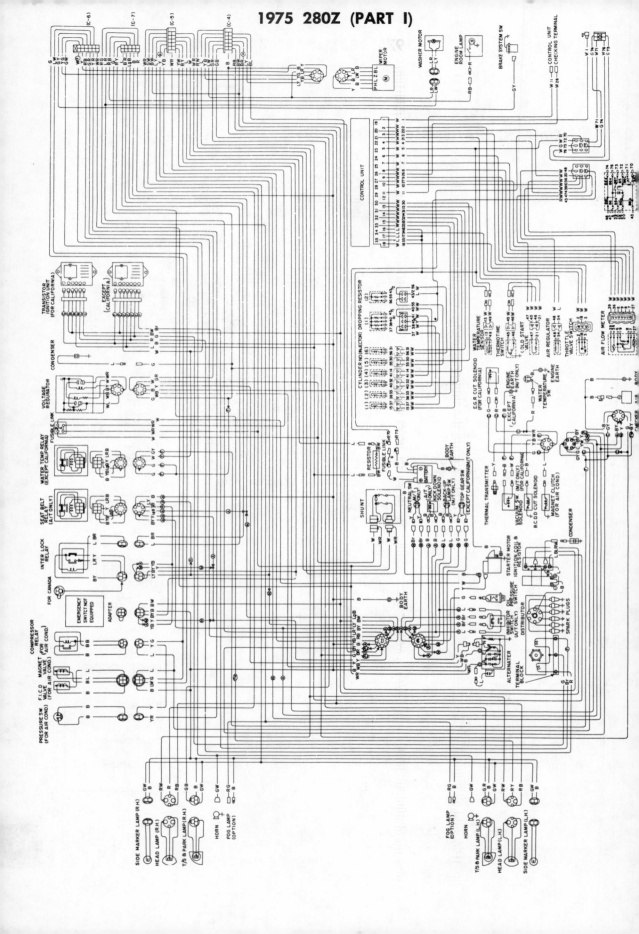

1975 280Z (PART I)

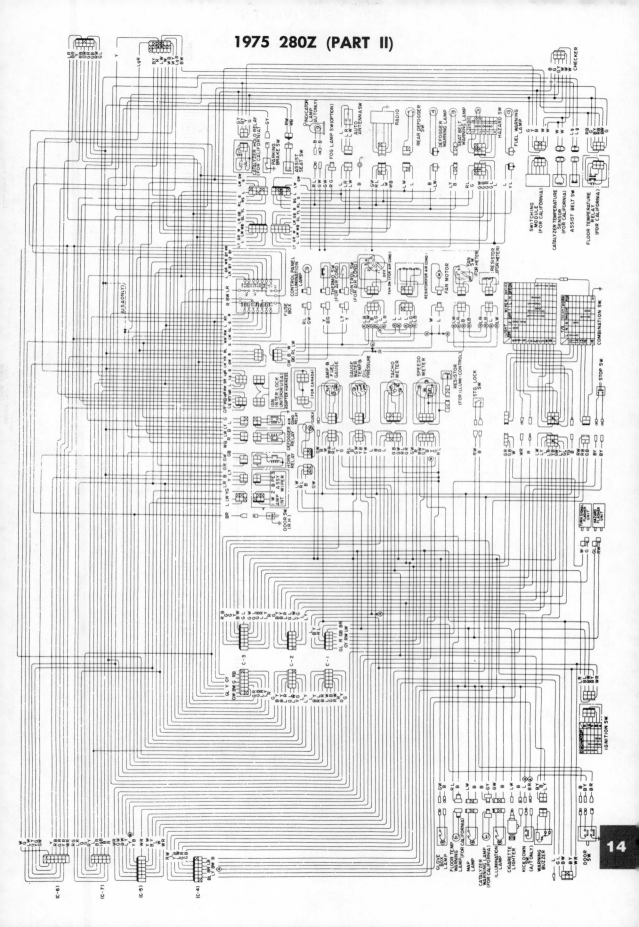

1975 280Z (PART II)

14

1975 280Z (PART III)

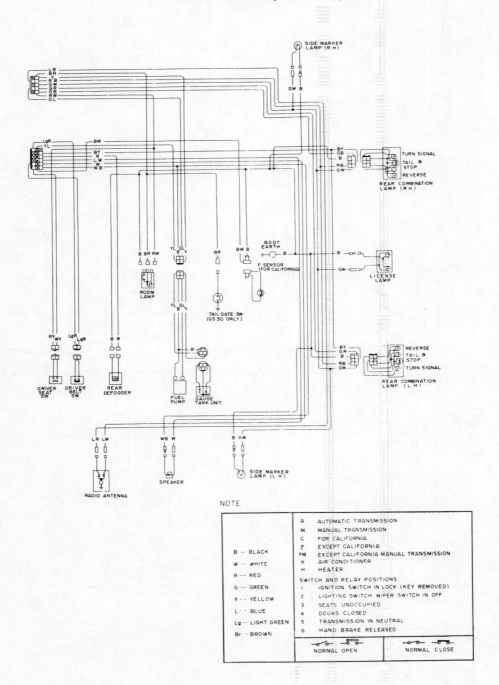

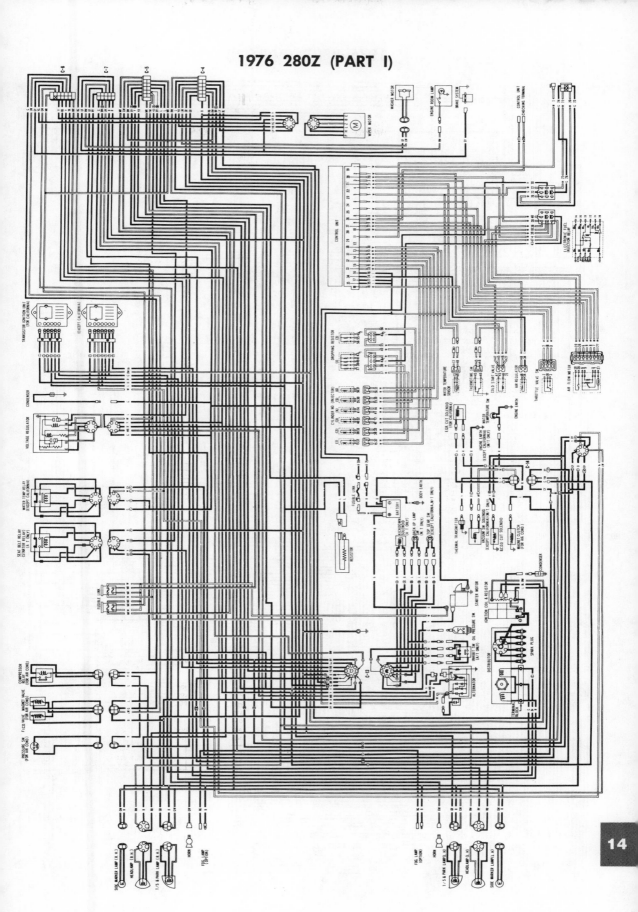

1976 280Z (PART II)

1976 280Z (PART III)

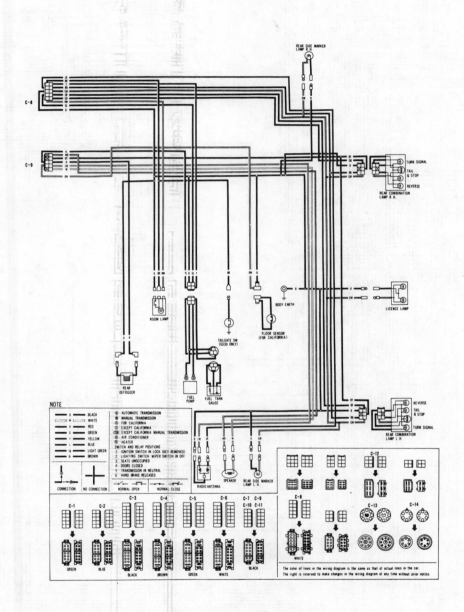

1977 280Z (Part I)

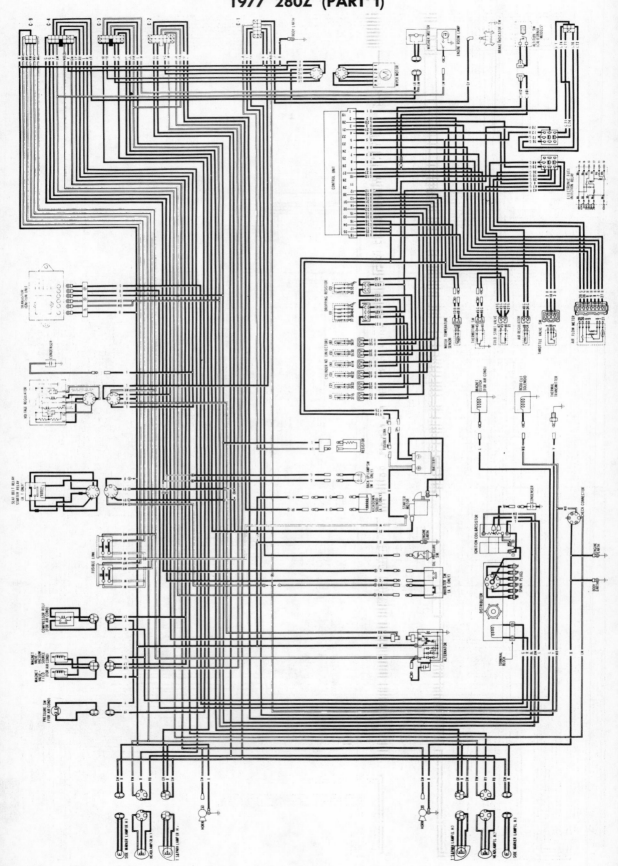

1977 280Z (PART II)

1977 280Z (PART III)

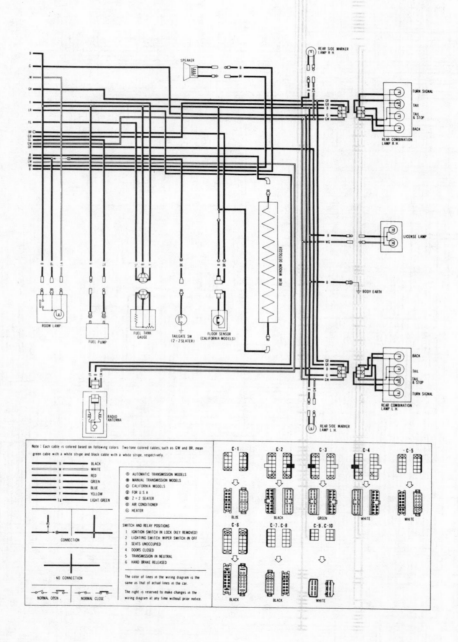

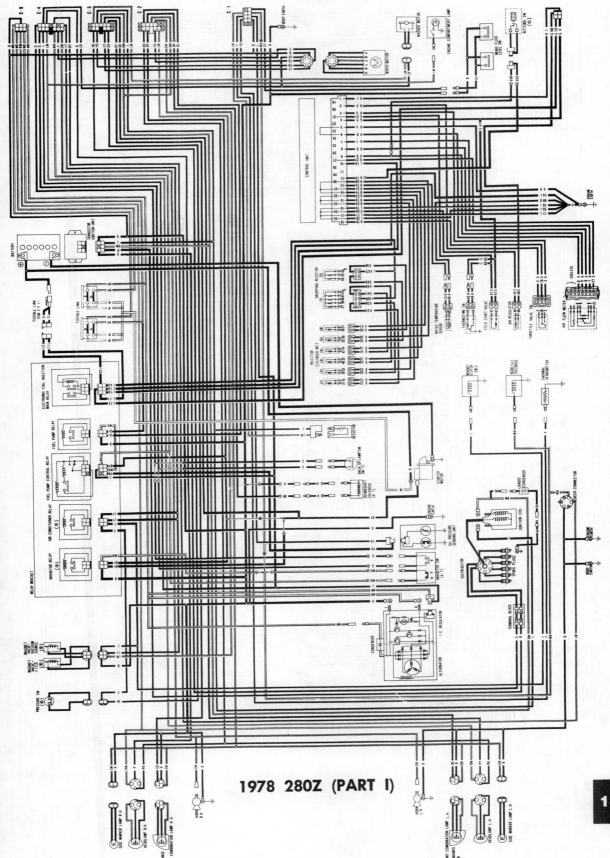

1978 280Z (PART I)

14

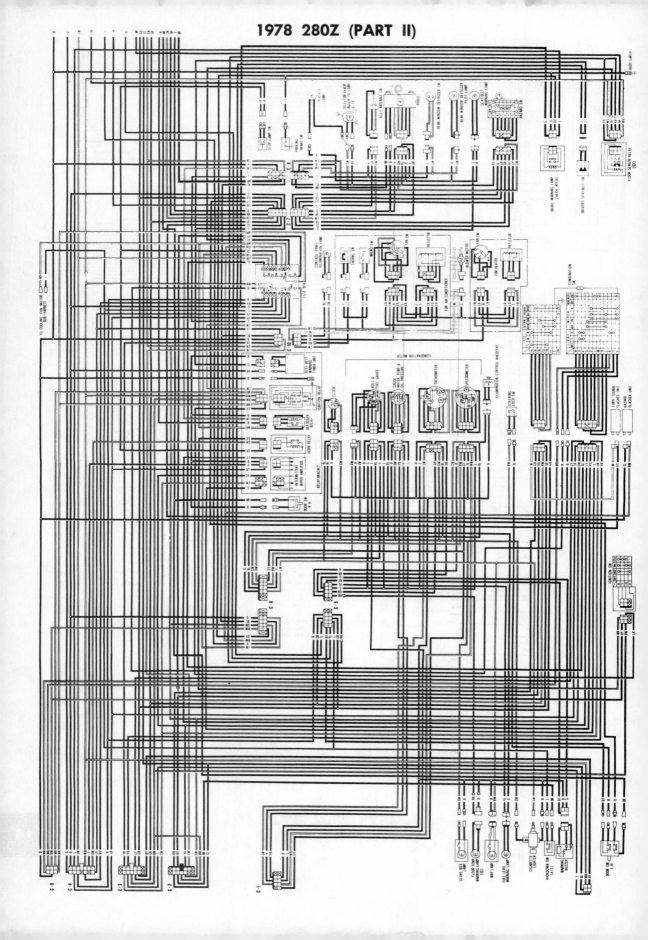

1978 280Z (PART II)

1978 280Z (PART III)

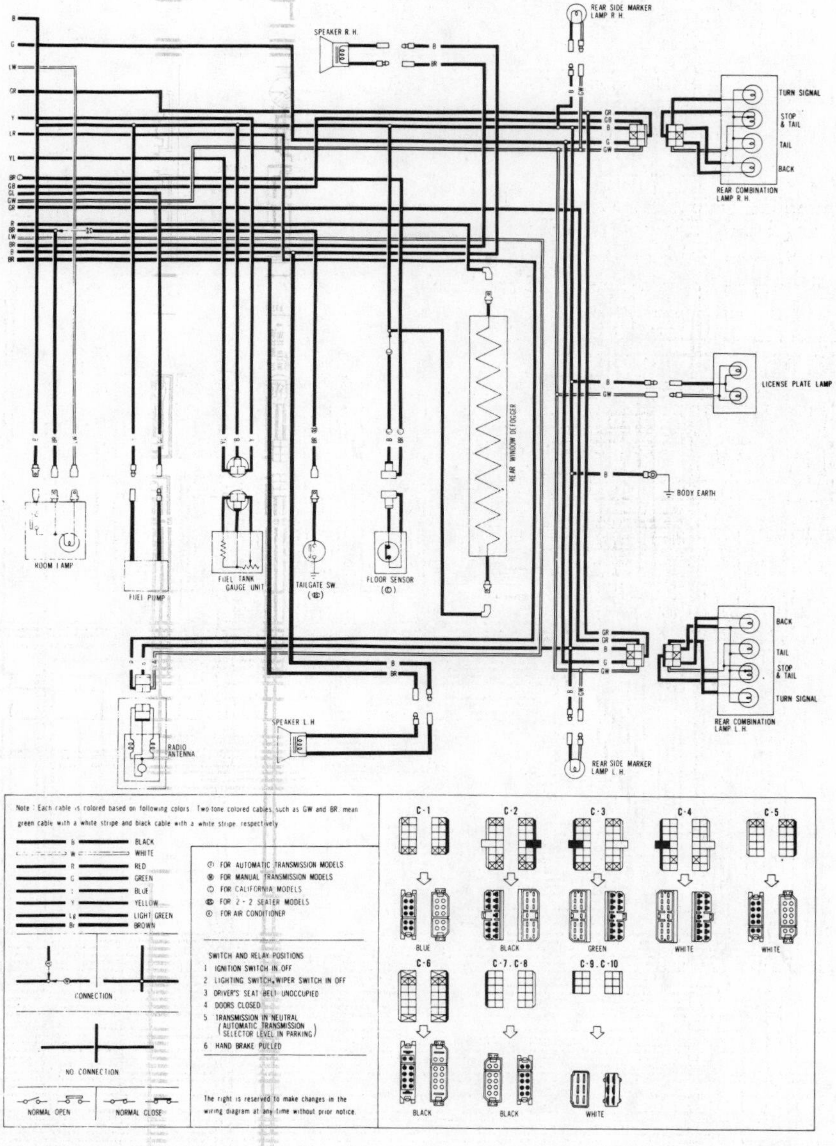

NOTES